Manu Goswami

Greg Grandin is the author of *Empire's Workshop*, *The Last Colonial Massacre*, and the award-winning *The Blood of Guatemala*. A professor of history at New York University and a Guggenheim fellow, Grandin has served on the United Nations Truth Commission investigating the Guatemalan Civil War and has written for *Harper's*, *The London Review of Books*, the *Los Angeles Times*, *The Nation*, *The New Statesman*, and *The New York Times*.

ALSO BY GREG GRANDIN

Empire's Workshop:
Latin America, the United States,
and the Rise of the New Imperialism

The Last Colonial Massacre:
Latin America in the Cold War

The Blood of Guatemala:
A History of Race and Nation

Praise for Greg Grandin's *Fordlandia*

A *New Yorker* Favorite Book of the Year
A *San Francisco Chronicle* Best Book of the Year
Amazon.com #1 History Book of the Year
A *Booklist* Top 10 Business Book of the Year

"Wonderful . . . Grandin tells a marvelous tale of colorful characters, some outsize and some just plain pathetic, misadventures, and fortunes made and lost on scales grand and puny."   —*Star Tribune* (Minneapolis)

"An excellent history . . . exhaustively researched . . . *Fordlandia* is keenly and emotionally observed and a potent record of the last hundred years of economic thinking and U.S./South American relations in the form of a blunt blow to the head."   —*Chicago Sun-Times*

"Grandin is one of a blessedly expanding group of gifted American historians who assume that whatever moral the story of the past may yield, it must be a story well told. *Fordlandia: The Rise and Fall of Henry Ford's Forgotten Jungle City* is precisely that—a genuinely readable history. . . . A fascinating historical narrative that illuminates the auto industry's contemporary crisis, the problems of globalization, and the contradictions of contemporary consumerism."   —*Los Angeles Times*

"Greg Grandin presents a nuanced explanation for Ford's dreams."
     —*USA Today*

"Grandin gives an exhaustive account of [Fordlandia's] failure and of the light it sheds on Ford."   —*The New Yorker*

"Written with a flair and deftness that one might expect to find in a well-crafted novel . . . Grandin brings to life the rogues and cranks who animate this tale. . . . Excellent."   —*The American Conservative*

"Fordlandia was, ultimately, the classic American parable of a failed Utopia, of soft dreams running aground on a hard world—which tends to make the most compelling tale of all. It's such an engrossing story that one wonders why it has never been told before in book-length form. Grandin takes full command of a complicated narrative with numerous threads, and the story spills out in precisely the right tone—about midway between Joseph Conrad and Evelyn Waugh."　　　　　　　　　　—*The American Scholar*

"An epic tale of a clash between cultures, values, man, and nature."
　　　　　　　　　　—*Booklist*

"Fascinating . . . In this lively history, Greg Grandin enlists a cast of union-busting thugs, a Norwegian sea captain, and a cranky botanist to tell the story of the short-lived Fordlandia plantation."　　　—*Mother Jones*

"The story of Ford's not-so-excellent adventure in the jungle is a writer's dream, and Greg Grandin takes full advantage of its dramatic potential. . . . His assessment of Ford is by turns critical and sympathetic, but always subtle."　　　　　　　　　　—*London Review of Books*

"Magic happens when a gifted historian and master storyteller finds a treasure trove of untapped materials to exploit. And Greg Grandin's book on Fordlandia is simply magical. Here is the truly epic tale of American adventurers dispatched by Henry Ford in 1928 to conquer and civilize the Amazon by constructing an industrial/agricultural utopia the size of Tennessee. Among the dozens of reasons I will be recommending *Fordlandia* to friends, family, colleagues, and students is the scale and pace of the narrative, the remarkable cast of characters, the brilliantly detailed descriptions of the Brazilian jungle, and what may be the best portrait we have of Henry Ford in his final years as he struggles to recapture control of the mighty forces he has unleashed."
　　　　　　　—David Nasaw, historian and award-winning biographer
　　　　　　　of Andrew Carnegie and William Randolph Hearst

"As a reader, I was fascinated by this account of Henry Ford's short-lived rain-forest Utopia, complete with golf course and square dances. As a writer, I envy Greg Grandin for finding such an intriguing subject—whose decline and fall has an eerie resonance at our own historical moment today."　　　—Adam Hochschild, author of *King Leopold's Ghost*

FORDLANDIA

FORDLANDIA

FORDLANDIA

The Rise and Fall of Henry Ford's Forgotten Jungle City

Greg Grandin

Picador

Metropolitan Books • Henry Holt and Company • New York

For information on Picador Reading Group Guides, please contact Picador.
E-mail: readinggroupguides@picadorusa.com

Designed by Meryl Sussman Levavi

Maps by Jeffrey L. Ward

The Library of Congress has cataloged the Henry Holt edition as follows:

Grandin, Greg, 1962–
    Fordlandia : the rise and fall of Henry Ford's forgotten
jungle city / Greg Grandin.—1st ed.
        p. cm.
    Includes bibliographical references and index.
    ISBN 978-0-8050-8236-4
    1. Fordlândia (Brazil)—History. 2. Planned communities—
Brazil—History—20th century. 3. Rubber plantations—Brazil—
Fordlándia—History—20th century. 4. Ford Motor Company—
Influence—History—20th century. 5. Ford, Henry, 1863–1947—
Political and social views. 6. Brazil—Civilization—American
influences—History—20th century. I. Title.
    F2651.F55G72 2009
    307.76'8098115—dc22

                                                    2008049642

Picador ISBN 978-0-312-42962-1

First published in the United States by Henry Holt and Company

To Emilia Viotti da Costa

Why, though, did we need a Mahagonny?

Because this world is a foul one.

—Bertolt Brecht
The Rise and Fall of the City of Mahagonny

CONTENTS

PART II: LORD FORD

PART III: RUBBER ROUGE

FORDLANDIA

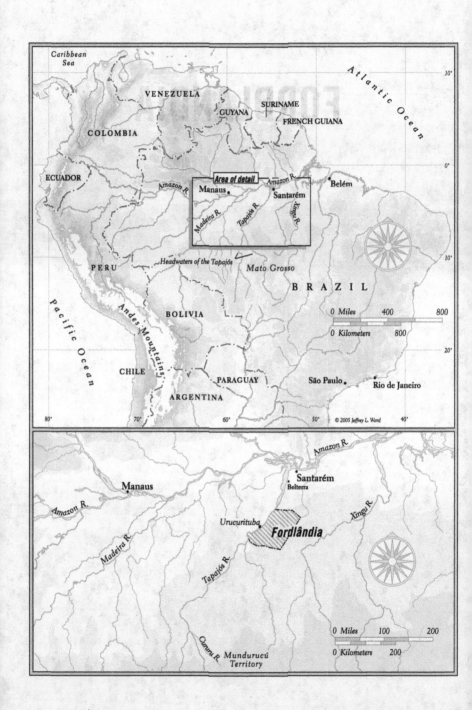

Caribbean
Sea

VENEZUELA

GUYANA   SURINAME

FRENCH GUIANA

COLOMBIA

Atlantic Ocean

10°

ECUADOR

0°

Amazon R.   Amazon R.   Belém

Manaus   Santarém

Madeira R.   Tapajós R.   Xingu R.

Headwaters of the Tapajós   Mato Grosso

PERU

B R A Z I L

Pacific Ocean

BOLIVIA

0 Miles   400   800

0 Kilometers   800

CHILE

Andes Mountains

PARAGUAY

São Paulo   Rio de Janeiro

ARGENTINA

80°   70°   60°   50°   © 2005 Jeffrey L. Ward   40°

10°

20°

Amazon R.

Santarém
Belterra

Manaus

Urucurituba   Xingu R.

Fordlândia

Amazon R.

Madeira R.

Tapajós R.

0 Miles   100   200

0 Kilometers   200

Cururu R.   Mundurucú
Territory

NOTHING IS WRONG WITH ANYTHING

JANUARY 9, 1928: HENRY FORD WAS IN A SPIRITED MOOD AS HE toured the Ford Industrial Exhibit with his son, Edsel, and his aging friend Thomas Edison, feigning fright at the flash of news cameras as a circle of police officers held back admirers and reporters. The event was held in New York, to showcase the new Model A. Until recently, nearly half of all the cars produced in the world were Model Ts, which Ford had been building since 1908. But by 1927 the T's market share had dropped considerably. A half decade of prosperity and cheap credit had increased demand for stylized, more luxurious cars. General Motors gave customers dozens of lacquer colors and a range of upholstery options to choose from while the Ford car came in green, red, blue, and black—which at least was more variety than a few years earlier when Ford reportedly told his customers they could have their car in any color they wanted, "so long as it's black."[1]

From May 1927, when the Ford Motor Company stopped production on the T, to October, when the first Model A was assembled, many doubted that Ford could pull off the changeover. It was costing a fortune, estimated by one historian at $250 million, because the internal workings of the just-opened River Rouge factory, which had been designed to roll out Ts into the indefinite future, had to be refitted to make the A. Yet on the first two days of its debut, over ten million Americans visited their local Ford dealers to inspect the new car, available in a range of body types and colors including Arabian Sand, Rose Beige, and Andalusite Blue. Within a few months, the company had received over 700,000 orders for the A, and even Ford's detractors had to admit that he had staged a remarkable comeback.[2]

The New York exhibit was held in the old Fiftieth Street Madison Square Garden, drawing over a million people and eclipsing the nearby National Car Show. All the many styles of the new model were on display at the Garden, as was the Lincoln Touring Car, since Ford had bought Lincoln Motors six years earlier, giving him a foot in the luxury car market without having to reconfigure his own factories. But the Ford exhibit wasn't really an automobile show. It was rather "built around this one idea," said Edsel: "a visual demonstration of the operation of the Ford industries, from the raw materials to the finished product." Visitors passed by displays of the manically synchronized work stations that Ford was famous for, demonstrations of how glass, upholstery, and leather trimmings were made, and dioramas of Ford's iron and coal mines, his blast furnaces, gas plants, northern Michigan timberlands, and fleets of planes and ships. A few even got to see Henry himself direct operations. "Speed that machine up a bit," he said as he passed a "mobile model of two men leisurely sawing a tree, against a background of dense forest growth."[3]

Though he was known to have opinions on many matters, as Henry Ford made his way through the convention hall reporters asked him mostly about his cars and his money. "How much are you worth?" one shouted out. "I don't know and I don't give a damn," Ford answered. Stopping to give an impromptu press conference in front of an old lathe he had used to make his first car, Ford said he was optimistic about the coming year, sure that his new River Rouge plant—located in Ford's hometown of Dearborn, just outside of Detroit—would be able to meet demand. No one raised his recent humiliating repudiation of anti-Semitism, though while in New York Ford met with members of the American

Jewish Committee to stage the "final scene in the reconciliation between Henry Ford and American Jewry," as the Jewish Telegraphic Agency described the conference. Most reporters tossed feel-good questions. One wanted to know about his key to success. "Concentration on details," Ford said. "When I worked at that lathe in 1894"—the carmaker nodded to the machine behind him—"I never thought about anything else." A journalist did ask him about reports of a price war and whether it would force him to lower his asking price for the A.

"I know nothing about it," replied Ford, who for decades had set his own prices and wages free of serious competition. "Nothing is wrong with anything," he said, "and I don't see any reason to believe that the present prosperity will not continue."[4]

FORD WANTED TO talk about something other than automobiles. The previous August he had taken his first airplane ride, a ten-minute circle over Detroit in his friend Charles Lindbergh's *Spirit of St. Louis*, just a few months after Lindbergh had made his historic nonstop transatlantic trip. Ford bragged that he "handled the stick" for a little while. He was "strong for air travel," he said, and was working on a lightweight diesel airplane engine. Ford then announced that he would soon fly to the Amazon to inspect his new rubber plantation. "If I go to Brazil," he said, "it will be by airplane. I would never spend 20 days making the trip by boat."[5]

Ford didn't elaborate, and reporters seemed a bit puzzled. So Edsel stepped forward to explain. The plantation was on the Tapajós River, a branch of the Amazon, he said.

Amid all the excitement over the Model A, most barely noted that the Ford Motor Company had recently acquired an enormous land concession in the Amazon. Inevitably compared in size to a midranged US state, usually Connecticut but sometimes Tennessee, the property was to be used to grow rubber. Despite Thomas Edison's best efforts to produce domestic or synthetic rubber, latex was the one important natural resource that Ford didn't control, even though his New York exhibit included a model of a rubber plantation. "The details have been closed," Edsel had announced in the official press release about the acquisition, "and the work will begin at once." It would include building a town and launching a "widespread sanitary campaign against the dangers of the jungle," he said. "Boats of the Ford fleet will be in communication with the property and it is possible that airplane communication may also be attempted."[6]

In the months that followed, as the excitement of the Model A died down, journalists and opinion makers began to pay attention to Fordlandia, as Ford's Brazilian project soon came to be called. And they reported the enterprise as a contest between two irrepressible forces. On one side stood the industrialist who had perfected the assembly line and broken down the manufacturing process into ever simpler components geared toward making one single infinitely reproducible product, the first indistinguishable from the millionth. "My effort is in the direction of simplicity," Ford once said. On the other was the storied Amazon basin, spilling over into nine countries and comprising a full third of South America, a place so wild and diverse that the waters just around where Ford planned to establish his plantation contained more species of fish than all the rivers of Europe combined.[7]

It was billed as a proxy fight: Ford represented vigor, dynamism, and the rushing energy that defined American capitalism in the early twentieth century; the Amazon embodied primal stillness, an ancient world that had so far proved unconquerable. "If the machine, the tractor, can open a breach in the great green wall of the Amazon jungle, if Ford plants millions of rubber trees where there used to be nothing but jungle solitude," wrote a German daily, "then the romantic history of rubber will have a new chapter. A new and titanic fight between nature and modern man is beginning." One Brazilian writer predicted that Ford would finally fulfill the prophecy of Alexander von Humboldt, the Prussian naturalist who over a century earlier said that the Amazon was destined to become the "world's granary." And as if to underscore the danger of the challenge, just at the moment Ford was deciding to get into the rubber business, the public's attention was captivated by reports of the disappearance of the British explorer Colonel Percy Fawcett. Having convinced himself, based on a combination of archival research, deduction, and clairvoyance, of the existence of a lost city (which he decided to name "Z") just south of where Ford would establish his plantation, Fawcett entered the jungle to find it. He was never heard from again.[8]

In the case of Ford, who had all the resources of the industrial world at his disposal, journalists had no doubt about the outcome, and they reported on his civilizing mission in expectant prose. *Time* reported that Ford intended to increase its rubber planting every year "until the whole jungle is industrialized," cheered on by the forest's inhabitants: "soon boa constrictors will slip down into the jungle centers; monkeys will set up a great chattering. Black Indians armed with heavy blades will slash down their one-time haunts to make way for future windshield wipers, floor mats, balloon tires." Ford was bringing "white man's magic" to the wilderness, the *Washington Post* wrote, intending to cultivate not only "rubber but the rubber gatherers as well."[9]

Since the sixteenth century, stories of El Dorado, an Indian king so rich that he powdered himself with gold, lured countless fortune hunters on futile quests. The word *quixotic* has its origins in a story set on the Spanish plains, in the same century when Europeans were first entering the Amazon. It's often applied to those entranced by the promise of jungle riches, as certain of the existence of the object of their pursuit as the Man from La Mancha was that the windmills he tilted at were giants. "I call it Z," said Colonel Fawcett of his fabled city, "for the sake of convenience."[10]

Ford, though, turned the El Dorado myth inside out. The richest man in the world, he was the gilded one—the "Jesus Christ of industry," one Brazilian writer called him, while another called him a New World "Moses"—and salvation of Brazil's long-moribund rubber industry and the Amazon itself was to come from his touch. The "Kingdom of Fordlandia," however, was decidedly secular, and its magic technological. Ford's move into northern Brazil took place on the cusp of two eras, as the age of adventure gave way to the age of commerce.[11]

Their time passing, explorers acted as Ford's John the Baptists, walking through a fallen land and heralding its deliverance even as they faded from the scene. Theodore Roosevelt's *Through the Brazilian Wilderness*—an account of the former president's last jungle expedition, taken in 1914, just a few years before his death, to survey a heretofore uncharted Amazon river—predicted that the treacherous rapids that nearly cost him his life would eventually provide enough hydropower to support a "number of big manufacturing communities, knit by railroads to one another." Francis Gow Smith, a member of New York's Explorers Club, was in Brazil searching for Colonel Fawcett when news got out that Ford had secured his Brazilian concession. In a lengthy dispatch from the field, Smith described his near lethal encounter with the "King of the Xingu"—a rich and ruthless rubber baron on the Xingu River who "typifies the feudal tyranny of plantation methods in Brazil just as his new competitor" Henry Ford "typifies North America's industrial enterprise." The "jungle millionaire" terrorized his "peons," keeping them in a state of perpetual debt, locking those who dared to challenge his authority in stockades, beating them unmercifully, and leaving them to lie for hours on the ground as vampire bats "feast upon their blood and hordes of ants gnaw at their bare skins." Henry Ford "has never met his jungle rival," Smith wrote, but his "Brazilian project will be the wiping out of the King of Xingu's rubber monopoly, the liberation of his peons and the dawn of a new day for Brazilian prosperity."[12]

THE AMAZON IS a temptress: its chroniclers can't seem to resist invoking the jungle not as an ecological system but as a metaphysical testing ground, a place that seduces man to impose his will only to expose that will as impotent. Nineteenth- and early-twentieth-century explorers and missionaries often portrayed the jungle either as evil inherent or as revealing the evil men carry inside. Traveling through the region in 1930, the Anglican lay leader Kenneth Grubb wrote that the forest brings out the "worst instincts of man, brutalizes the affections, hardens the emotions, and draws out with malign and terrible intention every evil and sordid lust." Theodore Roosevelt's account of his expedition, which first ran as a serial in Scribner's, likewise painted the Amazon as a malevolent place, where things "sinister and evil" lurked in the "dark stillness" of its groves. Ancient trees didn't just fall and decompose but were "murdered," garroted by the ever tighter twists of vines. Roosevelt described the jungle as being largely "uninhabited by human beings," portraying its challenges as nearly wholly natural, even preternatural, captured in gothic depictions of "blood-crazy" fish and "bloodsucking" vampire bats. The jungle was "entirely indifferent to good or evil," he wrote, working "out her ends or no ends with utter disregard of pain and woe." For those readers not familiar with the theology that hell is the absence of God, the Rough Rider left little doubt as to the analogy he was implicitly drawing: he began his tale with a detailed seventeen-page description of treacherous serpents.[13]

Even more recently, those who survive encounters with the jungle primeval are often compelled to search for some larger meaning in its severity, holding it up as a touchstone to expose the charade of human progress. "We are challenging nature itself and it hits back, it just hits back, that's all," said the German film director Werner Herzog of the hardships he encountered in making his 1982 film *Fitzcarraldo*. Herzog's notorious attempt to replicate the compulsion of his title character, played by Klaus Kinski, and pull a 340-ton steamship over an Amazon mountain (the movie is based on the life of Carlos Fermín Fitzcarrald López, who had the good sense to dismantle the boat before proceeding) leads him to ponder the ethical vacuity of the natural world: "Kinski always says [nature] is full of erotic elements. I don't see it so much as erotic. I see it more as full of obscenity. . . . Nature here is violent, base. I wouldn't see anything erotical here. I would see fornication, and asphyxiation, and choking, and fighting for survival, . . . just rotting away. Of course there is lots of misery but it is to say misery that is all around us. The trees here are in misery, the birds here are in misery. They don't sing, they just screech in pain."[14]

But Henry Ford, along with the men and women he sent down to build his settlement, proved tone-deaf to these kinds of musings, to the metaphors and clichés that entangle much of the writing on the Amazon. There was a stubborn literalness about the midwesterners, engineers mostly but also lumberjacks and sawyers, many of them from Ford's timber operations in Michigan's Upper Peninsula. Confronted by the jungle, they didn't turn philosophical. When they looked up in the sky and saw vultures, those rank, jowled carrion eaters that induced in other Amazon wanderers a sense of their transience, they thought of Detroit's pigeons. Life in the dense river forest was hard on many of the Ford staff. Boredom could be overpowering, and a few succumbed to disease and death. Yet rather than provoking thoughts of morality or mortality, the Amazon tended to instill melancholy in Ford's pioneers, a desire to re-create a bygone

America, an America that the Ford Motor Company played no small part in dispatching.

While he avoided the more feverish adjectives often attached to the Amazon, Ford nonetheless saw the jungle as a challenge, but it had less to do with overcoming and dominating nature than it did with salvaging a vision of Americana that was slipping out of his grasp at home. That vision was rooted in his experience growing up on a farm in Dearborn and entailed using his wealth and industrial method to safeguard rural virtues and remedy urban ills. He was in his sixties when he founded Fordlandia—or Fordlândia in Brazilian Portuguese, the circumflex indicating a closed, pinched vowel, the final three letters pronounced "jee-ah"—and the settlement became the terminus for a lifetime of venturesome notions about the best way to organize society.

Ford's idea of a worthy life was chivalrous, especially in its promotion of ballroom dancing. But it was distinctly not adventurous, in contrast to the privations of war, frontier living, and jungle exploration that someone like Theodore Roosevelt celebrated for their ability to strengthen character. "The man who works hard," Ford once said, "should have his easy-chair, his comfortable fireside, his pleasant surroundings." And so in the Amazon, Ford built Cape Cod–style shingled houses for his Brazilian workers and urged them to tend flower and vegetable gardens and eat whole wheat bread and unpolished rice. Coming upon Fordlandia after a trip of hundreds of miles through the jungle, the US military attaché to Brazil, Major Lester Baker, called Fordlandia an oasis, a midwestern "dream," complete with "electric lights, telephones, washing machines, victrolas, and electric refrigerators." Managers enforced Prohibition, or at least tried to, though it wasn't a Brazilian law, and nurseries experimented with giving soy milk to babies, because Henry Ford hated cows. On weekends, the plantation sponsored square dances and recitations of poetry by William Wordsworth and Henry Longfellow. The workers, most of them born and raised in the Amazon, were shown documentaries on African and Antarctic expeditions, including Admiral Richard Byrd's 1929 journey to the South Pole, as well as shorts promoting tourism in Yellowstone Park and celebrating the new, streamlined Lin-

coln Zephyr. "Henry Ford has transplanted a large slice of twentieth century civilization" to the Amazon, reported Michigan's *Iron Mountain
Daily News*, bringing "a prosperity to the natives that they never before
experienced."[15]

Over the course of nearly two decades, Ford would spend tens of
millions of dollars founding not one but, after the first plantation was
devastated by leaf blight, two American towns, complete with central
squares, sidewalks, indoor plumbing, hospitals, manicured lawns, movie
theaters, swimming pools, golf courses, and, of course, Model Ts and As
rolling down their paved streets.

Back in America, newspapers kept up their drumbeat celebration,
only obliquely referencing reports that things were not progressing as the
company had hoped. But there was one note of skepticism. In late 1928,
the *Washington Post* ran an editorial that read in its entirety: "Ford will
govern a rubber plantation in Brazil larger than North Carolina. This is
the first time he has applied quantity production methods to trouble."[16]

IT STILL TAKES about eighteen hours on a slow riverboat to get to Fordlandia from the nearest provincial city, as long as it did eighty years ago
when Ford first sent a crew of Michigan engineers and lumberjacks to begin construction on his town. I've made the trip twice, and the second
time it was no less jolting after hours of passing little but green to round a
river bend and come upon a 150-foot tower bursting from the forest
canopy holding aloft a 150,000-gallon water tank. Decades of rain have
since scrubbed off its cursive white Ford logo, yet at the time of its construction the tower was the tallest man-made structure in the Amazon,
save for a pair of now dismantled smokestacks that had been attached to
the powerhouse. It was the crown jewel of an elaborate water system that
daily pumped half a million gallons of filtered and chlorinated water drawn
from the river to the town, plantation, and ice plant. Miles of buried pipes
fed into indoor sinks and toilets, sewers carried away household waste,
and fire hydrants—still a novelty in even the largest Latin American
cities—dotted the town's sidewalks. The water system was run by an electric plant made up of steam boilers, generators, turbines, and engines

salvaged from decommissioned navy ships stripped down to scrap at the River Rouge plant a few years earlier, Ford being a pioneer in industrial recycling.

Fordlandia stands on the eastern side of the Tapajós River, the Amazon's fifth largest tributary. Flowing south to north and intersecting with the Amazon about six hundred miles from the Atlantic, the Tapajós is a broad river, with sloping sandy banks that give way to a gradual rise, and at no point on the trip does one feel that the jungle is closing in. It is home to a staggering number of fish, insects, plants, and animals. Yet the valley's big-sky openness often instills in travelers a sensation of tedium. "The prevailing note in the Amazon is one of monotony," thought Kenneth Grubb, "the same green lines the river-bank, the same gloom fills the forest. . . . Each successive bend in the river is rounded in expectancy, only to reveal another identical stretch ahead." But then one beholds Ford's miragelike industrial plant. "When the view is had from the deck of a river steamer," wrote Ogden Pierrot, a U.S. diplomat stationed in Rio, "the imposing structures of the industrial section of the town, with the tremendous water tank and the smokestack of the power house, catch the view and create a sensation of real wonderment."[17]

As my boat made its way to Fordlandia's dock, the wind cut the jungle humidity, which, in any case, really wasn't that bad. Up a hill from the river's edge stood the town's Catholic church, built after the Ford Motor Company abandoned the place. Ford's managers allowed priests to visit and minister to the population but refused the request of the local bishop to establish a permanent mission and run the town's schools. Farther back loomed the famous water tower, along with the empty lumber mill and power plant. Everything was peaceful and calm, and indeed much more suggestive of Ford's easy-chair arcadia than nature red in tooth and claw. It was difficult to picture the chaos that befell this shore eight decades ago.

The first years of the settlement were plagued by waste, violence, and vice, making Fordlandia more Deadwood than *Our Town*. The death rate from malaria and yellow fever was high. Bending to hack away at the underbrush with machetes, scores of frontline cutters died from viper bites. Those who fled the plantation brought with them tales of knife

"Landmarks are absent," wrote the lay Anglican leader Kenneth Grubb about his travels around the Amazon in the late 1920s, "and there is nothing by which progress can be marked." Fordlandia's water tower was a rare exception.

fights, riots, and strikes. They complained of rancid food and corrupt and incompetent overseers who defrauded them of pay and turned the forest into a mud hole, burning large swaths of the jungle without the slightest idea of how to plant rubber. In what was perhaps the biggest man-made fire in that part of the Amazon to date, burning leaves floated to the far side of the river as ash wafted across the sky, turning clouds of the rainy season sky into a blood orange haze. Building material sent from Dearborn rusted and rotted on the riverbank. Bags of cement turned to stone in the rain. Migrants desperate for jobs, many of them from Brazil's drought- and famine-stricken northeast, poured into the work camp on rumors that Ford would be hiring tens of thousands of employees and paying five dollars a day. They trailed behind them wives, children, parents, cousins, aunts, and uncles, building makeshift houses from packing crates and canvas tarps. Rather than a midwestern city of virtue springing from the Amazon green, local merchants set up thatched bordellos, bars, and gambling houses, turning Fordlandia into a rain forest boomtown. Managers eventually established sovereignty over the settlement and achieved something approximating their boss's vision. But then nature rebelled.

HUBRIS SEEMS THE obvious moral attached to Fordlandia, especially considering not just the disaster of its early years but also, even once order was established and the city was more or less functional, rubber's refusal to submit to Ford-style regimentation. Yet surveying what remains of it left me with an almost elegiac feeling. Despite the promiscuous use of fire by its first managers, along with the running of what was billed as the most modern sawmill in all of Latin America, the town doesn't so much invoke the plague of deforestation. That would be easy to rebuke. It rather brings to mind a different kind of loss: deindustrialization. There is in fact an uncanny resemblance between Fordlandia's rusting water tower, broken-glassed sawmill, and empty power plant and the husks of the same structures in Iron Mountain, a depressed industrial city in Michigan's Upper Peninsula that also used to be a Ford town.

About a mile and a half from the dock, on a hill hooked by a river bend, sits the abandoned "American neighborhood." The wood-framed buildings are properly Protestant and not too ostentatious, complete with shingled roofs, plank floors, plaster walls, decorative moldings, tile bathrooms, electric refrigerators, and wall sconces. Decrepit and overrun by weeds, as could be expected, the houses are now home to colonies of bats, which have left a patina of guano on the walls and floors. The residences flank "Palm Avenue," which is actually shaded by mango trees, a hint that the company made some concession to the jungle ecology. Elms or maples would have wilted in the wet heat. Yet concrete sidewalks, electric streetlamps, and those red fire hydrants confirm that it made such compromises reluctantly.

Closer to the river, Brazilians, including some surviving Ford employees, continue to live in smaller mill town bungalows, along three long avenues that follow the contours of the land. Though they have since been renamed, the street closest to the Tapajós was called "Riverside Avenue," the farthest, hugging the beginning of an incline, "Hillside." In the middle was Main Street. The powerhouse and sawmill, both with walls of floor-to-ceiling windows, separate the two residential areas. The turbines and generators have been removed from the engine room, but industrial ephemera are still scattered around the mill. Nuts and bolts fill wooden boxes carrying the name Standard Oil of Brazil, which did some exploratory work on the estate. About a dozen Landis Machine Company presses, dies, and stamps bear the mark "Made in the USA." Outside, buried in the jungle grass, are twisted rails, what's left of a three-mile train line that carried logs to the mill, though it's bewildering to think what force of nature or how the passing of time could have produced their current mangled state.

Fordlandia's most striking building is set back from the river, on a knoll about half a mile in. It's a wreck of a hundred-bed hospital built from a sketch by Albert Kahn, the architect of Ford's Highland Park and River Rouge plants. Gracefully proportioned, well ventilated, with generous eaves and dormer windows jutting out of a pitched roof, the long and narrow jungle sanatorium seems lower to the ground than it really is, much like Kahn's celebrated enormous Highland Park factory. Inside, two dormitory wings are united by a series of rooms marked by signs indicating their former function. Most of the beds are gone, but some equipment, made of metal and glass that today looks menacing but in the 1930s was state of the art, remains. In the sterilization room there's a large apparatus that suggests a front-load washing machine, and the gynecology room still has its examination table. The surgery and X-ray rooms are bare, but the laboratory has some bottles and test tubes lying around and the records of the hospital's last patients strewn on the floor.

Unlike nineteenth-century British writers who lamented the coming of industrialization, Henry Ford saw the machine not as defiling the garden but rather as harmonizing with it. And Ford's Amazon town does seem to complement its setting, perhaps because the conceit that underwrote Fordlandia has been muted by its weed-entwined buildings, rotten floor planks, and guano-glazed walls. This impression is reinforced by the memories of residents, most too young to have experienced the company firsthand, who speak approvingly about the good wages Ford offered and the free health care provided by the town's hospital. Things were *bom demais*, almost too good, says a man who moved to the town from downriver as a boy, when his father took a job on the plantation. Undoubtedly paternalistic, Ford's social program compares well with what is available to much of the world today. One doctor who accompanied a team of São Paulo medical students on a visit to the town in 2006 said contemporary Fordlandia residents who are sick have two options: those with money travel by river to a doctor; those who don't have money learn to suffer their illness. América Lobato, eighty-one years old on my first trip to Fordlandia, in 2005, was in the lucky group, but barely. She began working at the age of sixteen as a babysitter for a Ford administrator and therefore enjoyed a small pension from the Brazilian government. América remembers that the hospital didn't just treat company employees but took in patients from all over Brazil. "They couldn't do complicated operations like heart surgery," she said, but things like "the appendix or liver they took care of." América has since passed away, but during the last years of her life she had to travel nearly a full day by riverboat to a specialist to attend to her failing eyes and bad legs.[18]

THE FOND MEMORIES with which América and others recalled the heyday of Fordlandia are understandable, considering the lack of opportunities, decent jobs, and basic services available to most residents of the region. But there's something particular to Henry Ford that summons a deeper poignancy than one would hear from residents in similarly derelict company towns elsewhere in Latin America, ruins from a time when US corporations rapidly expanded their operations throughout the hemisphere, built around mines, mills, and plantations. In 1917, Milton Hershey began work on a sugar mill town outside the city of Santa Cruz, Cuba, which he named Hershey and which, when finished, included American-style bungalows, luxurious houses for staff, schools, a hospital, a baseball diamond, and a number of movie theaters. At the height of the banana boom of the 1920s, one could tour Guatemala, Costa Rica, Panama, Honduras, Cuba, and Colombia and not for a moment leave United Fruit Company property, traveling on its trains and ships, passing through its ports, staying in its many towns, with their tree-lined streets and modern amenities, in a company hotel or guest house, playing golf on its links, taking in a Hollywood movie in one of its theaters, and being tended to in its hospital if sick.

All of these enterprises of course say something about the way the United States spread out in the world, capturing in clapboard simplicity the assuredness with which businessmen and politicians believed that the American way of life could be easily transplanted and eagerly welcomed elsewhere. In the United States, company towns were hailed not just for the earnings they generated for their companies but for the benefits they brought Latin Americans, and many observers explicitly thought them a New World alternative to European imperialism—that is, run by private interests rather than government ministries. Just as the "conquest by Europe of the tropics of Africa, Asia, and the islands of the Pacific will be recounted by future historians as the monumental achievement of this age" for bringing "high civilization" to benighted lands, thought the business writer Frederick Upham Adams, so, too, would the United Fruit Company be celebrated for carving an "empire" in the "wilderness" that included not just modern industrial technology and up-to-date sanitary practices but "picturesque settlements," complete with "places of amusement, well-kept streets, electric lights, and most of the accessories of civilization."[19]

But the story of Fordlandia cuts deeper into the marrow of the American experience. Not because its trappings more faithfully represent the life and culture of the United States than those found in Hershey, Cuba, or in United Fruit Company towns: many of the features of Ford's Amazon town most commented on for their incongruity in a jungle setting in fact reflected eccentricities particular to the carmaker. Rather, what makes Fordlandia more quintessentially American was the way frustrated idealism was built into its conception.

Over fifty years ago, the Harvard historian Perry Miller gave his famous "Errand into the Wilderness" lecture in which he tried to explain why English Puritans lit out for the New World to begin with, as opposed to, say, going to Holland. They went, Miller offered by way of an answer, not just to preserve their "posterity from the corruption of this evil world" as it was manifest in the Church of England but to complete the Protestant reformation of Christendom that had stalled in Europe. In a "bare land, devoid of already established (and corrupt) institutions, empty of bishops and courtiers," they would "start *de novo*." The Puritans did not flee to America, Miller said, but rather sought to give the faithful back in England a "working model" of a purer community. Thus, central from the start to American expansion was "deep disquietude," a feeling that "something had gone wrong"—not only with the inability of the Reformation to redeem Europe but subsequently with the failure to achieve perfection, to found and maintain a "pure biblical polity" in New England. With the Massachusetts Bay Colony just a few decades old, a dissatisfied Cotton Mather began to learn Spanish, thinking that a better "New Jerusalem" could be raised in Mexico.[20]

The founding of Fordlandia was driven by a similar restlessness, a chafing sense that "something had gone wrong" in America. Other company towns, despite their much publicized altruism, lived and died by the economic logic that led to their establishment. Hershey, Cuba, supplied sugar to Hershey, Pennsylvania's chocolate factories for decades, until 1945, when it made more sense to purchase the crop from independent mills. Fordlandia, however, moved to rhythms set not by supply and demand but rather by the ups and downs of American life, which Henry Ford pledged to reform. Ford's frustrations with domestic politics and culture were legion: war, unions, Wall Street, energy monopolies, Jews, modern dance, cow's milk, the Roosevelts, cigarettes, alcohol, and creeping government intervention. Yet churning beneath all these annoyances was the fact that the force of industrial capitalism he helped unleash was undermining the world he hoped to restore.

FORDLANDIA'S LESSON WOULD seem to be particularly resonant today. With a surety of purpose and incuriosity about the world that seems all too familiar, Ford deliberately rejected expert advice and set out to turn the Amazon into the Midwest of his imagination. "What the people of the interior of Brazil need," he declared at the outset of the project, "is to have their economic life stabilized by fair returns for their labor paid in cash and their mode of living brought up to modern standards in sanitation and in prevention and cure of disease." This formula worked in Michigan and

Ford saw no reason it couldn't be exported to Brazil. "There will not be," Ford said, "any great difficulty in accomplishing these things." *Fordism* was a term that would go on to have many meanings, but its first usage captured the essence of cocksureness, defined by the *Washington Post* as "Ford efforts conceived in disregard or ignorance of Ford limitations."[21]

If anything, failure only made Ford and his emissaries more certain. The more Ford's errand to grow rubber, as originally stated, proved impossible to fulfill, the more he and his company revised their warrant, justifying their Brazilian mission in ever more idealistic terms, especially after the onset of the Great Depression, when the settlement was held up as a Ford-built solution for surviving hard times.

Two years into the construction of Fordlandia, after visiting the plantation site and witnessing firsthand the chaos that reigned there, one US diplomat stationed in Brazil wrote his superiors in the State Department to try to explain Ford's ongoing commitment to a "venture which apparently will never be commercially profitable":

> In the last few months, the writer has arrived at an opinion, based on a number of different facts, which seems to be the only theory which will fit all of these facts. This belief is that Mr. Ford considers the project as a "work of civilization." This very phrase has been used in correspondence of one of the higher officials of the Detroit office. Nothing else will explain the lavish expenditure of money, at least three million dollars in the last sixteen months, in laying the foundation of what is evidently planned to become a city of two or three hundred thousand inhabitants.
>
> On the basis of this theory, discarding any interpretation ascribing to the work the character of a purely commercial venture, it is possible to understand many things which are otherwise inexplicable.[22]

The journalist Walter Lippmann identified in Henry Ford, for all his peculiarity, a common strain of "primitive Americanism." The industrialist's conviction that he could make the world conform to his will was founded on a faith that success in economic matters should, by extension, allow capitalists to try their hands "with equal success" at "every other occupation." "Mr. Ford is neither a crank nor a freak," Lippmann insisted, but "merely the logical exponent of American prejudices about wealth and success."[23]

For Lippmann, Ford represented the essence of Americanism not just because he embodied a confidence born of money but also because he reflected "our touching belief that the world is like ourselves." "Why shouldn't success in Detroit," Lippmann asked, "assure success in front of Baghdad?"

And if Baghdad, then certainly Brazil.

Part I

MANY THINGS OTHERWISE INEXPLICABLE

CHAPTER 1

UNDER AN AMERICAN FLAG

①OVER A LONG LUNCH AT HENRY FORD'S DEARBORN HOME, FORD listened to Harvey Firestone complain about the British.

It was July 1925, and Firestone had thrown himself into a campaign to thwart Winston Churchill's proposed British rubber cartel. For decades, US industry had imported rubber from European, predominately British, colonies in Southeast Asia with little problem. But when prices started to tumble in 1919, Churchill, the British secretary of state for the colonies, endorsed a plan to regulate the production of crude rubber to ensure supply didn't outstrip demand. The future Tory prime minister would go on to gain a reputation as a steadfast friend of America. But at the time, politicians and industrialists denounced him as an archimperialist and protectionist. Speaker of the House Nicholas Longworth called Churchill's plan an "international swindle." Tennessee's Representative Cordell Hull, who would later serve as FDR's secretary of state, likened the proposed cartel to a "hold-up."[1]

Secretary of Commerce Herbert Hoover stoked the anger. The man who would soon be president believed America's rubber supply to be industry's choke point, more critical in many ways than oil. Petroleum was found in domestic fields in Pennsylvania, Louisiana, Oklahoma, Texas, and California, as well as in neighboring Mexico and Venezuela, within easy reach of US gunboats. But rubber came from a world away, from British, Dutch, and French plantations in Southeast Asia. Just as an increase in the demand for cotton in the nineteenth century reinvigorated America's slave plantation system, the growing US auto industry's thirst for rubber breathed new life into European colonialism, which had been weakened by World War I. Revenue from rubber—tapped and processed by cheap coolie labor—helped Amsterdam, London, and Paris bind their colonies in Indonesia, Sri Lanka, Malaysia, and Indochina tighter into their imperial system, with the profits from the sale of latex helping England and France pay off their war debt. Hoover warned American manufacturers—not just of cars but of any machine that used latex—that their supply of rubber was too dependent on old, imperialist Europe and that they could be subject to a "supercharge" of more than a half billion dollars if Holland and France were to join the proposed British cartel. He pointed out that if the United States adopted the same production restrictions and price controls that London was imposing on its rubber, the price of wheat would go from $1.50 to $8.00 a bushel in foreign markets. The secretary of commerce urged US manufacturers to invest in rubber cultivation in Latin America and funded scientific expeditions into the Amazon to offset their research costs. Business leaders, though, largely responded with indifference to Hoover's alarm. Except for Harvey Firestone and Henry Ford.[2]

"I am going to fight this law with all the strength and vigor that is in me," Firestone pledged, and he asked Ford to join with him in organizing a rubber association. He had tried this before. In February 1923, he convened a "national conference of rubber, automotive, and accessory manufacturers." Over two hundred industrialists, including Ford, gathered in Washington at the Willard Hotel to hear Firestone make his declaration of "economic independence" from London. "Rubber under an American flag," he proclaimed, as his audience listened politely to a plan to create an American Cooperative Association. Capitalized at $50 million, the cooperative would establish plantations in Latin America and the Philippines to bust the "small coterie of British shareholders in plantation interests." "We must," Firestone urged his fellow industrialists, "act immediately."[3]

But they didn't. Neither Hoover nor Firestone could raise much worry among America's corporate leaders. Firestone's colleagues at B. F. Goodrich, Goodyear, and U.S. Rubber worked closely with the British and didn't want to contribute to American Anglophobia, which seemed to be fueling much of the rubber feud. Besides, despite all their talk in support of free enterprise and open markets, they were generally in favor of the right to monopoly. Stuart Hotchkiss, president of U.S. Rubber, actually admitted to favoring Churchill's cartel. He thought it represented a mature rejection of a juvenile faith in the laws of free supply and demand and laughed at Firestone's warnings of war with Great Britain. It was so "unthinkable that if it should occur, there would not be much use in anything."[4]

Henry Ford, dependent as he was on rubber, shared Firestone's concern. The auto industry relied as much on vulcanized rubber as on oil, using processed latex not just for tires but for the hoses, valves, gaskets, and electrical wires needed to run the increasingly complex internal combustion engines, steering assemblages, and shock absorption systems, as well as for the machines that made the cars. The mileage of paved roads in the United States increased rapidly after World War I, reducing tire wear and tear. And during the first two decades of the twentieth century, design improvements extended the average life of a tire more than sixfold. Yet by 1925, the total number of tires sold in the United States hit an all-time high, and by the end of the decade the value of all rubber sold in the country surpassed a billion dollars, with more than 70 percent of it used to manufacture tires, about fifty million of them a year.[5]

Already by 1924, Ford had considered growing his own rubber in the "muck lands" of the Florida Everglades. Rumors of his interest in Florida prompted Detroit speculators to organize the Florida and Cape Cod Realty Company to scoop up and subdivide large tracts of land in the town of Labelle, offering lots for sale at seventy-five dollars a piece. "No doubt," wrote an investigator from the Michigan Securities Commission, "a good many Ford employees will be buncoed, as they will undoubtedly buy lots on the strength of Mr. Ford's supposed rubber experiment." But the project

Rubber-trust busters: Herbert Hoover, Henry Ford, Thomas Edison, Harvey Firestone.

didn't advance much beyond a few plantings of rubber figs and rubber vines to see if industrial amounts of sap could be tapped from their trunks.[6]

So through the course of lunch Ford listened to Firestone's harangue. He had heard it before, including Firestone's prophecy that the British would increase the price of rubber to an astonishing $1.20 a pound, even though at that moment it had floated down to about twenty cents. "Well, you know what to do about that," he finally shouted. "Grow your own rubber!"[7]

Ford liked Firestone and considered him not just an industry colleague but a friend. They had met in Detroit in 1895, when Ford walked into the Columbus Buggy Works, where Firestone worked as a sales agent, and ordered a set of sturdy carriage tires that wouldn't burst under his just built 500-pound gas-propelled automobile. Five years later, Harvey founded the Firestone Tire and Rubber Company in Akron, Ohio, and over the next two decades he worked in close partnership with Ford to develop tire technology—a detachable rim, diagonal nonskid thread patterns that allowed increased speeds, and a low-pressure balloon tire that dramatically increased mileage per gallon, thus lowering the cost of owning a car—that complemented Ford's goal of delivering a cheap, well-built car to the masses.[8]

But Ford was not an association man. Unlike northeastern corporate elites on the model of Hotchkiss, Ford, who grew up on a Dearborn farm, disliked collective action. In June 1926, despite a personal plea from General Motors' chairman, John Raskob, he refused to attend a meeting of Detroit's major car company executives called to figure out how to bypass antitrust legislation prohibiting the auto industry from importing rubber collectively. Raskob was an ally of Pierre du Pont, another GM director, and Ford had long felt persecuted by the patrician du Ponts. He did show up at Firestone's Washington conclave and funded a few joint projects with the tire maker to explore the possibility of growing rubber in Nicaragua. And the two men underwrote Thomas Edison's slow-going efforts to develop what Edison had taken to calling "war rubber"—that is, synthetic or organic alternatives to rubber, made from milkweed maybe or goldenrod. But he did nothing to help his friend realize his rubber association. "Mr. Ford," remarked his longtime personal secretary, Ernest Liebold, "wouldn't consider a thing like joining an organization of rubber producers. . . . He never wanted to ally himself with anybody else in connection with any specific activities."[9]

When the lunch was over, Ford held Liebold back out of earshot. "Find out," he whispered to his bespectacled aide, "where is the best place to grow rubber."[10]

Liebold threw himself into the task. He read everything he could on rubber, including reports supplied by the Department of Agriculture and Hoover's commercial attachés stationed in Brazil. He also took a crash course in African history and fairly quickly concluded that Liberia, where

Firestone, unable to rouse interest in his rubber collective, would soon establish a plantation, was too unstable to suit Ford's interest. Latex, thought Liebold, the American-born son of German Lutheran parents, should be cultivated "where the people themselves have reached a higher state of civilization." Ford's secretary decided that this ruled out Liberia, a country "composed entirely of Negroes whose mentality and intellectual possibilities are quite low."

"Rubber should be grown where it originated," Liebold concluded. And that meant the Amazon.

THE SOUTHERN HALF of the Amazon basin, running from the Atlantic mouth of the river through Brazil and into Ecuador, Bolivia, and Peru, is home to *Hevea brasiliensis*, the species of rubber tree that provides the most elastic and purest latex. From the early eighteenth century to the end of the nineteenth, the Brazilian Amazon supplied nearly all of the world's rubber, demand for which steadily increased as the Industrial Revolution in the United States and Europe took off. At the height of the rubber boom, in the second half of the nineteenth century, Amazonian latex made up 40 percent of Brazil's total exports and supplied most of the rubber used for gaskets, valves, belts, wire insulation, carriage, bicycle, and automobile tires, boots, shoes, raincoats, condoms, and elastic garters. Latex lords grew magnificently wealthy, building opulent palatial homes and gilded jungle cities. With their Beaux Arts palaces, neoclassical municipal buildings, electric trams, wide Parisian boulevards, and French restaurants, the cities of Manaus, located about nine hundred miles up the Amazon River, and Belém, the region's principal Atlantic port, competed for the title of "tropical Paris."[11]

Manaus is famous for its hulking Amazonas Theater, an opera house built of Italian marble and surrounded by roads made of rubber so the carriage clatter of late arrivals wouldn't interrupt the voices of Europe's best tenors and sopranos. Finished in 1896, it reportedly cost more than two million dollars to construct. Money flowed freely during the boom, and Manaus's better classes imported whatever they could at whatever price. American explorers found that they could sell their used khakis for five times what they paid for them at home, once they grew tired of parading

Manaos.   Theatro Amazonas.

A contemporary view of the opera house in Manaus, the tropical Paris.

around the city in their jungle gear.* With more movie theaters than Rio and more playhouses than Lisbon, Manaus was the second city in all of Brazil to be lighted by electricity, and visitors who came upon it from the river at night during the last years of the nineteenth century marveled at its brilliance in the midst of darkness, "pulsating with the feverish throb of the world." But not just light made Manaus and Belém, also electrified early, modern. Their many dark spaces provided venues for quintessentially urban pleasures. Roger Casement, Britain's consul in Rio, who later would become famous for his anti-imperialist and antislavery activities, wrote in his diary in 1911 about cruising Manaus's docks, picking up young men

---

*Unlike Brazilians, who upon returning from the jungle usually immediately bathed, shaved, and brought a new suit of clothes, Americans, one observer noted, had the "irritating habit of stalking through the streets, and calling on the highest officials" in their "ten-gallon hats, campaign boots, and cartridge-belts" (Earl Parker Hanson, *Journey to Manaos*, New York: Reynal and Hitchcock, 1938, p. 292).

for anonymous sex. Belém, for its part, wrote a *Los Angeles Times* correspondent in 1899, had an "amount of vice" that would shock the "reformers of New York," most of which could be found in its many cafes and cabarets, as well as its best brothel, the High Life Hotel, which is "devoted to the life of the lowest order" and which Brazilians pronounced, according to the journalist, as "Higgy Liffey."[12]

From start to finish, the production of rubber that made such affluence possible represented an extreme contrast to the industrial method pioneered by Henry Ford in Michigan. *Hevea brasiliensis* can grow as high as a hundred feet, standing straight with an average girth, at breast height, of about one meter in diameter. It's an old species, and during its millennia-long history there likewise evolved an army of insects and fungi that feed off its leaves, as well as mammals that eat its seeds. In its native habitats of Brazil, Bolivia, Peru, and Ecuador, it best grows wild, just a few trees per acre, far enough apart to keep bugs and blight at bay; would-be planters soon learned that the cultivation of large numbers of rubber trees in close proximity greatly increased the population of rubber's predators. The extraction and processing of latex, therefore, was based not on developing large plantations or investing in infrastructure but rather on a cumbersome and often violent system of peonage, in which tappers were compelled to spread out through the jungle and collect sap.

Tappers, known as *seringueiros*, lived scattered along the river, sometimes with their families but often alone, with their huts located at the head of one or two looped rubber trails that ran a few miles, connecting between a hundred and two hundred trees. In the morning, starting before sunrise, when the latex flowed freest through the thin vessels that run up the tree's bark, the tapper would make his first round, slashing each *Hevea* with diagonal cuts and then placing tin cans or cups to catch the falling sap. After lunch, and a nap to escape the worst of the heat, the *seringueiro* made a second round to collect the latex. Back at his hut, he smoked it on a spit over an earthenware oven fired by dampened palm nuts, which produced a toxic smoke that took its toll on tapper lungs, until it formed a black ball of rubber, weighing between seventy and ninety pounds. He then brought the ball to a trading post, handing it over to a

Two tappers smoking latex under a thatched lean-to.

merchant either as rent for the trails or to pay off goods purchased on credit. The rubber then made its way downriver to Belém's receivers and export houses. The excruciatingly unhurried drip, drip, drip of the sap into a battered cup, latched onto the tree with a piece of rope or leather, was about as far removed from the synchronized speed of Henry Ford's assembly line as one could imagine. Back in Michigan, Ford was obsessed with rooting out "slack" from not just the workday but the work year—trying to find ways to combine agricultural and industrial seasonal labor that maximized the efficiency of both. But along the Amazon, *seringueiros* often spent the "grey and sad" months of the rainy season, when latex ran too slow to tap, "in his hammock without any profitable occupation," accumulating more debt that they would never work off. Their thatched huts were often perched on poles, and as the water rose around them they passed the rainy days in isolation, as one traveler described, alone with "dogs, fowls, and a host of insects, all unable to move far owing to the water that surrounds them."[13]

It was a system that produced enormous riches when Brazil had a monopoly on the world's rubber trade and therefore largely set the global market price. But the wealth it created was fleeting and unsustainable. The tapping system itself could quickly deplete man and tree. As the seasons passed, cuts on the bark would scab over to be bled again, successively yielding less and less latex. With care, *Hevea* can produce for up to three decades, starting in its fifth or sixth year of growth, but under pressure to deliver more latex, *seringueiros* cut too often, too deep, causing stunted growth and early exhaustion. And profit was generated by what was essentially an elaborate pyramid scheme: at the apex were foreign commercial and financial houses; in the middle stood Brazilian merchants, traders, and a few exporters; and the whole thing rested on the backs of indebted tappers, who, as one critic put it, received goods on credit charged at fifty but in reality worth ten, in exchange for latex that the local merchant assessed at ten but that was actually worth fifty. As another writer noted, the "potentates of the forest have no credit beyond that on their books—against peons who never pay (unless with their lives)." Euclides da Cunha, one of the Amazon's great chroniclers, described the trade as the "most criminal employment organization ever spawned by unbridled selfishness."[14]

The first generation of early-nineteenth-century-boom rubber tappers came from the Amazon's native population. Things were bad for many indigenous communities prior to the rubber trade; slave raiding had already devastated many groups. "Every manner of persuasion," one anthropologist observed, "from torture to degeneration by cachaça"—a cheap rum distilled from sugar cane juice—was used to make natives collect wild jungle products. Prior to the expansion of the latex economy, these included nuts, feathers, snake skins, dyes, fibers, pelts, timber, spices, fruit, and medicinal herbs and barks, most notably from the cinchona tree, found in the higher reaches of the upper Amazon, which produced the antimalarial alkaloid quinine, indispensable in hastening the spread of European colonialism in Asia and Africa.[15]

But the rubber trade was by far more extensive, and thus more disruptive, than anything that had come before it, organizing under its regime the whole of the Amazon wherever *Hevea* was found. The Apiaca, for instance, were just one of many groups practically wiped out as a distinct tribal society, their men pressed into service either as tappers or to paddle or pole trading boats, and their women as servants or concubines. After native sources of labor were exhausted, migrants, mostly from Brazil's drought-prone northeast, made up subsequent generations of tappers. They arrived at Manaus and Belém by the boatful, withered, sunken-faced, and already bonded to pay for their transport. Between 1800 and 1900, the lower Amazon's population increased tenfold, with desperately poor, eternally indebted families living in small, isolated clusters of huts along the river's many waterways or in the sprawling shantytowns that spread out behind Manaus and Belém's Belle Époque façade.[16]

But by 1925, when Ford and Firestone were thinking of getting into the rubber business, this boom had long turned to bust, largely because of the actions of another Henry, who arrived in the Amazon over half a century earlier to commit what observers today call "bio-piracy," which would eventually unravel Brazil's latex monopoly.

Henry Wickham was a prime example of the kind of imperial rogue chronicled by Rudyard Kipling. Only Wickham didn't travel east to make a name for himself in Britain's formal colonies; instead he went west to Latin America, where London in the late nineteenth century was extending its commercial and financial reach. He landed first in Nicaragua, where he tried to turn a profit exporting colorful bird plumage back to his mother's London millinery shop, located on a small street just off what is now Piccadilly Circus. He was a bad shot, though, and soon decided to better his luck in Brazil.[17]

In 1871, Wickham and his wife settled in Santarém, where the Tapajós River flows into the Amazon. Attempting to establish himself as a rubber expert, he quickly fell into destitution, surviving only thanks to the kindness of a community of U.S. Confederate exiles who, moved by, as one of the Southern expatriates put it, Wickham's "aristocratic appearance" and "lonesome, melancholy aspect," took the couple in. A failure at most everything in life, Wickham enjoyed one reported success, the illegal spiriting of seventy thousand Amazonian seeds, gathered from a site not far from where Fordlandia would be founded, out of Brazil in 1876. These he turned over to London's Royal Botanic Gardens, where they were nurtured into the seedlings used to develop Asia's latex competition. Actually, Wickham's real success was in gaining fame for stealing the seeds, for historians of rubber have subsequently questioned key aspects of his derring-do story. Whatever the case, Queen Victoria knighted Wickham, securing his place in history as a British imperial hero and a Brazilian imperialist villain, and the Amazon began its long descent into economic stupor.[18]

The seeds Wickham collected and shipped to London provided the genetic stock of all subsequent rubber plantations in the British, French, and Dutch colonies. *Hevea* was able to grow closer together in Asia, and later Africa, because the insects and fungi that feed off rubber didn't exist in that part of the world. And when the trees began to run sufficient amounts of cheap latex to meet the world's demand, Brazil's rubber pyramid came toppling down. No matter how exploited the Amazonian tapper, the price of producing rubber in large estates was considerably lower than what it cost to extract it from wild groves. Asian plantations were close to major ports, which cut down on transportation expense. They used low-wage labor, often imported from China, and by the early twentieth century had selected and crossbred trees, leading to much greater sap yields. In 1912, estates in Malaya and Sumatra were producing 8,500 tons of latex, compared with the Amazon's 38,000 tons. Two years later, Asia was exporting over 71,000 tons. Less than nine years later, that number rose to 370,000 tons. Manaus fell into fast decline, its opera house ridiculed as an emblem of folly, of the excess wealth and European strivings of rubber barons who spent their money on gold leaf, red velvet, and murals of Greek and Roman gods cavorting in the jungle, rather than on developing a sustainable economy. Belém gave way to Singapore as the world's premier rubber exporting port, and the Amazon languished, subject of any number of plans to restore the region to glory—until Ford tried to make one happen.[19]

CHAPTER 2

THE COW MUST GO

ONE OF THE BOOKS ERNEST LIEBOLD READ IN HIS DELIBERATIONS on where best to grow rubber was *Through the Brazilian Wilderness*, Theodore Roosevelt's account of his triumphant Amazon expedition, in which he and his son Kermit almost lost their lives charting the unexplored thousand-mile-long River of Doubt. Roosevelt made only passing reference to the contracting rubber economy, mostly to relate the hard-luck life of tappers. But there was one passage that must have caught Liebold's attention.

In describing his journey to the headwaters of the Tapajós River, Roosevelt observed that the area's many fast rivers could provide nearly "unlimited motive force to populous manufacturing communities." Telegraph lines had to be run, followed by railroads, but there were no "serious natural obstacles" to either task. Once communication and transportation had been established, the "right kind" of settlers would arrive, followed by "enterprising businessmen of foresight, coolness and sagacity" willing to put the migrants to work for "an advantage that would be mutual." And thus would rise a "great industrial civilization."[1]

If anyone could make it happen—or at least if anyone was sure of his ability to make such a vision happen—it would be Henry Ford. When Roosevelt left for Brazil in late 1913, Ford was already well known as the creator of the world's first affordable, mass-produced automobile. But when he returned in early 1914, the industrialist had been catapulted to the heights of world fame, lauded as a "sociologist manufacturer" who didn't just attract the "right kind" of worker but assembled them from whole cloth. "The impression has somehow got around," said the Reverend Samuel Marquis, who for a time headed Ford's employee relations office, "that Henry Ford is in the automobile business. It isn't true. Mr. Ford shoots about fifteen hundred cars out of the back door of his factory every day just to get rid of them. They are the by-products of his real business, which is the making of men."[2]

SUCCESS CAME LATE to Ford. Born on a Michigan farm in 1863, he was forty years old when he founded the Ford Motor Company in Detroit, forty-five when he introduced the Model T, and fifty when he put assembly line production into place and began to pay workers a wage high enough to let them buy the product they themselves made. So while he came of age during the early stages of the Industrial Revolution, the America he lived in for the first half of his life was still mostly rural, and the changes he helped set in motion came stunningly fast.

Ford didn't invent the assembly line. He claimed he got the idea of having workers remain at one location and perform a single task from the "disassembly lines" found in Chicago's and Cincinnati's slaughterhouses, where butchers hacked off parts as pig and cow carcasses passed in front of them on conveyor hooks. Nor did he conceive the other central idea of modern mass production, that is, making parts as identical as possible to one another so that they would be interchangeable. But Ford did fuse these two ideas together as never before, perfecting the idea of a factory as a complex system of ever more integrated subassembly processes.

Most of this innovation took place in Ford's new Highland Park plant, opened in 1910 and designed by the architect Albert Kahn, who prior to his work with Ford had been associated with the anti–mass production arts and crafts movement. Located a few miles north of downtown Detroit along Woodward Avenue, the factory was enormous. It was four stories high, 865 feet long, 700,000 square feet in total, holding eight thousand machines, and was dubbed the Crystal Palace for the tens of thousands of windowpanes that bathed its shop floor in radiant sunlight. Highland Park was powered not so much by steam or diesel but, as historian Douglas Brinkley puts it, management's restless search to "save time, money, and manpower through further mechanization." Within eighteen months of the introduction in April 1913 of the first assembly line to make flywheels, every major component of Ford's car was being produced on moving lines, including the final confection of the finished product. Highland Park had become a machine itself, which by the midteens was dedicated to making one cheap yet sturdy thing: the Model T.[3]

The economics of Ford-style mass production were demonstrably simple. In 1911–12, it took just under seven thousand Ford workers to make 78,440 Model Ts. The following year, both production and the workforce more than doubled. Then in 1913–14, with the introduction of the assembly line and other innovations, the number of cars the factory produced doubled yet again, while the labor force *decreased* from 14,336 to 12,880 men. At the same time, the cost of manufacturing a Model T continued to decline, which allowed for a reduction in price, which increased demand, which generated more profit, which could be poured back into the factory to synchronize and mechanize production even further, to start the whole process over again. By 1921, Ford had captured more than 50 percent of the American car market, producing more than two million Model Ts a year at a production cost 60 percent cheaper than a decade earlier.[4]

In 1914, the British journalist Julian Street visited Detroit and described the raw energy of Ford's Highland Park plant:

> The whole room, with its interminable aisles, its whirling shafts and wheels, its forest of roof-supporting posts and flapping, flying, leather belting, its endless rows of writhing machinery, its shrieking, hammering, and clatter, its smell of oil, its autumn haze of smoke, its savage-looking foreign population—to my mind it expressed but one thing and that was delirium. . . . Fancy a jungle of wheels and belts and weird iron forms—of men, machinery and movement—add to it every kind

Highland Park's crankshaft assembly room, 1915.

of sound you can imagine: the sound of a million squirrels chirking, a million monkeys quarreling, a million lions roaring, a million pigs dying, a million elephants smashing through a forest of sheet iron, a million boys whistling on their fingers, a million others coughing with the whooping cough, a million sinners groaning as they are dragged to hell—imagine all of this happening at the very edge of Niagara Falls, with the everlasting roar of the cataract as a perpetual background, and you may acquire a vague conception of that place.[5]

For Street, the jungle trope was not to suggest, as it did for Upton Sinclair in his novel about the Chicago meatpacking industry, the anarchic brutality of capitalism, which drains the life out of workers and then casts them off to wither away like so many dead leaves. On the contrary, the British journalist saw the assembly line method as the taming of the industrial jungle, a "relentless system" yielding "terrible efficiency." "Like a river and its tributaries," Ford's integrated assembly lines flowed inexorably to their final destination: a finished Model T.[6]

"PEOPLE DON'T STAY put," Ford once said to explain why communism would never work in the Soviet Union. But neither did they remain still during the first decades of industrial capitalism. At the Ford factory, worker absenteeism averaged 10 percent a day between 1912 and 1913, and the yearly turnover rate of 380 percent was crippling the factory's production capacity. Ford's emphasis on synchronization and mechanization only aggravated the already high labor turnover. For the majority of Ford's ever growing workforce, the slightly better-than-average pay the company offered was not sufficient incentive to be turned into repeating machines.[7]

The second stage of Ford's revolution, then, had to do with human relations, with making people stay put. Ford came to believe that the key to creating loyal, more efficient workers was to help them find fulfillment, as he understood it, outside the factory. RULE

In early 1914, Ford made an announcement that sent seismic shocks across the globe. Henceforth, he proclaimed, the Ford Motor Company would pay an incentive wage of five dollars for an eight-hour day, nearly double the average industrial standard. The Wall Street Journal charged Henry Ford with class treason, with "economic blunders if not crimes." Yet his absentee and turnover rate plummeted and Ford was jolted into the ranks of the world's most admired men, "an international symbol of the new industrialization."[8]

But high wages alone were not enough to ensure either factory-floor efficiency or individual responsibility. A better salary could just lead to quicker dissipation through gambling, drinking, and whoring. There was no shortage of temptations in iniquitous Detroit. There were more brothels in the city than churches, and workers often lived crowded in fetid slums, in flophouses that fronted for gambling halls, bars, and opium dens. So Ford conditioned his Five Dollar Day plan with the obligation that workers live a wholesome life.[9]

And to make sure they did, the carmaker dispatched inspectors from his Sociological Department to probe into the most intimate corners of Ford workers' lives, including their sex lives. Denounced as a system of paternal surveillance as often as it was lauded as a program of civic reform, by 1919 the Sociological Department employed hundreds of agents who spread out over Dearborn and Detroit asking questions, taking notes, and writing up personnel reports. They wanted to know if workers had insurance and how they spent their money and free time. Did they have a bank account? How much debt did they carry? How many times were they married? Did they send money home to the old country? Sociological men came around not just once but two, three, or four times interviewing family members, friends, and landlords to make sure previous reports of probity were accurate. They of course discouraged drinking, smoking, and gambling and encouraged saving, clean living habits, keeping flies off food, maintaining an orderly house, backyard, and front porch, and sleeping in beds. They also frowned on the taking in of boarders since, "next to liquor, dissension in the home is due to people other than the family being there."[10]

The majority of the Ford Motor Company's workforce were immigrants, from Poland, Russia, Italy, the disintegrating Austro-Hungarian and Ottoman empires, the Middle East, Japan, and Mexico. In addition to attracting foreign-born workers, Ford's Five Dollar Day wage sparked a march of African Americans from the South who heard, correctly, that Ford paid equal wages to all male employees, regardless of skin color. The car industry's absolute need for labor was insatiable in the 1920s and mitigated racism, though African Americans were generally assigned the hardest jobs and the ones with the least potential for advancement. And though ecumenical in his hiring practices, Ford still charged his Sociological Department with Americanizing immigrants, conditioning ongoing employment on their attending English and civic classes. These courses were intentionally mixed by race and country so as to "impress upon these men that they are, or should be, Americans, and that former racial, national, and linguistic differences are to be forgotten." Commencement from the Ford school had the graduating workers, regaled in their native dress, singing their national songs and dancing their folk dances and climbing up a ladder to enter a large papier-mâché "melting pot." On the stage's backdrop was painted an immigrant steamship, and as Ford teachers stirred the pot with long ladles the new amalgamated Americans emerged in "derby hats, coats, pants, vests, stiff collars, polka-dot ties," singing "The Star-Spangled Banner."[11]

Consider the case of Mustafa, an immigrant who before taking a job with the Ford Motor Company had plowed the fields with his father in Turkey. When he first came to Detroit, he lived in a squalid downtown boardinghouse. Like the rest of his "countrymen," he washed his "hands and feet five times a day, as part of their religion before praying"—the hygiene of which impressed the sociological inspector less than the time it wasted troubled him (in 1914, Ford had fired nine hundred Orthodox Christians for missing a workday to celebrate Christmas in January). But after passing through Ford's Americanization programs and moving to "a better locality," Mustafa "put aside his national red fez and praying, no baggy trousers anymore. He dresses like an American gentleman, attends the Ford English school and has banked in the past year over $1,000.00." "Let my only son be sacrificed for my boss," the inspector claimed Mustafa said in gratitude for having had his life turned around. "May Allah send my boss Kismet."[12]

As Ford biographer Robert Lacey put it, the "Five Dollar Day raised the pain threshold of capitalism." But beyond an incentive to make workers stay put, it also became a model for how to respond to another crisis that plagued industrialism. The mechanized factory production that took flight during America's Gilded Age had promised equality and human progress but in reality delivered deepening polarization and misery, particularly in sprawling industrial cities like Detroit. Ford, advised by farsighted company executives such as James Couzens and John Lee, understood that high wages and decent benefits would do more than create a dependable and thus more productive workforce; they would also stabilize and stimulate demand for industrial products by turning workers into consumers.

To this end, the Sociological Department promoted spending. Yet not just any kind of spending. Employees were not to waste their money on what Ford dismissed as "trumpery and trinkets," goods made "only to be sold, and bought only to be owned," which performed "no real service to the world and are at last mere rubbish as they were at first mere waste." Ford's inspectors rather encouraged workers to purchase vacuum cleaners, washing machines, houses, and, of course, Model Ts.[13]

At least for some and at least for a time, the Ford Motor Company, then, managed to redeem capitalism's earlier promise of abundance. It created what was understood to be a closed, self-regulating circuit that both increased production and expanded consumption, whereby workers were able to purchase the products that they themselves made. "High wages," said Ford, "to create large markets."[14]

THE PUBLICITY GAINED from both his Five Dollar Day and Sociological Department combined with the popularity of the Model T allowed Ford to cultivate his image as a philosopher. Ford's almost preternatural mechanical talent had been evident since he was a boy. Yet now in the middle of his life he discovered a new skill. The carmaker turned out, as one reporter put it, to be an "unrelenting, unremitting" master self-publicist who, with the help of a loyal, close-knit group of handlers and hired writers, succeeded in spinning his social awkwardness into wise enigma. Through the 1920s, he enjoyed more press coverage than any other American except President Calvin Coolidge.[15]

Two contradictory threads ran through the fabric of Ford's homespun. One was a "Transcendentalists' belief in man's perfectibility." Ford was a pacifist, suffragist, and death penalty opponent who believed that he had "invented the modern age." "We don't want tradition," he said, "we want to live in the present, and the only history worth a tinker's damn is the history we make today." Not only did he take credit for ending society's reliance on the horse but, repelled by his own boyhood memories of farmwork, he wanted to do away with all barnyard animals. "The cow must go," he declared. In place of milk, Ford pushed soy milk. Instead of sheep's wool, he suggested linen made from flax.[16]

In the other direction ran nostalgia for the world he helped end, one rooted in his rural background. Aphorisms that stressed "self-reliance and rugged individualism" as solutions to social ills eventually evolved into a darker critique of a world that he played a large role in creating, one in which social relations were growing ever more complex, ever more in flux, and ever more shaped by forces beyond face-to-face contact. The "city" became a common object of his criticism, as did "Wall Street financers" and, increasingly starting in the 1920s, "the Jew."[17]

"I don't like the city, it pins me in," he said, "I want to breathe. I want to get out."[18]

For the rest of his life, Ford—who as a boy walked for a day from his Dearborn family farm to lose himself in the anonymous pleasures of urban Detroit yet as a man came to despise the city as degenerate—bounced back and forth between these poles. He was a suffragist who didn't offer women the same five-dollar-a-day wage he did men. He passionately advocated placing US sovereignty under the authority of the League of Nations and talked about the need to establish a "world government" well into the 1940s, but then condemned Jews for their "internationalism." He called for the nationalization of the railroads and telegraph and telephone service, yet he hated Franklin Delano Roosevelt and refused to abide by New Deal regulation. He exalted the dignity of the worker and fashioned himself a scourge of the "capitalist" but was violently opposed to unionism. And he was a radical pacifist who once conceded that one last great war might be needed to finally bring about world disarmament. At the vanguard of the industrial and consumer revolution responsible for many of the vices he condemned, Ford tried to transcend this dissonance with a self-regard bordering on the Promethean. He reveled in publicity that presented him as humanity's savior, once saying that if sent into an alley blindfolded he would lay his "hands by chance on the most shiftless and worthless fellow in the crowd" and "make a man out of him."[19]

It was, after all, an age of competitive redemptions. Socialist: the radical journalist John Reed in his *Ten Days That Shook the World* described the 1917 Russian Revolution as building an earthly "kingdom more bright than any heaven had to offer." Russians, he said, would no longer need priests to "pray them into heaven." Nationalist: T. E. Lawrence, better known as Lawrence of Arabia, in an account of his role in helping to spark the 1922 Arab revolt against the Ottoman empire, wrote that the rebellion was fought in the name of a "new heaven and a new earth."

Fundamentalist: the Reverend Billy Sunday held 40,000-strong revival meetings in the heart of Detroit in the years after the inauguration of the Five Dollar Day, vying with Ford for the press's attention. And capitalist: Ford too promised to deliver not just a cheap car to the "multitude" but a "new world, a new heaven, and a new earth."[20]

CHAPTER 3

ABSOLUTE AMERICANISMS

THE GOLDEN AGE OF FORD ARRIVED IN EARLY 1914, WITH THE thunderclap promise of the Five Dollar Day, heralding industrial peace and prosperity. The rest of the 1910s and most of the 1920s were a period of dizzying economic triumph for Ford. Having bought all minority shares in Ford Motor Company, with no dividends to pay, partners to consult, or banks to report to, Ford moved forward with the construction of a new factory complex, which he built along the Rouge River, in the county of Dearborn, near where he was born. When it was finished, the River Rouge would be the largest, most synchronized industrial plant in the world: sixteen million square feet of floor space, ninety-three buildings, close to a hundred thousand workers, a dredged deepwater port, and the world's largest steel foundry. Ford barges, trucks, and freight trains brought silica and limestone, coal and iron ore, wood and coal, brass, bronze, copper, and aluminum from Ford forests and mines in Michigan, Kentucky, and West Virginia to the Rouge's gates and piers, and everything was organized to achieve maximum efficiency in receiving the material and getting it to the complex's power plants, blast ovens, furnaces, mills, rollers, forges, saws, and presses, to be transformed into electricity, steel, glass, cement, and lumber. Where other factories processed raw materials once, Ford had the Rouge designed to allow for their intensive reuse. Rather than just burn coal for electricity and heat, coke ovens first broke down the rock into a high-burning compound that could be used in foundries to melt minerals to make castings. Only then was coke gas piped to the powerhouse to generate electricity. Wood chips were put to making cardboard, coal dust was swept off the floor and used to produce cement, metal scraps were tossed in the blast furnaces, and ammonium sulfate, another byproduct of the coking process, was sold as fertilizer. Refined raw materials then moved through a series of cranes, railcars, and crisscrossed covered conveyor belts to their final destination, the assembly plant—laid out on one floor to reduce unnecessary climbing. The Rouge was consecrated a "cathedral of industry," and Ford, one of the richest and most celebrated men in history, ordained the high priest of the modern age.[1]

But Ford's optimistic creed was tested by the outbreak of World War I, which had taken over a million lives by the end of 1914 and would eventually claim sixteen times as many. Historians have traced Ford's distaste for militarism to his mother, Mary Litogot Ford, who, having given birth to Henry in the middle of the Civil War, nurtured in her son a hatred of all things martial. But it's not hard to imagine Ford reading about European factories being used to mass manufacture ever bigger guns, larger-caliber ammunition, more lethal bombs, airplanes, submarines, mustard gas, and cars outfitted for battle and thinking that the hope of the Industrial Revolution had been turned inside out, that rather than deliver, as he kept saying it would, an easier, more satisfied life, it now made death possible on a scale heretofore unimaginable. The battle of Verdun alone consumed close to forty million artillery shells and over 300,000 lives. A half million died at the Somme, more than twice as many battle deaths as the entire Civil War.

Ford's failure to keep the United States out of World War I—a task he pledged to devote his entire fortune to—initiated a series of political defeats and compromises that, by the time he considered moving into the Amazon, left him without any major success apart from the considerable ones that bore his name: his cars, tractors, planes, factories, and method of production. The Great War forced Ford to revise his international utopianism, undermining his faith that the rational ordering of industrial capitalism and human relations could bring about a better, harmonious world, free of battles and borders. Ford flailed, blaming one group after another for society's ills. He continued to express an unbounded faith in the ability of technology to create human happiness, yet his proscriptions for reform became idiosyncratic and increasingly nativist. It is at this intersection of economic intoxication and political exhaustion that the idea of Fordlandia being something more than just a rubber plantation first took root.

FORD WENT PUBLIC with his opposition not just to World War I, or to war in general but to all preparation for war, which he said could only lead to war, in April 1915. "I am opposed to war in every sense of the word," he said; soldiers should have the word *murderer* embroidered on their uniforms. In the following months Ford would issue a stream of equally emphatic statements, thrusting himself into the position of the world's most famous pacifist, dedicated to both ending the European conflict and keeping the United States out of it. "I don't believe in boundaries," Ford told John Reed. "I think nations are silly and flags are silly too." He said he planned to pull down the US flag from his factory and "hoist in its place the Flag of All Nations which is being designed in my office right now."[2]

Jane Addams, another prominent peace activist, thought such pronouncements flamboyant. Yet they weren't at odds with much of mainstream thought of the time. Many thought, on the eve of World War I, that pacifism was on the verge of triumph. A strong antiwar sentiment had emerged in all the world's major religions, including in the growing Christian evangelical movement in the United States, making common cause with politicians in Europe, the United States, and Latin America to reorient the purpose of diplomacy away from militarism and dominance toward the resolution of conflict and the maintenance of peace. A respectable number of the world's most prominent intellectuals, businessmen, politicians, and clergy could seriously argue that a world of perpetual peace, governed by the dispassionate rule of law, was within reach.

Ford reflected this début-de-siècle optimism but parted company with those who saw progress as being driven by politicians and governments.

"History is more or less bunk," Ford once famously said, by which he meant the kind of great-man or great-nation history that made it into textbooks. It was not just the "bankers, munitions makers, Kings and their henchmen" who pushed people into war, Ford thought, but "school books" that glorified battles as engines of historical movement. Ford was not averse to American expansion. He in fact had a pronounced belief in his and the United States' ability to rejuvenate the world. Just not at the point of bayonets. "If we could put the Mexican peon to work," Ford said in reference to the turmoil of the Mexican Revolution, which broke out in 1910, "treating him fairly and showing him the advantage of treating his employers fairly, the Mexican problem would disappear. There would be no more talk of a revolution. Villa would become a foreman, if he had brains. Carranza [another Mexican revolutionary] might be trained to be a good time-keeper."[3]

Ford's vision of a world made whole and happy by trade and industry is captured in his favorite poem, Lord Alfred Tennyson's "Locksley Hall":

For I dipt into the future, far as human eye could see,
Saw the Vision of the world, and all the wonder that would be;
Saw the heavens fill with commerce, argosies of magic sails,
Pilots of the purple twilight, dropping down with costly bales;
Heard the heavens fill with shouting, and there rain'd a ghastly dew
From the nations' airy navies grappling in the central blue;
Far along the world-wide whisper of the south-wind rushing warm,
With the standards of the peoples plunging thro' the thunder-storm;
Till the war-drum throbb'd no longer, and the battle-flags were furl'd
In the Parliament of man, the Federation of the world.
There the common sense of most shall hold a fretful realm in awe,
And the kindly earth shall slumber, lapt in universal law.*

---

*Ford also appreciated Victor Hugo, jotting down in his notebook a translated paraphrase of a fairly obscure quote from his fellow world-government advocate: "I represent a thing that does not yet exist the party of the revolutionary civilization will come in the 20th century," giving rise first to "the United States of Europe and then the United States of the world" (BFRC, accession 1, box 14, folder 8).

It was technology, production, and commerce that made history, and it would be not gunboats or marines that would tame the world but his car. "In Mexico villages fight one another," Ford said, but "if we could give every man in those villages an automobile, let him travel from his home town to the other town, and permit him to find out that his neighbors at heart were his friends, rather than his enemies, Mexico would be pacified for all time." And to back up his point, he announced that any employee who left his job to join General John Pershing's expedition to capture the Mexican revolutionary Pancho Villa would not find work waiting for him on his return.[4]

THE OUTBREAK OF war in Europe in August 1914 shattered the illusion that the battle flags of the world would soon be furled. Rather than dousing the dream, however, the European conflict provoked ever more desperate efforts to realize it, like Henry Ford's "peace ship."

Ford had seized on the notion of chartering an ocean liner to float a "people's delegation" to Europe to negotiate an end to the conflict in November 1915, after an associate raised the idea in passing, and he threw himself into the endeavor with the same impetuous energy he brought to his other, more mechanical passions. "I will do everything in my power to prevent murderous, wasteful war in America and in the whole world," he said, committing to stay in Europe as long as it took to bring peace to the continent. "I will devote my life to fight this spirit of militarism." Working closely with members of the world peace movement, Ford arranged to rent the Scandinavian-American Line's *Oscar II* and set up a command center in New York's Biltmore Hotel, sending out a barrage of invitations to the best names in American politics, society, and industry to join his "international peace pilgrimage." "We're going to try to get the boys out of the trenches before Christmas," was the slogan Ford adopted for the campaign, having come to appreciate the publicity value of a succinct, well-turned phrase.[5]

Ford's flair for bombast was more than matched by the theatricality of the fifteen thousand people who crammed a Hoboken pier to send off his "peace ark." A band played "Battle Hymn of the Republic" and "Onward, Christian Soldiers," as the crew of the *Oscar* tried to sort out who was legitimately part of the Ford entourage and who was trying to stow away. Most of the country's prominent liberal internationalists, intellectuals, and religious leaders, like William Jennings Bryan, William Howard Taft, and Louis Brandeis respectfully declined the industrialist's invitation to join his odyssey. "My heart is with you," apologized Helen Keller for not being able to make the trip. Jane Addams did accept but fell ill and couldn't sail. That left Ford with an odd and volatile assortment of lesser-known dissenters, vegetarians, socialists, pacifists, and suffragists as companions. That the voyagers seemed more at home under a carnival tent than in the halls of diplomacy was underscored by the arrival of a gift of two caged squirrels — "to go with the nuts," some wag said. Ford himself, swaddled in a full-length overcoat, stood on the ship's deck in the winter wind with beatific pink cheeks and a frozen smile, bowing over and over again to well-wishers. One reporter asked him what his supporters should do while he was away. "Tell the people to cry peace," he said, and "fight preparedness." Among those gathered on the dock was Mr. Zero, the street-performance name of anti-hunger activist Urbain Ledoux, who would later be known for staging "slave auctions" of unemployed workers in the Boston Common. When he tried to do the same in New York's Bryant Park, cops rioted and beat the assembled crowd with billy clubs, provoking a nightlong melee in which thousands of the jobless marched through Broadway's theater district chanting "Hurrah for the army of the unemployed!" and demanding to know "When do we eat?" As the *Oscar* pulled away from the dock and the band struck up "I Didn't Raise My Son to Be a Soldier," Mr. Zero leapt into the cold Hudson waters. Fished out of the bay, he told reporters that he was "swimming to reach public opinion."[6]

The mission proved a bust. In the middle of the voyage, President Woodrow Wilson announced that he would call on Congress to increase the size of the standing army, a policy shift that split the delegates into competing factions, between those who felt they needed to call off the mission in deference to Wilson and those who insisted on pressing forward. Ford joined the militants but, laid low by a flu and realizing that he was in over his head, sequestered himself in his cabin until the *Oscar* arrived in −12° Oslo on December 18. He returned to the United States nearly immediately, leaving his fellow delegates to make their futile "people's intervention" on their own. "Guess I had better go home to mother," he told them, meaning his wife, Clara. "You've got this thing started now and can get along without me."

The voyage of the *Oscar* revealed the unwillingness of many of America's most influential intellectuals and politicians, despite their nominal commitment to peace, to challenge a president whom they saw as a fellow internationalist, first when Woodrow Wilson promised to use his office to press for arbitration in Europe and then when he began his military buildup. But it also exposed Ford's vision of Americanism to a powerful backlash, led by Theodore Roosevelt.

WHEN THEODORE ROOSEVELT returned from the Amazon in May 1914, he was thinned by parasites and fever. During the trip, an infection had eaten at his flesh and despair had brought him to the edge of suicide. He had lost three men to murder and the river and had almost lost his son Kermit. Yet Roosevelt, who served as president from 1901 to 1909, recovered enough to lecture on his adventures, and once he convinced skeptics that he had discovered a new river—now flowing under the name "Roosevelt"—he began again to concern himself with social issues, including the new Five Dollar Day plan Ford had put in place while he was away. He wrote to Ford to suggest they have lunch or dinner the next time Ford was in New York. Roosevelt wanted to know a "great many things" about his factory system—not just how Ford was handling his "workmen from the purely industrial and social side" but also his "method of dealing with the immigrant workingmen."[7]

Both men contributed, in their own way, to the triumph of the "Progressive Era" over the abuses of the barons and trusts that emerged from America's first period of industrial expansion. They shared a number of friends, including Thomas Edison and the naturalist John Burroughs, and Roosevelt, the first president to ride in a car, felt "not merely friendliness" toward Ford "but in many respects a very genuine admiration." But the meeting did not take place, for as Ford became the voice of a frustrated pacifism, Roosevelt's admiration soured into scorn and "cutting sarcasm." "Mr. Ford's visit abroad," he said of the peace ship, "will not be mischievous only because it is ridiculous."[8]

Roosevelt and Ford represented distinct traditions of Americanism, especially with respect to expansion beyond America's borders. Where Ford believed the country should move forward to the steady hum of a well-organized factory, Roosevelt thought that the nation should march outward to the beat of a military bass drum. The Rough Rider urged men to live at the extremes, and he hailed the hard, besieged life of the frontier — whether in the Dakota badlands or in a tropical jungle — as essential in both building character and defining morality. "The most ultimately righteous of all wars is a war with savages," he wrote in *The Winning of the West*, even though he admitted that such a war was "apt to be also the most terrible and inhumane." His distaste for the flaccid commercialism of American society is well known. In 1899 he warned citizens against being lulled into a "swollen, slothful ease and ignoble peace" and seduced by the "over-civilized man," by which he and other militarists meant feminized, excessively cerebral intellectuals who believed that man's baser instincts had been forever subdued by the triumph of bourgeois politics and economics. To counter these threats, Roosevelt prescribed war as a regenerative remedy. "He gushes over war," wrote the psychologist William James, one of Roosevelt's Harvard teachers, "as the ideal condition of human society, for the manly strenuousness which it involves." The burdens of the presidency contained Roosevelt's enthusiasm for battle and empire as an expression of national glory, and he even lent his support for an international arbitration court to be established in The Hague. Yet he nonetheless presided over an extraordinary expansion of the government and the armed forces in the realm of foreign policy.[9]

Ford, born on a farm, resentful to the point of paranoia of America's eastern elite, and scornful of their bourgeois conceits, could hardly be considered "overcivilized." Yet that's exactly why his "pussyfooting" pacifism, as Roosevelt put it, represented such a threat to the ex-president's martial nationalism. Neither an old-line isolationist nor an intellectual pacifist, Ford promoted an expansive heartland Americanism that sought to break the equation, often made by radicals, between industrial capitalism and militarism. He insisted that you could have the former without the latter. Although he was ridiculed in the press after his return from Norway in January, Ford's pacifism continued to resonate with many Americans, not just dissenters but mainstream Christians and, before Ford went public with his anti-Semitism, Jews. "Henry Ford and his party are but swelling the ranks of 'fools' and 'madmen,'" said Philadelphia rabbi Joseph Krauskopf in his Sabbath sermon to mark the sailing of the *Oscar*, "but they are in good company. . . . Would to God, we had more of their sort of foolishness." Ford even beat both Roosevelt and Wilson in a St. Louis straw vote for president.[10]

Ford didn't win that nomination, but he didn't run. His candidacy was entered without his approval and he didn't make speeches, engage in debate, or attend the nominating convention held in Chicago in June. Still, in the months leading to the convention, he received an outpouring of encouragement from farmers and industrial workers urging him to "fight the munition manufacturers." "I am just a humble farmer," one letter said, "but my three greatest desires are to vote for Ford, own a Ford, and see Ford elected president by the greatest majority given any man." Residents of Parker, South Dakota, distributed handbills proclaiming that "no names are greater in the whole universe than George Washington, Abraham Lincoln, and Henry Ford."[11]

This last encomium must have irked Roosevelt, for he often invoked Lincoln to scold pacifists. He sent Ford a letter in February 1916, telling him that by putting "peace above righteousness" he had made pacifism the "enemy of morality." "Righteousness if triumphant brings peace," he wrote, "but peace does not necessarily bring righteousness."[12]

THREE MONTHS LATER, Roosevelt took his cause to the home of Fordism. He arrived in Detroit early on a May morning to the cheers of over a thousand well-wishers. The Michigan Republicans who organized the visit urged him to ignore Ford. But Roosevelt couldn't contain himself, saying that he had come "girded to fight the pacifism of Ford." Nearly all of his comments were aimed, either directly or indirectly, at the industrialist. At the city's Opera House, an overflow crowd fought with police and firemen for an opportunity to hear the Bull Moose, who received a standing ovation when he called Ford an enemy of the "welfare of the country and its people." "I've got two sons to go," yelled a woman from the balcony in response to Roosevelt's call for universal military service.

"Madam," he responded, "if every mother in the country would make the same offer, there would be no need for any mother to send her sons to war"—a reference not lost on the crowd since Ford's son, Edsel, had not enlisted.[13]

Roosevelt enjoyed a reputation as a progressive, a buster of trusts and promoter of government regulation over industry. But by the time he reached Detroit he had largely abandoned his earlier advocacy of "social justice." He had learned a lesson taught to many a would-be reformer: the drive to achieve a more equitable domestic society is too divisive a crusade—it is much easier to focus outward, on external threats, to achieve unity than to fight for fairness at home. Roosevelt's preparedness campaign therefore meant more than national defense. It meant national identity.

Thus Roosevelt, even as he urged vigilance against Germany, could admit that he admired his Prussian adversaries for their discipline. "The highest civilization can only exist in the nation that controls itself," he told his Opera House audience. "Above all, we must insist upon absolute Americanism." Roosevelt's vision of praetorian nationalism was directed squarely at Ford and his kitsch civic pageantry, and the praise he had earlier heaped on Ford's Sociological Department for breaking down "hyphenated Americanism" had given way to contempt. In his call for universal conscription that May day, Roosevelt railed against the notion that "Americanism" could be forged on the factory floor, in the industrial city, or in the theatrics of papier-mâché melting pots and derby hats. What Roosevelt called the "great factories of Americanism" were to be found not in Highland Park but in the collective effort of war, or at least in the collective effort needed to prepare for war. "I believe the dog-tent would be a most effective way for democratizing and nationalizing our life," he said, "quite as much so as the public school and far more so than the American factory."[14]

Ford responded by casting Roosevelt as an anachronism from the past martial century, a wandering old soldier looking for one last battle to fight. "Ordinarily one considers an ex-president a little different from the everyday citizen," remarked Ford. "It has been seven years since he was President, and in that time he has entirely failed to understand the trend of events and the sentiments of the people. I consider Roosevelt so antiquated that the 'ex' business does not mean anything. I consider him just an ordinary citizen because he does not keep up with the times."[15]

He then left Detroit to go fishing, abruptly ending speculation as to whether the two Americanists would meet.

The United States entered World War I in April 1917, but that didn't stop the feud. In 1918, Ford announced he was making a bid for Michigan's seat in the US Senate in order to support Wilson's proposed League of Nations. He lost that election too, though he did come within a few thousand votes of winning, again without having campaigned or spent any money electioneering.[16]

Roosevelt worked for Ford's Republican rival, condemning Ford's pacifism as treasonous, making an issue of Ford's earlier comment that he thought the American flag "silly."[17] Politicians and journalists joined in denouncing Ford as "criminal" and "insane," unfit for public office. "Upon some of the biggest questions of Americanism," wrote the *Chicago Tribune*, "Henry Ford is, to our way of thinking, wrong. He is dangerously wrong. We agree with Theodore Roosevelt." Roosevelt even called on Ford to sacrifice Edsel to atone for having opposed America's entrance into the war, since the fighting would have been over in ninety days and many lives spared "if we had prepared." Ford belonged not in the Senate, he said, but "on the mourners' bench."[18]

Roosevelt died in early 1919, having lived to witness Ford's pacifism, seemingly triumphant in 1915, wilt in the face of the fervor in which Americans marched into war. Roosevelt also saw Ford turn his factory over to war production, leading many who had simply considered the carmaker a fool to now think him a hypocrite. And he even bested Ford with his death: Ford had planned to run a "scathing" indictment of him in the inaugural issue of the *Dearborn Independent*, a local newspaper Ford purchased in 1918, but he was forced to scrap it on news that the ex-president had passed.[19]

FORD WAS IMMUNE to the emotions of nationalism and deaf to the grievances of history. The motor force of his internationalism, the one true thing that moved him, was constructive, rationally ordered activity, which he believed could be transplanted to any country to help mute political passions. What did it matter that India was colonized by Great Britain if its people were at work making things? Would Serbians care that they were oppressed if they had factory jobs to go to? What did matter was war, for it was an absolute mockery of everything Ford stood for. He was appalled by the destruction, by the insanity of using factories, machines, and men to kill rather than to make. "Every time a big gun was fired, it cost almost as much as a Ford car," wrote a contemporary to explain Ford's disgust. "A rifle cartridge cost almost half as much as a spark-plug. The nitrates burned up in explosives would fertilize all the worn-out farms in the world." One day during the war, Ford, having learned that twenty thousand men had been killed within the previous twenty-four hours, quickly figured that if those wasted men had worked for him for a year they would have earned $30 million. Capitalized at a standard rate of 5 percent, Ford calculated, that meant that $600 million was lost in a single day.[20]

World War I, along with Ford's failure to stick to his own convictions when the US entered it, prompted a gradual revision of his internationalism. He still continued to insist that his balm of hard work, high wages, and moral living could be universally applied, regardless of country or creed. Yet through the 1920s, Ford would back away from his high modernist disdain for "tradition," coming to believe that if the world was to be saved it needed to look for solutions rooted in the small-town values of America's past.

CHAPTER 4

THAT'S WHERE WE SURE CAN GET GOLD

HENRY FORD DIDN'T MUCH LIKE TO READ. READING WAS LIKE A "dope-habit," he said. "Book-sickness is a modern ailment." He delegated most of the reading and writing required to run his company and keep up his public persona to his subordinates, as Ford himself admitted when one or another of his pronouncements got him into trouble. "Mr. Delavigne wrote that," was Ford's fallback defense when criticized for undermining American military preparedness; Theodore Delavigne, his "peace secretary," ghostwrote many of Ford's pacifist manifestos. "Why should I clutter my mind with general information," he once asked, "when I have men around me who can supply any knowledge I need?"[1]

Ford wasn't illiterate, as his detractors claimed, though he did pass on several opportunities to prove otherwise. In 1919, Ford sued the *Chicago Tribune* for libel for having called him an "anarchist" yet in his testimony refused to read passages from documents entered as evidence. He forgot his spectacles, he said, or his eyes were too watery from "the hay fever." He claimed he didn't care that he gave the impression that he couldn't read. "I read slowly, but I can read alright."

Doesn't care what others think

Ford was in fact an impressionistic reader, and he was animated by big ideas. He insisted that his dog-eared copy of Orlando Smith's *A Short View of Great Questions*, which popularized for an American audience highbrow German anti-Semitism and Oriental metaphysics, "changed his outlook on life." And he continued to quote "Locksley Hall" until the end of his life.[2]

Ford's cultivation of himself as a heartland sage dispensing folksy wisdom owes much to the influence of William Holmes McGuffey's *Eclectic Reader*, his childhood civics textbook. The early twentieth century was swollen with books—many of them still found, underlined and annotated, on the shelves of his estate, Fair Lane—that defined what it meant to be modern, ideas concerning diet, exercise, reincarnation, and politics that Ford often passed on to friends and employees. "Mr. Ford wouldn't discuss the books he read or anything like that," said Albert M. Wibel, head of the company's purchasing division. "He just did it enough to make me think, 'What the heck is he talking about? I'm going to find out.'" Though not always with enthusiasm: "I hated those God damn soybeans and didn't want any part of them," he said about one of Ford's more enduring obsessions.[3]

Ford liked to keep his advice short and simple yet his interest in matters philosophical led him to expand his vocabulary. The Ford Archives hold dozens of his "jot-it-down" pocket notebooks, which Ford kept at the ready to save his thoughts and occasionally list variations of words:

Met a phys ic
Met a phys i cal
Met a phy si cian
Met a fi zish an
Met a phys ics

Coming upon his boss in his Fair Lane sitting room reading Ralph Waldo Emerson, Reverend Marquis, the minister who headed the Sociological Department, asked Ford what he thought of the "Concord philosopher." "Emerson's a pup," Ford replied. "Why a 'pup'?" Marquis asked. "Well," Ford said, "I just get comfortably settled to the reading of him, when he uses a word I don't understand, and that makes me get up and look for a dictionary."[4]

Of all of Henry Ford's many intellectual influences, Emerson was his most enduring muse. Ford appreciated the Concord philosopher's optimism and celebration of individualism and self-reliance. But he also found in Emerson a useful corrective to the writings of other nineteenth-century pastoralists, who saw industry as a violation of nature. William Wordsworth, for instance, protested the coming of the railroad to England's lake country in 1844, warning against the spread of the mechanical "fever of the world." "Is then," he asked, "no nook of English ground secure from rash assault?" Emerson, in contrast, celebrated steam power, railroads, and factories as rejuvenating forces that would help man fully realize the wonders of the natural world. Mechanization opened up the West, dissolved Old World hierarchies and stifling customs, turned deserts into gardens, and freed the mind from meaningless labor to allow more contemplative thought. In answer to the poet who feared that the railway and the "factory-village" would break the "poetry of the landscape," Emerson insisted that both "fall within the great Order not less than the beehive or the spider's geometrical web. Nature adopts them very fast into her vital circles, and the gliding train of cars she loves like her own." In the years after World War I ended the optimism of the Progressive Era, Ford would prescribe a similar holism as a solution for America's problems, setting out on an increasingly manic quest to restore order to a world off-kilter.[5]

THE IMMEDIATE CATALYST for Ford's initiative was America's 1920 recession. The downturn lasted less than two years, short compared to either the six-year contraction that began in 1873 or the great desolation that would come in 1929. Yet the drop in economic output was acute, revealing the vulnerability of both urban and rural society under the new regime of mass consumer capitalism. Banks failed and businesses closed. Unemployment skyrocketed in cities and families went hungry. The recession and its aftermath were a blow to one of Ford's mostly loyal constituencies, farmers, who still made up about a third of the US labor force. The price of agricultural products plummeted by as much as 40 percent, never to fully recover, even after the economy began to grow again in 1922. It was the first serious downswing since Ford had put his industrial and social system into place in Detroit the decade previous, and it galvanized him into action. For the rest of his life he would commit a good part of his great wealth to addressing the problem of industry and agriculture by trying to harmonize the two. "We cannot eat or wear our machines," said Ford. "If the world were one vast machine shop it would die. When it comes to sustaining life we go to the fields. With one foot in agriculture and the other in industry, America is safe."

Ford increasingly began to preach, and then tried to implement, what he called his "village industry" program. More and more after 1920, his conversations with reporters were dominated by different iterations on one topic: a way to reconcile farm and factory work. A return to the fields, he said, would solve urban poverty, the application of industrial technology to farm life could relieve rural drudgery, and decentralized hydroelectric plants could liberate manufacturing and farming communities from the high prices charged by the parasitical "energy trusts." Having helped do away with the horse as a source of transportation, he believed that in the "future farm animals of all kinds will be out. We don't need them. We will be better off without them." And to prove his point, he set up a small, fully mechanized farm just outside Dearborn. But mechanization was part of the problem, for the formula that provided Ford so much success in Detroit and Dearborn—machinery to lower prices, lower prices to increase demand, increased demand to make up for slimmer profit margins—didn't work for agriculture. New mechanized farm equipment, including Ford's Model Ts and Fordson tractors, might have relieved the slog of farmwork, but it continued to drive down prices by increasing yield. Corn, wheat, and other commodities poured into America's great industrial centers, selling at prices well below what many small to midsize farmers could live on.[6]

Ford hoped to solve this problem by finding industrial uses for agricultural products, and he directed his chemists to synthesize beans, corn, flax, and wood chips into grease, fuel, paint, artificial leather, organic plastics, and assorted chemical compounds. "I believe," Ford said, "that industry and agriculture are natural partners. Agriculture suffers from lack of a market for its product. Industry suffers from a lack of employment for its surplus men." The time would come, he thought, when "a farmer not only will raise raw materials for industry, but will do the initial processing on his farm. He will stand on both his feet—one foot on soil for his livelihood; the other in industry for the cash he needs. Thus he will have a double security. That is what I'm working for." No crop better promised to achieve this balance than soybeans, and over the next two decades Ford would spend four million dollars on soy research and more than twice that amount on soy processing equipment and physical plant facilities. His laboratories turned its oil into car enamel and house paint, varnish, linoleum, printer's ink, glycerin, fatty acids, soap, and diesel, and its meal and stalks into horn buttons, gearshift knobs, distributor parts, light switches, timing gears, glues and adhesives, and pressed cardboard. Ford even began to talk about the possibility of "growing cars" and had the body of one made entirely of plastic. Dubbed the "soybean car," it was ditched soon after it became clear that the strong mortuary smell from the formaldehyde used to process the plastic was not going to subside.[7]

Ford also promoted soy as a wonder food. He hired Edsel Ruddiman, a childhood friend and scientist after whom he named his only child, to develop novel foodstuffs from soy. He forced his associates to eat soy "biscuits,"

Henry Ford, sitting in a wheat field, dressed in a suit made of soy fiber.

described by one employee as the "most vile-tasting things you ever put in your mouth," and served his dinner guests soy banquets, course after course of dishes made from soybeans, including puree of soybean, soybean crackers, soybean croquettes with tomato sauce, buttered green soybeans, pineapple rings with soybean cheese, soybean bread with soybean butter, apple pie with soy crust, roasted soybean coffee, and soymilk ice cream. Ford thought soy's most promising food use would be as vegetable shortening, oleomargarine, and, of course, milk, which would allow him once and for all to eliminate cows. "It is a simple matter to take the same cereals that the cows eat and make them into a milk that is superior to the natural article and much cleaner," Ford said in 1921. "The cow is the crudest machine in the world. Our laboratories have already demonstrated that cow's milk can be done away with and the concentration of the elements of milk can be manufactured into scientific food by machines far cleaner than cows."[8]

FORD'S FIRST SUSTAINED attempt to put his "one foot in agriculture, one foot in industry" program into effect took place in Michigan's remote and sparsely populated Upper Peninsula, a region connected to Wisconsin in the west and bounded by Lake Superior to the north, the St. Mary's River to the east, and Lake Huron to the south. The Upper Peninsula's economy was based largely on copper and timber, both of which had been exploited to the point of exhaustion by the time Ford, in 1919, dispatched an agent to buy large tracts of land, sight unseen, in the region—just as he would do later in the decade in Brazil. By the mid-1920s, he had purchased property in the Upper Peninsula roughly the size of what he would a few years later own in the Amazon, sprawling across four counties and encompassing a number of small mill towns, including Pequaming, Munising, L'Anse, and Iron Mountain. The economic motive was to acquire the forests to provide the lumber needed for his Model T. Each car required 250 board feet of hardwood, the price of which was rising steadily as industrial demand increased and timber stocks decreased.[9]

"I was forced to get ahold of the forests," Ford said.

Yet as would be the case in the Amazon, Ford's objective was much more ambitious than merely gaining direct access to a single raw material.

While every component of his expanding empire was to feed into the Rouge, he imagined each to be a model of integration on its own, generating hydropower if possible and finding new uses for its byproducts — updating Emerson's ideal of self-sufficiency for the industrial age.

At Iron Mountain, an economically depressed city of eight thousand residents — most of its mines had been shut down and the surrounding forests had been stripped of their valuable hardwoods — Ford built a state-of-the-art industrial sawmill, the most efficient and modern the United States had yet seen. Dubbed the River Rouge of the North, the complex included fifty-two dry kilns, three factories making parts for the Model T, and its own electricity plant powered by a Ford-built dam. Ford had become obsessed with the potential of hydroelectricity as a way of freeing industrial communities from the grip of "energy trusts." On his camping trips with his friends Thomas Edison and John Burroughs, Ford would walk up and down every stream they came across, speculating how much horsepower could be harnessed from its currents, and by the end of the 1920s he had built or acquired at least ten hydroelectric plants throughout the US.[10]

Unlike the lumber barons of the late nineteenth and early twentieth centuries who ravaged northern Michigan's yellow pine groves, leaving behind cutovers of high stumps and waste, Ford saw himself as a conservationist. He insisted that, wherever possible, his lumbermen use "selective logging" practices to prevent deforestation, cutting only mature trees or targeted species. In areas where a clear cut was required, he ordered his lumberjacks to saw trees as low to the ground as possible, no more than six inches high, as opposed to the two-foot or higher trunks the logging companies left. These clean forest cuts allowed for quicker and fuller second growth, limited forest fires, and made it possible for Ford's managers to conduct reforestation experiments, something that the "commercial mills" — as Ford's men labeled other logging companies operating in the Upper Peninsula — rarely practiced. Much of Ford's conservation instinct came from his childhood growing up on his father's Dearborn farm, which maintained large forest reserves from which timber for construction was culled. "We don't want to destroy all the growth there is there just because we are going to operate this mill today," Ford told the head of his Iron Mountain operations. "Look out for tomorrow, next month, next year."[11]

Iron Mountain also included a five-story chemical laboratory. As at the Rouge, Iron Mountain managers and chemists pursued a restless quest to recycle all waste products. They used "every part of the tree except the shade," as historian Tom McCarthy puts it, producing $11,000 worth of value every day from mill waste, including 125 pounds of acetate of lime, sixty-one gallons of methyl alcohol (one-fifth of America's total production), antifreeze, artificial leather, and fifteen gallons of tar, oil, and creosote. Sawdust, underbrush, branches, wood chips, and cull lumber—that is, defective logs pulled from piles of otherwise serviceable timber—were turned into charcoal "briquettes" (which today continue to be sold under the brand name Kingsford) or burned to power steam engines and heat worker bunkhouses.[12]

THE LAND FORD purchased in the Upper Peninsula came with people. Iron Mountain was a relatively large city for the region, full of mining and timbering old-timers and new arrivals hoping to make good on the coming of Ford. Ford could react only piecemeal to its boom-bust-boom problems—its shortage of adequate housing, its speculators driving up land prices, its lack of health care, schools, and sanitation, and its many brothels, speakeasies, and morphine dens. But elsewhere in the Upper Peninsula Ford acquired large tracts of virgin timberland, dotted with small, remote lumber camps and mining towns. He imagined them to be blank canvases on which to paint his vision of industrial-rural wholeness.

"Your vacation is over, boys," announced Ford's manager to the thirteen workers who ran a very small mill in the village of Pequaming, purchased by Ford in 1923. Nearly overnight the hundred or so families saw their backwater village transformed, as the Ford Motor Company became the de facto municipal authority, responsible for its sanitation, schools, power, and even churches. Ford paid Pequaming lumberjacks and sawyers more than double the prevailing wage, but he would also impose Ford-style regimentation. "One was not even permitted to lean against a lumber pile or sit down for five minutes to figure up a lumber tally," remembered one sawyer. "It was compulsory to stand up perfectly straight on two feet."

Smoking was prohibited while on the clock, and town commissaries were forbidden to sell tobacco products and alcohol. All workers were required to undergo a medical examination, the cost of which was deducted from their newly increased salaries.

There were other deductions as well, for laundering, for instance, even if the worker didn't avail himself of the service. The idea was that if he paid for it he would use it and therefore wear clean clothes. Ford raised rents, more than compensated for by better wages, and he used the money to completely make over the villages. In Pequaming and other towns and villages, construction crews repaved streets, built new schools, and repaired and reroofed buildings. And they painted. "Paint, paint, paint. He had six or eight men painting the year 'round," said one worker in Ford's Upper Peninsular operation. "They painted every house and every one of the company shops. Then they'd go back and start all over again." In grimy mining towns, "lawns were cut and flowers were planted."[13]

Located on the shores of Lake Superior, rustic Pequaming became a Ford favorite. He built a summer bungalow there, traveling to the town at least a few times a year, reviewing the modernization of its sawmill and its experimental plantings of soybeans, potatoes, and other crops. He and his wife, Clara, took a personal interest in Pequaming's schoolhouse. By this point in their lives, the Fords were patronizing a number of experimental schools throughout the Midwest, rejecting mass public education in favor of small, personalized classrooms and experiential learning, which were to cultivate not just job skills but manners and character. Ford's curriculum emphasized "learning by doing"—in addition to reading, writing, and math, girls were instructed in homemaking skills, and boys in vocational training, and all children were taught how to garden. Pequaming's school became a model of Ford pedagogy, and Ford himself would participate in teaching the children old-style dances like the quadrille, the five-step schottische, and, Ford's favorite, the varsovienne, a Polish round dance with a polka beat. "Unless Mr. Ford asked for something special," remembered Oscar Olsen, a fiddler hired by Ford as Pequaming's music instructor, "we would just dance along like we always had," teaching the children how to round and square dance.[14]

At times one Ford idea would contradict another. In Pequaming, for instance, he hoped to restore the importance of community in industrial life, yet children were no longer allowed to enter the mill to bring lunch to their fathers. He wanted to nurture self-reliant "farmer-mechanics," giving his lumberjacks, sawyers, and miners garden plots to grow their own vegetables. But he also was committed to the idea of creating integrated consumer markets. So he ordered families to tear down their picket fences, which were used to corral cows, chickens, and pigs in their front yards. With their increased salaries, Pequaming's residents were now expected to buy their own meat, eggs, and milk.

Then there were the villages and camps Ford had built from whole cloth, deep in the woods, the "likes of which no sober lumberjack had ever dreamed," wrote one company historian. Ford had the idea of founding one such town when he was driving through a densely wooded and isolated area of the Upper Peninsula between Pequaming and Iron Mountain. Coming upon a site he thought especially pretty, Ford ordered his men to dig an artificial lake and build a lumber mill. Deep in a remote hardwood forest, Alberta, as the settlement was named, became another of Ford's Upper Peninsula showcases, its dozen or so workers all expected to divide their time lumbering, milling, and farming. Unlike the filthy, cold, and vermin-infested rough cabins woodsmen were used to, Alberta was an electrified oasis of modern America. It sported indoor lighting, streetlamps, cement sidewalks, showers, clean, screened private bunks, recreation rooms, and movies. The company put into place an innovative steam heat system to keep the bunkhouses warm during the extremely cold winters and served wholesome food "in a large, clean dining hall." "It is spick-and-span all over," said one observer of Alberta. "You don't see sawdust and bark and dirt. It is always clean. It is a lovely little setting there in the woods by the man-made river pond. There are some beautiful homes. From that standpoint it is marvelous."[15]

But from another standpoint, it was more Potemkin village than practical model for how to organize society. In Alberta, there were too few families to build the relations and institutions that integrated and tied a community together, and residents felt isolated, having to travel miles to buy anything beyond the most basic necessities, to see a doctor, or to attend church. And Alberta, along with Pequaming and other small Ford-subsidized communities, made little economic sense, as whatever milled wood it provided could be cut more economically at Ford's industrial plants in L'Anse or Iron Mountain. It was, as historians Allan Nevins and Frank Ernest Hill put it, all the "stuff of a backwoods fairy tale." Yet through the 1920s, Ford purchased or created scores of similar small towns in Michigan and elsewhere, including nineteen on rivers within the vicinity of his River Rouge complex. These lower Michigan villages were more directly integrated into the production of Ford cars than Upper Peninsula lumber towns. "Farmer mechanics" took the summer months off to go farm, cut hay, pick berries, tend gardens, and raise squab and spent the rest of the year manufacturing small parts that Ford outsourced from Highland Park and the River Rouge, such as valves, ignition locks, keys, carburetors, starter switches, and lamps.[16]

SHORTLY AFTER LAUNCHING his village industry program in Michigan, Ford made a bid to realize his industrial pastoralism on a large scale in a depressed river valley—not in the Amazon but in Muscle Shoals, along a stretch of the Tennessee River in northwestern Alabama. The valley connected with the lower Mississippi and served as the drainage basin of the southern Appalachian mountains, home to over four million people, most of them farmers who lived lives of isolation, disease, and poverty.

During the war, the US government had started but never completed building a series of nitrate factories and hydroelectric dams. Ford promised to finish the factories and build a dam as majestic as the Nile's Aswan dam in Egypt, completed two decades earlier. Taming the unruly Tennessee River would stop its fearsome floods, make it navigable, and provide cheap electricity to the surrounding region. He also said he planned to establish a seventy-five-mile-long city, as thin as Manhattan but five and a half times its length. Other chaotic, unplanned cities grew in sprawls, in a "great circle" that trapped residents, never giving them a chance to "get a smell of the country air or see a green leaf." Those who lived in Ford's river metropolis, in contrast, would never be more than a mile from rolling hills and farmlands. The city—which some were calling a "Detroit of the South"—would exist symbiotically with the surrounding agricultural villages, drawing seasonal labor. In exchange, the Ford Motor Company would supply low-interest mortgages so workers could buy land to build a home (prefabricated to reduce cost) and farm. Ford factories would pay high wages, serve as a market for crops, provide affordable fertilizer, and organize the cooperative use of machinery like tractors, binders, threshers, and mills. Ford schools would teach wives home economics and children a useful trade. Shops, churches, and recreational centers would line a meandering road that tethered one end of the imagined community to another—an "All Main Street" city was how one magazine described Ford's vision.[17]

The benefits of the project would ripple out in concentric circles, supporters of the plan said, from southern Appalachia to the wider South, then to the Midwest and all of America. And sure enough, by 1922 vegetable and fruit production had increased throughout the valley, in expectation of the government's granting Ford the concession. The *New York Times* reported that former slaveholding families who had kept their stagnant, undeveloped plantations "as a matter of sentiment ever since the Civil War" were selling them to entrepreneur farmers. As a result, a vibrant, dynamic population was "already being assembled for the city of Ford's dreams." The *Atlanta Constitution*, a New South tribune that had long advocated industrialization as a way of overcoming the Confederacy's manorial legacy, praised the project, writing that it would revive steamboat commerce on the Tennessee, Ohio, and Mississippi rivers. "Within 500 miles of Muscle Shoals there are fifty large progressive cities and towns that would be vitally affected by the development of the Tennessee valley," including Indianapolis, Columbus, Cincinnati, Louisville, St. Louis, Kansas City, Chattanooga, Birmingham, Montgomery, and Jacksonville.[18]

For Henry Ford, Muscle Shoals would do this and more, pulling together the many threads of his social philosophy into one audacious bid.*

---

*Despite the peculiarity of many of Ford's ideas, contemporary social reformers offered similar schemes to commingle urban life and nature and reconcile if not Emersonian then Jeffersonian democracy with the industrial world. Frank Lloyd Wright, for instance, shared Ford's criticisms of the modern city, particularly the way its immense scale and density threatened to wipe out community and individualism. Wright was directly influenced by Ford's proposed valley city. He often cited it as inspiration for his own Broadacre

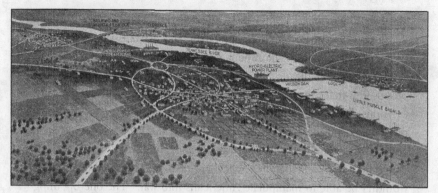

Frank Lloyd Wright remarked that Ford's valley city, imagined above in an illustration published in Scientific American *in 1922, was "one of the best things" he had ever heard of. Ford was "going to split up the big factory," Wright said. "He was going to give every man a few acres of ground for his own."*

He offered not the "city on a hill" that looms so large in American mythology but rather a "city in a valley," powered by hydroelectricity, which would liberate residents from the energy trusts—in this case, from the Birmingham-based Alabama Power Company, which monopolized the region's power supply. Cheap fertilizer could help end poverty and revitalize the agricultural sector: "There are too many people in this country—too many mouths to feed, too many bodies to clothe—to permit any soil to become exhausted." His ribbon city would refute the idea that there "exists an essential conflict between industry and the farm." "The farmer is idle through part of the year, and consequently has to live on his hump," Ford said. "The worker in an industrial center is idle through part of the year, and he, too has to live on his hump." The way to overcome this waste was, he believed, "to fit agriculture and industry together so that the farmer may

City, a planned community meant to showcase an architectural style that would blend organically with the landscape and allow "all that was human in the city to go to the country and grow up with it" (Frank Lloyd Wright, *Frank Lloyd Wright on Architecture: Selected Writings, 1894–1940*, ed. Frederick Gutheim, New York: Duell, Sloan, and Pearce, 1941, p. 144; Frank Lloyd Wright, *Modern Architecture: Being the Kahn Lectures for 1930*, Princeton, N.J.: Princeton University Press, pp. 108–9).

also be an industrialist and the industrialist may also be a farmer." And the development of hydroelectricity would truly make World War I the war to have ended all wars. "If the American people once can catch the idea of what water power means," he said, "they never again will submit to the proposition that to get power they must pay tribute to Wall Street." Ford even raised the idea of printing his own "energy dollar"—a regional currency based not on the gold standard but on the kilowatt output of the area's dams—as a way to break the power of banks. Since the moneymen would have no "part either in financing or operating Muscle Shoals," they wouldn't be able to manipulate Americans into war. "The one big thing which I see in Muscle Shoals," he said, "is an opportunity to eliminate war from the world." Dirt-poor farmers who until then knew the river only as a source of danger and flooding and workers hoping for a wage-paying job agreed, and they rallied to support Ford's proposal. One grassroots petition demanding the government hand over Muscle Shoals to Ford called the carmaker the "Moses for 80% of us."[19]

"If Muscle Shoals is developed along unselfish lines," Ford predicted, "it will work so splendidly and so simply that in no time hundreds of other waterpower developments will spring up all over the country and the days of American industry paying tribute for power would be gone forever. Every human being in the country would reap the benefit. I am consecrated to the principle of freeing American industry." "We could," he said, "make a new Eden of our Mississippi Valley, turning it into the great garden and powerhouse of the country."[20]

NEVER FAR FROM Ford's sunny vision of an industrial arcadia as a solution to America's problems, and indeed inseparable from it, was a darkening opinion as to who was causing those problems. In the early days of his public fame, Ford's exhortations to achieve the kind of self-reliant individualism celebrated by Ralph Waldo Emerson seemed folksy. As he aged and many of his reforms either failed to solve or actually aggravated social problems, they sounded downright Nietzschean: "Prayers are a disease of the will," Ford quoted Emerson's "Self-Reliance" essay in his pocket notebook. Most Americans in the mid-1920s still thought of Ford as the Ford of

1914, the reformer who with his Five Dollar Day and Sociological Department promised to put into place a new industrial humanism, to cultivate virtuous, productive workers through civic education and the
inducements of high wages conditioned on proper living. Yet Ford had
pretty much abandoned his liberal paternalism. His company, particularly his new River Rouge plant, had grown too big for such hands-on nurturing. Ford still paid better than most industrial companies, but he
came to rely on two quite different tactics to increase productivity and
enforce labor discipline in his far-flung Michigan empire. The first tactic was the speedup, which pushed the idea of synchronized assembly
lines to the limits of human endurance and made working for Ford, as
one employee who quit the line put it, a "form of hell on earth that
turned human beings into driven robots." "The chain system you have is
a *slave driver*," wrote the wife of one worker to Ford. "That $5 a day is a
blessing," she said, "a bigger one than you know but *oh* they earn it." Every
day it seemed like the belt moved a little faster, as performance technicians, armed with stopwatches, shadowed workers, figuring out ways to
shave off seconds here and there from their motions. Intellectuals and social critics began to draw attention to the dehumanization of the line.
"Never before," wrote a contemporary observer, "had human beings been
fitted so closely into the machines, like minor parts, with no independence or chance to retain their individual self-respect." Ford's factory
turned workers into "mere containers of labor, like gondola cars of coal.
They arrived full; they left in the evening as empty of human vitality as the
cars were empty of coal. The trolleys which crawled away from Highland
Park at closing time were hearses for the living dead." "It's sickening to
watch the workers bent over their machines," wrote Louis-Ferdinand
Céline, based on his firsthand study of the physical and mental health of
Ford workers. "You give in to the noise as you give in to war. At the machines you let yourself go with two, three ideas that are wobbling about at
the top of your head. And that's the end. From then on everything you
look at, everything you touch, is hard. And everything you still manage to
remember more or less becomes as rigid as iron."[21]

Fear was the second tactic, needed to forestall the discontent that such a system inevitably generated. It was instilled largely by Harry Bennett, a former pugilist but inveterate brawler who presided over the company's so-called Service Department, nominally the employment office but in reality a three-thousand-member goon squad—described by the *New York Times* as the "largest private quasi-military organization in existence"—made up of spies and thugs armed with guns, whips, pipes, blackjacks, and rubber hoses otherwise known as "persuaders." Hired in 1916 to work security, Bennett quickly caught Ford's attention with his gamecock confidence, and he soon became not only Ford's enforcer but his near constant companion, one of the most powerful men in the company, whose authority was based not on any engineering or marketing knowledge but on his ability to terrorize workers, to make them conform to the Rouge's perpetual speedup. The former navy boxer used his connections with Detroit's Mafia to weave "the Ford Motor Company into a network of underworld connections with hoodlums of largely Italian origin, and the unholy alliance came into its own in the battle which Ford fought against the unions with increasing ferocity as the decade went by," wrote Robert Lacey. Where Ford in the press was touting his village industries as nurturing healthy communities, in the Rouge Bennett, according to historian Douglas Brinkley, used fear and intimidation to keep its "workforce of 70,000 as a group of isolated individuals, and not let them create a community." The terror spread out from Dearborn to encompass Ford's dispersed assembly plants, as Bennett cobbled together an interstate consortium of antiunion toughs. In Dallas, Texas, for instance, Bennett converted the Ford plant's champion tug-of-war team into a security unit, headed by one "Fats" Perry, who by his own estimation handed out scores of savage beatings. "If it takes bloodshed," the plant management told its workers during a forced mass meeting, "we'll shed blood right down to the last drop" to keep the plant union free.[22]

It was not just physical violence, which Brinkley says Bennett dispensed with "brutish zeal," but the distrust generated by constant surveillance that kept workers in line. Bennett claimed that one in three line workers was an informer. "The whole city," recalled one union organizer, "was a network of spies that reported every whisper back to Bennett," allowing him to stalk workers not just within the Rouge's gates but in their "private life as well." He carried out Ford's edict that workers stop drinking, even in their own homes, and forced workers, at the pain of losing their jobs, to buy a Ford car.[23] For Ford employees, then, Fordism went from being a system in which they were paid enough of a wage to be able to buy the products they made to being one where they had little choice in the matter.[24]

Throughout the 1920s, most Americans, aside from those who worked inside a Ford factory or who had family who did, were unaware of Bennett's brutality. But they couldn't help know of Ford's anti-Semitism, which first erupted in public in 1920. Over the course of the next seven years, the *Dearborn Independent*, a local newspaper Ford purchased a year earlier, blamed the Jews for nearly all that was wrong with America, the degradation of its culture, the corruption of its politics, and the distortion of its economy through monopolies, trusts, and the "money system." It was Ford, and not his admirer Hitler, who popularized the *Protocols of the Elders of Zion*, a document concocted by Russia's tsarist government to fuel belief in the existence of a worldwide Jewish conspiracy. Most observers have located the roots of Ford's anti-Semitism in midwestern populism's critique of bankers and the gold standard, aggravated by Ford's tendency to reduce the complexities of the world to their most simple, mechanical terms. The historian Richard Hofstadter called his hatred of Jews and Wall Street "the foibles of the Michigan farm boy who had been liberally exposed to Populist notions." Ford's anti-Semitism, however, was not just a holdover sentiment from America's receding agrarian past but also one element of a larger sinister appraisal of the world he helped create.[25]

In another of his notebooks, Ford scribbled a reference to Gustave Le Bon, a French sociologist who died in 1931, and his 1895 book, *Psychology of Crowds*. It's a telling notation, for many have noted that both Mussolini and Hitler were influenced by Le Bon's argument that the "irrational crowd" was the defining feature of modern life, something that needed to be controlled lest it lead to degeneration. Ford was sympathetic to Nazism, and he seems to similarly have taken to heart Le Bon's warning that the "claims of the masses" were "nothing less than a determination to utterly destroy society as it now exists." Yet what stopped Ford from turning into a full-fledged fascist was that he took the opposite lesson from Le

Bon than did Mussolini and Hitler. Where the two fascists drew from Le Bon to mobilize the masses—through political pageantry, mass communication, and, in the case of Hitler, an eliminationist racism—Ford put most of his energies into dispersing the threat, through his many proposals to "decentralize" industrial production.[26]

By the mid-1920s, the man who had assembled together in one factory the largest concentration of industrial workers in history had pronounced the crowded metropolis "doomed," crumbling under the weight of traffic, pollution, vice, and the cost of "policing great masses of people."[27] Previewing the kind of antiurban sentiment that would become commonplace among the right in the United States in the years after World War II, Ford started condemning the city as "untamed and threatening," an "artificial," parasitical "mass" that "some day will cease to be." Throughout the 1920s, as the "claims of the masses" became impossible to ignore, particularly in Ford's own factories, where workers were beginning to contest the speedup and Bennett's terror, Ford fused his three great hatreds—of Jews, war, and unions—into a single conspiracy: "Unions are organized by Jewish financiers, not labor," he said. "Their object is to kill competition so as to reduce the income of the workers and eventually bring on war." "People can be manipulated only when they are organized," Ford insisted.[28]

The man who once repudiated tradition and declared himself the executor of the modern world was having published under his byline in the *Dearborn Independent* articles that denounced "change," which he warned was "not always progress." "The trouble with us today is that we have been unfaithful to the White Man's traditions and privileges," one article said. Having thrown open his factory gates to workers from across the world and declared that he didn't like borders of any kind, he now looked warily at Ellis Island, with its "horde of people who have been systematically beforehand taught that the United States is a 'capitalistic country,' not to be enjoyed but to be destroyed." Ford would continue to condemn war and those who profited from it, yet the man who once scolded Theodore Roosevelt for his antiquated militarism now cautioned his "race" that it needed to maintain "unrelenting vigilance" against two threats: one was a "corrupt orientalism" that was "breaking down the rugged directness of the White

Man's Code," the other a "false cry of 'Peace, Peace' when there is no peace."[29]

BEYOND THE PROBLEMS and abuses that Ford himself couldn't solve, created, aggravated, or compromised on—depressed agricultural prices, labor violence, anti-Semitism, the dehumanization of machine work, and war—it became apparent throughout the 1920s that both his car and his factory system worked against the world he hoped to bring into being.

Ford imagined his method as a powerful integrator: the rational application of technology would allow for the holistic development of industry and agriculture; the tractor and other advances in mechanization would relieve the drudgery of field and barn, the car and truck would knit regional markets closer together, providing new sources of income for hard-strapped farmers; radios and telephones would overcome rural isolation (starting in the 1930s, Ford broadcast from a company studio in Dearborn his *Sunday Evening Hour*, which featured "familiar music, majestically rendered," as well as editorials reflecting the "philosophic views of the Founder"); and grounding it all was a faith in the alchemic power of high wages to create prosperous, healthy working-class communities, with private profit dependent on the continual expansion of consumer markets. "Our buying class is our working class," Ford said clearly and simply, and "our working class must become our 'leisure class' if our immense production is to be balanced by consumption." At his most eccentric, Ford insisted that the fulfillment of this vision would result in a restoration of small-town America.[30]

But Fordism, and the product it was first associated with, was also a potent dissolving agent.* The car transmuted sexual mores and loosened

---

*The term *Fordism* evolved after the *Washington Post*, condemning Ford in 1922 for briefly shutting down his factory rather than pay high coal prices, defined it as "Ford efforts conceived in disregard or ignorance of Ford limitations," a category in which the paper included the peace ship. Around this time, the term was often interchangeable with *Taylorism*, after Fredrick Taylor, the pioneer of motion analysis who aimed to extract ever greater productivity out of workers through the isolation of the individual tasks needed to make a product. It also denoted standardization, efficiency, and mass production. By the late 1920s, Fordism began to take on its more comprehensive meaning, used to suggest a modernization of economic thought that appreciated the value of high wages as a motor the bonds between men and women, children and parents. It alleviated the burden of farmwork and brought points on the map closer together, yet the automobile also began the transformation of human settlements and migration patterns, broadening the social horizon of people's lives. Daily commutes grew longer, and families spread out. The extension of paved highways, the widening of existing thoroughfares, and the sprawl of industrialized metropolises were visible threats to the rural communities so treasured by Ford as the repository of American virtue. By 1920, the county Ford's wife grew up in, Greenfield Township, was absorbed by Detroit, and later in the decade he had to move his childhood home to save it from destruction due to the planned expansion of a county road. He relocated it to a model American town he had begun building near his River Rouge plant, which he named Greenfield Village. As an industrial method, too, Fordism had embedded within it the seeds of its own undoing. The breaking down of the assembly process into smaller and smaller tasks, combined with rapid advances in transportation and communication, made it easier for manufacturers to break out of the dependent relationship established by Ford between high wages and large markets. Goods could be made in one place and sold somewhere else, removing the incentive employers had to pay workers enough to buy the products they made. While it would be decades before the implications

of industrial growth. And sociologists and intellectuals, particularly those in industrialized European countries, started using it in tandem with *Americanism*. In 1927, for instance, an article in London's *New Statesman* identified Americanism/Fordism as an industrial system in which the pace of the factory determined productivity (as opposed to pace being set by a wage system that rewarded output): "The worker under Fordism is speeded up, whether he likes it or not, by the pace at which the factory runs, by the endless stream of articles ceaselessly propelled toward him by the remorseless chain of machines. He must work at the factory's pace, or go; and go he will, unless he is offered a special inducement to remain." But the article also acknowledged that high wages, in addition to serving as an inducement to remain on the line, actually created large markets, which allowed industrialists to increase their takings even as profit margins were reduced: "It was found, not merely that high wages were fully compatible with low costs of production, but that the offer of higher wages still might be so used to stimulate a further fall in cost. High wages therefore became, with some employers, not merely a necessity that had to be faced, but a positive policy" (reprinted in *the Living Age*, May 15, 1927). By the 1950s, the term *Fordism* had worked its way into social science terminology, as scholars began to consider the foundations and implications of the United States' unprecedented postwar economic expansion.

of this change would become fully apparent, already by the 1920s the component elements of the economy that in Ford's mind operated as a symbiotic whole—land, labor, resources, manufacturing, finance, and consumption—were drifting apart.

Ford responded by committing even more to his village industries, which he hoped would slow the flow of migrants to the cities, save farms by bringing wage-paying industry to rural areas, and keep families intact— with women in the kitchen and men on the shop floors and in the fields. They also allowed Ford to continue to play humanity's redeemer, even as he was fending off criticism that his anti-Semitism was perilously inflamma- tory and his factory system had become a soul-crushing thing. "I sometimes think that the prejudice and narrowness of the present day," he said, "is due to our intense specialization." Get workers out into the country. Have them work under an open sky. "If we saw more sides of life . . . we should be better balanced," he observed. "I think farmers are going to disappear in the course of time. Yes, and factory workers too. Every man will be a farmer some day, and every man will work in a factory or office. We've proven that already. I've built little factories along the little rivers."[31]

Yet his little factories along the little rivers were no match for the raw power of the changes taking place in American society, politics, and cul- ture in the 1920s, and in any case, Congress, after years of debate, had de- finitively rejected his Muscle Shoals proposal. An alliance of economic and regional political interests made the case that the US government was about to hand to Ford too good, too vague a concession. Would he own the mineral rights to the land? What about timber? What would happen to the project when Ford died?

Building on the criticism, Nebraska's Republican senator George Norris led the charge against the deal. A committed Progressive—and, particularly irksome to Ford, a close ally of the late Theodore Roosevelt— Norris believed that a project of the scope Ford was proposing should be carried out under the auspices of the federal government and not private interests. The senator was disturbed by the wild land speculations that had gripped the Tennessee Valley upon rumors of Ford's interest. The Muscle Shoals Land Corporation, founded in Detroit, staked out a tract of land on the banks of the Tennessee River, laid out boulevards with names such as

Dearborn Avenue and Michigan Street, and incorporated the site as a city, dubbed "Highland Park." A group of newspapermen in Detroit pooled their money and bought up a square mile of the "dreamland," hoping to flip it for a profit. In New York, another start-up cashed in by selling twenty-foot lots of land. "Would you, if you could," promotional material asked potential customers, "associate yourself with the world's greatest manufacturer and industrial genius—HENRY FORD? Thousands of people have become independently wealthy through the development of Ford's gigantic industrial plants in Detroit, Michigan. Mr. Ford has recently stated that he would employ one million men and build a city seventy-five miles long at MUSCLE SHOALS." After reading of Ford's plans for the Tennessee Valley in the African American *Chicago Defender*, East Texas bluesman George Thomas captured the get-rich-quick spirit of the times in a song recorded by Bourbon Street–born Lizzie Miles: "Hurry up, Papa, we must leave this town, got the blues for Muscle Shoals, that's where we sure can get gold."

Norris was especially repelled to hear poor Southern farmers chanting, "'When Ford comes, . . . when Ford comes,' as if they were expecting the second coming of Jesus Christ." Muscle Shoals, he said, was the "most wonderful real estate speculation since Adam and Eve lost title to the Garden of Eden." Ford's offer to buy Muscle Shoals passed the House, but Norris and other Progressives opposed to the privatization of national resources, such as Wisconsin's Robert La Follette, killed it in Senate committee in mid-1924. The streets of Highland Park, with not one house built, soon "disappeared into cotton fields," wrote an observer, "the sidewalks, under brambles."[32]

So Ford began to look abroad to implement a plan of reform that was failing at home. Having been denied the opportunity to redeem a poor rural river valley in Appalachia, he would find another in the Amazon.

CHAPTER 5

FORDVILLE

SHORTLY AFTER HIS SUMMER LUNCH WITH HARVEY FIRESTONE
where they discussed the proposed British cartel, Henry Ford granted a
long-sought audience to Brazil's New York–based consular inspector, José
Custódio Alves de Lima. The Brazilian diplomat had been courting Ford
for two years, since reading about his interest in growing rubber in the
Florida Everglades, and had sent him samples of Amazon rubber and
minerals along with an elegantly carved cabinet made out of assorted rare
rain forest hardwoods, all with the purpose of turning his attention to
Brazil. De Lima had received permission from the governor of Pará—one
of the largest of the Amazonian states—to offer Ford "special inducements," tax and land concessions, in the hope that the industrialist would
help revive the regional economy, depressed since 1910, when Brazil lost
its rubber monopoly to Asia.[1]

As he traveled from New York to Dearborn by train, de Lima reflected
on Ford and what his investment in the Amazon would mean for Brazil.
By that point, the Model T was more than a car: its speed, simplicity, and
durability chanted freedom, its affordability spoke democracy. And Ford

Motors had become more than a company. Notwithstanding the criticism its assembly and speedup had provoked, its method of industrial relations, for many the world over, it had become synonymous with modern life, offering the promise of not only efficient production but the increased leisure time needed to enjoy the fruits of efficiency. Fordism, *fordismo, fordismus*, or *fordizatsia*—in whatever language, countries hoping to shake off the scent of farm animals and catch up with the United States adopted some aspect of the system pioneered in Detroit and Dearborn. In countries with strong artisanal and mechanic traditions like France, England, Germany, and even the United States, intellectuals and craft unionists condemned Fordism for replacing the craftsman and skilled worker with mindless "jerks, twists, and turns." Yet by the early twentieth century, the world was increasingly divided between the industrial and the hoped-to-be-industrial. And in the larger latter half, few harped on the downside of steady wages and mass, standardized production of low-cost goods.[2]

Ford himself, lanky, "incessantly moving," "swift as a shadow," as the journalists John Reed and John Gunther respectively described him, embodied for many the vitality and quickness of the modern age. Carl Sandburg said that "one feels in talking with Ford that he is a man of power rather than of material riches." His half-cultivated, half-innate Delphic opaqueness—"I'm going to see that no man comes to know me," he wrote in one of his notebooks—allowed his followers to pick and choose what they liked from his philosophizing, uniting admirers as diverse as Lenin and Hitler, Trotsky and Mussolini.[3]

By the time of de Lima's Dearborn visit, the Ford Motor Company was well established throughout Latin America. In 1914, it already operated sales offices in Argentina, Uruguay, Brazil, Chile, and Venezuela, and when World War I closed Europe off to business, the region served as the site of Ford's first extensive overseas expansion. Production began in Buenos Aires in 1917 and in São Paulo in 1920 and quickly spread to most major Latin American cities. By 1925 Ford had a near monopoly on the car and truck trade in Brazil—60 percent to 17 percent for General Motors—with over four million in sales and dealers throughout the country, including in Belém, the Amazon's major Atlantic port. Three years later, Ford would have seven hundred agencies and more than two thousand service garages in Brazil. The sturdy, high-off-the-ground Model T was particularly popular in the country's rugged backlands, serving, as it did in the rural United States, as an all-terrain vehicle for unpaved and rutted roads. Ford dealers sent caravans of cars, tractors, and trucks on publicity tours, parading them before audiences of up to a hundred thousand people in dozens of cities and towns during the day and screening films depicting Ford assembly lines and factories at night. In some regions, Ford trucks were converted into public buses and Model T engines were used to run cotton gins and sugar mills.[4]

Consul de Lima was from southern São Paulo, the prosperous heart of his country's industrializing south, whose elites viewed the equatorial Amazon much the way northern US industrialists looked at southern states, as torpidly rural, economically backward, and beset by racial conflicts. Ford's first autobiography, *My Life and Work*, had recently been translated into Portuguese and was widely read among members of São Paulo's business and political class. Throughout the 1920s, *paulistas*, as residents of São Paulo are called, took the lead in building Brazil's modern highway system and practically erected a cult of Henry Ford, understanding Fordism to be the antithesis of what the rest of Brazil was and the model of what it needed to become if it was to progress: industrial, rational, wage-based, and prosperous. A graduate of Syracuse University and a longtime resident of New York, de Lima had to have known Ford's opinion of Jews. He nonetheless pronounced the carmaker the "Moses of the twentieth century," who would turn the Amazon into the Promised Land. Ford's translator, José Bento Monteiro Lobato, also from São Paulo, called him the "Jesus Christ of industry" and described his life story as the "Messianic Gospel of the Future."* "For Brazil," he said,

---

*The work of fiction most associated with Henry Ford is Aldous Huxley's 1932 *Brave New World*, which describes a future in which a dystopic Fordism reigns supreme: babies are manufactured on assembly lines, the T has replaced the Christian Cross, and "History is bunk" stands as the official motto of an indolent, purposeless society overcome by a narcissism spawned by technological abundance. But six years earlier Lobato wrote a novel set in 2228, in an America transformed by Ford's "pragmatic idealism" into an exemplar of mechanical efficiency and wealth, one that has allowed for the transcendence of class conflict. "Ford proved," Lobato writes, "that there was no antagonism between capital and labor." Yet "The Clash of Races," as the novel was originally called in Portuguese, is "there is no literature or study more fruitful than Henry Ford's book." Farther north of São Paulo, in the provincial town of Uberabinha, around the time of de Lima's campaign to woo Ford's attention, a local newspaper worked with business leaders to raise money to erect a statue to Henry Ford, in honor of the role his car played in opening up the backland states of Goiás and Mato Grosso.[5]

FOR HIS PART, Ford must have welcomed de Lima's attentions and the unreserved admiration of men like Lobato and other *paulistas*. He was sixty-one years old in 1925 and, though unparalleled in wealth and prominence, had, starting with his opposition to World War I, suffered a string of political rebukes. And having been denied Muscle Shoals by, in his opinion, shortsighted and self-interested politicians, he must have viewed the cooperation offered by de Lima and other Brazilian statesmen as evidence that the Amazon valley provided a better opportunity to realize his industrial pastoralism than did the lower Tennessee River.

Ford greeted Consul de Lima in his office at the new River Rouge complex and, though still uncommitted, took the opportunity of the meeting to recapture a lost innocence. On display for the Brazilian diplomat in Dearborn that day was not the Henry Ford who swore by the veracity of the *Protocols of the Elders of Zion* and increasingly defended a "white man's code." Nor was it the man who loosed Harry Bennett's "service men" on his factory floor, with their "guns, sticks, and other weapons, . . . enforcing obscure rules at their whim" and refusing to let workers sit, ever. It was

---

as bleak as Huxley's. Despite predicting the suppression of class struggle, the book imagines a world in which racial conflict has yet to be resolved. Its narrative focuses on a presidential contest where, as a result of a split in the white vote between a white man and woman, Jim Roy, an eloquent, intelligent black candidate, becomes president. The backlash against Roy's victory leads to the sterilization of all African Americans and, in unclear circumstances, the president-elect's death, which results in a restoration of white political power. Despite Lobato's faith in Ford's redemptive powers, his book, written in 1925, before Ford committed to the Amazon, envisioned a troubled future for the region: what was Brazil would be split in half, divided into a progressive and prosperous south, joined by Argentina and Uruguay, and a northern, stagnant "tropical republic" (José Bento Monteiro Lobato, *A onda verde e O presidente Negro*, São Paulo: Editora Brasiliense, 1956, pp. 202–6, 214).

not the Ford who presided over a factory where workers, not allowed to talk, learned how to speak without moving their lips, a skill they called "fordization of the face." It was not the Ford of the speedup, the man who by the late 1920s embodied the inhumanity of assembly line production, which turned the workers themselves into machines. Not the Ford who by that time was condemned in countless exposés and novels as the sponsor of the worst dehumanizing effects of mass industrial production.

Rather, de Lima met a Henry Ford thrust back to the mid-1910s, a man confident that he could wed industrial efficiency to human fulfillment. The Brazilian recounted the "simple speech and modest manner" with which Ford received him. Throughout their meeting, Ford remained standing, which a more observant guest with firsthand knowledge of the Rouge would have taken as an example of Ford's ability to turn his own manias into industrial policy, a subtle caution against the promises to come. But de Lima was an enthusiast, and he saw Ford's restlessness as vitality. After the two men discussed the nuts and bolts of the matter, how much land Brazil was willing to concede to the motor company, along with tax and tariff issues, Ford became expansive.

He asked the Brazilian about the wages rubber tappers received. Thirty-six to fifty cents a day, de Lima answered; Ford replied that he had "no doubt that he would pay up to five dollars a day for a good worker." Brazilians, he said, had the right to work as "free men," not as "slaves." His principal concern was not the number of hours he got for his wages but the productivity of the labor force. True, he told de Lima, he strove for efficiency and took no stock in charity. Yet he asked that each worker only give to the job what he could. His factories, he said, employed the "blind, crippled and dumb," who "work only three hours per day, without feeling humiliated about it."

Also making an appearance at that meeting was the Ford who absolutely believed that his system of industrial fairness was all that was needed to prevent wars and revolutions. When "Peter tries to rob Paul of that which he prizes most, making him do extra work without due compensation, then naturally reaction ensues," he said. Ford even rehearsed his old Tennysonian internationalism for his Brazilian guest, telling the diplomat that when he did business he forgot that he was an American, "because a business man knows no country. He is born by chance in this or that country." For Ford, the Amazon offered a fresh start in a place he imagined to be uncorrupted by unions, politicians, Jews, lawyers, militarists, and New York bankers, a chance to join not just factory and field but industry and community in a union that would yield, in addition to greater efficiency, fully realized men.

"There will be schools," Ford said of his plans for the Amazon, "experiment stations, canteens, stores, amusement parks, cinemas, athletic sports, hospitals, etc. for the comfort and happiness of those who work on the plantation."

IF DE LIMA, quoted widely in the Brazilian press on the success of his Dearborn meeting, was the public face of the campaign to draw Ford to the Amazon, Jorge Dumont Villares played a stealthier role. From a wealthy and politically connected São Paulo coffee-growing family, Villares had arrived in Belém, the capital city of the Amazonian state of Pará, in the early 1920s. Despite the collapse of the rubber economy, there was still money to be made in the many schemes floated to revive the trade. As the nephew of the famed aviator Alberto Santos-Dumont, the man Brazilians insist invented the airplane only to have the credit stolen by the Wright brothers, Villares, partial to linen suits and Panama hats, was relatively well known in elite circles. He was tall, thin, and a bit fussy, and he had a flair for the covert. Shortly after his arrival, he began to cobble together a loose confederacy of politicians, diplomats, and Ford officials, all with their own interests in luring Henry Ford to Brazil.[6]

Villares's first and most important ally in getting things moving was William Schurz, who served as Washington's commercial attaché in Rio, though to the annoyance of the US ambassador he spent most of his time in the Amazon. "Generations of little men have nibbled, like mice, at the edges of the Amazonia," Schurz later wrote in a book he authored on Brazil—a remark that could be taken as autobiographical. Schurz had joined the Department of Commerce in the early 1920s, just at the moment that its secretary, Herbert Hoover, was greatly expanding its reach. Hoover tripled Commerce's budget and added three thousand employees, many of them attachés like Schurz, traveling salesmen of America's growing economic ambition. These "hounds" for American business, as Hoover called them, tended to ignore the big-picture geopolitics that so occupied State Department diplomats. Instead they lobbied, often with a *Glengarry Glen Ross*–like aggressiveness, on behalf of a narrower range of interests specific to US corporations—as well as to themselves.[7]

Schurz had been a member of the 1923 commission organized by Hoover's Department of Commerce to study the possibility of reviving rubber production in the Amazon, part of Hoover's campaign to counter Churchill's proposed cartel. It was most likely from his experience on this commission that Schurz first realized the possibilities for profit, especially after the 1925 announcement by Pará's new governor, Dionysio Bentes, that he would make jungle property available at no cost to anyone willing to cultivate rubber. As a US diplomat, Schurz couldn't petition for land directly, so he allied with Villares, with the idea that they would use Hoover's rubber crusade to sell their concession to an American corporation. Joining Schurz and Villares was Maurice Greite, an Englishman who lived in Belém and called himself "captain," though no one knew of what. A longtime resident of the Amazon always on the lookout for the main chance, be it a lead mine or a land scheme, Greite quickly became more of a burden than an asset to Villares. But he did perform one useful service. He introduced Villares to Belém's mayor, António Castro, and to Governor Bentes, two men whose allegiances would need to be secured if the plan was to have any chance of success. In exchange for a cut of the money, both officials pledged their support. The mayor promised not to oppose the transaction and the governor, in September 1926, granted Villares, Schurz, and Greite an option on 2.5 million acres in the lower Tapajós valley—one of the many places experts considered suitable for large-scale rubber cultivation. The three men had two years to either develop or sell the property. If they failed to do one or the other, they would lose their option and the land would revert back to the state.[8]

At first, Schurz, from his embassy office in Rio, tried to interest Harvey Firestone. But when Firestone settled on Liberia, he turned his attention to the Ford Motor Company, writing letters to both Ford and his secretary, Ernest Liebold, hyping the possibilities of Amazonian rubber. As commercial attaché, Schurz had access to US government-funded research being carried out on rubber, which he passed on to Liebold before the Commerce Department could process it and make it available to other potential investors. At the same time, both he and Villares established contact with two men, W. L. Reeves Blakeley and William McCullough, whom Ford had sent to Belém after his meeting with de Lima to scout out potential locations for a rubber plantation. There is no evidence that Blakeley took money, yet documents indicate that McCullough did. Villares promised to pay him $18,000 for whatever help he could provide in making the deal move forward.[9]

In the Amazon, Villares also began to enlist the services of the Belém-based US consul, John Minter. In this case, no money was proffered. But Villares's conspiratorial air had a way of pulling in confidants. He whispered to Minter that plans were afoot to infect Southeast Asian rubber plantations with South American leaf blight, a fungus native to the Amazon that was often lethal to rubber trees. It would take only one epidemic of blight, in Ceylon or Malaysia, Villares told the US diplomat, to restore Brazil's domination of the global market. "A word to the wise is sufficient," Villares said to the consul. He fed Minter bits and pieces of information regarding his negotiations with US corporations, including the contacts he had made with the Ford Motor Company, drawing the American official into his intrigues. He said that he had "secretly planted a nursery of 500,000 seedlings on hidden unclaimed property adjacent to that which Ford is likely to take up," so that Ford would have a ready stock of *Hevea* to begin planting once he committed to the project. The reason the nursery had to remain a secret, Villares said, was that powerful local interests were conspiring to stop the deal from going forward. Before long, Minter was cabling his superiors back in the State Department telling them that he was putting his office and staff at the service of Villares in his dealings with Ford. Villares's next step, in late summer 1926, was to travel to Dearborn to pitch his proposal directly to Henry and Edsel Ford, having secured an audience probably through either McCullough or Blakeley, with whom Villares had established a friendship.

Villares was a skilled sycophant, and in his meeting with father and son Ford, he tacked back and forth between fear and flattery to make his case. The Brazilian presented them with a rough-drawn map of the property, which included two towns named "Fordville" and "Edselville."[10] Building on Schurz's spadework, he painted a fantastical picture of what could be accomplished in the Amazon, "the most fertile and healthy region in the tropical world." The Brazilian drew up a wish-list contract, naming himself executor of the project and granting the company the unfettered right to extract gold, oil, timber, and even diamonds. Villares also promised Ford that he could harness hydroelectricity, import and export any material free of taxes and tariffs, and build roads, including two that would run three hundred miles up both banks of the Tapajós "into the vast wild rubber forests" of its headwaters, which would give Ford a complete monopoly over the valley's latex production. He told Henry and Edsel that he would greatly prefer to make the land available to an American, but if no one came forward he might be forced to transfer it to other interests before his option expired. It was painful, Villares told the Fords, to "even think that some of my homeland will go into the hands of Japs, Britishers, and Germans." "The call has been heard," Villares concluded his presentation, "and the surest guarantee that the enterprise will be a great success is that the *first* to answer the call was *Ford*. He never retreats. He never fails."[11]

The meeting left Villares hopeful. From Detroit's Cadillac Hotel, he wrote his fellow conspirator Greite and urged him to be patient: "Say nothing," for things with Dearborn were going well. "Tear this letter up," he instructed the captain.[12]

Ford seemed to be hooked. Still, Villares was anxious. He left Detroit for New York, where he composed another letter, this one to Blakeley. If Ford didn't act quickly, he wrote his closest ally in the company, "Some one will realize it soon." "When you were down there," he asked, "did you notice a curious thing: 'The faith everyone has in Ford?' The magic in that name has penetrated into the hearts of the most humble; it has got into mine. They have faith in Ford, so have I. Thousands await his coming; he will come."[13]

CHAPTER 6

THEY WILL ALL DIE

FORD REMAINED UNDECIDED, BUT HIS MEETING WITH JORGE Villares did prompt him to send Carl D. LaRue, a botanist at the University of Michigan's Ann Arbor campus, to Brazil to "find a good area somewhere" to plant rubber. LaRue had been to the Amazon once before, in 1923 as the head of Herbert Hoover's Department of Commerce–sponsored expedition aimed at surveying locations for rubber production, the same one US commercial attaché William Schurz was on. On that trip, the botanist covered a wide radius of over 25,000 miles, and his findings, along with those of other expeditions, identified several suitable locations scattered up and down the Tapajós River. These were mostly on public property, which Ford could have obtained directly through a government concession at little or no cost. This time, though, LaRue didn't revisit any of the sites he had scouted earlier but rather made a beeline for a fifty-mile strip along the east bank of the Tapajós, part of the land optioned to Villares, Schurz, and Greite. Later, once the details of the deal surfaced—a deal in which Ford essentially purchased property he probably could have gotten for free—rumors started to circulate that the Michigan professor was part of the con. LaRue denied the allegations, yet Ford never trusted him again. "Do not think we would benefit any by using him," was Ford's handwritten comment in the margins of LaRue's subsequent offer to help get the rubber plantation up and running.[1]

Whether or not LaRue was involved in Villares's swindle, his report—the main source of most everything Ford would know of the Amazon before committing to his rubber project—was like catnip to the industrialist-philosopher. Its first half made the botanical case for the Tapajós valley. "The vegetation is very luxuriant," with plenty of rainfall and good drainage, LaRue wrote. Its soil was rich, a palette of dark hues, red and yellow. "We saw very fine old trees," and "there is no question" that many of them would yield up to a gallon of latex a day. The site sat high enough to be out of the reach of mosquitoes, composed mostly of plateaus cut with a few streams and no swamps, making it a perfect place for a settlement. The forests could be timbered for profitable export to the United States, and the potential for hydropower was "considerable." The Tapajós valley, LaRue concluded, was superior, often vastly so, to other established rubber-producing regions, such as Sumatra in Southeast Asia.[2]

But it was the second section of the report, laying out the living conditions of the valley, that must have entranced Ford. It was his vision of hell.

TRAVELING ALONG THE Tapajós during the second decade of Brazilian rubber's long twilight, LaRue painted a picture Dickensian in its attention to misery, one that in every way was the opposite of the world Ford believed he had created back in Michigan. "The people are everywhere poor and forlorn," the botanist wrote Ford, "most of them are penniless and without hope for the future. Many of them have not even had a piece of money in their hands for years." Children enjoy "no school, no play, no advancement and no hope even of life itself, for they are doomed to an early death from hard work, poor food and disease," he recounted. "Thin, yellow and weak," with "drawn set faces," they have "nothing" but despair "until death overtakes them. They have ceased to hope for any amelioration of their lot."

During the previous decade, Ford, as part of his broader restructuring of industrial and human relations, had become interested in health care and worker safety. However much his concern may have been driven by a desire to create a more efficient workforce, Ford's unrivaled wealth allowed him to move beyond self-interest to provide decent medical services to many in the larger Detroit community. In 1915, he established his flagship namesake hospital, filled with state-of-the-art equipment and renowned for its expertise, where "everyone, rich or poor, paid the same nominal fees for the best care possible."[3]

So LaRue was careful to record the health condition of the jungle's rubber tappers and nut gatherers who would make up Ford's labor force. "Some of these men are magnificent specimens," the botanist said, "but one sees a great many fever-stricken bodies among them. Many also have horrible wounds and sores on their legs and feet. They are always nearly naked, covered merely by rags which have been mended upon mended until the whole costume is fairly quilted with patches; the patches themselves being full of holes." LaRue would "never forget" the "sight of a little nursing baby quite naked and completely smeared over with clay from the wet dirt floor," reporting that each household at any moment had at least one person laid low with malaria, groaning and tossing in bed.

The majority of children suffered from hookworm, a disease that had received much attention from public health reformers in the United States, where it was prevalent among poor dirt farmers in Georgia, Mississippi, and Alabama. Left untreated, it resulted in extreme anemia, distended stomachs, and, as one study put it, a "craving for eating earth and all sorts of unnatural things." LaRue told Ford that he saw many, many children in the "clay eating stage" of the infection who had only a "few weeks to live." Matters were made worse by the poor diet—when "there is any food at all to be had"— consisting nearly entirely of dried pirarucu, an Amazonian catfish, and manioc. Milk and butter were "unknown," bread was found "only in larger towns," there was no fruit, not even bananas, and green vegetables were "very scarce." Medicine, including quinine for malaria, was sold at prohibitive prices, out of the reach of most. The afflicted sought relief in "bark and leaves," local remedies that LaRue allowed might have minor remedial benefits but were more likely "totally worthless, if not even injurious."[4]

LaRue explicitly linked the misery he witnessed to the region's system of debt peonage, which he knew would be of particular interest to Ford. Born the year the Emancipation Proclamation went into effect, Ford liked to contrast his industrial wage system with slavery (there was always a porous border between how he viewed the US South and the Amazon). And so did LaRue, who echoed a genre of reform writing common to the time, which opposed America's rural, impoverished southern states to the industrialized and prosperous north. Rubber tappers, he told Ford, were "worse off than slaves were in any decent slave-keeping country," since "slaves, like horses, had to be treated decently to make them profitable." Cash, he explained, was practically never used to pay for rubber, as tappers handed over their latex to "some Syrian on the river" to pay off a previously advanced "grub-stake"—food, clothing, a rifle and ammunition, knives to tap the trees, or some other necessity of life. By Syrian, LaRue was referring broadly to the Arab and Jewish immigrants from North Africa and the Levant who stepped in to take over a good part of the rubber trade after the economic collapse wiped out the larger Brazilian merchants. These traders advanced "lowest in quality merchandise at three to twenty times its retail value, while buying nuts and latex at well below market price. Thus the rubber tapper was "enslaved through debt," constantly "working to pay for produce he has already bought."[5]

LaRue illustrated his point with this story: "A man brought about a hundred pounds of Brazil nuts into a shop. The dealer threw them into a store room without even weighing them and asked the man what he wanted. He wanted some rope and took about thirty feet of smaller rope. Then he wanted some food. The buyer asked if he had any more nuts and said those he had brought only paid for the rope." And this: "A man brought rubber on board a launch . . . on which we were traveling. The rubber was in small balls strung on light sticks. The stick weighed not over five pounds, but the buyer docked the man about three dollars for the wood and took two hides he had brought also, without allowing anything for them. The man protested and asked where his pay for the hides came in, but they were in the hold then, and the buyer merely shrugged his shoulders."

"Instances such as these," LaRue told Ford, "could be found every day."

Ford certainly recognized this system, not just because when he saw "Syrian" he probably read "Jew," but because he had confronted one like it back in Detroit, where "petty empires" run by ethnic bosses took advantage of the high wages Ford paid to immigrant workers, charging exorbitant amounts for apartments and retail goods. To free his employees from these mini-fiefdoms, Ford established a credit union, both to encourage savings and to make low-interest loans available so workers didn't have to go to an "outside Shylock for assistance." He also opened up factory pharmacies and commissaries, which, unlike the infamous "company store" that kept workers perpetually indebted, provided employees a wide array of high-quality products at low prices, often below cost.[6]

Debt slavery, LaRue wrote, left frontline Amazon workers uncared for and disposable. Most were uneducated and illiterate, living in "mere huts" thatched with palm leaves. "Dirt floors are universal and when dry are not so bad, but when wet with the leakage from the roof, are terrible." The workers went months without seeing other human beings, he said. "The loneliness is appalling." Beds or any kind of furniture were uncommon, and a "family is lucky if there are hammocks enough to go around"; most slept "two or three to a hammock." Children sold themselves to riverboats, "glad to work, like dogs for nothing but their food."

LaRue told Ford that his team tried to give quinine to a man with malaria "almost in dying condition" only to have it snatched away by his creditor, who "laughed at the poor devil as he drove him back to work. It made our blood boil, but we were helpless."

Above the traders stood Brazil's aristocratic elite, "young men of wealth" who lived in the Amazon's provincial cities, unconcerned with "bettering the condition of the forest people." Indeed, the very word *upriver* filled them with "dread." Here again LaRue's account seems finely tuned to Ford's fixations, for the carmaker must have imagined Belém to be the Amazon's version of Detroit's Grosse Pointe, home to the pampered scions of inherited wealth—Ford called them "parasites"—untroubled in their manors and mansions by the problems of the world from which they profited. If the Amazon's urban rich were to brave the jungle's "terrors and

Native rubber-tapper family on the Tapajós, around the time of Carl LaRue's trip.

discomforts," LaRue wrote, it would be to execute a program not of reform but of exploitation. Most of the local elite occupied themselves with "dress and dissipation," a Brazilian variation of the trumpery-and-trinket consumerism Ford preached against at home, or with "politics," which for Ford was indistinguishable from corruption.[7]

The real lords of the rubber trade, LaRue told his boss, were the foreign-owned export houses and financial firms, which were "utterly heartless toward their victims." Because of their monopoly, they paid next to nothing to the traders who floated the latex downriver to Belém. Of these foreign interests, LaRue singled out the British as being particularly indifferent to the value of human life. Whether or not this was true, his charge of British callowness tapped into Ford's Anglophobia. LaRue's account was particularly resonant in the wake of the two-decade-old Putumayo scandal, which in 1907 exposed the profiting of a British rubber corporation from the enslavement, torture, starvation, murder, and rape of thousands of Amazonian Indians. These atrocities occurred much farther to the west, in the borderlands that separated Ecuador, Peru, and Colombia, but LaRue suggested that London's mercantile ruthlessness continued unabated on the Tapajós. British companies were sending "families up the Tapajós to collect rubber without any provision for their care and shelter whatever." When Ford's emissary inquired as to how these people, especially the children, would fare, a company representative cavalierly said, "Oh, none of these children will ever come back anyway."[8]

LaRue ended his report with a prediction sure to arouse Ford's self-image as a man with the power to pull humanity from the brink: "They will all die."

A DECADE HAD passed since Ford's feud with Theodore Roosevelt over their competing visions of Americanism, and Ford seemed to be at the top of not only his industry but American, and therefore world, capitalism. Yet as is often the case in the course of great empires, periods experienced as triumphs can be understood with the benefit of hindsight as quietly marking a change in fortune; 1927 was such a moment for Ford's motor company.

At the end of that year, the company rolled out its Model A. The new car was a critical and commercial triumph, putting the company again in the forefront of its industry, taking over 45 percent of the market by the eve of the Great Depression. But in retrospect, the switchover forced Ford to revise a number of his most cherished beliefs.

For years, Ford had ignored the advance of rivals like General Motors, led by Alfred Sloan, who cut into Model T sales by offering cars with shock absorbers, gas gauges, gearshifts, and speedometers. Ford believed his competitors' use of cheap credit and their yearly stylistic changes were perversions of the consumer society he had helped create. "We have lost our buying sense and fallen entirely under the spell of salesmanship," Ford said. "The American of a generation ago was a shrewd buyer. He knew values in terms of utility and dollars. But nowadays the American people seem to listen and be sold; that is, they do not buy. They are sold things; things are pushed on them." Cheap credit was distorting the market, he thought. "We have dotted lines for this, that and the other thing—all of them taking up income before it is earned." He remained committed—at times violently so—to his ideal of manufacturing one infinitely interchangeable product year after year. Once, while he was away on a trip to Europe, Ford's engineers made a number of style changes to the Model T, stretching it out a few inches and giving it a smoother ride. On his return, Ford circled the new model a few times and then proceeded to destroy it, ripping off its doors and shattering its windows before walking away. He repeated throughout the first months of 1927 that "the Ford car," sales of which by that point had plummeted to an all-time low, "will continue to be made the same way."[9]

Until it wasn't. In reluctantly agreeing to abandon the car he had made for two decades and had built the River Rouge to make for two decades more, Ford accommodated himself to the new consumerism. Henceforth, he would have to learn how to satisfy the diverse tastes of consumers rather than lecture them about what their tastes should be. He began spending heavily on advertising, pitching yearly superficial style changes as part of his company's sales strategy. Ford also grudgingly accepted the fact that future sales growth was no longer based on driving the sales price of a new car as low as it would go—which only led to competition with America's growing stock of used cars—but on expanding the customer base for new automobiles through easy loans. So Ford established the Universal Credit Corporation, which allowed Americans to sign on the dotted line and purchase a new $550 Model A roadster for $150 down and $12.50 a month. Yearly style changes also meant he had to abandon a cherished component of his village industry program: the policy that allowed factory workers to take off part of the year (usually May to August) to go farm. When Ford was making the same car year in and year out, it was possible to overproduce parts and then stockpile them for use during the months the worker would be in the field. But after 1927, workers had to stay at the factory year-round, as such stockpiling was no longer possible (the production of parts had to be closely calibrated to the rhythm of actual sales) and the assembly line had to be annually retooled to make the next year's model part.[10]

The year 1927 also marked the completion of the River Rouge plant, hailed the world over as a monument to industrial modernism. But it also meant the ascension of Harry Bennett and the complete defeat of the humane industrialism that for many, particularly those outside Detroit, Ford came to represent with his Five Dollar Day. Workers at Highland Park had already experienced both the speedup and increased coercion and surveillance. Yet those were nothing compared with the monstrous pace of the new factory.

"Highland Park was civilized," said Walter Reuther, who as head of the United Auto Workers union was the man most responsible, years later, for ending Bennett's reign of terror, "but the Rouge was a jungle." With the transition to the Rouge also came the purging of a number of the company's best engineers and officials, often for no reason other than that they represented a threat to Bennett's power or because their intelligence and independence challenged Ford's autocracy. The firings were vicious and cruel, and most often carried out by Bennett himself. In a notable instance, Bennett asked Frank Kulick, a respected engineer who got on Ford's bad side for having suggested, a few years earlier, that the T be upgraded for more power, to take a look at a car that was supposedly making an odd noise. When Kulick climbed on the fender and bent his head under the hood, Bennett stepped on the gas and sped the car out the factory gates, swerving so that Kulick was thrown to the ground. Bennett then turned the car back into the factory yard and locked the gates, and the engineer was never allowed in again. Another twenty-year Ford man, driving with his family on vacation in Michigan's Upper Peninsula, was pulled over by a state trooper who relayed a message that his job was terminated. Ford repeatedly humiliated William Knudsen, the engineer credited with creating a network of Model T assembly plants around the world, pushing him to quit and take a job with GM, where he would turn its Chevrolet division into one of Ford's chief competitors. Ford felt Knudsen was too independent and too allied with his son Edsel, who was trying to modernize the company. "I let him go," Ford later admitted in a moment of candor, "not because he wasn't good, but because he was too good—for me."[11]

The migration of the lion's share of production to the Rouge, Ford's purging of many of the men who made the T a world phenomenon, his growing dependence on Bennett and other thugs, his increasing resort to shop-floor intimidation, and his growing nativism coincided with a psychic turn inward. By 1927, Ford was into the sixth decade of his life, and what was in the past taken as shy awkwardness had rigidified into fortresslike solitude, garrisoned by blasts of intense paranoia and cruelty, increasingly directed at his only son, whom he taunted and tormented mercilessly. Ford constantly embarrassed him in public, countermanding his initiatives and making it clear that while Edsel was nominally the company's president he had no real authority save that granted by his father. When Edsel, for instance, as part of his effort to rationalize the company's notoriously anarchic bookkeeping system, had a new office building constructed at the Rouge to house accountants, Henry vindictively abolished the Accounting Department. Increasingly, the kind of expansive goodwill on display for Consul de Lima was reserved exclusively for public relations spectacles. "The isolation of Henry Ford's mind is about as near perfect as it is possible to make it," was how Samuel Marquis, the minister who headed the Sociological Department in its early, benevolent years, described his aging former employer.[12]

It was also in 1927 that Ford's anti-Semitism finally caught up with him. Since 1924, the *Dearborn Independent* had focused much of its anti-Jewish venom against Aaron Sapiro, a lawyer and activist who had organized farm cooperatives throughout the United States and Canada. In Sapiro, Ford undoubtedly saw a competitor for the affections of farmers, someone who produced more tangible results in helping them obtain better prices for crops than any of Ford's many schemes could. "Jewish Exploitation of Farmers' Organization," ran the headline of the inaugural attack on Sapiro. "Monopoly Traps Operate under Guise of 'Marketing Associations.'" The organization, the article explained, was "born in the fertile, fortune-seeking brain of a young Jew"—Sapiro. After suffering months of similar attacks, linking him to a broader conspiracy intent on subordinating American farms to Jewish money interests, Sapiro filed suit against Ford, claiming defamation and demanding a million dollars in damages. The press salivated at the idea of seeing Ford on the witness stand, hoping for a repeat of the kind of spectacle that occurred in 1919 when Ford sued the *Chicago Tribune* for libel and gave the impression that he was illiterate. Ford had avoided the process server for weeks, until one day, while he was sitting in his car watching planes take off from Ford Field with his window rolled down, a summons dropped in his lap. The carmaker said that he would refuse to appear but finally settled on a March 31 court date after being threatened with legal action. In the week leading up to his scheduled testimony, thousands of people crowded the small Michigan courtroom in anticipation, while the *New York Times* issued a challenge: "If Mr. Ford is convinced, as he must be if he is an honest man, that the matter printed in the *Dearborn Independent* truthfully states an abhorrent and appalling menace to the people of the United States, it is hard to see how he can refrain" from using the publicity generated by the trial to paint "the danger in such colors before the eyes of this entire country, and in fact of the whole world, that the facts will be established beyond challenge." But if he didn't truly believe the threat was real, the *Times* continued, he needed to denounce the "race calumny" that had brought "pain and suffering" to "millions of American citizens." The trial offered Ford an unparalleled opportunity to clearly state his belief. "Will he seize it?" the paper asked. "Will he rise to it?"[13]

He didn't. On the eve of his scheduled appearance, while driving home on Michigan Avenue, Ford claimed, he was sideswiped by a Studebaker and pushed off the side of the road. Many at the time, and a number of historians since, believe the accident, which sent him to the hospital but spared him his court date, to have been staged. His lawyer rescheduled his appearance, but in the end Ford settled out of court.[14]

Ford also agreed to issue a statement apologizing for his anti-Semitism, written by Louis Marshall, head of the American Jewish Committee and one of Ford's chief critics. It was "pretty bad," said Harry Bennett, who tried to read Marshall's prepared text over the phone to his boss. "I don't care how bad it is, you just settle it up," Ford cut him off. The retraction was published worldwide on July 8, 1927, carried by Hearst newspapers, the International News, the Universal Service, the Associated Press, and the United Press news services: "I deem it to be my duty as an honorable man to make amends for the wrong done to the Jews as fellow-men and brothers, by asking their forgiveness for the harm that I have unintentionally committed, by retracting so far as lies within my power the offensive charges laid at their door." Later that year, Ford shuttered the *Independent* and sold off its presses.[15]

It is in this context of domestic constraint, contraction, and compromise that Ford sought out a new space of freedom.

CHAPTER 7

EVERYTHING JAKE

As if to confirm that the logic pushing Ford to the Amazon had moved beyond the laws of supply and demand, by the time Carl LaRue issued his report on the Tapajós valley, the economic rationale behind Ford's interest in rubber no longer held. Two years earlier, just after his lunch with Firestone, Ford was told by one of his men that high prices had stimulated rubber planting on such a large scale that the cost of latex was bound to fall. Also the Dutch were clearly not going to join the British cartel after all, which rendered Churchill's proposal toothless. It made more sense, Ford was advised, to forgo the plantation idea and just open a purchasing office in the Amazon. And sure enough, even before Ford gave the final go-ahead, world rubber prices began to tumble; soon the cost of latex would be substantially lower than it was in the 1910s.[1]

Ford pressed forward. In June 1927, he assigned power of attorney to two of his employees, O. Z. Ide and W. L. Reeves Blakeley, and dispatched them to Brazil. The men were charged with negotiating a land concession with the governor of the state of Pará, the jurisdiction where the property recommended by LaRue was located, and incorporating a subsidiary company under Brazilian law to oversee the plantation.

IDE AND BLAKELEY, both thirty-seven years old, and their wives traveled to New York by train in late June. If Ford thought himself an internationalist, his far-flung company provided him with a useful foreign service. For whatever mission, his agents could rely on Ford dealers to organize the trip, establish contacts, arrange accommodations, and provide transportation— a Lincoln if status warranted, otherwise a Model T or A.

In Manhattan, the Dearborn emissaries were shepherded around in a "Lincoln car" by "Mr. Leahr, of the branch," who helped them obtain their visas and prepare for their departure on the British Booth Line's SS *Cuthbert*. The two couples took in the city and enjoyed a few meals, including one at the Waldorf-Astoria. They also caught Oscar Hammerstein's *Desert Song* at the Casino Theater, the story of a French general sent to Morocco to suppress an anticolonial Arab uprising led by the mysterious "Red Shadow," who turns out to be the general's son. Ide wrote in his diary that it was "as pretty and interesting an operette as I have ever seen."

Ide was enjoying himself. But just before setting sail he got a sense of his partner's temperament and what he saw didn't bode well for the success of their charge. Blakeley got "hot" when shown his sleeping quarters. They weren't up to his standards, he said, and he threatened to call the whole trip off. Blakeley, of course, didn't have the power to do anything of the kind, but he did bully the captain to move a ship officer out of his stateroom. Placated, Blakeley and his wife boarded the ship.

On the *Cuthbert*, Ide eyed Blakeley warily, yet the two-week cruise to Belém was uneventful. Blakeley had already been sent to Brazil once before by Ford, on a trip where he had met Jorge Villares. But it was Ide's first sea voyage, and as the ship pulled away from the Brooklyn dock and sailed out of the Narrows, he wistfully noted the "filigree of Coney Island and Atlantic City." He brought a dictionary with him and tried to learn Portuguese, but his interest soon waned. Ide's "flesh and spirit" proved "a bit too weak to overcome the blissful lethargy and temptation to do nothing." He surrendered to an endless bridge game, and within a few days the ship's passengers, with the conventions of shore life behind them, gave up wearing their coats and neckties.

On July 7, the *Cuthbert* entered the Baía de Marajó, one of the Amazon's many mouths, so enormous that land was not sighted until the eighth. Roughly four thousand miles long and beginning just a sliver east of the Pacific Ocean, the Amazon is the largest river system in the world, comprising about 15 percent of all the earth's river water. The Mississippi discharges 41 percent of the runoff of the continental United States, but the Amazon expels twelve times as much—fifty-seven million gallons of water per second. Oceangoing vessels can travel deep into it, as far west as Iquitos in Peru.

Like the Mississippi, the Amazon and its tributaries have been worked on over the centuries. Man-made canals and footpaths have transformed nature's baroque into human rococo, weaving an already bedazzling ecology of waterways into an even more intricate set of nested trading systems, connecting nine (of thirteen) South American countries—Brazil, Venezuela, Peru, Bolivia, Ecuador, Colombia, Suriname, Guyana, and French Guiana—and, via Venezuela's Orinoco River, numerous Caribbean nations. Retaining walls protect settlements from the tides and seasons, as do dams, which permit the drying of wetlands and seasonal floodplains. Dredges keep sediment from building up around ports and buoy lights guide ships, especially during low water. But the Mississippi is truly an industrial river; its stepped locks, levees, dikes, dams, navigation signals, and excavated channels make it the most managed and manipulated water system in the world. In contrast, the Amazon, despite its grandeur, is—as it was at the time of Ide and Blakeley's arrival—an artisanal river. Its pilots rely on a lifetime of experience and skill to navigate shifting bars, fast-changing depths, and a powerful tidal bore that could travel inland from the Atlantic, rushing "up the river in a sheer wall with a rumble like a regiment of light artillery on the stampede" as far as ten miles, raising the largest of ships and leaving them aground on its recession. And unlike the delta of the Mississippi, which over the last two centuries has been reduced from a patchwork of barely navigable bayous, islands, shifting sandbars, and estuaries into a rationalized sluice, the Amazon's terminus remains democratic, with many metamorphosing paths in and out.[2]

ONE OF THE calmest entry points in terms of the tides, and thus the most trafficked, is the Baía de Marajó, along with the smaller Baía de Guajará, which gives way to a water channel that connects inland to the Amazon proper. On the southeastern shores of the Guajará presides Nossa Senhora de Belém—Our Lady of Bethlehem. As the *Cuthbert* closed on the city, the shimmering constant green of the dense jungle gave way to red tile roofs and blue- and cream-colored walls. Though the rubber boom had ended more than a decade earlier, the port was still busy. The harbor was crowded with many different kinds of ships, from single-masted canoelike sailboats, called *vigilengas*, and flat-bottom barges that served as floating markets, filled with fish, turtles, birds, vegetables, and fruit, to ocean liners bound from Portugal or New Orleans to Iquitos or Manaus, cities that, like Belém, had flourished during the boom but had since lost much of their shine. The most distinctive vessels were the multileveled steamboats, known as *gaiolas*, "birdcages," whose hammock-lined bowed decks made it seem as if they were sagging in the middle.

Everything felt "strange and new," Ide thought, as the Ford party transferred to a small government launch to take them to shore. The entourage proceeded to a long stone water wall, above which worked cranes, winches, steam trolleys, and stevedores. Along the quay sat a line of metal-roofed brick cargo warehouses flanked by the customs building, and terminals for the major shipping companies, like the Booth Line. To the right of the warehouses was the city's fish market—known as *ver-o-peso*, or "check-the-weight"—a green metal and concrete cavern, its four-cornered ornate turrets a reminder of the city's military origins. Inside, mongers working over makeshift butcher blocks sliced from Amazonian hardwood trees sold an array of the river's harvest, including incalculable variations of catfish. Farther back from the water stood a row of three-storied export houses, shops, and merchant homes, behind which, on Rua Gaspar Viana, the Ford Motor Company would open an office to coordinate the arrival of cargo from Dearborn and the hiring of laborers.

On shore to greet the Ford delegation was John Minter, the American consul, and Gordon Pickerell, a local Ford dealer who had himself just retired from a thirteen-year run as US consul. Also present was Jorge Villares, whom Blakeley greeted warmly, which Ide thought peculiar since he didn't recall his partner's mentioning any contacts on his previous trip other than Pickerell and Minter. Blakeley made the introductions, yet he did so in an awkward way, only mumbling Villares's name.

The sun glared and the heat felt intense as the Dearborn emissaries left the dock, turning onto the broad Boulevard of the Republic, which took them to their hotel. Ide had never traveled much beyond Michigan, so he took care to record his impressions of his arrival in Belém in a diary. They passed shops selling turtle shells, baskets, snake skins, parrots, monkeys, and "strange birds of beautiful plumage." The streets were filled with "handsome dark men in white suits, strikingly pretty girls of doubtful cast, probably half breed," and "niggers or natives with great loads on their heads." The midwestern Ide thought the architecture "odd," almost "oriental or Mexican," by which he was probably referring to the glazed bluish tiles that adorned the faces of many of Belém's best buildings. He recognized the buzzards, though, that flew high over the city. They reminded him of Detroit pigeons. And the potholes that filled the streets made him think of Detroit's notoriously bumpy Gratiot Avenue.

As in any diplomatic corps, divisions and rivalries at the home office played out abroad. Since its founding, the Ford Motor Company was famed for its factionalism, which created competing spheres of loyalty among employees. Henry Ford's delegating yet incorrigibly controlling and manipulating managing style aggravated the divisions, as did his reliance on men with strong personalities and even stronger egos. The company's most famous schism — described by historians as Shakespearean — was between Edsel, Ford's only child, and Harry Bennett, the head of Ford's Service Department.

Edsel, just twenty-six when his father made him the nominal president of the company in 1919, and Harry were polar opposites. Bennett, about the same age as Edsel, was a thug with organized crime connections and a reputation for getting into fistfights—during his boxing days in the navy he fought under the name Sailor Reese—car chases, and gun battles, stories of which delighted Henry. Ford "liked the look of the man—the colored silk shirts, the Western belt buckle, and the snap-brim felt hat. He liked the Damon Runyonesque quality—the fact that Bennett had real experience in a masculine world." And he liked his loyalty. "If Mr. Ford told me to blacken out the sun tomorrow," Bennett once said, "I might have trouble fixing it. But you'd see a hundred thousand sons-of-bitches coming through the Rouge gates in the morning all wearing dark glasses."[3]

In contrast, Edsel, interested in the aesthetics of industrial design and modern art, forever disappointed his father, though many now credit him with holding the company together through the twenties and thirties. "Where Edsel was gentle," the historian Thomas Bonsall remarks, "Henry saw weakness. Where Edsel was imaginative, Henry saw frivolity." If Bennett ruled the factory floor as if industry were an extension of the Wild West, Edsel with his "martyr's smile" quietly worked to bring professionalism to the company, to mitigate not just Bennett's violence but the arbitrariness that governed Ford's labor relations. Much to his father's contempt, he even admired Franklin Delano Roosevelt and moved to accommodate the company to the New Deal. During the 1930s, Henry would come to despise FDR, not just for being a member of the East Coast elite (and Theodore Roosevelt's cousin) and for supporting legislation making it easier for unions to organize. Roosevelt's New Deal, which extended the power of government to regulate industry, in effect directly competed with Ford's decentralization and village industry program for how best to tame capitalism. It was, for example, FDR's Tennessee Valley Authority, largely a nationalization of Ford's Muscle Shoals proposal, that would bring electricity and jobs to the poor farmers of lower Appalachia.[4]

Of the two men, Henry didn't hide whom he preferred. Not only did he do nothing to douse the fires that burned between Bennett and Edsel, he fanned them. The elder Ford backed Bennett in his fights with Edsel in a way to encourage jealousy, while telling Bennett, at any sign of rapprochement, "Harry, you think you're getting along with Edsel, but he's no friend of yours." Once, while Edsel was in the process of

having a new row of coke ovens built at the Rouge's foundry, Ford told
Bennett, "Harry, as soon as Edsel gets those ovens built I'm going to tear
them down." And he did.[5]

WILLIS LONG REEVES Blakeley was a Bennett man, and he acted it.
Born in 1890 in Bowling Green, Kentucky, Blakeley, after serving in
World War I, joined the march of migrants up the Ohio Valley to the factories of the Midwest, and he found a job in Bennett's Service Department as an assistant employment manager. On the *Cuthbert*, he tried to
boss Ide around, peacocking like a "big shot" and telling everybody on the
boat about their mission even though Henry Ford himself insisted that
"this thing should be kept secret until we got well into it."[6]

Blakeley took well to Belém, which combined the grandeur of an old
colonial city, energized by rubber riches and then exhausted by their
evaporation, with the ribald pleasures of a boomtown, still considerable
despite the economy's collapse. Its architecture might have been European, but its soul was New World frontier. The writer José Maria Ferreira
de Castro, around the time of Blakeley and Ide's visit, called the city the
"Mecca of the world's harlotry," its brothels filled with Parisian and Eastern European courtesans. Much of the wealth that could be pulled out of
the Amazon passed through its port, and it attracted adventurers and fortune seekers from the world over. They gravitated toward one another, fre-
quenting the same casinos, bars, and brothels.

Blakeley quickly gained a reputation among the rogues and expatriates
as a drunkard and an exhibitionist. He stayed in the best corner suite on the
second floor of the Grande Hotel, Belém's finest, with a veranda and floor-
to-ceiling windows, the shutters of which he left open as he walked around
naked and made love to his wife. The hotel, since demolished, was located
on the city's central plaza, and Blakeley's room faced the majestic Theatro
da Paz, where the city's gentry promenaded every evening, coiffed and be-
decked in formal wear. "Everyone on the street could see," complained the
hotel manager to Ide. To make matters worse, Blakeley's window was just
above a major taxi stand, and the drivers circulated gossip about the scandalous behavior of the Ford man throughout the city. "It's the talk of the
town," said the manager, who tried unsuccessfully to evict Blakeley.[7]

Like his boss, Bennett, who as his power grew in Dearborn brokered contracts with outside suppliers in which he received healthy kickbacks, Blakeley saw a convergence between his interests and those of the company. He began to work on a plan with Consul Minter in which as Ford's representative he would buy bonds issued by Pará's deeply indebted state treasury, with the idea that their value would soar once word got out that Ford had committed to investing in a rubber plantation. Minter told his superiors in the Department of State that he thought it a win-win-win proposition: "taking over the bonds at or near their recent quotation would not only mean ultimate profit to the Ford Motor Company" but also entrench the company more "solidly in this state, increasing its prestige and power therein." This, in turn, would please the Brazilians, who, Minter believed, "would prefer to have the state developed by American capital than by British."[8] It is doubtful that Dearborn would have approved of any transaction that might have exposed the company to charges of engaging in speculation. And given Henry Ford's well-known aversion to finance capital, it's likely that the bond scheme was wholly initiated by Blakeley. In any case, the State Department quickly nixed the idea, instructing Minter to "strictly confine" his activities on behalf of Ford's representatives to the provision of statistical information, "without comment or advice."[9]

IDE, OR OZ as he was called (O. Z. was his complete first name), worked in Ford's legal division, a branch of the company loyal to Edsel and considered a bastion of professionalism. Taciturn where Blakeley was brazen, the lawyer at first didn't pick up on why his partner was acting so strange on the dock when he introduced him to Consul Minter and the Ford dealer Pickerell. But then he realized it was because Blakeley was trying to hide from them the fact that Ide also worked for Ford. "They thought I was just someone he had met on the boat," remembered an irritated Ide. He didn't make much of it until later that night, when he learned that Blakeley had kept him from being invited to a reception at the consul's house. Villares, too, was a mystery. Ide had never heard mention of Blakeley's elegant friend, who, since meeting them on their arrival, was always around, offering his services as interpreter and general liaison and seeming to know more about the mission than Ide himself did.

Ide, of course, was unaware of the role Schurz and Villares had played, with an assist from LaRue, in pushing the idea that a specific strip of land along the right bank of the Tapajós River was the best place to grow rubber, though he quickly identified Villares as an "opportunist" who had managed to obtain an option on that land. Whatever his opinion, Ide had little choice but to cooperate with his colleagues. He could try to work around them by enlisting Consul Minter, but Henry Ford didn't want the US government to know of his affairs, much less participate in them. He could try to negotiate an agreement with the governor on his own, but having spent his time on the *Cuthbert* playing bridge instead of learning Portuguese, Ide was lost in the local language. That left the ubiquitous Villares, whom Ide eventually came to like. He even later defended the Brazilian, believing that the money he and his partners would make was simply the price of doing business. "Between them," he recalled, "they had to pay off the Governor and the other political boys who had something coming to them."

Despite these machinations or, as Ide soon realized, because of them, discussions went smoothly with Brazilian officials. Villares, Blakeley, and Ide met with Governor Dionysio Bentes—the man who granted to Villares, Schurz, and Greite the option to the land in question—to begin negotiations. There wasn't much to negotiate. Bowing, nodding, and smiling to bridge the language gap, Bentes told the men they could have anything Ford wanted. The concession required approval by the state legislature, but that, he assured them, was a formality. He then sent the delegation off, as Ide remembered, to "prepare a bill to be presented to the legislature, setting forth in this petition exactly what we wanted."[10]

One of the first things they needed to do was draw up a legal description of the designated property. For this, they went to the mayor of Belém, António Castro, who Ide thought looked "kind of like a monkey." Castro was already promised some money by Villares, but he was happy to offer his services as a civil engineer for an additional fee.

Ide had not been to the property—it was a six-day boat ride from Belém. But in his meeting with Castro he unfolded a map of the Tapajós valley and with a heavy black pencil traced out a seventy-five-mile line up the river, then inland seventy-five miles, then another line parallel to the first, and then finally back to the starting point. A total of 5,625 square miles.

That's an "awful lot of land," exclaimed the surprised mayor. "That's not your problem," Ide shot back. "I just want you to give us a description."[11]

Next on the agenda was to sit down with Samuel McDowell, the local Ford dealership's lawyer, to hash out the terms of the contract. On a "yellow tablet" Ide, Blakeley, and Villares wrote "just what we wanted in the bill that was going to the legislature." They had only vague instructions from Dearborn, so they asked for everything they could think of: the right to exploit the land's lumber and mineral reserves, the right to build railroads and airfields, to erect any kind of building without government supervision, establish banks, organize a private police force, run schools, draw power from waterfalls, and "dam up the river in any way we needed to." They exempted the company from export taxes, not just on rubber and latex but on any products and resources the plantation would want to ship abroad: "skins and hides, oil, seeds, timbers, and other products and articles of any nature." "We thought of a lot of things there that we had never heard of before," said Ide, and "as we got into it, we'd think of these things and put them in."[12]

In return for Bentes's generosity, Ford's negotiators obligated the company only to plant a thousand acres of the grant with rubber within a year. They did this to preserve the "symmetry and equilibrium" of the contract and to provide a show of good faith that Ford really did intend to cultivate rubber and not just mine the land for gold or drill for oil. Blakeley assumed that he would be named manager of the estate and that he could easily clear and plant as much as three thousand acres within a few months. McDowell then "dressed the contract up in the proper language" and had it translated into Portuguese. When the team passed it along to Governor Bentes, they expected him to balk at some of the requests. But the governor presented the bill to the legislature with nary a comment, complete with everything asked for by the Ford team. "Much more," wrote Ide, "than we hoped to get."[13]

All told, the state of Pará ceded Ford just under 2.5 million acres, a bit less than what the Dearborn lawyer sketched out on the map but, at close to the size of Connecticut, still a vast dispensation. Half of this was from the Villares claim, for which Ford was to pay $125,000, a pittance considering the company's enormous wealth. Public land covered the other half, which Ford received for free.[14]

As they waited for the legislature to ratify the deal, Ide took care of unfinished business. He and McDowell incorporated the Companhia Ford Industrial do Brasil as the legal owner of what quickly came to be called Fordlândia—the Portuguese word for Fordville. Then he and Blakeley sailed to Rio to work out the terms of the tariffs the company would pay to import material and machinery. At the time, Brazil's constitution was a model of "extreme federalism" that invested in state governors the power to grant the kind of generous concessions Bentes gave to Ford. Import duties, however, fell within the national government's jurisdiction. But before Ide had a chance to conclude his negotiations with federal officials, he was called back to Belém. So he left Blakeley to wrap things up. When Blakeley returned to the Amazon, he claimed to have obtained from the federal government a deal that "everyone said impossible"—that is, the right to import all machinery and goods completely free of customs duties. As it turned out, "everyone" was right. He received nothing of the kind.[15]

But the problems caused by Blakeley's overconfidence lay in the future. Back in Belém, things were moving along nicely. Bentes was as good as his word, and the state legislature, on September 30, 1927, ratified the concession exactly as the Ford men composed it. It took under three months to negotiate and finalize the deal, a far cry from the fruitless years wasted on trying to get the US Congress to approve Ford's Muscle Shoals project.

With his work finished, Ide made arrangements to return home. He wired his wife, who, not having fared well in Belém's heat, had left for the United States a few weeks earlier: "Everything jake sailing on Hubert tonight love Oz."

He also telegrammed Dearborn, urging the home office to compensate Villares: "I am thoroughly sold on Villares, both as to his professional knowledge of tropical horticulture and ability and also as to his reliability and honesty."

For his part, Villares, eager to pay off Greite, Schurz, Bentes, and the other "political boys" who made the deal possible, followed up with his own cable.

"Great joy enthusiasm among people," he wrote. "Send funds."[16]

CHAPTER 8

WHEN FORD COMES

O. Z. IDE RETURNED TO DEARBORN TO DEBRIEF COMPANY OFFI-
cials. He tried to warn Edsel and Henry Ford about Harry Bennett's protégé, complaining of Reeves Blakeley's exhibitionism and other rough
behavior while in Belém. Yet Henry Ford, with the same leniency and
perhaps fondness he had for Bennett—who just then was increasing his
cruelty on the factory floor as well as solidifying his influence over his
boss—nonetheless decided to tap Blakeley to head the plantation. Along
with a number of other Ford employees, including John R. Rogge, a lumberjack from the Upper Peninsula, and Curtis Pringle, the former sheriff
of Kalamazoo, Blakeley returned to the Amazon in early 1928 to begin
work and prepare for the arrival of two Ford-owned cargo ships containing
heavy equipment and other material needed to establish a small city.

In Belém, the advance team was joined by Jorge Villares, who for a
few months after the concession was ratified enjoyed a good reputation in
Dearborn. Blakeley and Villares formed an unlikely partnership. The Ford
man was arrogant and filled with purposeful energy, the Brazilian fretfully
effete. Yet their shared sense of confidence papered over these differences

in style. Blakeley bought a launch and the expedition set out up the Amazon, stopping in the town of Santarém, at the mouth of the Tapajós. After purchasing provisions and hiring a work crew of twenty-five laborers, the group pushed off from the town's pier, towing a thatch-roofed barge that served as a makeshift kitchen for Tong, a Chinese cook, and his assistant, Ego, and headed up the Tapajós River, to found Fordlandia.

Blakeley and Villares had already selected the site for the new settlement, a village named Boa Vista, which means pleasant view in Portuguese, based on their reconnaissance of the area during Blakeley's previous trip to the Amazon. It sat 650 miles from Belém and about 100 from Santarém, at a point where the river stayed deep right to the shore, which would save on dredging expenses and allow the unloading of heavy equipment. The bank quickly rose fifty feet within a hundred yards of the river, continuing to climb another two hundred feet over the course of the next mile.

It was a providential location high enough to afford protection from mosquitoes and other insects, Blakeley insisted in his report to Dearborn, though he consulted no entomologist to support his claim. And it was rich in trees and resources. One could find about twenty exportable trees on any given acre, he said, including the redwood massaranduba, a dark reddish brown heartwood called angelim, and Spanish cedar, in addition to old-growth wild rubber trees. There was, Blakeley believed, a strong possibility that they would find oil, along with gold, silver, platinum, ores, and possibly diamonds. The Cupary River, a tributary of the Tapajós that ran twenty miles into the estate, would be, Blakeley said, a perfect spot for a hydroelectric dam. And until the planted rubber matured to produce sap—which takes about five years—a number of company outposts could easily be established at key points to buy wild rubber. Blakeley told Ford that the Tapajós valley produced fifteen hundred tons of latex a year and it would be relatively easy to "capture all of that." With fair treatment and higher prices, the river's tappers would happily abandon their "Syrian patrons" and sell their rubber to Ford's agents.[1]

But before Blakeley, Villares, and their crew could start work in Boa Vista, they needed to sort out competing claims to the land along the riverbank where they wanted to base their operation. When O. Z. Ide was researching the Amazon's property registry during the concession's negotiation, he noticed that there existed a few hundred deeded lots within the boundaries of the land granted to Ford. About seventy-five or so families lived along the bank of the Tapajós River, another fifty up the Cupary River, and more scattered throughout the estate, mostly rubber tappers who worked a trail or two. Some had title to their land, but many paid rent to local merchants who held the deed, like the Franco family, who lived just across the Tapajós, or the Cohen family, just downriver in the small town of Boim. Most were descendants of boom-time migrants who settled in the area during the height of the rubber trade. They were generally known as *caboclos*, or "copper-colored," the term used to refer to the rural poor of mixed ancestry, a blend of Portuguese, Native American, and African. Also scattered throughout Ford's two and a half million acres were a number of small communities of Tupi-speaking people, who hunted and gathered, farmed and fished, living on cassava and other jungle fruits. "I met Indians there," John Rogge, the lumberjack on Blakeley's advance team, wrote home to the Upper Peninsula, "and ate everything but monkey meat."[2]

Ide wasn't too concerned. They were "just squatters," he thought, who lived in little shacks on "very, very small patches of land along the river. If anybody had any property right where we were going to clear," their land would just be purchased and they would be moved somewhere else. Back in Dearborn, Ernest Liebold agreed, thinking they were just "some native tribes" that didn't "stay in one place very long." Ide decided the best thing to do was to "forget about those fellows" until operations were under way, and he wrote into the Bentes contract a clause that would allow Ford to buy title to any property within the boundaries of the concession.[3]

It was hard, though, to "forget about" the Franco family, since they owned the entire village of Boa Vista. They were descendants of Alberto José da Silva Franco, a Portuguese migrant who a century earlier had been one of the region's most prosperous rubber traders. How Franco came to the Tapajós is bound up in one of the most brutal chapters in Amazonian history.

ALBERTO FRANCO ARRIVED in the Amazon from Lisbon in the early nineteenth century, wealthy but not enough to enter into Belém's *elite lusitana*—the prosperous Portuguese class that controlled the city during the colonial period. So he settled in provincial Santarém, establishing himself as a slave-owning merchant. But he was soon on the move again, in flight from the Cabanagem Revolt, or the War of the Cabanas, Brazil's bloodiest uprising.[4]

The rebellion broke out in 1835, when thousands of *mestizos*, *mulattos*, Africans, and Indians marched on Belém, which before it would be celebrated for its tropical Beaux Arts buildings and boulevards was associated with another French tradition: revolution. The ranks of the insurgents came from the city's majority destitute residents, who lived in the adobe and wood-planked hovels, *cabanas*, which gave the rebellion its name. The red-shirted rebels declared the city independent and ran it for a year, emptying prisons, outlawing forced labor of all kind, distributing the wealth of merchants, setting up a communal food distribution system, and terrorizing landlords and merchants, especially if they were Portuguese. Beneficiaries of what a Prussian prince then touring the region called "the fruits of ceaseless oppression," the Portuguese were known by a set of regionally specific derogatory names, including *caiado* ("chalk skin") and *caramuru* ("fish face"). The white-faced cebus monkey was popularly known as the *macaco português*. The British navy helped Brazil's newly independent federal government blockade the city, yet it still took troops more than a year to retake Belém. The insurgents were finally forced to give up the city, but the rebellion spread throughout the vast interior, as far west as Manaus and deep into the Amazon's many tributaries, including the Tapajós.[5]

Martial law was declared throughout the lower Amazon, and soldiers hunted down the revolutionaries, now joined by rural African and indigenous slaves, with a vengeance that made the violence against the Portuguese pale in comparison. Troops engaged in mass drownings and mass shootings, festooning themselves with rosaries made of the strung-together ears of the executed. Insurgents occupied Santarém in 1836 for a few months but eventually retreated up the Tapajós, which became the scene of the rebellion's drawn-out final stage. For five years, the rebels engaged in a rearguard hit-and-run guerrilla war with federal troops before finally surrendering, at a trading post just upriver from where Ford would found his settlement. As many as 30,000 out of a regional population of 120,000 were killed, most of them at the hands of government soldiers.

The Cabanagem uprising and its repression had a lasting effect on the valley. As historian Barbara Weinstein writes, the violence weakened the control of white Portuguese elites over the rural population. Runaway slaves deserted plantations en masse, founding fugitive communities throughout the forest. But the breakdown of social relations also allowed provincial merchants and traders to fill the vacuum, especially once federal troops got the upper hand against the rebels. These new regional elites leveraged the assault on Portuguese power to set up trading outposts and claim large parcels of jungle land, laying the foundation for the impending rubber boom. Once established, they began to resort to a variety of mechanisms to erode the autonomy of peasant communities. Pará's government passed vagrancy laws aimed directly at driving smallholders who didn't have deeds to their property into debt to merchants. Indigenous communities were particularly hard-hit, and many soon found themselves on the edge of cultural and often physical extinction, having suffered slave raids, tribal dispersal, and forced relocation. Men were conscripted as tappers and boatmen, while women were forced into domestic service or into concubinage. Survivors sought refuge deep in the jungle, leaving the Tapajós's main trunk and tributaries to the poor migrant families that came from Brazil's impoverished northeast — the forebears of the unfortunates so graphically described by LaRue.[6]

Memories of the rebellion lingered for decades. In 1866, the conservationist and poet George Washington Sears, more famous for his descriptions of canoe trips through the Adirondacks, traveled up the Amazon and spoke with rebel survivors. Having grown up among Native Americans in upstate New York and himself having just fought for the Union in the Civil War, Sears was moved by their stories to write an ode to the insurrection. The historical precision of "Tupi Lament" is haunting, capturing the rueful pride in having staged the revolt but also the shame of defeat and sexual subjection that underwrote what Amazonian scholar Susanna Hecht has called "terror slavery":

We sing the noble dead to-night
Who sleep in jungle covered graves.
We sing the brave who fell in fight
Beside the Amazona's waves,

The white man counts us with his beasts,
And makes our girls the slaves of priests.
Woe, woe for the Cabano!
. . . .
We swept their forces at Para,
But English ships were on the waves.
And still our girls are serfs and slaves.
Woe, woe, for the Cabano!
We drove them from the Tocantins,
We swept them from the Tapajoz.
A feeble race with feeble means,
Our courage conquered all our foes.
. . . .
We were a fierce avenging flood
That no Brazilian force could stem.
We reddened all their towns with blood,
From Onca's isle to Santarem,
But ah, our best are in their graves
And we again are serfs and slaves!
Woe, woe, for the Cabano![7]

FAMILY LORE SAYS that Alberto José da Silva Franco, along with his wife, his children, and a handful of loyal slaves, barely escaped Santarém, fleeing up the Tapajós. After nearly a week paddling on the river, as they took shelter from a storm in a marshy inlet of a large island named Urucurituba, a bass jumped out of the river and into the boat, which Alberto José took as a divine sign that the island was where his family should stake their new life. The revolt was still roiling the valley. Just a year after his landing on Urucurituba, insurgents slaughtered forty residents of the village of Aveiros, an hour downriver, on the opposite bank. So the Francos kept a low profile, building a small house with an adjacent chapel to Saint Peter, whom Alberto José designated as the island's patron. Once the insurrection was put down, Alberto José began to spread out, soon becoming one of the Tapajós's most important landlords and merchants, well placed to profit from the pacification of the valley and increasing rubber trade. He registered the island, as well as land on both banks of the river, in his name and planted sugar to distill and sell *cachaça*. The rum was valuable not just as a tradable product but for its effectiveness in weakening the will of those who tried to hold out against falling into debt. He also built a statelier Casa Grande, a hacienda. The new house had six airy rooms, one consecrated as a chapel to Saint Peter, right next to the office where rubber was weighed and debt recorded, and a twelve-posted terracotta-tiled veranda that ran along the entire length of its front. Where his first modest home was set in an inconspicuous cove, this one was built on a prominent knoll, framed by a row of grand Havana palms. When he died, he left Urucurituba, along with his other holdings, including Boa Vista, opposite the island on the Tapajós's right bank, to his many sons.[8]

Alberto José's great-grandson, Eimar Franco, is still alive, and he remembers the coming of Ford to the Tapajós as "provoking a true revolution up and down the valley." He was seven years old in 1928 and had only twice traveled beyond Santarém, when "all of a sudden modern boats were plying the river in all directions and immense tractors were roaring day and night, digging up the dirt, pulling down trees, opening roads," he says. On "our side of the river we were still living like our ancestors did, with a few alterations." Eimar's memories accord with those of David Riker, who was just a boy when his Baptist father, along with other Confederate "cavaliers" and "roughs" who preferred exile rather than submission to the terms of Appomattox, settled near Santarém after the Civil War. Riker described the coming of Ford as shaking the Tapajós "to its foundations." It was like a "blood transfusion," he said, jolting alive a moribund economy with an injection of money, electricity, and internal combustion engines in a region that still relied mostly on barter, debt, and wood-burning steamboats to circulate goods and people. Nearly overnight there was a cash "market for anything negotiable."[9]

One thing that had not been negotiable for a long time was land, as its value had plummeted to almost nothing in the trail of the rubber bust. But as Blakeley and Villares pitched camp and began preliminary clearing, Henry Ford sent a trusted accountant (he didn't trust too many accountants), James Kennedy, up the Tapajós with a satchel of cash to buy whatever land Blakeley indicated was necessary to advance operations. And since the Francos had fallen on hard times with the collapse of rubber, they welcomed not just the cash Ford's accountant was offering but the possibility of making money by provisioning the work camp.

As in Muscle Shoals and the Florida Everglades, wherever Ford or his company went, or was believed to be going, land prices skyrocketed and speculators bought up property to resell at jacked-up prices. When word got out in Iron Mountain, Michigan, that Ford was opening a sawmill, rents jumped from fifteen dollars a month to fifty-five and the prices of houses increased threefold. Boa Vista's value just a few months earlier was negligible, but now, in 1928, the Ford Motor Company was buying it in cash for four thousand dollars.[10]

The sale took place on Urucurituba, in the first modest house built by Alberto José ninety years earlier. James Kennedy, along with his satchel, arrived on the island, accompanied by a notary to officiate the sale and David Riker to interpret the proceedings. Helping foreigners get by on the Tapajós had become something of a tradition for the Confederates and their descendants; a half century earlier, David's father had lent a hand to down-on-his-luck Henry Wickham, just before Wickham lighted out for London with the seeds that would doom the Brazilian rubber trade. A large crowd of Urucurituba's residents—the equivalent of sharecroppers, who paid the Francos rent in rubber and other jungle products—gathered around the house, which stood next to the already crumbling chapel of Saint Peter. "An almost religious silence" fell over the assembly as the notary began to recite the terms of the transaction from an "enormous book." When the reading was finished, Kennedy opened his bag and handed the money to Eimar's father, Francisco. Francisco was standing proxy for his young nephew, Luiz, who had just inherited Boa Vista from his father. The boy looked on wide-eyed as his uncle counted out the bills, one by one, on the dining room table. When Francisco finished the tally, he handed the money to a trembling Luiz, who took the payment under his arm and left for his house, with a large procession in tow. "Nothing like that," Eimar said, "had ever happened on the Tapajós!"[11]

NEWS THAT FORD had completed the deal prompted wild speculation as to his ability to revive the Amazon's economy. Modernizers, both those from São Paulo like Consul de Lima but also many from the Amazon, hoped that Ford's plan for capital-intensive, high-wage industrial development would overcome the jungle's poverty and backwardness, which many understood to be rooted in its extractive debt economy. National and local newspapers reported that Ford would build a railroad linking the interior to the Atlantic, roads that would flank the jungle's many rivers, and electric trolley lines running up and down both banks of the Tapajós, all allowing easy access to the Atlantic market for the state's agricultural products.* Rumors circulated in the press about how big Ford's city would be (the biggest in the Amazon, most agreed), the amount of money he intended to spend ($40 million, reported one paper), and how many workers he would hire (at least fifty thousand, wrote another). The Amazon would finally become, as Humboldt predicted, the "world's granary." On news of Ford's imminent arrival, Belém's municipal government paved roads, filled potholes, and laid new sidewalks; the city began to rouse itself, "just like an old broken-down fire horse when he sniffs smoke. The moment somebody says 'rubber' out loud there is a sudden stir in all the old river towns."[12]

In the press frenzy surrounding the concession, Ford was a symbol of hope but also a flashpoint of conflict, as many began to question his motives. Members of Brazil's intellectual and political class were often strongly nationalistic. They admired US industry and needed US capital, but they distrusted Washington's intentions. Not an unreasonable fear, considering that even as Ford was organizing his rubber project, US marines were occupying Nicaragua, Haiti, and the Dominican Republic. And the death of Henry Wickham—now generally known around Belém

---

*Brazilians were not the only ones to see opportunity in Ford's project. Dearborn received letters from around the world offering to sell Ford cheap land or share visionary ideas. Leslie Evans, of Battle Creek, Michigan, for example, wrote to the carmaker of his plan to create a system of rail and river transportation throughout Brazil completely powered by biofuel made from the babassu palm nut, which "grows abundantly in a wild state" in the Amazon. The idea was "worth millions," according to Evans, who said that he himself would build the babassu-powered trains and ships and all Ford would have to do to earn a part of the proceeds was to put him in touch with the proper Brazilian officials and guarantee that the lines would not operate at a loss (BFRC, accession 74, box 13, "General Correspondence").

as "Henry the First"—in September 1928, widely reported in the Brazilian press just as Ford's men were getting under way, reminded many of an earlier treachery.[13]

The tension between the promise of development and the fear of loss of sovereignty was especially acute in the Amazon, over which Rio had but a precarious hold—as witnessed by the prolonged Cabanagem Revolt. The vast rain forest seemed to attract international intrigue, both rumored and real. In 1850, Matthew Fontaine Maury, the head of the US Naval Observatory, floated perhaps the first of what would be a long history of schemes to transfer the Amazon to some jurisdiction other than Brazil's.* In the hope that the United States could both avoid a civil war *and* keep its expanding cotton industry, Maury proposed that Washington transfer the entire southern plantation economy—slaves, slavers, and livestock—to the lower Amazon valley. The question Maury asked was whether the Amazon would "be peopled with an imbecile and an indolent people or by a go ahead race that has the energy and enterprise equal to subdue the forest and to develop and bring forth the vast resources that lie hidden there."†

---

*Brazilians understandably chafed when Al Gore recently said that "contrary to what Brazilians think, the Amazon is not their property, it belongs to all of us." During World War II, Nelson Rockefeller recommended building a series of large canals connecting Venezuela's Orinoco delta to the Amazon and beyond to Argentina's Rio de La Plata, as a way of making sure that Latin American raw materials could get to US factories directly, without having to travel the German submarine–infested Atlantic. And in 1965, the futurist Herbert Kahn, founder of the conservative Hudson Institute think tank, recommended that the United States, as part of its anticommunist economic modernization policy for Latin America, dam the Amazon to create five "Great Lakes," to spur industrial development and generate electricity, not just for Brazil but for all of South America (Herman Kahn, "New Focus on the Amazon," New York: Hudson Institute, 1965; Michael Goulding, Nigel J. H. Smith, and Dennis J. Mahar, *Floods of Fortune: Ecology and Economy along the Amazon*, New York: Columbia University Press, 1999, p. 47; Gerard Colby and Charlotte Dennett, *Thy Will Be Done: The Conquest of the Amazon; Nelson Rockefeller and Evangelism in the Age of Oil*, New York: HarperCollins, 1996).

†Maury's proposal reflected the US South's hope that expansion into the Caribbean or Latin America, by seizing Cuba or parts of Central America, could save slavery. Its politicians and merchants pushed Brazil to allow for free navigation up the Amazon, arguing that the South American river was really an extension of the Mississippi. In 1849, the Richmond, Virginia–based *Southern Literary Messenger* wrote that since Atlantic currents sweep its waters north into the Gulf of Mexico, the Amazon "may very properly be regarded as one of the tributaries" to "this our noble sea," the Caribbean. Just as the Mississippi Valley worked as the "escape valve" for slavers migrating from abolitionist states, believed the Virginian Maury, "so will the Amazon Valley be that to the Miss."

"How men from the Mississippi would make things hum along the Amazon," waxed another American observer in 1910.[14]

And so after an initial flush of enthusiasm the press in Rio and Pará criticized the concession's vagueness and undue generosity. It was a "monstrous contract," wrote the initially sympathetic *Folha do Norte*, a "most shameful document."[15] That Ford was required to plant rubber on only one thousand of the two and a half million acres granted led some to suggest that what the "multimillionaire Yankee" was really interested in was not latex but oil, gold, and political leverage. Much of this early criticism was really an attack on the man who originally brokered the concession, Governor Dionysio Bentes, a powerful local party boss with many friends, quite a few enemies, and higher political aspirations. Critics blasted the secrecy in which the concession had been negotiated and its lavish tax and tariff exemptions. They noted that the estate's autonomous bank, schools, and police force violated Brazil's sovereignty. It was, they pointed out, as if Ford had the right to run Fordlandia as a separate state.[16]

In provincial Santarém, newspapers reported on the debates with wry detachment that seemed to have eluded their more earnest counterparts in Belém or Rio. "When Ford Comes" is the "catchphrase of the day," one wrote of the excitement that was building over the arrival of the carmaker, with everybody dreaming of the money to be made and the marriages to be had. The same kind of Christ-like hope placed by rural people in the coming of a redeemer that so troubled Senator Norris in Tennessee was not lost on the Santarém press, which occasionally referred to the savior as São Ford—Saint Ford. "We use the word Ford," wrote one columnist, "as if it were an amulet, a protective talisman, if not to get rich than at least to get out of the tight situation we find ourselves in." He went on to suggest that perhaps sausages and toilet paper should bear the name of Ford, as well as a new cocktail, made up of *açaí*—a local berry believed to be an aphrodisiac—and American "*uísque*," that is, "whiskey."

But the scorn and sarcasm were largely lost on the many who continued to believe that Ford's arrival meant the salvation of the Amazon.[17] A Ford car was a cultural symbol the world over, weighted with meaning and familiar to even those who existed on the margins of survival, even if they lived in a place empty of roads, dirt or otherwise, like the Tapajós River valley. "Now I am finally going to learn how to drive," was one tapper's response to the news that Ford was starting a rubber plantation there. And throughout the lower Amazon, those looking for work simply said they were on their way to "Ford"—or, rather, "For," as it was pronounced in the regional Portuguese. They might use the masculine "*o For,*" to refer to the man, or the feminine "*a For,*" to indicate the company or plantation, but either way the meaning was clear: "*Eu vou prá For*"—"I'm going to Ford."[18]

And they hoped Ford would come to them as well, to see Brazil and the wondrous Amazon firsthand. Consul de Lima kept promising he would deliver Ford. He said the carmaker was to have visited as early as 1922 but a failed military uprising interrupted his trip. "With the approach of the winter," de Lima wrote Dearborn in November 1925, "I wonder if you could inform me at about what time you would be ready to leave for Brazil?" Ernest Liebold's response was not encouraging: "I could not say definitely at this time whether Mr. Ford will be able to undertake this trip to Brazil." Another secretary followed up yet another inquiry: "Mr. Ford has not yet made any definite plans concerning the trip you mention, consequently we are unable to give you the desired information." Not to worry, the consul assured his fellow countrymen in late 1927, for now that the negotiations surrounding the rubber concession had been concluded to everyone's satisfaction, "it is in the cards that very soon we may have a visit from Mr. Ford," most likely in his "famous yacht that goes 20 knots an hour." "Perhaps," de Lima hoped, "he will come with his old friend Mr. Edison."[19]

Ford said he would come. "I certainly intend to visit," he promised in 1928, "though I cannot now say how soon."

Part II

LORD FORD

CHAPTER 9

TWO RIVERS

SHORTLY AFTER THE NEW YEAR'S DAY THAT FOLLOWED THE
ratification of the land grant, Henry Ford wired Governor Bentes to wish
him well for 1928 and to thank him for the "fine assistance" he had extended to Ide and Blakeley. "We are at present working out plans," he
wrote, "and are fitting up a ship of our own for the voyage" to the plantation to "inaugurate the nucleus of a project which we trust will contribute
to the prosperity of North Brazil."[1]

The ship in question was the _Lake Ormoc_, one of 199 decommissioned merchant marine vessels purchased in 1925. Throughout the 1920s,
River Rouge managers pioneered techniques of industrial recycling, scour-
ing through the detritus of government and commerce for reusable resources. Ford was obsessed with finding as many ways as possible to use
nature's bounty. Just a few months after wiring Bentes, for instance, Ford
was in England to promote his new Model A. Told that a garbage dump in
Dagenham, Essex, had been burning for over a thousand years, he proposed building a powerhouse on the site to transform its heat into steam to
run his nearby factory. "This dump goes back to prehistoric times," he said.

"Those fires have been burning away, wasted absolutely, all these centuries. I would like to see them working for man."[2]

In the case of the *Ormoc*, the ship was part of a fleet of "lakers" decommissioned by Washington after World War I and sitting rusting for years in seaports along the East Coast, until Ford acquired them at a cut rate. Under the direction of Charles Sorensen, Ford's legendary engineer who ran production at the Rouge, the ships were towed to Dearborn, stripped of brass, copper, piping, wires, and wood, then sent through a massive half-mile-long aquatic disassembly line. The line was composed of ten positions fitted with wrecking cranes, industrial torches, and giant shears, each charged with shredding a different ship section: masts, deck cabins, boilers, engines, hulls, and keels. Boilers and engines were refurbished and used elsewhere, and cabins became tool sheds and stockrooms. Railcars rolled the sheared steel to the Rouge's pig-cast building, where it was melted in enormous blast furnaces and shipped to the foundry. It took less than a week to render what it took months to build, leaving only a shadow of "oil and rust on the water." "What we call waste is only surplus," Ford once remarked, "and surplus is only the starting point of new uses."[3]

Two ships were spared. Rouge workers gave the *Lake Ormoc* a new diesel motor, a machine shop, and water distillation plant, both for drinking and boiler use. They refitted the ship's mechanics, reducing the number of men needed to sail it from twenty-four to six. The captain's desk and dining table, his shower, and bedsprings for the crew's mattresses were all made of material recycled from other salvaged ships. As the proposed "base ship" until Fordlandia was up and running, the *Ormoc* was equipped with a hospital and an operating room, chemistry lab, refrigerators, laundry, a "well stocked library," lounge, and screened, relatively spacious cabins. The *Lake Farge* was converted into a tow barge, to be used to haul most of the makings of Fordlandia to the Tapajós.[4]

In early July, boxcars began to pull alongside the Rouge's slip and cranes and winches started to fill the holds of the *Ormoc* and *Farge* with the machinery and material needed to start and maintain the plantation: a steam shovel, electric generators, road-building machinery, tractors (some with threaded wheels), picks, shovels, a stone crusher, a huge ice-making machine, hospital equipment, concrete mixers, a sawmill, pile drivers and stump pullers, a diesel tug, smaller river launches, prefabricated buildings, an entire disassembled warehouse recycled from Ford's Highland Park factory, piles of structural steel precut and fitted for the quick construction of buildings, asbestos to be used as a roofing material to deflect the sun's rays, plumbing fixtures, office supplies, clothes, medicine, and food, including a "huge supply of frozen beef" and vegetables to "obviate any necessity of recourse to native tropical diet." There was even a railroad—a locomotive, rails, and ties—salvaged from Ford's Upper Peninsula sawmill operations, which by then used mostly Ford trucks to transport timber. It was a million dollars worth of goods all told.[5]

Unfortunately, the Rouge's synchronized industrial efficiency didn't always spill over to the company's administration. No one told Sorensen that an underwater rock ledge cut across the Tapajós fifty miles downriver from where they planned to establish the plantation, making it impossible for ships the size of the *Ormoc* to reach the site during the dry season, when the water was low.

"Where are you going to send this boat?" Ernest Liebold asked Sorensen, who had called Ford's secretary over to the Rouge to have him take a look at the newly equipped *Ormoc*.

"Down to the plantation," Sorensen replied.

"You can't get up there."

"Why not?"

"You've got a rock ledge that goes across there, and you've only got nine feet for navigation."

"How did you find that?"

"Well, that information was available. If you had told me you were going to send the *Ormoc* down there, I might have told you."[6]

Sorensen didn't believe Liebold, so he asked Einar Oxholm, a Norwegian sea captain sent by Ford to do advance work to check it out. Oxholm reported back that there was indeed a "shoal in the river" that made it "impossible for anything over nine feet in draft to move up at low water period."

ANYWHERE BETWEEN SIXTY and a hundred inches of water fall in the Amazon every year, mostly during the high-water season, which runs from December to June but often lingers on through July and August. To keep with the standard most often used by the Ford men, that's four times more precipitation than what the US Midwest gets in any year. Rain combines with melting Andean snow to swell the Amazon and its tributaries during these months, and rivers rise as much as thirty-six feet, overflowing into the jungle's floodplains, or *várzea*, leaving behind a coating of rich mountain soil that during the subsequent low-water season will nourish cultivated manioc, corn, beans, and other jungle crops. During the flood months, the jungle takes on a netherworld, shape-shifting quality, as plateaus and hills become islands and trees seem to float erect, each an ecosystem to itself, alive with lichens, moss, algae, insects, snakes, bats, and mammals. From December to June, much of the Amazon basin forms a vast but seasonal freshwater lake, what the Portuguese called a sea river, that constantly reworks the contour of the land. During these months, the *Ormoc* and *Farge* could easily make it up the Tapajós to the plantation site.

But the ships were ready to go at the end of June, and back in Brazil Blakeley and Villares's advance team had already started to clear the plantation site and they needed the heavy equipment. So Ford decided to dispatch the *Ormoc* and *Farge* despite Oxholm's advice to wait until the rainy season. They would at least make it as far as Santarém, about a hundred miles downriver from Boa Vista, the sleepy river village of a few dozen families picked to be the "capital of Fordlandia." In these early days, "Fordlandia" referred not to the plantation settlement but rather to the entirety of Ford's 2.5 million acres.[7]

With Captain K. E. Prinz at the helm, the *Lake Ormoc* left the Rouge dock on July 26, three days before Ford's sixty-fifth birthday. Its departure was an event momentous enough to earn front-page applause in most every major US daily. All of Brazil, announced the *Detroit News*, was eagerly awaiting the two ships loaded with "science, brains, and money." "Brazilian Area Bigger Than New Jersey Expected to Yield Gum to Make Tires for 2,000,000 Cars Yearly," ran the *Washington Post*'s headline. The *Christian Science Monitor* said that Ford planned to plant five million acres with rubber, while the *New York Times* predicted that the estate would eventually produce "five times the total world production estimated by experts for this year," or "6,000,000,000 pounds of rubber a year, enough to make nearly 1,000,000,000 Ford tires."[8]*

Despite this fanfare, Ford, usually loath to miss a publicity opportunity, skipped the send-off. A week earlier, he and Edsel had taken the *Ormoc* out on a trial run down the Rouge River into Lake Erie. But now, a heat wave had settled over lower Michigan, killing scores of people. Defying the Amazon's dry season from a world away was one thing. Suffering Detroit's humidity in the flesh was another, so Ford escaped the city by taking off on one of his road trips.

By this point in his life, Ford had become an ardent antiques collector, another one of his eccentricities that the press enjoyed reporting on. The *Detroit News* ran a steady stream of stories detailing his purchases of old furnaces, musical instruments (particularly violins), clocks, books, tools, kitchen utensils, London churches—anything that could be shipped back to an overflowing warehouse in Ford's tractor factory. Just that year, Ford had Thomas Edison's Fort Myers, Florida, workshop—a house built by the inventor's father in 1884—disassembled and rebuilt in Greenfield Village, a model town Ford had started building in Dearborn composed of important landmarks in American history.

Now, in his flight from the heat, Ford first headed to a train depot in Fraser, Michigan, where he hoped to acquire the key on which a young Edison had learned how to transmit telegraph messages.

"What do you want for it?" he asked the stationmaster.

"Well, I'd like to get delivery on my new Ford. It was ordered a long time ago."

"We can fix that up."

Ford got his "relic" and the next day the stationmaster received his newly painted Model A. Ford then continued on to New Jersey to celebrate his birthday with the aging Edison in person.[9]

Returning to Dearborn a few days later, Ford held a press conference where he told reporters that he himself had driven a good part of the seven-hundred-mile trip in the new Model A. Ford's birthday corresponded to the

---

*Though an improbable amount, both the *Times* and the *Los Angeles Times* reported this six billion figure, most likely provided by a company press release.

silver anniversary of his company, which now employed well over 200,000 men in operations on six continents. It had gone from producing less than two thousand cars a year in its old Mack Avenue workshop to over nine thousand in a single day. "The company's 25th birthday," wrote the *Wall Street Journal*, "finds Henry Ford in the midst of the most intensive period of activity since he first began to dream of horseless carriages." "Isn't there an age limit somewhere?" he was asked by a reporter on his return from New Jersey, about not just his endurance behind the wheel but his steerage of his company. "I haven't found it yet," Ford answered. He said he expected to "do more in the next five years than I have in the last 20." "You have got to keep going and doing," Ford wrote in his notebook.[10]

THE *ORMOC* CUT across Lake Erie to the Welland Canal and Lake Ontario, then out the St. Lawrence to the Atlantic, docking at Kearny, New Jersey, in New York Harbor. There it joined the slower moving *Lake Farge*, which had left Dearborn two weeks earlier pulled by the tug *Bellcamp*. The ships picked up additional supplies, along with fourteen passengers—the plantation's staff and their wives—who had arrived from Detroit by train: a doctor from the Henry Ford Hospital, an electrical engineer, a chemist, an accountant, and "several competent managers." The *Ormoc* had plenty of science, brains, and money on board. What it didn't have was a horticulturalist, agronomist, botanist, microbiologist, entomologist, or any other person who might know something about jungle rubber and its enemies.[11]

The ships averaged about a hundred miles a day, stopping in Belém for a few days and then arriving in Santarém in mid-September, in time for a jungle heat wave that for the next three months raised temperatures ten degrees higher than normal. It was an exceptionally dry season, and the Tapajós's banks were drawn low, exposing a two-meter strip of sand, rock, and cracked clay. As predicted, it would be at least two months, probably longer, before the ships would be able to make the final hundred miles to Boa Vista.[12]

For months local newspapers had talked about what would happen "when Ford comes." Now, a year after the concession's ratification, the

Ford executives on the deck of the Lake Ormoc. *Left to right:* William Cowling; Edsel Ford; Einar Oxholm; Henry Ford; Pete Martin, *in charge of production at Highland Park;* Charles Sorensen; *and Albert Wibel, head of company purchasing.*

moment had finally arrived. Santarém was founded as a fort in the early seventeenth century, when Portuguese slavers pushed up the Amazon River, obliterating the peaceful Tapajó Indians. Home to a few thousand people in the late 1920s, the city is located where the impressive Tapajós River comes to an end, giving way to the even more imposing Amazon. The juncture of the two rivers sits where the rocky bluffs of Brazil's southern alluvial shield butt up against the lower and flatter alluvial plain, creating a sheer drop just off Santarém's shore that allows large vessels like the *Ormoc* and *Farge* to pull up close. But despite a natural advantage that made the inland town a deepwater port, residents were used to big ships ignoring them, stopping only for a moment, or not at all, on their way to Manaus or Iquitos. Decades later, Elizabeth Bishop, poet laureate of the United States, visited Santarém and wrote an eponymously titled poem that captured the town's languid, time-stopping qualities:

> That golden evening I really wanted to go no farther;
> more than anything else I wanted to stay awhile
> in that conflux of two great rivers, Tapajós, Amazon,
> grandly, silently flowing, flowing east.
> Suddenly there'd been houses, people, and lots of mongrel
> riverboats skittering back and forth
> under a sky of gorgeous, under-lit clouds,
> with everything gilded, burnished along one side,
> and everything bright, cheerful, casual—or so it looked.
> I liked the place; I liked the idea of the place.
> Two rivers. Hadn't two rivers sprung
> from the Garden of Eden? No, that was four
> and they'd diverged. Here only two
> and coming together. . . .

A long river beach—which Bishop described in a letter to a friend as made of "deep orange sand"—and wharf served as the heart of the city, whose irregular cobblestoned streets, then lined with a mix of close-cropped blue and red stucco and tile houses and thatched straw huts, rise gently from the beach, like aisles away from a stage in an amphitheater. The town had one car, an old rusted Ford truck, and had recently built a small electric plant, which powered a few straggling streetlamps. Facing the river stood the bleached blue and white Nossa Senhora da Conceição, Our Lady of the Conception, the town's turreted cathedral built in the eighteenth century.[13]

The scene rarely changed. Women beat dirty laundry on the beach rocks. Freighters, steamships, fishing boats, and the occasional timber raft vied for dockside space. Small boats filled with birds, monkeys, fruits, and "turtles of mammoth dimension" paddled to intercept ocean liners heading to Manaus. Dockmen hoisted steers onto cattle boats with a harness and a pulley rope. "Two rivers full of crazy shipping—people / all apparently changing their minds, embarking, / disembarking, rowing clumsy

A faded view of Santarém's waterfront, 1928.

dories," Bishop's poem continues. There was also the strange confluence of the blue green water of the Tapajós and the muddy brown of the Amazon, each keeping its own color, flowing like two bands for miles without blending. Occasionally, a boat would discharge a fortune seeker or naturalist: Henry Wickham lived just outside the city before gathering the seeds that would doom the Brazilian rubber trade; Henry Walter Bates, Alfred Russel Wallace, and Richard Spruce made significant contributions to nineteenth-century evolutionary theory by using Santarém as a base of operations to send samples of plants and insects back to London's Kew Gardens.* And during the high-water season, a parade of up-valley debris, the bloated carcasses of alligators and manatees, fallen trees, and even

---

*It was Spruce who identified and delivered to London a potent variety of cinchona, used to begin cultivation in India to make quinine—described by one official with the East India Company in 1852 as the most valuable medicinal drug in the world, "with probably the single exception of opium." At Santarém, where Spruce lived for over a year, he documented the local use of guarana—a caffeinelike stimulant prescribed for nervous disorders and thought to be a prophylactic for a variety of diseases—believing it could be introduced into European pharmacies, perhaps as a supplement to tea or coffee (Mark Honigsbaum, *The Fever Trail: In Search of the Cure for Malaria*, London: Macmillan, 2003, p. 5; Richard Spruce, *Notes of a Botanist on the Amazon & Andes: Being Records of Travel on the Amazon and Its Tributaries*, London: Macmillan, 1908, p. 452).

whole islands made of river grass, bromeliads, vines, moss, and philoden-drons, floated past the town as the river made its way to the Atlantic.[14]

But that September there was a new show, as onlookers took in the Ford ships and waited to see what they would do next. The *Ormoc* and *Farge* were hearty American vessels, about 250 feet long and nearly 50 across. Well provisioned and newly painted, they spoke for Ford's serious-ness of purpose and proven capability. Yet they seemed rather forlorn as they sat in the Tapajós's massive "mouth-lake"—twelve miles wide and ninety long—which intersected with the Amazon River to create a body of water one anthropologist compared to an "inland sea or one of the North American Great Lakes." One could, observed a Ford employee, "drop Lake Houghton, the largest of Michigan's inland lakes," into the Tapajós "and still have miles of margin left over."[15]

CAPTAIN OXHOLM, WHO had taken over command from Prinz upon the ships' arrival in Brazil, considered his options. He could wait a month or so for the waters to rise, but impatient Dearborn wanted to see progress. That meant he had to transfer most of the cargo to smaller launches and use the *Bellcamp* to tug them to the plantation site. One local company, affiliated with the British Booth Line, offered to do the job for six dollars a ton. This was perhaps the last time Oxholm would be quoted a fair esti-mate, for in the months ahead, after Ford made the captain chief manager of the plantation, he developed a reputation as a "soft touch" easily fleeced for goods and services. In this instance, though, he declined a reasonable bid. He opted instead to rent lighters and hire labor directly, which not only wasted much valuable time but cost, according to a subsequent au-dit, roughly thirty-five dollars a ton. With a capacity of 3,800 tons, Ox-holm paid out about $130,000 to unload just the *Farge*.[16]

The transfer was slowed because the "special cranes" needed to re-move the heavy equipment were packed first, "below all other freight on the ships." In future shipments, managers urged Rouge workers to "en-deavor to use good judgment" in filling the *Ormoc* so that "articles of gen-eral use or which might have several uses can be easily found." Another reason for delay was that it took at least two days for the *Bellcamp* to make it up to the construction site and back, teaching the Ford staff an early lesson in the slow rhythms of Amazon life. And even if the tug could go faster, the makeshift dock the advance team had constructed was too small to handle such a massive shipment of material and too wobbly for much of the heavy equipment. Nor was enough of the riverbank cleared to receive the cargo, which led to more bottlenecks. Then there was the confusion of Portuguese-ignorant foremen supervising local laborers, making for what one eyewitness described as good "material for a super Charlie Chaplin film." *Modern Times* meets *Fitzcarraldo*.

On October 4, the plantation's representative in Belém cabled Charles Sorensen in Dearborn good news: "*Lake Ormoc* left Santarém last night bound for plantation." But later that day he sent a correction: "Report *Ormoc* leaving Santarém for plantation in error due to misunderstanding. *Ormoc* still at Santarém." Then a third: "Water going down instead of rising."[17]

At the end of November, there were still over a thousand tons of equipment on the *Farge*, and the general chaos of the work got on the crew's nerves, yielding to "nasty accidents" and scuffles. On the last day of the cargo transfer, "Sailor Stadish" was on the deck of the *Ormoc* operating a steam winch and teasing "Fireman Patrick," who was in the hold supervising local workers in a final cleanup. Stadish said something he shouldn't have, or at least not to someone in the hold of a ship on a day when the thermometer had well passed ninety degrees. He looked up and saw Patrick coming after him with an iron bar. Taking a step back, Stadish fell into an open hatch twenty-five feet, fracturing his skull and breaking a few ribs.[18]

It was not an auspicious beginning for a company that hoped to, as Edsel Ford put it, bring "redemption" to the Amazon. It took nearly until the end of January to finally get the ships up to Boa Vista and fully unloaded. And then the trouble really began.

CHAPTER 10

SMOKE AND ASH

As they waited for the *Ormoc* and the *Farge* to reach them, Blakeley and Villares set about establishing a work camp just outside the hamlet of Boa Vista and started to clear the jungle. True to the kind of optimism typical of the Ford Motor Company in the 1920s, reinforced by Villares's constant assurances that he had plantation experience, Blakeley was convinced that the rain forest and its people would soon yield to a "great industrial city" housing twenty-five thousand workers and a hundred thousand residents. The proposed location for this metropolis, on a rise sloping gently to the river, "lends itself well to an economical development of sewage." Though Blakeley was no more an engineer than his immediate boss, Harry Bennett, he thought building a city would be "a more or less simple matter." His plan was to allow arriving workers to live in temporary quarters set apart from the main settlement, until pronounced fit by Ford doctors to move into Fordlandia proper. Under company supervision, Brazilians, Blakeley proposed, should be allowed to build their own homes according to local traditions, though he would insist on the construction of proper and sanitary outhouses, which would be an important step in bringing "forth a new race." He told the American consul in Belém that Ford had given him "carte blanche" to spend up to twelve million dollars, not just to "show some profit for the company" but to "do good" for the Amazon.[1]

In a preliminary report to Dearborn, he suggested paying workers between twenty-five and fifty cents a day and teaching them how to grow vegetable and fruit gardens to diversify their diet. Schools and churches would be built later, as the tappers were long used to living and working in isolation, free from religious and educational institutions. Unlike at the Rouge, he did not foresee a discipline problem; Brazilian workers are "most docile," he wrote. Among his crew, he hadn't heard the "slightest murmur of Bolshevism." Not even the execution of Sacco and Vanzetti—which took place just as he and Ide were negotiating the concession with Bentes—aroused their sympathy, Blakeley said.[2]

Yet also true to the Ford tradition, Blakeley quickly developed a reputation as an autocrat. During his short reign at Fordlandia "his word was law." He had set himself up in an old Boa Vista *fazenda*—Portuguese for hacienda—that was decrepit but well ventilated while the laborers slept outdoors in hammocks or in palm lean-tos and his foremen crammed into a quickly erected, sweltering, malaria-ridden bunkhouse, each given "one room with one door and no window and no bath." Dearborn first got an inkling that something was wrong when Blakeley tried to take control of the subsidiary corporation Ide had set up as the legal owner of the plantation. "You have not explained why," company officials wrote him pointedly, "it was necessary to elect yourself managing director."[3]

But where autocracy in other realms of the Ford empire tended to produce some concordance between vision and execution, in the jungle it led to disaster.

THE FORD MOTOR Company enjoyed a well-deserved reputation for industrial immaculateness. Hundreds of workers painted the Detroit plants on a regular basis. Cleaners scrubbed them as if they were operating rooms, making sure even the most remote corners were well lit, to prevent spitting. "One cannot have morale," Ford said, "without cleanliness."[4]

Imagine, then, Dearborn's reception of this very first notice on Fordlandia's progress: "No sanitation, no garbage cans, flies by the million, all filth, banana peels, orange rinds and dishwater thrown right out on the ground. . . . About 30 men sick out of 104, no deaths but plenty of malaria. . . . Flies abounded in kitchen in all food and on tables and dishes until you could hardly see the food and tables. No screens for men to sleep under, no nets." The report was filed by São Paulo's Ford dealer, Kristian Orberg, after a visit to the camp. Orberg told Dearborn that two creeks bordering the main work site had been converted to a dump, breeding flies and mosquitoes that led to a severe outbreak of malaria. As a result, work came to a standstill for nearly the whole month of August. Food rotted. "They need ICE worst of all," he said.

The impending arrival of the *Ormoc* and *Farge* promised tractors and other heavy equipment that would ease the work involved in land clearing. But in the meantime Blakeley and Villares tried to make do. In Belém, Blakeley had purchased a few power saws and a small tractor, which he had delivered to the work site. Yet he quickly ran out of gas, so the machines sat idle. After months of labor, with workers cutting and dragging logs by hand, only a few hundred acres of trees had been felled.

To add to the difficulties, the two men had picked the wrong time of the year to begin work. Ideally, the clearing of jungle for planting or pasture should be done during the dry season, between June and October, when the downed trees can be left to dry for a few months before being burned. But Blakeley and Villares had started felling trees during the wet season. When they tried to torch the waste wood, daily rains would extinguish the fire, leaving soaked piles of charred scrub. So they had to use copious amounts of kerosene to start a second burn, bigger than any yet seen on the Tapajós—or in most other parts of the Amazon, for that matter. The jungle was turned inside out, as flames rose over a hundred feet, forcing tapirs, boars, cougars, boas, pit vipers, and other animals into the open, "crying, screaming, or bellowing with terror." Toucans, macaws, and parrots took flight, some of them falling back into the flames.[5]

"They burned hundreds of hectares of primitive forest," remembers Eimar Franco, who watched the progress of Fordlandia from across the

Charred trunks and stumps after an incomplete burn.

river. "They started a fire that lasted for days and days," he remembers, invoking both an image associated with today's Amazon—the forest laid waste by fire—and the smokestack and forge fires of nineteenth-century factory industrialization: "It terrified me. It seemed that the whole world was being consumed by flames. A great quantity of smoke rose to the sky, covering the sun and turning it red and dull. All that smoke and ash floated through the landscape, making it extremely frightening and oppressive. We were three kilometers away, on the other side of the river, and yet ash and burning leaves fell on our house."[6]

DEARBORN WAS GROWING increasingly distrustful of Blakeley. No archival evidence proves that Blakeley took a profit from the machinations surrounding the Bentes concession, yet the fact that he kept his dealings with Villares, Greite, and Bentes, as well as his knowledge of kickbacks, a secret couldn't have sat well with Henry Ford, who learned about the swindle from State Department officials in early 1928.[7] For

Blakeley's part, whatever opportunities he saw arising from Ford's rubber enterprise were fanned by a growing sense of grievance. He began to resent the fact that the company was not rewarding all his good work with adequate compensation, and he sent Charles Sorensen a letter asking that his salary be increased to "A" level. His long stays in Brazil, he complained, had forced him to sell his Dearborn house and lose track of his investments. He reminded Sorensen that he had given up much American-style pleasure and comfort in order to "accomplish things in a country such as this." He began to pocket plantation cash, money that should have been used to buy quinine for the fever-ridden or gas for the power saw and tractor. He even refused to buy a horse for the fifty-four-year-old Raimundo Monteiro da Costa, a local rubber man hired to scout out the concession. During the hottest part of the day, the "old man" was making two four-mile tours on foot. And though Blakeley promised workers free room and board, he deducted the cost of transportation to the site from their first payment and charged them forty milreis, about four dollars, for hammocks that cost half that. Dearborn didn't get wind of this petty graft until much later, yet in July a witness had emerged, a fellow passenger on the SS *Cuthbert*, who supported Ide's account of Blakeley's coarse behavior "in every particular."[8]

Dearborn recalled Blakeley and dismissed him in October, and his sudden departure led to a collapse of what little authority there was at the work camp. The remaining Americans bickered among themselves. Villares tried to leverage the bedlam to his advantage. No one was clearly in charge, so no one took responsibility for feeding and paying the camp's labor force, which had grown to 380 men. A month of bad food, no money, long workdays, and increasingly insulting behavior by increasingly desperate foremen were aggravated by a heat wave that made the jungle hotter than usual.

In the best of conditions, clearing jungle is brutal, close-in work. But as October ran into November, high temperatures were hitting 106 degrees. Exhaustion and sickness overcame the contracted laborers who made up Fordlandia's first crew as they hacked their way into the dense, dank wood with machetes and cutlasses. They worked stripped to the waist: throughout the day, as the sun rose and the humidity increased, their

Workers clearing the jungle pose for a photo.

bodies, covered with sweat, were scraped by thorns and branches and punctured by the bites of ticks, jiggers, black flies, and ants. The workers were not provided hats though these were indispensable when making the first pass at jungle clearing, as often the chopping of a creeper or a vine could disturb insect nests, raining scorpions, wasps, or hornets on those below. Just a touch of a branch or a vine and within seconds a swarm of ants could cover a body, leaving workers red with festering bites. The mortality rate was high, as workers, bending low to chop the undergrowth, died quickly from snakebites or suffered a more prolonged wasting away from fever, infection, or dysentery.

In early November, with the *Ormoc* and *Farge* still stuck in Santarém, tensions came to a head. When the crew's cook served yet another meal of rotten meat and stinking fish, "hell was loosed." Demanding "good food the same for all," they sacked the kitchen and storehouse. The rioters armed themselves with the machetes and cutlasses and chased the Americans into the woods or out into the river on boats. In a letter to his former comanager, Blakeley, now in Dearborn, Villares claimed credit for restoring calm, saying that he slaughtered two steers to feed the men and brokered a deal in which they would get their wages if they promised not to hurt the Americans or destroy plantation property. There were, he pointed out, hundreds of gallons of kerosene and two hundred pounds of dynamite within their reach.[9]

But like most other things having to do with Villares, it was hard to figure out where the line separating fact and self-promotion lay. Even before the riot, the Americans, particularly John Rogge and Curtis Pringle, had lost patience with the Brazilian. At first they thought him to be "energetic and capable." Yet at the plantation site Villares proved to be supremely impractical. He displayed little knowledge of agriculture, while Brazilian workers, who relied on him as an interpreter to communicate with the Americans, found him haughty. Villares knew enough about the Amazon to know that what the Americans were doing—especially when it came to clearing and burning the jungle during the rainy season—was wrong. But he didn't know enough to say clearly what should be done and so only contributed to the work site's confusion. During the riot a gang of workers chased him into the woods, where he fell into a ditch and fractured his finger and nearly broke a leg. He made his way to Belém, only to be ordered to leave the country immediately, by his coconspirator Governor Bentes, in a last-minute bid to suppress a brewing scandal that was about to reveal to all of Brazil the shady dealings that went into granting Ford his land concession.

It turns out that Captain Greite did not tear up the letter Villares had sent him two years earlier from Detroit's Cadillac Hotel, after the meeting with the Fords where Villares pitched the idea of "Fordville" and "Edselville." He instead made a copy of it, along with every other document related to the Ford swindle. Believing that his partners were shortchanging him, Greite handed them over to a local newspaper, which passed them on to Brazil's Communist Party's newspaper, A Manhã, for publication in Rio.

In early 1929, the story of the kickbacks and payoffs behind the concession exploded in the press. It all came out: the "ghoulish motives" of

Jorge Villares, back left, and work crew with axes and machetes.

Greite, the "puerile tactics" of Schurz and Villares, the cash to Bentes and others. "While Greite and Villares received a good share of the opprobrium attached to the transaction," the American consul in Belém wrote to the State Department, "Bentes and the Ford Company received the brunt of the blame." The press expressed its indignation at the bribery that led to the concession, but US diplomats thought the graft trivial compared with the corruption that usually attended the expansion of American corporations abroad. It was common practice for US companies to put local officials on the payroll for nonexistent consulting services, to disperse company shares to politicians, and to give outright bribes. In establishing his rubber plantation in Liberia, Harvey Firestone, for instance, floated a $5 million loan to government officials that helped things go considerably more smoothly for him in Africa than they did for Ford in Brazil. "Nearly all large companies," wrote US commercial attaché Carlton Jackson, who replaced William Schurz, "have learned to be 'practical.'" But the Ford Motor Company bribed just enough to provoke a scandal but not enough to keep it quiet. The controversy's real damage, then, was not to Ford's reputation for honesty but rather to his reputation for competence. The great man, it seemed, was snookered by a syndicate of bungling and bickering provincials into paying for land that was being given away free.[10]

VILLARES PROBABLY DIDN'T welcome the scandal's publicity. Yet for the nephew of Alberto Santos-Dumont, who Brazilians insist was robbed of the credit for inventing the airplane, there were worse fates than to be known as the man who bested Ford. Claiming to be suffering a nervous break-down, Villares, induced by "threats, together with the payment of a sum of money"—both courtesy of Governor Bentes—boarded a steamer headed for France to retrieve his aviator uncle, who really had suffered an emo-tional collapse.[11]

The disappointment of Alberto Santos-Dumont's life was not that he didn't get credit for inventing flight, though he did resent that the Wright brothers won all the acclaim. His real heartbreak was that he lived long enough to see the machine he helped develop be used as an instrument of death. Santos-Dumont wasn't an ideological pacifist like Henry Ford, but he did hope that airplanes would knit humanity closer together in a new peaceful community, just as Ford had believed that his car, along with other modern machinery, could bring about a warless world and a global "parliament of man." Both were of course proven wrong by World War I, which broke the conceit of many like Ford and Santos-Dumont that tech-nology alone would usher in a new, higher stage of civilization. "I use a knife to slice gruyere," Santos-Dumont said when war broke out in Eu-rope, "but it can also be used to stab someone. I was a fool to be thinking only of the cheese."[12]

Ford dealt erratically with the fact that, after all his high-handed op-position to World War I, he turned his factories over to war production. He continued to speak out provocatively against war, maintaining his po-sition that soldiers were murderers and quoting Tennyson's "Locksley Hall" to the end of his days. Yet Ford's faith in America as a revitalizing force in the world led him to say that he would support another war to do away with militarism. "I want the United States to clean it all up," he said.

No wonder the Topeka *Daily Capital* said that Ford put the "fist in paci-fist."[13]

Santos-Dumont, in contrast, was crippled by just his mere association to a machine that was used for mass murder. He held himself "personally responsible for every fatality" caused by his "babies," that is, airplanes. "He now believes that he is more infamous than the devil," commented a friend. "A feeling of repentance invades him and leaves him in a flood of tears."[14] After the war he vainly called on governments and the League of Nations to "demilitarize' the airplane (a call that the surviving Wright brother, Orville, didn't support. Orville invoked a different kind of tech-nological utopianism, insisting instead that the plane itself "has made war so terrible that I do not believe any country will again care to start a war"). But the slaughter continued, and death from above became a constitutive fact of modern life. Britain, for instance, encouraged by Minister of War and Air Winston Churchill, regularly bombed and strafed Arabs as a way of maintaining cost-effective control over its colonies. And on July 16, 1927, just a week after Ide and Blakeley arrived in Belém, US marines in Nicaragua staged their first dive-bombing campaign, against the rebel Au-gusto Sandino. Marine pilots descended to three hundred feet to fire four thousand rounds of ammunition and drop twenty-seven bombs on any-thing that moved. Hundreds were killed in the slaughter.[15]

Throughout the 1920s, Santos-Dumont found himself checking in and out of various European sanatoriums, refusing to eat and losing weight. Death seemed to pursue him. Persuaded by his nephew Jorge to return to Brazil, Santos-Dumont arrived home a hero. A dozen of Brazil's leading politicians, intellectuals, and engineers boarded the *Santos-Dumont*, a bi-motored seaplane, to meet the steamship that carried the flyer and his nephew as it entered Rio's harbor. But celebration turned to tragedy when one of the plane's motors exploded, plunging its passengers and crew members to their deaths and Santos-Dumont deeper into depression. When the ship landed at the quay, the aviator was "greeted with profound silence by the multitude."[16]

And the killing continued. War broke out in early 1932 between Bo-livia and Paraguay over a stretch of worthless, hellishly hot scrubland thought to hold oil. It was a fully mechanized slaughter, with both sides borrowing copious amounts of money from foreign banks and petroleum companies to purchase tanks and planes. By the time it was over, more than a hundred thousand Bolivians and Paraguayans were dead. That same year, after witnessing the aerial bombing of his beloved city of São Paulo by federal forces putting down a regional revolt, Santos-Dumont committed suicide. Having sent his nephew Jorge out on an errand, he spoke his last words to an elevator operator as he returned to his room to hang himself: "What have I done?"[17]

BACK IN THE Amazon, Bentes had left the governor's mansion for the federal senate just before the scandal broke, yet the controversy effectively ended his political career. His replacement as governor, Eurico de Freitas Valle, took office in February 1929 and immediately announced that he would review, and revise if necessary, the Ford concession.[18]

A committed nationalist who was fearful of a Ford monopoly over either rubber or lumber, Governor Valle first canceled the grant's across-the-board export tax exemption. The Ford Motor Company took this gravely. While officials hoped that the property would hold oil or valuable minerals such as gold and maybe even diamonds, they knew it was rich in hardwoods and Dearborn assumed that the sale of lumber would cover the plantation's startup costs. Adding to their aggravation, Valle decreed that only rubber cultivated at Fordlandia—and not latex tapped from wild trees on the property or purchased from tappers working elsewhere—would be covered by the tax exclusion.

Valle's moves had an immediate impact. Shortly after he announced his revocation of Ford's tax exemption, the governor of Amazonas—the state to the northwest of Pará whose capital was Manaus—had twenty-four cases of rubber seeds destined for Ford's plantation seized and impounded. Ford intended to ship the seeds to California or the Philippines, he claimed—implicitly but none too subtly associating Henry Ford with the usurper Henry Wickham.[9]

These seeds had been obtained by Ford agents in the upper Amazon, on the advice of Carl LaRue, who thought the western region was home to a purer and more productive strain of *Hevea* than what was found around Fordlandia, even though it was he who had recommended the southeastern bank of the Tapajós as the best place to grow rubber. In any case, the embargo of the seeds, combined with the delay unloading the Ormoc and Farge, left plantation managers scurrying to find local seeds. If they didn't succeed in planting a thousand acres by the end of July 1929—a stipulation of the Bentes contract intended to ensure that Ford's proposed rubber plantation was not simply a cover for a quest for oil, diamonds, or gold—then Valle would have grounds to revoke the concession.

Caught between Belém and Manaus, the plantation also had to answer to Rio. Contrary to Blakeley's assurances that the federal government had released the company from most import taxes, customs officials insisted that Ford pay duty on all material and machinery not directly related to rubber cultivation. When the Ormoc and Farge first arrived in Belém, Oxholm had left a deposit of $12,000 to be used against future levies. Port authorities didn't want to hold up the ships by inspecting their crammed holds, so they waved them through. But now they said that Ford owed an additional $58,000 for the initial shipment and that henceforth all shipments would have to pay assessed duties in full before proceeding upriver.[20]

From 1929 to 1931, the Ormoc made successive round-trips, bringing material from Detroit to the Amazon and stopping in British Guyana on the way back to load bauxite for the Rouge's metal works. As the cargo piled up on Belém's docks, the company's tax bill soared. Ford lawyers argued that *all* material brought in was ultimately to support the cultivation of rubber, but port authorities interpreted the law narrowly, disqualifying the equipment needed to build the town, cut wood, sink wells, run train lines, construct houses, and lay roads. Company officials negotiated to release some imports, thereby allowing construction to proceed. Yet by March 1931, sixteen thousand tons of Ford goods—paint, steel, train rails, shelving, furniture, tools, stationery, hospital machines, surveying equipment, lab instruments, electrical parts, enameled sinks, and many other things—still sat unused in a customs warehouse.[21]

These setbacks took place in the shadow of the worsening press coverage leveled at Bentes's "mercenary" contract, which for a "miserable handful of dollars" allowed "the vessels of the multimillionaire to transport everything without paying a single cent to our empty treasury." Ford, the papers said, was given a "concession for dominion."[22]

The tone was outrage, the style exposé. One report after another documented not just the corruption that surrounded the original transaction but the complaints of workers who had left the plantation about low pay, putrid food, abuse of workers, forced evictions, and, particularly damning for Ford's name, ineptitude.

The American consul wrote Dearborn that the Manaus and Belém newspapers were accusing Ford of having "commenced the prophesied subjection and exploitation" of Amazonian workers. One ex-Fordlandia clerk absconded with a number of documents that he claimed showed a large differential in the wages paid to Brazilians and Americans, peddling them to various newspapers for a "monetary reward." In early 1930, customs agents boarded and searched the *Ormoc* on its return to the States, acting on a tip that it was smuggling cases of diamonds out of the country. It was now "common gossip," wrote the consul, that Fordlandia's managers were paying workers just thirty cents a day, while entering eighty in the account books and pocketing the difference. (The gossip continues to this day: I was told by a resident of Fordlandia that plantation managers hollowed out tree trunks that they used to sneak gold past port authorities.)[23]

The consul had these stories translated into English and passed them on to Henry Ford directly. They were "patently false," he told Ford, yet "your company is not altogether without fault in the matter."[24]

CHAPTER 11

PROPHESIED SUBJECTION

FOLLOWING REEVES BLAKELEY'S DISMISSAL AND THE NOVEMBER riot, Charles Sorensen suggested to Henry Ford that he appoint Captain Einar Oxholm as Fordlandia's manager. Born in 1892 in Fredrikshald, Norway, near the border with Sweden, Oxholm ran away from home when he was thirteen to join the merchant marine, working his way up from cabin boy to deck hand, then to command of his own ship with the New Orleans–based United Fruit Company. After reading a notice in a local paper in early 1928 that the Ford Motor Company was hiring ship crews, he traveled to Dearborn. Henry Ford gave him a job on the spot and sent him to the Amazon with Blakeley's advance team. Word had not yet reached Dearborn of Oxholm's clumsy unloading of the *Ormoc* and *Farge*, so the carmaker took Sorensen's recommendation.

Oxholm had no experience in tropical botanics or plantation management. But this didn't trouble Ford, who disdained specialization and expertise. He liked to brag that his company never employed an "expert in full bloom" because they "always know to a dot just why something cannot be done." "None of our men are 'experts,'" Ford said. "We have most unfortunately found it necessary to get rid of a man as soon as he thinks himself an expert—because no one ever considers himself expert if he really knows his job."[1]

Much of this contempt was pure posture, for Ford in fact hired experts, from lawyers and doctors to sea captains. Yet he did have famed luck entrusting complex missions, even industry-transforming tasks, to people with intuitive engineering intelligence. It was not a trained metallurgist but a former factory sweeper, John Wandersee, who perfected the alloy process for vanadium, the breakthrough lightweight steel compound that made the Model T possible. Ford's "pioneering spirit," as Albert Wibel, the company's purchasing chief, put it, allowed him to take chances on unproven men. "He thought of it in terms of common sense."[2]

For Ford, the Lutheran Oxholm did have one quality that made him perfect for the job: a reputation for absolute honesty. Stories from Brazil of corruption and kickbacks troubled Dearborn officials, as did reports of drinking and prostitution, not just by Brazilians but by Ford men.

Ford, then, charged Oxholm not just with taking over what Blakeley had started but putting an end to what he had let fester. It was Sorensen, a fellow Scandinavian, who gave Oxholm his brief: "I am of the opinion that the difficulties you are up against will gradually clear up if you confine yourself strictly to the principles of the Ford Motor Company, which are absolutely honest in every direction you are dealing," he wrote. "It is on this one point that I am depending so much upon yourself, because at home, while we feel your lack of experience in matters of this kind, we are, however, strongly of the opinion that we can depend upon your honesty. The experience that is required will come by keeping this point in mind at all times, and doing the work in accordance with strict Ford principles."[3]

OXHOLM MAY HAVE been honest, but honesty is not a required jungle virtue. Nor would strict Ford principles help him interpret local expectations.

He refused the reasonable bid by a shipping firm to unload the *Ormoc* and *Farge*, instead spending over a hundred thousand dollars to do himself what others would have done for a fraction of the cost, because he didn't want to seem an easy mark. Worse still, his strict reading of his orders inflamed the import duty issue. Little contretemps that could have been settled with a bit of charm in his hands turned into an exhausting fight that lasted three years. Brazilian law stated that when custom inspectors needed to travel outside their stationed port of entry to examine cargo, the owners of the merchandise were responsible for paying about $2.50 for their room and board. But when Belém's inspectors, having traveled to Santarém to inventory the holds of the *Ormoc* and *Farge*, requested the fee, Oxholm thought he was being tapped for a bribe. He indignantly refused to pay it, leading the port authorities to harden their assessment on future Ford imports.[4]

A "big man" with a "weak mind," as one of his assistants remembered him, Oxholm, having wasted nearly three months unloading the *Ormoc* and *Farge*, only continued Blakeley's "chaos" and "mismanagement" at Fordlandia, according to the US consul in Belém.[5] By January, with the *Ormoc* and *Farge* finally at the plantation site and order restored after the riot—thanks to a "quantity of arms and munitions, including machine guns," sent by Brazilian authorities, as one local newspaper reported—Oxholm began to hire more men.[6] By the end of 1929, the Brazilian workforce at Fordlandia had grown from a few hundred to over a thousand. Workers poured in from all over the country, and boats arrived every day bringing more. "We are steadily increasing the force," Oxholm told Dearborn. Yet even as the number of employees continued to climb, progress toward making the plantation an efficient productive unit faltered.

Oxholm had started construction on an administrative office, a makeshift hospital, and workshops, hoping to establish a temporary settlement until a good patch of jungle could be cleared and enough rubber planted to meet the terms of the contract. Then he would devote himself to surveying a street grid for the town and building "proper houses according to blue prints." But in the meantime, single workers crammed into hastily built, poorly ventilated bunkhouses, and married families threw up ramshackle houses along the work site's edge, using discarded planks from packing crates for walls and palm thatch or canvas tarps for roofs. "We are having a hard time," Oxholm admitted to Dearborn in December 1929, making "this place look as a Ford plant should."[7]

* * *

THE CAPTAIN'S MAIN problem was labor: getting it, keeping it, and managing it. It would be years before the estate needed rubber tappers, but the company still required as many men as it could hire to clear the jungle. Oxholm had to have at least a thousand acres planted by July 1929, as per the terms of the concession. He also needed men to level roads and the bed for the railway and to build the physical plant and town residences.

In the first months of his tenure, Oxholm hired thousands of workers. But he had trouble retaining them. During some weeks in 1929, particularly through June, July, and August, the turnover rate equaled that of the Ford Motor Company back in Highland Park in the years prior to the Five Dollar Day. Three times as many workers were quitting as were being hired, which meant that the plantation's managers and foremen had to spend a good part of their day training new workers to adjust to the regimentation of plantation labor.

Oxholm couldn't tell Dearborn why he was having such a hard time building and keeping a steady labor force. "We have lately lost quite a number of men without being able to obtain any special reason," he wrote to the home office in June. Foremen were powerless to stop workers getting on boats and leaving. Most refused to say why they were quitting, but Oxholm believed they didn't want to work during the dry season, which was also the insect season, "when the fever is most prevalent." He tried to make "these people understand that this place is far healthier than the places where many of them live, swampy regions, where nothing is done to subdue the mosquitoes, and where there is no medical attention within reach." But perhaps having survived, or heard of, the malaria epidemic that crippled the camp the year before—when Blakeley refused to provide the sick with quinine—they didn't listen.

Other Americans who spent time on the plantation thought the low retention rate had to do with the fact that living was too easy in the bountiful jungle, or at least they thought it was. A long tradition of Amazon travel writing attributed the region's supposed lethargy to its fecundity, which, by easily yielding its nutritional riches, was said to encourage idleness. Though the genre would become mostly associated with nineteenth-century Victorian travel and naturalist writers, one of the first Europeans to appreciate the satiating richness of Amazonian life was the man for whom the Americas were named, Amerigo Vespucci, who upon sailing up the Amazon in 1499 said that he "fancied himself to be near the terrestrial paradise." "One turtle suffices to satisfy the largest family," wrote Father Cristóbal de Acuña a century and a half later. "These barbarians never know what hunger is." If daily life could simply be picked off a tree, there was little incentive to harness the resources of the jungle to set productive forces loose. "When they got a little money they would just take off," the Michigan wife of one early Fordlandia administrator recalled. Workers would amble into the woods and bring "out avocados which grew wild. Wild bananas are sweet, yellow and are used for desserts. The natives would bring back grapefruits, oranges and papaya and lima beans. . . . Beans grow about ten times the size of their Michigan relatives. The orange was bigger than the grapefruit. . . . Fishing was wonderful. This gives you an idea of how simple it was for the natives to live." The sawyer Matt Mulrooney thought the natives the "richest people in the world. . . . All they had ever seen was the woods and water. They didn't know anything about work." Having come to the United States as a boy with his family from Ireland to escape famine, Mulrooney, but a generation removed from peasant labor himself, appreciated the Amazon's abundance. "There is pears, oranges and bananas," he said. "Right in front of the house where I lived, bananas were growing." People "could go out Sunday and kill monkeys. They had monkey meat there the year around. The woods was full of them. You could go out there with a gun and in twenty minutes have a monkey. They didn't have guns. They got them with a slingshot."[8]

That Ford paid wages, as opposed to advancing credit, did seem to undercut the plantation's ability to ensure a stable labor force. Once a worker accumulated enough savings to live on for a few months, there was little incentive to stop him from returning home to his family and tending to his crops. "There was nothing down there to absorb their earnings," said Ernest Liebold, acknowledging that the Amazon lacked a key ingredient of Fordism: something to buy. David Riker, who for a time served as one of Fordlandia's labor recruiters, had a similar view. He had difficulty finding workers, since as long as Brazilians could live without wages they resisted the "Ford machine."[9]

Others attributed worker flight to abusive foremen, bad food, and continued poor housing conditions. Years earlier, Ford, during his animated conversation with Brazilian diplomat José Custódio Alves de Lima, said he had every intention of paying his celebrated Five Dollar Day wage, a promise de Lima repeatedly published throughout Brazil to build support for the coming of Ford. But in its many overseas operations, the Ford Motor Company tended to pay a notch above the prevailing wage, which is what it intended to do in the Amazon, notwithstanding Ford's showboating.

This, thought the American consul in Belém, was possibly one of the reasons for the high turnover rate, as workers who showed up thinking that they would be getting five dollars a day were disappointed to receive thirty-five cents.[10]

LABOR RECRUITERS FANNED out through the region's maze of rivers, creeks, and lakes but found the going exasperatingly slow. "It is hard to get around as fast as one would like," said James Murray, a Scottish recruiter who was sailing around the confluence of the Tapajós and the Amazon near Santarém. Traveling through Lago Grande, just up the Amazon from Santarém, Murray's steamship ran aground for three hours. A "terrific storm" then delayed it another four. He finally arrived in the town of Curuai and rounded up thirty-three recruits. Then at midnight, the boat hit bottom again. By seven in the morning, it was still trying to break free. And while riverboats could be used to travel to the main river towns, many of the settlements dispersed along the banks of lesser rivers, streams, and lakes could be reached only by smaller crafts.[11]

Murray tried to send advance word through priests, traders, and steamboat pilots that he would be arriving in a given village on an approximate date so that those who lived inland looking for work could gather in their village plaza. But he found local elites none too cooperative. Many feared that the Ford Motor Company, and the cash it paid, would disrupt the patronage relations that governed life on the river.

When Murray landed in the town of Monte Alegre, he had hopes that he would be able to find some workers among what appeared to be a largely idle and poor population. But he had a run-in with the mayor, who not only "flatly refused to help in any way" but threatened to charge the company a tax of fifteen dollars for every inhabitant Murray took from his town. An election was coming up, and the politician didn't want to lose any potential voters. On the town's outskirts, the recruiter spoke with a number of migrant families who had settled in Pará because of severe drought in their home states of Ceará and Maranhão. They were interested in Fordlandia work. But they were indebted to the state government for the land and tools advanced them and were not permitted to leave, as their labor was contracted to a local cotton plantation owner.

Then there were the steamboat operators who shuttled recruiters around river towns and carried contracted labor back to Fordlandia. That Ford agents might have to spend days in a forlorn village waiting for a boat to arrive tended to weaken their ability to negotiate reasonable fares. When the *Santa Maria* finally showed up in Parintins, an island town in the Amazon River, Murray went aboard and asked how much it would cost to take him and the twenty-three men he had signed up back to the plantation. The captain first said he was too busy to take the job. Then, when pressed, he quoted a price of four dollars a head. Murray said he was crazy and walked away. But stuck on an island with few other options, he returned to the dock and pleaded the price down to three dollars. Murray tried to pass this expense on to his recruits, but they balked. Twenty of them changed their minds and decided not to take the job. Two others said they would get to Fordlandia in their own canoe.

Murray also saw many men who seemed to be unoccupied in the town of Alenquer, across the river from Santarém, so many that he wrote the plantation to say that he had "a feeling of confidence that labour is available." But he was quickly disappointed. "There are many men around, but when you talk to them and suggest working a hoe they tell you flatly that this type of work does not interest them." Instead of the constant work Fordlandia was offering, Murray reported that local residents preferred seasonal labor, tapping rubber or gathering nuts on expeditions financed by local merchants. Most showed "little interest in Fordlandia. Claim passage rates too high, too far from home, and high cost of living." Likewise in Santarém, another Ford man complained that while there were "hundreds (maybe 2000) idle men" who didn't "have one thin dime," they didn't "want to work."[12]

Steamboat on the Tapajós.

Henry Ford sent instructions that Fordlandia was to pay at least 25 to 35 percent more than the local wage. But it was impossible for Fordlandia's staff to translate that differential into cash, since so much of the river economy was calculated in kind and credit. "No fixed scale of wages exist," Murray wrote. "What the *caboclo* earns is secondary to him." How much, he asked, was to be added to a Ford wage that would compensate a worker for the ability to throw a line into the river and fish for that night's dinner, even as he sat on a dock and sorted brazil nuts for some merchant who hired him for the day?[13]

If Ford paid too little, he wouldn't attract enough workers to begin with. If he paid too much, there was nothing to stop those who did come from melting back into the jungle once they earned enough to live for a few months without work. Labor in exchange for goods advanced on credit created a familiar set of expectations, against which pure cash wages and a fixed schedule often couldn't compete. Murray wrote that what tappers "like is to be free and go and come when they think fit." It's a sentiment confirmed more recently by anthropologist Edviges Marta Ioris. In the course of fieldwork in rural communities in the Tapajós National Forest, which today overlaps with what was Fordlandia, she met a few surviving Ford workers who told her that they would stay on the plantation for a time but leave when they needed to "plant the field crops, go fishing."[14]

Murray and other recruiters mostly scouted among the river *caboclo* communities, made up of descendants of migrants from Brazil's northeastern departments who had come to the region during the rubber boom. These communities, whose economy rested solely on rubber tapping, were hard-hit when the latex economy crashed. Ford, however, was arriving nearly two decades after the bust, when some of them had managed to revive and diversify their survival strategies, planting crops, keeping animals, and fishing to provide a basic level of subsistence, taking jobs with local patrons as needed.

But there were also settlements of desperately poor, hungry indigenous peoples around the Tapajós who had managed to survive, just barely, rubber's heyday. Whether or not Fordlandia would have been able to draw a significant amount of labor from these communities is debatable, as a combination of racism and ignorance precluded anyone's even trying. At one point, a labor recruiter indicated that there was a group of "2000 starving Indians" recently settled by the government on the banks of the Xingu, a river running roughly parallel to the Tapajós, to the east, and that they would probably welcome working at Fordlandia, which would provide them with "free housing, free medical attention, free hospital, good water, free school, and a steady job for steady men." Yet before an agent could be dispatched to the Xingu, Edmar Jovita, an Oxford-educated Brazilian who worked for the company but was then traveling, sent a telegram urging the plantation to "have nothing to do with these Indians as they are not tamed." Fordlandia wired back asking if Jovita thought that just a hundred men could be hired, with the "distinct understanding that they are subject to discipline." But the Brazilian responded forcefully: "Today more than ever have the opinion that we should not have any [Indians] in the plantation either these or others. . . . You would have trouble ahead. Even if they were tame they are lazy and undisciplined. Besides all other defects they are treacherous, even the tamest." Fordlandia relented. "Okay on Indians. We repeat we don't want them. Glad you got right information."[15]

FROM BEYOND THE Amazon, where wage labor was more institutionalized, many impoverished Brazilians did travel to Fordlandia at their own expense, too many for Oxholm to handle, either as plantation manager or town administrator. Soon more than five thousand people lived in and around the plantation, about double Santarém's population. There existed little infrastructure to support such a fast-growing community. Through 1929 and into 1930, there was no permanent dock or reception hall for Fordlandia's new arrivals. So when job seekers got off the steamboats, they spread out along the riverfront, setting up family camps, building cooking fires, and hanging their hammocks. A jungle shantytown quickly took shape. "Sometimes it is several days before they present themselves at the employment office," complained one foreman.

The migrants were a varied lot, described by one observer as made up of "the hopeless, the lame, the blind, the unemployed and everything else, along with some good men." Some were hired. But those who weren't stayed anyway, as did many who were initially employed yet quit soon after; with a 300 percent turnover rate, Fordlandia had to make about six thousand hires to keep a payroll of two thousand. Many of these new arrivals took up residence in the small villages that predated the Ford contract and dotted the periphery of the plantation, such as Pau d'Agua, a settlement of sharecroppers located about a half mile upriver from the cleared riverfront that, like Boa Vista before its sale to the company, was owned by the merchant Franco family. A whole service economy sprang up in these villages, and the plantation became, as one observer sent by Dearborn to see how Ford's namesake town was progressing put it, a "mecca for all undesirables, even criminals, of the entire Amazon Valley." These "troublemakers," the Ford official went on, "endeavored in any way conceivable to make a living off of the men who were working for the company." The sudden influx of cash gave bloom to "filthy small cafes, restaurants, meat and fruit shops," gambling houses, and thatched bordellos established by local merchants and staffed mostly with women from Brazil's poor northeast. Riverboats pulled up to Fordlandia's makeshift dock daily, and workers "swarmed aboard" to buy beer and cachaça.[16]

Captain Oxholm and James Kennedy, Ford's accountant, tried to have these villages destroyed, but they ran into resistance. Though the Francos had been willing to part with Boa Vista, they insisted on holding on to Pau d'Agua, which provided the family a useful monthly revenue in rubber, pigs, hens, ducks, and, increasingly as Ford's wages began to seep into the local economy, cash. In addition to the Francos, a number of other landowners along the Tapajós and up the Cupary River refused to move or sell, even though property values had increased dramatically. What made this standoff even more intractable was that the Ford Motor Company refused to compensate residents who did not have a clear and legal deed. This meant that those who had occupied their land for decades without titles, a common enough situation in the Amazon, had little incentive to move. Kennedy wrote to Dearborn saying that he had managed to buy out a few families who did have deeds. Yet they refused to leave their homes, and when the accountant tried to have them evicted they complained to the press that Ford had swindled them, buying their land from illiterate family members without their authorization. The Ford Motor Company didn't always get its way—Ford was, after all, frustrated at Muscle Shoals—yet it often did. In Michigan in 1923, when property owners refused to sell land where Ford wanted to build a hydro-electric dam to power one of his village industries, the company got the state legislature to pass an eminent domain law that allowed it to expro-priate the property. But in the Brazilian state of Pará, with Governor Valle's anti-Ford campaign in full swing, a judge issued an injunction or-dering Kennedy to cease his eviction threats.[17]

PROHIBITION WAS ONE of the Ford principles Oxholm was sworn to up-hold. It had been the law of the land in Michigan since 1916 (a law that Ford lobbied for, telling reporters that he would convert Detroit's breweries to produce alcohol fuel for his cars) and in the United States since 1920. Prohibition of course didn't stop drinking but rather provided fertile op-portunities for the extension of organized crime. Detroit and Dearborn sprawled with bars and speakeasies. In Michigan's Upper Peninsula, Iron Mountain, where the Ford Motor Company paid high wages to a large workforce, also saw the spread of "unparalleled conditions of vice and pros-titution." Mob gangs with ties to Detroit's Mafia moved in to set up whiskey "joints," casinos, brothels, and morphine dens along its midway. "One pretty 18-year-old miss," reported a local newspaper, "has found that there are shadows as well as bright lights along the primrose path of jazz," having succumbed to the town's ample supply of "white powders."[18]

But the problems created by the criminalization of alcohol failed to di-minish Ford's sense of virtue. With reports coming in about drunken revel-ries in the Amazon, he insisted that what was law in America be company policy in Brazil. "Mr. Ford constantly impressed me with the fact that he didn't want anyone around addicted to liquor," Ernest Liebold recalled. "We were in prohibition, and he wanted it enforced, as far as our employees were concerned. Even though it was a foreign country, I think it was largely in line with Ford policy to carry it into that country. If we were to permit promiscuous use of liquor on our plantation, why, the employees might on certain occasions get beyond our control."[19]

It was Ford's will, but Sorensen was his enforcer. He fired off one di-rective after another to Oxholm, demanding strict compliance with Prohi-bition. "We absolutely will not have it," meaning alcohol, "on our property. We know from events that have happened during the past year that drinking has taken place." He insisted on "absolutely no tolerance."[20]

In truth, Oxholm was powerless to stop the debauchery. He couldn't even keep a leper named Castro from camping on the dock to solicit alms. Shooed away, the mendicant simply returned when the captain's attentions were elsewhere. Similarly, when Oxholm did manage to shut down a few bordellos and bars, the proprietors simply set up shop on an island just off Fordlandia's banks, building their brothels on stilts because the island was half wetlands and prone to floods. It was ironically dubbed the "Island of Innocence" since, as Eimar Franco put it, "no one on it was innocent."

Besides, Oxholm himself developed a fondness for *cachaça com limão*. Many afternoons, even before the workday had come to a close, he'd take a fast launch over to the island of Urucurituba to visit his friend Francisco Franco, who after his nephew Luiz used the money from the sale of Boa Vista to move to Belém, had taken over the main hacienda. Swaying on a hammock on Franco's veranda, right in front of the chapel to Saint Peter, Oxholm sipped rum and watched Fordlandia's bustle.[21]

BACK ON HIS side of the Tapajós, Oxholm found himself governing a community of ailing migrants. By late 1929, the workforce had grown considerably, yet on any given day about a hundred would be in the hospital sick. The "amount of medical attention for the approximately 1300 men on the payroll," he wrote Dearborn, "is way out of proportion to what one would expect." During the rainy season, the numbers of sick increased, taxing the hospital "to the limit." Its beds filled with workers with suppurating sores on their feet and legs. The medical staff was charged not just with treating the sick but with screening recruits. Potential employees stripped naked in front of a Ford doctor, who examined their eyes and ears, recorded their weight and height, and took their urine.[22] The company rejected 5 to 10 percent of all applicants. Some were turned away for illnesses ranging from cirrhosis and bronchitis to paralysis, hernias, and leprosy. One was blind in the right eye. Another in the left. And at least one job-seeker was too short.[23]

That didn't mean everyone who got a job was healthy. More than 85 percent of job seekers had in the past suffered from at least one disease: syphilis, malaria, beriberi, dysentery, parasites, typhoid, ringworm, filariasis—caused by a mosquito-borne thread worm that infects the lymphatic system and leads to a thickening of the skin—or yaws, skin ulcers caused by bacteria. But Oxholm couldn't afford to turn anybody with such "garden variety" illnesses away since "nearly everyone has them." By December, a third of the hired workforce had to pass some time in the hospital before even getting started.[24]

He also had to deal with the employees who had contracted venereal diseases, running at a rate of about nine a month, in the camp's bordellos. When a Ford doctor visited one of the brothels, he found that seven of its nine prostitutes had an active gynecological infection. Oxholm ordered the following sign posted around the work sites and villages:

> It is a serious matter to contract venereal disease during the period of employment in this Company and the Company wishes to discourage it. Any employee having contracted venereal disease must immediately report the fact to the Medical Department. In case it is decided to hospitalize him the Company reserves the right to charge a reasonable amount to cover this service. At intervals there may be a Medical Inspection of employees to ascertain if there are any unreported cases. The disposition of these cases will be at the discretion of the Company.

As to the women, Oxholm would not treat them: "We do not want to have anything to do with them, and have absolutely refused treatment in any way, shape, or form. We hope that by doing so they will be forced to leave."

The families of migrant workers put yet another strain on Fordlandia's already overwhelmed health services. Plantation administrators factored into the cost of transport one wife and three children per worker. But they soon realized that workers from northeast Brazil, where many migrants to the Amazon originated, were, as one labor recruiter put it, "very prolific and 5 children should be reckoned." The medical staff was completely unprepared to deal with the influx of these children, many of whom were malnourished and suffered from hookworm, intestinal illnesses, and jungle fevers. "While we make it a practice to examine men who enter

our employ," the captain reported to Dearborn, "we have not been examining the women and children who live in the native camp, and every
river boat which reaches our property is bringing more of them. The boats
are also bringing in friends and relatives of employees." Oxholm had to
relent, allowing the hospital to set up a children's ward, which was never
without a severe case of malnutrition.

To offset all these expenses, Oxholm suggested that the company *Rule*
abandon its promise of free medical care. He set up a payment scale that
would cover job applicants who needed hospital treatment before they
started working, family members who required care, and those employees
who contracted venereal disease despite the posted warnings. He wanted
to deduct fees from salaries, yet there was no bookkeeping system in
place that could manage such accounts. It took some time to locate the
office supplies that were packed in the *Farge*, and once they were found,
typewriter carriages had rusted and paper had grown moldy from the humidity. The roof of the accounting office poured in water so that every
time it rained "all records have to be gathered up and put away and the office force has to evacuate the building until the rain has ceased." In any
case, when Oxholm told Dearborn officials of his plan, they overruled
him, insisting that medical care should remain free.

IN HIS SEARCH for labor, Oxholm also looked to the British Caribbean,
which had a long history of supplying workers to large-scale construction
projects throughout Latin America, such as the Panama Canal. In the first
couple of months he managed to attract a number of West Indians from
the upper Amazon who had survived the construction of the 228-mile
Madeira-to-Mamoré train line, one of the most brutal and ill-conceived industrial projects ever executed. The line was started in the 1870s at the
height of the rubber boom with the idea of bypassing a series of formidable rapids that hindered the use of the upper Madeira River, which ran
roughly parallel to the Tapajós, farther west. An engineer for the first company to undertake this task called the Amazon a "charnel house," with
workers "dying like flies" as they tried to build a rail line that "ran through
an inhospitable wilderness of swamp and porphyry ridges." Even with the
"command of all the capital in the world and half its population, it would

be impossible to build the road." A series of other companies were engaged to finish the job until one finally did, in 1912, just as the boom collapsed. All told, it cost $30 million and took ten thousand lives—one, it is said, for every tie that was laid.[25]

When the line was completed, workers, including a number of West Indians, were left abandoned in the railroad work camp of Porto Velho, which had grown into a small, destitute city. At the news that Ford was hiring, many headed down the Amazon and then up the Tapajós to the plantation. Added to these stranded West Indians rail workers were migrants who came directly from Jamaica, Barbados, and Saint Lucia.

They arrived at a camp where many of the same conditions that sparked the riot in late 1928 continued—poor housing and working conditions, particularly for those hired to clear the jungle, confusing pay schedules, and bad food—aggravated by strident attempts to regulate hygiene and enforce Prohibition. In June 1929, a knife fight broke out between a Brazilian worker and Joseph Hippolyte, a migrant from Santa Lucia, as the two men waited on line to receive their wages. Hippolyte stabbed the Brazilian, whose friends retaliated by nearly beating the Santa Lucian to death.

In his report to Sorensen, the increasingly beleaguered Oxholm seized the moment to showcase his decisiveness. He blamed the brawl on Brazilian racism, saying that it was impossible to make native workers toil alongside "foreign Negroes." As Villares did the previous year, Oxholm claimed that his quick actions had headed off a riot, telling Sorensen that he gave all of Fordlandia's West Indians some travel money, loaded them on a lighter, and sent them downriver.

"We think you will agree with us," he wrote, hedging behind the plural, "that on such occasions as these a quick and decisive policy is better than dilly-dallying and waiting for events which may prove to be disastrous."

The British consul in Belém disagreed. He wrote to Henry Ford saying that Oxholm's emphasis on Brazilian prejudice diverted attention from his already well-known incompetence. The diplomat pointed out that for decades West Indians had worked on large-scale railway and public works projects throughout the Amazon valley "on friendly terms along-side their Brazilian fellows." He also contested Oxholm's claim that the plantation had covered the travel costs of the exiled workers to "wherever they wanted to go." At least half paid their own fare to Belém, where they found themselves "strangers in a land of which they did not speak the language." Many were stranded at the mouth of the Amazon in a "more or less destitute condition." As a result of Oxholm's actions, he said, Ford could no longer count on His Majesty's assistance in securing Caribbean workers.

"I invite the company," the consul concluded, "to consider whether, in the circumstances described, in preference to sacrificing justice to expediency, they do not feel themselves bound, at least morally and equitably, if not legally, to assume some responsibility for the loss [to the West Indian workers] their action has involved."[26]

Oxholm, though, had more pressing matters to worry about. Rubber planter, construction manager, town planner, health care provider, Prohibitionist, the sea captain had yet another responsibility to discharge: undertaker.

By the end of 1929, ninety people had been buried in the company cemetery, sixty-two of them workers and the rest "outsiders who had died on the property." Most of the deaths were from malnutrition and common disease. But lethal snakebites, from vipers especially, infections from ant, hornet, or vampire bat bites, and, before proper shelters were built, jaguars, which occasionally snatched babies right from their hammocks, all made the plantation especially dangerous during those early years. Oxholm's maid had her arm bitten off by a caiman and bled to death while bathing in the Tapajós. And the company was responsible for interring all who died on the plantation, not just workers. As Oxholm explained to Dearborn, Brazil's civil code required that "if strangers come to our property and we render them aid we are responsible for their burial in the event of death"—a law that invoked a bond between death, community, and soil reminiscent of Gabriel García Márquez's observation, made in a novel about the foundation of another doomed town, that "a person doesn't belong to a place until there is someone dead underground." A year later, there were three times as many graves—including four that contained Oxholm's own children.

BY THE END of 1928, it seems that Ford—who once claimed to have invented the modern world and all that went with it—found himself in much the same position as did Spanish and Portuguese conquistadores centuries earlier: presiding over an enormous land grant populated by quite a number of dependents. Friend Ford had become Lord Ford.

CHAPTER 12

THE FORD WAY OF THINKING

To Ford's people back in Dearborn, the confluence of events in Brazil hampering the development of the plantation — threats to revoke export tax exemptions, seizure of seeds, levies of import duties, rebellious workers, and relentless bad press — seemed like a conspiracy, a confirmation of preexisting prejudices many of them had about doing business in Latin America. What to do? The decision to invest in rubber cultivation had been based on the assumption that Ford's Amazon operation would pay for itself, not with latex at first but with the sale of lumber or minerals. But mounting costs and floundering construction proved such a forecast wildly optimistic. Already by the beginning of 1929, Ford had spent over a million and a half dollars with little to show for it. An even greater concern than the money was Ford's reputation, for newspapers and newsreels had already announced the imminent rescue of the Amazon from the "scrap heap of civilization." So with Henry Ford "exercised" about import duties, and Charles Sorensen "annoyed" by Oxholm's inability to resolve matters, the company did something Ford had always been loath to do: it turned to Washington for help.[1]

The Ford Motor Company had extensive overseas business interests. Yet remarkably it had no contacts, either formal or personal, with anyone in the State Department. Edsel had to go to Herbert Hoover, now president, while the company's chief lawyer, Clifford Longley, approached Attorney General William Mitchell, asking to be put in touch with the right people. Out of these inquiries, Sorensen obtained a meeting with Dana Munro, the assistant secretary of state for Latin America. But when he traveled to Washington to ask for help in putting pressure on Rio, Munro treated Sorensen coolly. This was perhaps to be expected considering the company's long history of cold-shouldering US diplomats. Whatever the reason, the assistant secretary considered Ford's Brazilian tax problem routine and simply sent off a perfunctory directive to the embassy in Brazil to render whatever assistance possible. To little effect. The American ambassador, about to sail to Europe on his summer vacation, had left his considerably less influential deputy to handle the matter.[2]

With no help from Washington forthcoming, Ford appointed William Cowling as his personal representative and dispatched him to Brazil to make things right. A loyal "Fordling"—as midlevel executives without official title were known—Cowling was but the first of many such fixers Dearborn would send to Brazil over the next couple of years.[3]

Cowling arrived in Rio on August 8, 1929, and spent the next nine days meeting with government officials and other "people of importance." He wasn't looking for a quick settlement. He sensed that the game would not be won by legal or moral righteousness. Although Sorensen and other company officials saw Ford's problems in Brazil as all connected, Cowling knew they sprang from different sources, especially from confused lines of authority separating state and federal jurisdiction. It was the national government that imposed import duties and embargoed building material sent from Dearborn, while the state governments applied export taxes. Who had the power to impede interstate commerce and seize Ford's seeds was anybody's guess, and Cowling left that issue to be decided by Brazil's Supreme Court.

Cowling, who both in allegiance and in manner was decidedly not a Harry Bennett man, quickly understood that the issues at play were not necessarily captured in the reports and newspaper clippings sent to Dearborn.

He moved carefully and in his meetings with officials didn't push for an immediate answer on specific matters like the import duty dispute, preferring to let the lawyers who worked for the Ford dealership in Rio resolve the matter. The larger problem, he guessed, was that Ford agents, particularly those in Belém associated with the plantation, mostly kept to themselves, doing little to establish friendships with Brazilian politicians and businessmen. He decided to focus on making contacts, building goodwill, and so laying a "thorough foundation for future action." Cowling hoped to "educate Brazil to the Ford way of thinking," not arrogantly, as that phrase suggests, but rather by convincing local opinion makers of the sincerity of Ford's motives.[4]

As HE LEFT Rio, sailing north on a slow boat around Brazil's eastern bulge, past the city of Recife to Belém, Cowling had time to reflect on what he believed was the root of the company's problem. He put down his ideas in two lengthy letters to Henry Ford and other top-level company officials.[5]

First off, Cowling wrote, Fordlandia was located far from Rio de Janeiro, the center of "Brazilian thought," and what people there "know about it, or think they know, comes to them in an underground way, full of scandal of all sorts, detailing the worst improprieties on the part of plant managers and other Americans." Outrage over the revelations of kickbacks and bribes was not really the issue; the "fact that we paid for certain worthless concessions" was appreciated as "good business ability on the part of those who sold to us." "Official Brazil" was not so much indignant over the corruption as disappointed in Ford's business skill. And that Ford subsequently made a big deal of "absolute honesty" in all transactions, of refusing to indulge in "petty graft," only added to the disenchantment. It seemed the carmaker had followed up credulity with naïveté.

This, Cowling believed, led to a second, more serious perception problem. Many "higher-up Brazilians," having read Ford's books and interviews, couldn't reconcile what he said with the stories they heard from Fordlandia, tales of lost opportunities, mismanagement, wild parties, and "drunken revelry, not by natives but by our own men." Such gossip wouldn't matter for any other company. But Ford's self-promoted reputation for rectitude and efficiency set a high bar.

When Cowling assured Brazil's minister of agriculture, who hailed from Pará and was an ally of Governor Valle, that Henry Ford was "taking a personal interest" in Fordlandia, the minister said that he was glad to hear it for he "feared up to this time that he was not." Cowling asked him to explain, and the minister replied because he had "read Mr. Ford's books very carefully" and therefore had the idea that Ford's "success was due chiefly to the fact that nothing was allowed to be wasted." And yet there were reports of the squandering of resources in the Amazon, including "thousands of dollars worth of wonderful trees which had been burned in clearing the land." If the United States didn't need the lumber, the minister said, surely Brazil could use it.

Cowling warned Ford not to underestimate the political intelligence of Brazilian officials. "We must never get the idea that those in power in Brazil are not shrewd," he said. They "match up very well with those we meet in Washington." But neither should Ford equate this cunning with mere venality. Whatever problems the company had in Brazil, they had little to do with corruption. "They never forget Brazil," he said of the country's leaders, revealing an ability to appreciate the complex issues facing local politicians usually beyond the reach of most Ford men. If "they are corrupt, it is not in such a small way as in interfering with us. There are always bigger things than playing with one industry."

The problem was rather the company's actions, which had nurtured a bemused detachment among Brazil's political class. Every politician Cowling met with seemed to be reading from the same script. They first expressed great admiration for Henry and Edsel and graciously accepted the gift of signed photographs of the two Fords that Cowling presented on Henry's behalf. Then they apologized for not being able to help since the concession didn't fall under federal jurisdiction. Next they claimed that they hadn't really been following events along the Tapajós. Then they offered telling criticisms and recommendations. "They know more about our progress," wrote Cowling, "than some of us do, but they never admit it, for to do so would be to place themselves in the position of having to express an opinion"—and so far the bungling of the Ford Motor Company didn't deserve such a commitment.

"And so," Cowling concluded, "out of all this chaotic talk has come a sort of indifference on the part of political influences, a decided suspicion on the part of newspapermen that we were not all we claimed to be, and back of it all the idea that in the end we would do what every one else has done before us, exploit the country to the fullest extent."

UPON ARRIVING IN Belém, Cowling shifted tactics. In Rio, Brazil's political and cultural capital, not wanting to seem imperious, he wisely decided not to push the issue of import duties, preferring to let the matter wind its way through the courts. But in the provinces, Cowling's solicitousness gave way to a hard line. He met with Valle, letting him know in clear terms that Ford would pull out of the Amazon if the governor's harassment continued. Valle blinked, and on the key issue of export taxes the two men reached a compromise: the plantation would hold off from exporting anything for two years, after which it would be exempt from duties, as per the terms of the original concession. Following this settlement, a month later, Brazil's Supreme Court ordered the release of Ford's seeds—though this was a symbolic victory, since most of the gathered seeds had germinated.[6]

Much encouraged, Cowling next traveled to Fordlandia to see for himself if what Brazilian officials had told him was true, if the plantation was really in as bad shape as they said it was. And sure enough, what he found after a long and listless trip up the Amazon, first to Santarém on a steamer, and then to the estate on a company launch, made a mockery of everything the Ford Motor Company and its state-of-the-art River Rouge plant stood for: efficiency, synchronization, orderliness, smart use of resources, discipline, and independence.

Within a few weeks of Cowling's September 1929 visit to Fordlandia, Henry Ford would preside over Light's Golden Jubilee, a celebration to mark the fiftieth anniversary of Thomas Edison's invention of the incandescent lamp. Five hundred invitees attended the commemoration, including John D. Rockefeller, Marie Curie, Orville Wright, Will Rogers, Gerard Swope, the president of General Electric, Julius Rosenwald, the head of Sears, Roebuck (who years earlier had been singled out in the

Dearborn Independent's anti-Semitic campaign), J. P. Morgan (whom Ford had attacked as a warmonger), President Herbert Hoover, and, of course, the eighty-two-year-old Thomas Edison, who had taken a break from work at his Fort Myers, Florida, laboratory, where he was still trying to find substitutes for tropical rubber. The event nominally took place at Ford's recently constructed Greenfield Village, the model town near the Rouge composed of historical homes and buildings imported from other locations. But the celebration really took place all over America and beyond. Albert Einstein addressed the crowd by radio from Germany. In a live coast-to-coast broadcast, an NBC announcer dramatized the moment that Edison lit the first electric bulb in his Menlo Park, New Jersey, laboratory. Across the country, Americans were urged to participate by shutting off their lights, gathering around their radios in the dark, and then switching them on when they heard the cue: "Mr. Edison has two wires in his hand; now he is reaching up to the old lamp; now he is making the connection. . . . It lights! Light's Golden Jubilee has come to a triumphant climax." The extravaganza, which was held on October 21, a week before the stock market crash, was to mark not just the invention of electric light in 1879 but the half century of dizzying technological innovation that had followed, including the telephone, motion pictures, the internal combustion engine, and the automobile.[7]

Back on the Tapajós, Oxholm was having trouble keeping lit the string of bulbs that hung over the few bedraggled streets he had carved out of the jungle. Equipment and tools unloaded from the *Ormoc* and *Farge* lay scattered around the grounds, and there had been no attempt to do an inventory or set up a checkout system. Theft was rampant. Oxholm had still not constructed a permanent dock or central receiving building, so additional material shipped from Belém or Dearborn piled up on the riverbank, likewise unsupervised. Bags of concrete sat on the banks, "hard as a rock."[8]

Trees had been cut back from the riverside, but the underbrush remained untouched. In the thousand acres cleaned and burned for planting, charred, black stumps, which Oxholm didn't bother to pull up, mingled like darkened tombstones among the emerging seedlings, making the plantation look like an untended graveyard. The captain had built some houses, but not nearly enough to meet the needs either of workers or of managers and their families. The hospital building had "sunk on its foundations and leaked terribly." The soggy office doubled as a residence for its staff, with luggage stored on the porch for lack of closet space. There was no place for visiting Brazilian officials to sleep, so they strung their hammocks where they could. One married American couple slept in an "old seed shed." Another threatened to leave if the company didn't provide them with a decent house. As Oxholm had yet to assemble the refrigeration plant, keeping food fresh for a labor force now well over a thousand remained a problem.[9]

Throughout May, June, and July, Oxholm had rushed to meet the concession's July 1929 deadline for planting a thousand acres with rubber. But Manaus's seizure of Ford's seeds forced him to use local seeds of dubious quality, and he did so at the beginning of the dry season, the worst time to plant rubber. In his haste to meet the terms of the contract, Oxholm sent gangs of workers to spread out across the cleared jungle armed with sticks, one end whittled to a point, which they jabbed into the ground to make planting holes. A second team followed behind, dropping either hastily gathered seeds or seedlings from a makeshift nursery that one British observer said were "ruthlessly torn out of the ground" and then left under the "hot sun" for "two, three, and even four days." In agreeing to a July deadline, Ide and Blakeley had no idea, and if Villares had he didn't let on, that the clearing of tropical jungle best takes place in the dry season and the planting of rubber in the wet. Having started work on Fordlandia in early 1928, the Ford men had only one dry season (June to December 1928) to prepare a thousand acres for planting during the subsequent rainy months, which in effected shortened the July deadline to April or May. That Oxholm was planting at the beginning of the dry season was of course not his fault, considering the mess Blakeley left him, the difficulty of securing a stable labor force, and Manaus's seed embargo. Nor could he have known that Blakeley's abundant use of gasoline to fire the felled jungle had scorched the soil of the first lot cleared, adversely affecting its ability to nurture healthy rubber. It didn't help that a few months earlier Oxholm had driven Raimundo Monteiro da Costa, one of the few people with rubber experience in Ford's employ, off the estate after an argument over planting techniques. By the end of 1929, it was

A terraced hillside in Fordlandia planted with rubber.

clear that, while having met the concession's requirements, Fordlandia's first planting would have to be plowed under and "planted with better seeds at the right time."[10]

The sawmill posed problems for Oxholm as well. Blakeley before him had indeed, as the minister of agriculture complained to Cowling, begun clearing land during the rainy season. The plantation was littered with "huge piles of green wood" that could be neither burned nor cut into lumber because the felled wood was too big, too soft, or too wet. In addition, neither Blakeley nor Oxholm had properly graded the 2½-mile road leading from the plantation clearing to the sawmill. When the rains turned the road into mud, as they did most every day, the plantation's tractors couldn't haul the logs to the mill. Even when workers lay cut trees over the worst stretches, creating what lumberjacks call a corduroy road, it was still slow going. And when they did get through, they could transport only about eight to ten logs at a time. With gasoline at forty-eight cents a gallon, the cost of moving wood within the plantation alone was proving to be prohibitive.[11]

Like Michigan's Upper Peninsula, the Tapajós valley is filled with mixed stands of broad-leaved trees about a hundred feet in height, with robust, shade-providing crowns and straight trunks relatively free of branches. Yet unlike in Michigan, where most species were neither too hard nor too soft and fell within a profitable range, much of the wood in the Tapajós was either too pulpy or too dense to be usable. Some of the largest trees, like angelim, were often hollow. And Michigan saw blades, when they didn't rust from the humidity, were no match for the hardest of Brazilian hardwood. A "round-saw would scream halfway through a giant log and stop dead," reported a manager, while a "band-saw would melt into smoke." Being Ford men the managers did what Ford men do when confronted with an obstacle: they ordered a speedup. Running double fast, the "saws shook down their stations and almost wrecked the mill," blowing out the electric generator and delaying work until Dearborn could send hardened blades.

Also unlike the Upper Peninsula, which counted on average about six different tree types per acre, the Tapajós contained about a hundred different species within the same space. Sawyers quickly realized that potentially profitable trees were never grouped together but scattered throughout the forest. And the forest was so thick with trees, climbers, and vines that four or five trees would have to be cut and yanked before a clearing could be made for a free fall. "It cost too much," remembered one lumberjack, "to get in here and there through the timber to get the

Making a high cut on a big tree.

kind of wood that was any good. You couldn't walk ten feet into the woods without cutting your way. It is just a mass of jungle and vines."

So Oxholm began to purchase lumber for his construction needs, which meant that the plantation was not only failing to generate income from timber but actually losing money to purchase it. And since the unsettled customs duty issue made the importation of value-added material expensive, Oxholm had no choice but to buy raw timber in Brazil and mill it at the plantation. He ended up purchasing wood from local indigenous villages. The Ford Motor Company may have been bringing the techniques of centralized and synchronized mass industrial production to the Amazon, but for at least a time it relied on jungle dwellers using little more than crude hand axes to supply its would-be rubber plantation with lumber.[12]

At this point, Henry Ford, who had pioneered innovative conservation methods in his timberlands in the Upper Peninsula, intervened directly. He ordered an end to the burning of wood, demanding that logs be milled and stored until "such time as world prices make it salable at this end, and at a profit." But Fordlandia's sawyers had little experience storing hardwood in a humid environment, and the sun-dried lumber quickly rotted and warped. Edsel Ford quietly countermanded his father, allowing for the burning of all wood that was "worm-eaten and rapidly decaying."[13]

And Oxholm had no more luck than did Michigan officials enforcing Ford's "absolutely no tolerance" liquor policy. He tried to evict the "squatters," as company officials now called titleholders who wouldn't sell, and to shut down bars and brothels. But faced with what the *New York Times* described as "small uprisings" of machete-wielding protesters, he backed down. Efforts to keep workers off liquor boats also resulted in the threat of "armed resistance on several occasions," according to Oxholm, who turned to Brazilian authorities for help. But all they did was point out that Prohibition was a US, not a Brazilian, law. They also criticized his hypocrisy since, as they pointed out, the Norwegian captain and his foremen were known to like their drink. Balking at the attempt by Fordlandia's managers to "apply Prohibition to Brazilian workers without accepting it themselves," a local magistrate ordered Oxholm to let the liquor boats dock alongside Ford's property. When plantation managers turned to the itinerant Catholic priest to help preach against drinking, he refused. "For heaven's sake," he said, "I'm not a Baptist."[14]

So despite the concerns of Brazilian nationalists who thought that the concession granted too much autonomy to Ford, the plantation found itself caught in a relationship with the rest of the Amazon similar to the one Third World countries often have with the First: extreme dependency. Oxholm depended on a detachment of Brazilian soldiers equipped with machine guns and other arms to keep order. Stuck in the middle of a rain forest yet requiring a steady flow of money to pay workers and suppliers, he depended on the Belém-based Bank of London and South America for twice-monthly cash shipments. Nowhere near close to the standard of self-sufficiency Ford set for his village industries back in the United States, Oxholm depended on Indians who lived along the Tapajós to supply the camp with fish and produce and on local merchants for cattle and other food. Though he had access to a few boats, including a speedy Chris-Craft, to go back and forth to Santarém (and Urucurituba), Oxholm depended on local ancient wood-burning steamers to bring goods and people to the plantation. "The words slow, inadequate, aggravating, etc. hardly express what could be said regarding this matter," was one Dearborn official's description of his trip up the Amazon.[15]

Over and over, Fordlandia's managers found themselves reliant on outside support, unable to replicate either the extreme independence pioneered by Ford and Sorensen at the Rouge or the Emersonian ideal of self-reliance embodied in Ford's community factories and mills.

THE DAY BEFORE he left the estate, Cowling summoned its staff and "lectured them severely for their lack of organization and efficiency." He was harsh on Oxholm, whom he found overbearing and arrogant and unwilling to offer direction to his managers and foremen. Cowling condemned the lack of organization that had produced "waste of various kinds which is appalling." With no leadership or plan for moving forward, the plantation's foremen, he said, were turning in circles. On numerous occasions during his short stay, Cowling had seen four or five members of the staff deep in conversation for extended periods of time over matters of relatively little importance, and even then they often didn't come to a decision about what to do next.

"Many things," Cowling scolded Oxholm, "are begun and then not followed up and to say that your entire operation is costing at least fifty percent more than it should is putting it mildly."[16]

Cowling urged the Norwegian captain to act in a way that would repair the "moral reputation of the Ford Motor Company" and to live up to a "higher sense of duty to the Company as well as a keener idea of personal responsibility in your work." "You are a long ways from your old home, but you must carry on just as if the eyes of the home office were upon you."

The home office, in fact, never took its eyes off Oxholm, and Sorensen followed up Cowling's visit by firing off cable after cable demanding an accounting.

"Do you yourself use intoxicating liquors of any kind?" Sorensen asked Oxholm. "Have you any intoxicating liquors in your possession, either in your home or elsewhere on our property? What was the trouble on this liquor question? What about conduct of other officials of the company with reference to this same question that I applied to you? Do any of them use intoxicating liquor? What is the reason for this long delay in answering letters?" Sorensen ended this barrage demanding immediate answers "without any evasion."[17]

Oxholm had had enough. His sister Eleanor and wife, Cecile Hilda, had joined him toward the end of 1928, along with his son Einar and three daughters, Mary, Marcelle, and Eleanor. By the end of 1929, three of his children—Einar, Mary, and Eleanor—had died in an epidemic of an unnamed fever. In early 1930, a second son, also named Einar, died at birth. Sorensen's cables grew increasingly shrill, but by then Oxholm had stopped replying to them. In May he either quit or was fired—company records are silent on the matter—boarding the *Ormoc*, along with his brokenhearted wife and their surviving daughter, Marcelle, to sail back to the United States. Upon arriving in New Orleans, he continued on to Dearborn, where he met with Henry Ford, debriefing him on the rubber plantation and asking if there was another ship he could captain. Ford said no, and Oxholm returned to New Orleans to once again work with the United Fruit Company.

Fordlandia, Oxholm would later say, was "the hardest proposition I have ever tackled in my life."[18]

WILLIAM COWLING LEFT Fordlandia in late September for Rio and sailed for Dearborn on October 2. A request from a *New York Times* reporter for an interview before he left was met with refusal, which the paper "interpreted as indicating he found conditions discouraging." Though he had managed to establish some goodwill in Rio, negotiate a compromise on the issue of export taxes, and identify what the problems were in Fordlandia, other troubles persisted. Governor Valle continued to refuse to read the concession as giving Ford the right to expropriate the property of settlers who wouldn't sell. Nor would he force Francisco Franco, the merchant patriarch of the island of Urucurituba, across the river from Fordlandia, to part with Pau d'Agua, the small village that the Ford Motor Company felt had become the source of much of the plantation's vice. And while the import duty issue was supposedly settled through the intervention of Ford's Rio representative, customs inspectors at Belém were still holding up material that they deemed unrelated to the "refining of crude rubber or the manufacture of rubber products."[19]

Then the company's fortunes received an unexpected boost. In October 1930, a revolution brought Getúlio Vargas to power. Vargas, a reformer who would dominate Brazilian politics for the next two decades, creating the modern Brazilian welfare state, is often compared to Franklin Delano Roosevelt. The Vargas government passed labor legislation, regulated the financial sector and other areas of the economy, and generally presided over the strengthening of the central government. In the United States, Ford would come to detest FDR and his New Deal for implementing many of the same policies. Yet in Brazil, Vargas's ascension meant mostly good news for Ford, as it signaled the end of the excessive federalism that had the Ford men tied in knots trying to address problems in Belém, Manaus, and Rio.

The ripples of the revolution were immediately felt in the state of Pará. Though the revolutionaries were nationalists and therefore suspicious of foreign capital, they were also modernizers, hostile to the regional oligarchs who ruled each state as if it were their own personal fiefdom. Ford posed a particular conundrum. He was both a modernizer, promising to bring capital-intensive development to the backwater Amazon, and a man who wanted to run his namesake property with sovereign autonomy, like the rubber lords who didn't like Rio meddling in their affairs. Vargas cut through this dilemma. Soon after coming to power, he replaced Valle with someone sympathetic to Ford. He also confirmed Ford's land concession, a good sign considering that he canceled all foreign contracts in Pará except for Ford's and one other. It took somewhat longer to resolve the sundry tax issues, as Ford lawyers continued to debate with officials how to interpret the minutiae of Brazil's custom tax law. Eventually, in a series of decrees in 1932 and 1933, Vargas granted Fordlandia its long-sought import and export duty exemptions—retroactively, which was key since by the time of Vargas's dispensation the company, according to Cowling, had a "couple of million dollars charged" against it.[20] For the foreseeable future, Ford could count on a relatively supportive government and a predictable tax structure.[21] RULE

CHAPTER 13

WHAT WOULD YOU GIVE FOR A GOOD JOB?

HENRY FORD, EVER READY TO CHALLENGE COMPANIONS TO A foot race or a fence-jumping contest, represented, as both icon and huckster, the freedom of movement that distinguished American industrial capitalism from its European equivalent. "All that is solid melts into air," Karl Marx wrote in the middle of the nineteenth century to describe the revolutionary potential of capitalism to break down feudal hierarchies and the superstitions that justified them. But Europe took a considerably longer time to thaw than the United States: in no other country had national identity become so closely associated with movement—whether horizontal, that is, the march west and then overseas, or vertical, the idea that those born to the lowest ranks could climb power's peaks.

There would be inventors of faster machines than his motor car. Yet nobody could claim to have transformed, at least in such a noticeable way, nearly every realm of daily life, from the factory and field to the family. And for capitalism's sake he did so in the nick of time. Just as industrial amalgamators like John D. Rockefeller were declaring that "the age of individualism is gone, never to return," Ford came along to put the car—a supreme symbol of individualism—in reach of millions. "Happiness is on the road," Ford said. "I am on the road, and I am happy."

Ford peddled change as if he were the head not of a motor company but of the Metaphysical Club. "Life flows," he remarked in his cowritten autobiography. "We may live at the same number on the street, but it is never the same man who lives there." The myth, of course, didn't come close to matching the reality, for what some came to call a "new industrial feudalism" intensified existing prejudices and created new forms of exclusion and control, including those perfected by Ford himself. "The Ford operators may enjoy high pay, but they are not really alive—they are half dead," mourned the vice president of the Brotherhood of Electrical Engineers in 1922. Ford responded by justifying his antiunionism not in the language of reaction or even primarily in that of efficiency but rather by assigning to it the essence of true "freedom": "The safety of the people today," he said, also in 1922, is that they are "unorganized and therefore cannot be trapped." But if most of his employees had been reduced to cogs in the greater machine called Fordism, for a few mobility was more than a promise.[1]

Charles Sorensen—handsome as Adonis, thought a colleague, and "masculine energy incarnate," wrote a historian—started out working at Ford's foundry pattern shop in the old Highland Park plant. By the 1920s, his engineering intelligence had combusted with a "burning passion for advancement" to catapult him to the pinnacle of company power. Sorensen jockeyed for position with Ford's other lieutenants, including Edsel Ford and Harry Bennett, and became the executive force behind Rouge production, as well as assuming a large role in the running of Fordlandia.[2]

Others who didn't make it that high nonetheless had new vistas opened to them. Victor Perini, a twenty-year-old son of Sicilian peasant immigrants, was apprenticing as a toolmaker with the Richardson Scale Company in Passaic, New Jersey, when he heard from a friend that the Ford Motor Company needed workers. So he and his wife, Constance, headed for Detroit. It was 1910, and the company was still operating out of its first plant on Piquette Avenue, then producing a hundred Model Ts a day.

"Can you use a toolmaker?" Victor yelled through the plant's gates. "Oh yes, we can use a toolmaker," came the answer. He was hired at thirty-five cents an hour.[3]

As Perini's engineering know-how matured into a reserved yet meticulously observant managerial style, he was promoted to help run Ford's copper radiator factory and hydroelectric dam on Green Island, in the Hudson River near Troy, New York, then sent to Manchester, England, where he oversaw the manufacture of the British Model T, and on to Iron Mountain, where he built an airstrip before becoming manager of Ford's state-of-the-art sawmill.

"We covered a lot of places during the years that my husband was at Ford's," Constance recalled of Victor's career. "The company was more than generous in arranging accommodations for our comfort and convenience. We always went first class." She remembered with gratitude that "because of this the entire family has had experiences that are not often duplicated." But there was one not-so-comfortable place Ford sent them.

VICTOR FIRST LEARNED about Fordlandia from Henry Ford himself, when his boss visited the Perinis at their home in Iron Mountain in late 1929. "You would think that he owned everything around here," said Henry to Constance as he surveyed the photographs of Ford factories that hung on their living room wall. Over their kitchen table, Ford, having himself been recently debriefed by Cowling, told Victor about the mess Oxholm had made of things in Brazil and asked him to check on the sea captain and relieve him of his duties if necessary. Perini immediately said yes.

The first thing Perini did was tap other workers he wanted to bring with him, and he did so with the same kind of informality that got him his first Piquette Avenue job. One morning a few weeks after Ford's visit to his home, Perini, along with another Iron Mountain manager named Jack Doyle, ran into the tousle-haired second-generation Irish sawyer Matt Mulrooney on his way to work.[4]

"What would you give for a good job, Mulrooney?" asked Doyle.

"A cigar," Mulrooney responded without missing a beat.

"Come on and give it to me."

"I haven't got the cigar on me. Mr. Perini, you've got some in your pocket. Lend me one."

Perini did and Mulrooney handed it to Doyle, who "sprung this proposition" on him "about going to South America."

"What do you say?" they asked the sawyer.

"I haven't got anything to say. If I'm of more use to the company down there than I am here, I'd be a damn poor stick if I wouldn't go. They've been feeding me here quite a while. It would be a good thing to go down there and eat off them for a while."

"Well, that's pretty good," said Perini, who later described Mulrooney as a "gentlemanly young man."

"Don't say anything about it now for a while," Perini told his recruit, "later on, we'll see."

Mulrooney proved more obliging than did Perini's wife. Constance was tired of packing up house as they moved from one post to another and wanted to "live at the same number on the street" for just a bit longer. "You go by yourself this time," she told her husband.

"Okay, you can stay here," Victor said. But Ford overruled him. Dearborn had by then received word that the drinking and gambling of Fordlandia managers was mitigated somewhat by the "presence of American women." Wives were having a "beneficial effect on the general appearance of all the men here," a Fordlandia manager wrote. Even the "whiskermania" that had gripped Americans cut free from Michigan's clean-shaven decorum waned in their presence. Ford's men and machines would civilize the Amazon, but Ford's women were needed to civilize his men.[5]

"Where you go," Ford told Perini when the two men met later in Dearborn to discuss specifics, "your family goes with you." Victor nodded and phoned Constance back in Iron Mountain. "I guess you better get ready."

THE PERINIS' TRIP, in early March, was nothing like Ide and Blakeley's gentle roll to Belém two years earlier. Off the coast of Florida, the *Ormoc* ran into a hurricane. Lashing rain drenched the ship, whose motors were no match for the whitecaps washing over its deck. Unable to make steer-

The Perini family.

ageway, the boat drifted hundreds of miles into the Atlantic. Pitching and rolling "all day and night," the *Ormoc* tossed cargo into the sea as the passengers huddled in their cabins.

It took two days for the ship to right its course, and another two weeks to arrive in Belém. The Perinis and their three children stayed at the Grande Hotel, which was the best in the city yet still a place where spiders could be found in the bedclothes. Belém's Ford agent, James Kennedy, told Constance to get used to it. In the Amazon, he said, "the cockroaches follow the ants, and the mice follow the cockroaches. Everything takes care of itself, don't worry about it."

After a rough night in a soft bed, which gave out under Victor's weight, the Perinis were "glad to get back on the *Ormoc* because it was nice and clean there, even though traveling was rough." Both the Amazon and the Tapajós are broad rivers, in places vastly so. In a work published just that year, the Brazilian writer José Maria Ferreira de Castro noted that the Amazon makes perspective impossible. Instead of appreciating its vast panorama, first-time observers "recoil sharply under the overpowering sensation of the absolute which seems to have presided over the formation of that world." And as the Perinis made their way up to the plantation, the wide sky combined with long stretches of dense forest to weigh on Victor's mind. He complained of the tedium as they passed endless low banks with "no hills of any kind and nothing but trees and vines visible." The view was interrupted only by occasional villages, most derelict and some deserted. The family was traveling during the rainy season, when the Amazon just below Santarém is at its widest and the constant green of the shore at its most distant. During these months, the floodplain spills over into the forest, creating half-submerged islands and a "vast flow of muddy water," as the writer Roy Nash, who made the trip just a few years before, described his impression. Sailing as close up the middle of the waterway as possible, voyagers on oceangoing ships often miss the sublime, radiant sensation many experience under the rain forest canopy; traveling on a crowded boat, wrote Nash, one is even cheated of the "poignancy of solitude."* After leaving Santarém, the *Ormoc*'s captain, unfamiliar with the Tapajós's shifting channels that make it difficult to travel even when the water is high, ran the ship aground and was pulled free by a tug only after "considerable effort."[6]

Victor was even less taken with Fordlandia, and whatever recoil he might have felt on his voyage from the human emptiness of the jungle was intensified when he confronted the amount of work the place needed. His first impression upon leaving the dock was of tractors and trucks "wailing in

---

*More than a half century earlier, Henry Wickham wrote about the sensation of sitting in the forest and gazing up at the "leafy arches above" and becoming "lost in the wonderful beauty of that upper system—a world of life complete within itself." The British explorer Charles Luxmoore, traveling up the Tapajós in 1928 trying to locate Percy Fawcett, complained incessantly in his journal about everything he encountered—people, food, insects, heat, and the landscape. Yet upon taking a hike in the forest, "lit up by the sun," he pronounced it "very beautiful." "I would not have missed this part of the journey for anything," Luxmoore conceded. (Joc Jackson, *The Thief at the End of the World: Rubber, Power, and the Seeds of Empire*, New York: Viking, 2008; 99; Devon Record Office, Exeter, UK, Charles Luxmoore, Journal 2, 1928, 521 M–1/SS/9.)

mud," slipping and sliding on roads that weren't graded, drained, or surfaced properly. The rain was constant, and the wet heat, without the relief of a river breeze, overpowering. "There is so much to be done that it looks hard to decide where to start. . . . It will be necessary," he thought, "to start a railroad line at once," along with houses, schools, and a receiving building.[7]

DESPITE PERINI'S INITIAL impression, and despite first Blakeley's and then Oxholm's clumsy administration, Cowling's lecture had had a galvanizing effect on Fordlandia's managers and the project of transforming the jungle into a settlement and plantation had advanced considerably. The labor situation had stabilized somewhat, and by the end of 1930 Fordlandia employed nearly four thousand people, most of them migrants from the poverty- and drought-stricken northeast states of Maranhão and Ceará. Before he departed, Cowling delegated more authority to the engineer Archilaus Weeks, who had arrived in Fordlandia in 1929 from Ford's L'Anse lumber mill, located on Lake Superior in Michigan's Upper Peninsula, to take charge of construction.[8]

Under Weeks's direction, a recognizable town had begun to take shape along the Tapajós to replace Blakeley's work camp. Having pulled up the stumps and burned the undergrowth along the river frontage, Weeks organized a more efficient system to receive material and process potential employees. Workers had begun to lay pipes and wires for water, sewage, and electric systems. The sawmill and powerhouse had been completed, and the water tower was rising. About thirty miles of roads crisscrossed the property, pushing into the jungle. Work was under way on a 3,200-square-foot dining hall to replace the shambles of a mess hall left by Blakeley. The old lopsided hospital was torn down, and in its place was built a sleek new clinic designed by Albert Kahn. And soon after his arrival, Perini took charge of supervising the construction of what would be a three-mile-long railroad, cutting through the estate's many hills and linking the sawmill to the farthermost field camps, which were charged with clearing more land for rubber planting.[9]

Dearborn had also finally sent a topographer down to do a proper survey and identify the best location for a "city of at least 10,000 people to cover about three square miles." Though Fordlandia was going on its third

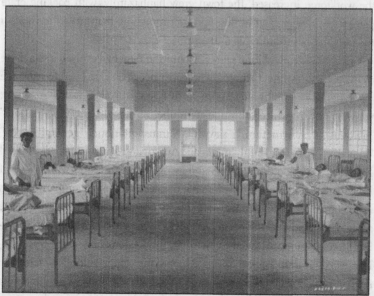

Top: An "ambulance" arrives at Fordlandia's hospital, designed by Albert Kahn.
Below: The scene in the hospital ward.

year, the construction of permanent houses for its Brazilian workers had not yet begun. Single laborers lived in bunkhouses or in holdout towns like Pau d'Agua along the plantation's periphery. A few took up residence across the river, on Urucurituba island, and paddled to work every morning. Married workers mostly lived in the ever metastasizing "native village" stretching along the river. The largest, rambling part of this settlement was made up of the families of the plantation's common laborers. They slept and cooked in one-room thatch houses, some of them reinforced with planks pried off discarded packing crates. Children, mothers, fathers, and other relatives hung their hammocks like radiating spokes from a central pole; the cooking fire's smoke damaged their lungs but protected them from mosquitoes. Better-paid workers—hospital orderlies, coffee roasters, cooks and their helpers, waiters, log loaders, swampers, deckmen, firemen, gardeners, painters, oilers, janitors, sweepers, clerks, bookkeepers, stenographers, teachers for the Brazilian children's school, draftsmen, boat pilots, meatcutters, tinsmiths, and blacksmiths—lived in slightly nicer houses, often made of milled wood, but also with thatched roofs and dirt floors. As the workforce increased, the town grew haphazardly, with packing crate planks recycled as boardwalks, laid over a midway that turned to mud in the rain and baked into ruts in the sun.

By 1930, the plantation's lines of administration had evolved into a more or less settled routine. Oxholm, who either decided or was told to leave the plantation two months after Perini's arrival, was still the nominal manager, yet work was organized through a number of departments: "plantation," "gardens," "construction," "sawmill," "transportation," "general stores," "kitchens," "clerical," and "medical." Americans, Europeans, and skilled Brazilians presided as managers and assistant foremen over work gangs of Brazilian laborers, who mostly remained nameless as far as company records were concerned so long as they didn't try to organize a union, steal, or cause some other kind of trouble. Archie Weeks oversaw the largest part of the labor force, the men who did the hardest, most exhausting, and often deadliest work, beating back the jungle, quarrying stone, cutting underbrush, sawing trees, burning the wood waste, tilling the ash and soil, and planting new blocks of rubber. Weeks developed a "rare knack of training the natives to do his work," according to his personnel file. He was a "driver," but in a way that "made his men like it," which may very well have been the case since most credited him with whatever progress Perini saw upon his arrival.

In other areas of plantation life, however, efforts to accustom a fast-growing labor force to Ford-style regimentation, discipline, and hygiene generated tensions, often aggravated by brusque and antagonizing managers. Oxholm, for instance, had organized a ten-man "service department" to enforce Prohibition, dispatching his agents to do spot searches of the bunkhouses and bungalows and to confiscate any stashed liquor. Kaj Ostenfeld, who was from Denmark but had worked for five years as a cashier in a Rio Ford dealership, was put in charge of the camp's payroll. His rude impatience in explaining certain deductions from biweekly wages, including for food service, compounded the resentment single men already felt about having to eat in a crowded mess hall (married employees who lived in the plantation's riverside village were allowed to eat at home). And though Dr. Colin Beaton was respectful in his dealings with his patients, his efforts to make the plantation village conform to certain hygienic standards were felt to be radically intrusive. Before coming to Fordlandia, most of the workers had been destitute but at least had the freedom of living as they saw fit.[10]

At Fordlandia they found themselves subject to the dictates of "sanitation squads" and "medical teams" that roamed the camp, draining and oiling potential mosquito breeding sites, killing stray dogs, checking for gonorrhea, and swatting flies. Inspectors swept into homes to make sure that food was correctly stored, that latrines were kept clean, and that all knew how to use, and properly dispose of, company-provided toilet paper. Their efforts to prevent families from sleeping in the same room where the cooking fire was kept not only were impractical, since the company had not built multiroom houses, but ignored the local practice of using the smoke to protect from insects. Inspectors fined families that didn't keep the small, crude pig and chicken corrals in front or on the sides of their houses clean and insisted that women hang wet laundry on clotheslines. Dr. Smith, a pathologist Dearborn sent down to assist Dr. Beaton, believed that the common practice of laying items flat on the ground to dry helped transmit hookworm and other soil parasites.

* * *

Dr. and Mrs. Smith show off a collection of butterflies, tarantulas, and other jungle fauna.

BEHIND THE NATIVE village, to the left if one's back was to the river, stood a dozen or so clapboard bungalows where European, American, and Brazilian engineers, foremen, and sawmill workers lived. Among them, working in the plant and seed division, was David Serique, the son of Julio Serique, a Tangiers-born Jewish émigré who helped Harry Wickham gather the Tapajós seeds that ended Brazil's dominance of the world's rubber supply. Also at the estate were a few of Santarém's Southern Baptist Confederates, who in an odd historical turn first encountered northern industrial regimentation in the Amazon. During the plantation's first bungling years, members of this community provided indispensable support, provisioning it with goods and interpreting local language and culture for its managers. David Riker acted as a translator and also ran the plantation's cattle yard and stockyard. Pushing seventy, he is described in his personnel file as an "older man than the Company would usually employ to put in charge of so large a work." Yet his intimate knowledge of the Tapajós, along with the fact that since his father had established a small rubber farm on the outskirts of Santarém he was one of the only people around with experience in cultivating *Hevea*, compensated for his age.

"Healthy and active," with "several good years ahead," Riker, aside from his service as labor recruiter and interpreter, presided over the "cleanest native camp on our premise." Three of his sons moved to Dearborn, where they took jobs at the River Rouge. As the oldest man in the camp, Riker had the honor in early 1928 of planting Fordlandia's symbolic first seedling in a patch of cleared forest. A dozen or so workers stood in a circle as the old man pushed his spade into the soil with his foot, turned it, set the seedling in the hole, and patted the soil back in. He then said a few quiet words asking that the Lord bless the tree and make prosperity, for the plantation and the valley, flow from its bark.[11]

Many of Fordlandia's skilled workers were "prosperity boomers," who, having arrived in Latin America to help dig the Panama Canal twenty years earlier, passed from one job to another. They traipsed through the jungle and desert frontiers, finding easy work in the US-owned mines, railroads, oil fields, and plantations that were spreading out across the continent. At each new job, they waxed about the glories of the last, and at the end of the day, over beer and whiskey, they "persisted in digging the Canal again" in tales that grew taller with every retelling. Others first came to the Amazon to work on the Madeira–Mamoré railroad and then stayed on. Texas cowboy Jimmy James, for example, had been living in Belém when he befriended Reeves Blakeley and signed on to his work crew. Fordlandia also attracted a number of "American and European renegades" fleeing their pasts. The Frenchmen Yves Efira, who did Fordlandia's clerical work and was considered a "splendid linguist," was rumored to be an escapee from Devil's Island, the prison island located just off French Guiana. Additionally, the plantation hired a number of veterans who for one reason or another had landed in Brazil after the war. One of them, a machinist named Sullivan, "never missed an opportunity" to talk about "Paris and the wonderful French girls." But he didn't get along with Mueller, an Austrian draftsman. Tensions between the two men boiled over, and after one fight the machinist took the Austrian's clothes and suitcases from the bunkhouse and threw them "outside in the mud from the torrential rain." Mueller quit the plantation soon after.[12]

Most of these migrants were engineers and mechanics, bringing years of experience working in the jungle to the plantation. But it was hard to check credentials on the Tapajós, so a few professed to have talents that they didn't. A Dane named Simonsen claimed to be a rubber expert and said that the best way to protect seedlings from insects was by rubbing Vaseline on their trunks. "He succeeded in getting rid of the insects, but the trees died too, so he was given a pink slip," according to one personal account.[13]

By the time Fordlandia got fully under way, life for quite a few "tropical tramps" had turned desperate. In the 1910s and 1920s, they had "boomed from job to job," ever ready to quit one because they knew they could always "find work at the end of the trail." But after 1929, Europeans and Americans were likely to arrive at the mines, plantations, and railroads less boisterous and more hungry, searching not for adventure but for steady work no longer available in their home countries. Increasingly during the Great Depression, they found work sites to be unaccepting of the indulgences and pleasures associated with the drifting life of skilled itinerants. Mining and plantation companies had learned the importance of hiring married men, beholden to women and children, as a way to maintain a stable and responsible labor force. Corporate-run company towns grew "more and more respectable, more and more conscious of the ugliness of sin," as a travel writer who passed through the region put it.

Fordlandia's puritanism was especially hard on Jack Diamond. Like Jimmy James, Diamond first arrived in Brazil to build the Madeira–Mamoré railroad, before moving on to other large infrastructure projects, eventually drifting over the Andes to take a job in Chile's copper mines. With the onset of the Depression, though, Diamond found himself out of work and stranded. Bumming his way back to the Amazon, he hoped to get work again on the Madeira–Mamoré line, only to find it "virtually dead," practically killed, first by the collapse of rubber prices and then by the global recession. After all the human lives wasted to build it, it was by 1930 running only one train each way every two weeks. He traveled down the Madeira River to Manaus. There, a group of expatriates raised a collection to stake him a ticket to Fordlandia, since "Henry Ford had a reputation of never refusing work to any man who came to his rubber plantation in search of it." But Diamond couldn't reconcile himself to Ford's "new morality," including his attempt to ban drinking and smoking. The shock was not of physical withdrawal: everybody from the head manager to common laborers got around Ford's prohibition, and Diamond could always find a drink on what the skilled workers called rum row—the boats, barges, and canoes that served as floating bars and gambling houses bobbing just off the plantation's shore—or on the Island of Innocents. It was rather, as one of his contemporaries put it, that Fordlandia's strictures forced on him the realization that he had "outlived his day," that "time had passed him by and that there was no longer a place for him in this world."[14]

So he quit the plantation and boarded a cattle steamer back to Manaus. As the ship slowed to approach the city's dock, Diamond looked down from its upper deck into its brown waters and saw his way out. He climbed over the railing and leaped into a congregation of crocodiles.

SET EVEN FARTHER back from the river were the "modern wooden houses" that Oxholm had built for the American staff, with porches and sloping front yards, on a wide street lined with mango trees, sidewalks, and streetlamps. These residences sat on a high spot on a bend in the river about a mile and a half from the dock and had stunning views in two directions of the Tapajós. Within a few years, this neighborhood would have a clubhouse where the men played cards and pool, a hotel for visiting guests, a tennis court and swimming pool, a movie theater, and a golf course. Compared with the "veritable Babel" of the skilled workers' international camp, as Eimar Franco described it, this compound, aside from the occasional European like Oxholm, tended to be insular and homogeneous. The Texan Jimmy James married Oxholm's sister and Kaj Ostenfeld wedded his Brazilian secretary, yet those who came directly from Ford's Michigan operations tended to keep to themselves. Having visited the town with his father, Eimar Franco remembers walking in and thinking the Americans to be a race apart. "They were very white, blond with blue eyes, and spoke a different language," he recalls. "It was as if the earth had been invaded by beings from another planet." One traveler through the area at the time compared them unfavorably to the Confederates, who though they built their own Baptist churches lived huddled together in a group and maintained their southern drawl and faded gentry manners, married Brazilians, and produced new generations of "American faces and gray eyes chattering Portuguese on Santarém's streets." In contrast, the midwesterners at Fordlandia had erected a "wall of provincialism" around themselves.[15]

Most never really mastered Portuguese, beyond learning how to conjugate the imperative form of a small number of verbs. A joke among Brazilians who lived on the plantations went: "What do the Americans learn how to say after their first year in the Amazon?" "*Uma cerveja.*" A beer. "And after two years?" "*Duas cervejas.*"[16]

In the United States, the men and women Ford sent to the Amazon were decidedly working- or lower-middle class, accustomed more to showing deference than to receiving it. Even those who had a certain amount of status back home, like Dr. Beaton, who before being transferred to Brazil worked in Detroit's Henry Ford Hospital, were not used to sitting at the absolute top of the social ladder as they did in Fordlandia. For men like Perini and Weeks, charged with building a plantation and company town, the change in class position probably elevated their sense of self-worth. For the women, however, the shift was disconcerting. Suddenly finding themselves serviced by a complete domestic staff, including cook, washerwoman, housecleaner, nanny, and "choreboy," they quickly succumbed to boredom. Illiterate in Portuguese, the wives couldn't even enjoy the pleasure of speaking the language of command to their servants, who competently went about their jobs with little direction. "Frankly, I believe that one of the troubles with the ladies," wrote one staff member back to Dearborn, is that "for them it is a listless, useless life, nothing to do, and they have not the energy to do anything, due to the climate, which is undoubtedly of an insidious nature."

Some Americans, in particular children, took happily to the adventure the Amazon offered. Leonor Weeks, Archie Weeks's daughter, was eight when she arrived at the plantation. She loved her time at Fordlandia and today considers it the most interesting part of her long life. She remembers swimming in the American pool, which was right by her house, and playing golf with her father. She suffered from one bout of malaria but didn't think it much worse than the flu. She did hate the "horrible hairy spiders" that often got in her house. If she ever came across a snake,

PIONEERS ON WAY TO SETTLE IN FORD'S JUNGLE EMPIRE

Ford pioneers on their way to the Amazon but dressed for Michigan winter.

she just did what her father taught her and let it pass. Unlike their parents, American boys and girls socialized with Brazilians, attending the plantation's schools along with the children of Brazilian workers, and some, like Charles Townsend, who was born in Fordlandia in 1938, grew up speaking Portuguese as their first language. (When Townsend returned a few years ago to visit the house he lived in, now home to hundreds of bats, he couldn't believe that he had survived such humidity.) The younger Leonor was tutored at home, but she too learned Portuguese and rode bikes with the children of her servants. Her fondest memory of the time at Fordlandia is of Chico, her pet monkey, which she describes as different from most, with "long black hair and bangs." Leonor took Chico with her when she returned to the United States, much to the delight of her Michigan schoolmates.[17]

As to the adults, Curtis Pringle, a lean ex-sheriff from Kalamazoo, Michigan, who sported a thin Clark Gable mustache and was described by a colleague as "absolutely fearless in the jungle," stayed for over a decade, earning a reputation as a practical-minded foreman. Dr. Beaton, thirty-one and single, also enjoyed the assignment, sweetened as it was by having his pay tripled from what he earned in Detroit. When his first tour was up, he signed on for another two-year turn. He put himself to learning Portuguese and soon spoke the language more fluently than any other Michigan transplant. "Extremely well liked," his personnel file said; Beaton "fit his job like an old shoe." And, importantly considering the high attrition rate of Americans due to jungle illnesses (he replaced Fordlandia's first doctor, who couldn't stand the heat), he enjoyed good health.[18]

The sawyer Matt Mulrooney was also never sick, not even for a day during his year in Fordlandia. His immediate supervisor thought he had a "chip on his shoulder," but what was interpreted as disaffection was in fact a wry Irish sense of the absurd. Mulrooney thought it was funny that he could turn on his radio and listen to American music patched in from the United States via relays in Managua, Nicaragua, and Santa Marta, Colombia. One night, he and his wife danced to a Rudy Vallee concert broadcast live from Green Bay, Wisconsin. America's original pop idol, Vallee was the first singer to master the intimate, disembodied tone of new radio technology. At the time of his Green Bay concert, he was riding high on a parade of movie musicals and hit songs, including "I'm Just a Vagabond Lover" and "Deep Night," the lyrics of which wafted through Fordlandia's American village, as Mulrooney held his wife close:

Deep night, stars in the sky above
Moonlight, lighting our place of love
Night winds seem to have gone to rest
Two eyes, brightly with love are gleaming.
. . . .
Deep night, whispering trees above
Kind night, bringing you nearer and nearer and dearer
Deep night, deep in the arms of love.

"Where others have played to thousands," ran the ad for one of the singer's movies, "Vallee sings nightly to millions," including those who

The Mulrooneys.

found themselves deep in the Tapajós valley, his voice competing with the nighttime sounds of howler monkeys, frogs, and a cacophony of crickets.[19]

MANY OF THE Americans, though, did not welcome their posting to the Amazon. The jungle pressed heavy on them, with its incessant rains that gave way to baking sun. "It was like living in a steam bath!" thought Constance Perini. There were flying bugs with "claws just like lobsters," heat rashes and sunburns, insect bites, ticks, skin funguses, and dysentery. The Ford staff was introduced to an array of minor pests bearing strange names, such as *piums*, small biting black flies, as well as minuscule fleas that dug under fingernails, leaving their eggs to fester and infect the skin. At night, vampire bats often worked their way past window screens to feed, and since their razor-sharp incisors could painlessly pierce flesh, the Americans would sleep through an attack, waking up to find their toes and ankles bloodied. And if malaria didn't get you, the nightmares brought on by the daily quinine pills would. "Dope every day," was how Mulrooney remembered the prophylactic.

Illness, often the kind of undiagnosed fevers that took the lives of

Oxholm's children, became a chronic condition. William Cowling was just one of the company officials who returned to Dearborn gaunt after some time in the Amazon. Malaria became as common as a Detroit cold, and many of the men and women spent their days recovering from an attack or expecting a new one. "Some had malaria two or three times," recalled one worker. "Rogge had it three times. Bricker had it I don't know how many times. Casson had it. They all had it."

Dr. Beaton sent a steady flow of telegrams to Dr. Roy McClure, his Dearborn superior and head of surgery at Detroit's Henry Ford Hospital:

Mrs. Oxholm has had recurring attacks apparently cholelthiasis (gallstones) probably also functional nervous disturbance. One aggravates other. Needs also considerable dental work her daughter needs tonsils extracted. Recommend both go Ford hospital soon.

Mr. Carr's son had a recurrent attack of acute rheumatic fever with cardiac decompensation during the voyage up the Amazon River.

Advisable to return Mr. Babcock by first available boat he continues to lose weight.

Mrs. Johnston keeps losing weight, she was 127, and is now 106. I have tried to persuade her to go home, but she is not keen about that, however.

Mr. and Mrs. Runge are leaving for Miami. Mr. Runge did not get along too well in this country but that may be the fault of the country.

Mrs. Bradshaw has suffered during the month from gastric hyperacidity with attacks of dull hunger like pain accentuated if anything by meals and relieved temporarily by alkalis. At times the highly acid stomach contents are vomited with relief. . . . [Her illness is] provoked by the nervous strain inherent with life here. She is very soon returning to the States. . . . The unrelieved stretch of two years work under tension in a tropical climate is too long and its effects continue to manifest themselves. The cities of Belém and Manaus are no health resorts but visits to them or . . . quiet rests on ranches, hunting trips, etc. . . . would steady nerves, calm ruffled tempers, distract attention from petty exasperations and infuse one with new and more worthwhile interests.

For some, the isolation of the plantation increased fears born of loneliness, making some feel as if they were "prisoners." Moody and unable to concentrate, Mr. Groth, a chemist doing lab work on parasitical infections for the plantation, kept asking to be allowed to return to the United States. His supervisor dismissed his complaints as "imaginary ills" stemming from a fear of catching some of the diseases he was studying. "Take hold of yourself," he scolded Groth, telling him that "as a man thinks so he is." This may not have soothed the chemist's nerves, but it did keep him quiet for a while. But when he again demanded to be allowed to leave, management relented. "We are not trying to persuade him any more. We believe he is lonesome and has had some trouble with his sweetheart and he feels that he can't carry on."[20]

The most striking defection was Victor Perini's. Henry Ford had hoped Perini would turn things around, but Perini couldn't take the Amazon heat. He hated the jungle and from his first day in Belém began to suffer from "edema of legs and puffiness of face."

"Awaiting instructions," a distressed Dr. Beaton wired Dearborn, "on what to do with Victor Perini." Diagnosed with chronic exhaustion, Victor eventually took his family and sailed back to Dearborn in May 1930 on the *Ormoc*, only two months after his arrival.

MOST OF THE rubber Oxholm had planted in the middle of 1929, during the dry season, under the hot sun in burnt ground, with seeds and seedlings of doubtful quality, had come up weak. And in April, before he left the plantation, Perini had decided to plow the field over and start again. Which meant that it would be at least another five years before Fordlandia would produce latex. The lumber mill, too, was a mess, its blades and saws ill suited for the very hard or very soft jungle wood. Hired to be a sawyer, Matt Mulrooney felt more like an undertaker: "They averaged about a man a day dying. I used to get orders every so often to cut this lumber for coffins. There was a certain thickness and a certain width

Fordlandia cemetery.

they used to make the coffins out of. They'd bring an order up every so often and give it to me. I'd say, 'What, some more of them gone?' 'Yep, better fix up for about ten, Matt.'"

Like many of the other men Ford sent to Brazil, Mulrooney belonged to the generation of skilled carpenters, miners, and lumberjacks that had presided over the transformation of Michigan's natural resources into wealth; they had seen the conversion of the state's forests, minerals, and waterways into the energy and capital that fed the great industrial factories and cities of the Midwest. Sawyers like Mulrooney had witnessed in their lifetimes the seemingly inexhaustible white pine forests of upper Michigan thin out, leaving first inferior stocks of yellow pine, birch, and deciduous aspen and then wastelands of cutovers, trunks, shrubs, and branches of no economic value. Yet they also saw the rise of cities that spoke of prosperity enjoyed not just by the lords and barons in the manor houses of Chicago and Detroit but by increasingly affluent working- and middle-class communities that spread out from these cities.[21]

So Mulrooney could take pride as the gnarl of the Amazon gave way, slowly, to the order of the plantation. "You know, an old sawyer likes the looks of a sawed log," he said. "There was some nice-looking logs there, some nice-looking timber, awful nice-looking. To go out and look at a bunch of that timber cut up in the woods, it was really a picture to look at, straight and not a limb or a knot in it."

But the sawyer also knew that a "very, very big percentage" of the cut wood was "no good." Watching the absurdity of it all—Oxholm's bungling, the silliness of trying to impose Henry Ford's ideas concerning diet and morality, the enormous expense and waste of resources, the impossibility of making the mill work right—Mulrooney had a distinct sense of futility. At the end of the workday, he and his pal Earl Casson, also from Iron Mountain, would "grin and wonder how we'd ever wound up in a madhouse, or if we'd ever win. We tagged it as a game."

CHAPTER 14

LET'S WANDER OUT YONDER

IT IS ALMOST IMPOSSIBLE TO TELL THE STORY OF FORDLANDIA WITH-
out invoking Joseph Conrad's *Heart of Darkness*, that great, indelible alle-
gory of European colonialism in general and Belgian brutality in
particular. Here, the Rouge River stands in for the Thames, the starting
point of Conrad's tale, and the *Ormoc* for the *Nellie*, which carries Marlow
to his rendezvous with tropical madness. Any number of Ford agents—
Blakeley, for instance, or Oxholm—could double for Kurtz, defying the
"whited sepulchre" of Dearborn puritanism and giving in to their lusts.

Yet there's something more Mark Twain than Joseph Conrad, more
Huckleberry than homicidal, about the stories of Ford men lost in the
wilderness. Consider Mr. Johansen, a Scot, and Mr. Tolksdorf, a German,
dispatched to gather rubber seeds in September 1929 by Ford's envoy
William Cowling. Their mission was urgent. After the disaster of Captain
Oxholm's first planting, the two men were charged with locating groves of
high-yielding rubber trees, gathering their seeds, and returning in time to
plant them by the coming May, before the rains ended. Traveling with a
Brazilian assistant named Victor Gil and a "Negro cook" named Francisco,

the two Europeans cut loose their Brazilian underlings a month into the trip. Gil they abandoned in a two-hut village, and Francisco they put ashore on an uninhabited island.[1]

Johansen and Tolksdorf headed to Barra, a small rubber town at the headwaters of the Tapajós. With the idea that it would be "nice to have a highball or two" on the coming New Year's Eve, they ordered wine, whiskey, and beer and paid for it with company funds. They proceeded to get "intoxicated and remained that way most of the time throwing money away and making fools of themselves in general." One night, Johansen stumbled into a trading post, where he purchased several bottles of perfume. He then headed back out to the town's one street, swerving back and forth as he chased down cows, goats, sheep, pigs, and chickens. Baptizing the livestock with the perfume, he repeated the benediction "Mr. Ford has lots of money; you might as well smell good too."

After about a week, the two renegades contracted a launch, loaded it with Ford-bought whiskey and a prostitute they hired as a cook, and set off on what sounded more like a "vagabond picnic than a rubber seed gathering expedition." They continued their riverine ribaldry from village to village, one smaller than the next, until they landed in a government area set aside for the Mundurucú Indians, centered on a Catholic Franciscan mission. There Johansen established himself as the "rubber seed king of the upper rivers," using a crew of about forty Indians to clear underbrush and gather seeds.

FORD MANAGERS, LIKE European colonialists in Asia and Africa, were fixated on race. Ernest Liebold, after all, advised Ford to plant rubber in Brazil and not in Liberia largely because of his low opinion of Africans. "She has just a touch of the 'tar-brush,'" wrote O. Z. Ide in his diary after meeting the Brazilian wife of a Belém-based British exporter. Others who followed Ide used the words *nigger* and *negroes* freely and, according to historian Elizabeth Esch, plotted workers by skin color on a spectrum that ranged from "tameness" to "savagery." When Archibald Johnston, who would shortly become Fordlandia's manager, wanted to send Henry Ford and other company executives some samples of rain forest wood, he had a "little wooden nigger boy" made from different specimens of trees found on the estate. Johnston said in a note accompanying the gift that its color was "all natural." Its cap, coat, teeth, and collar were made of pau marfim, a dense, cream-colored wood. Its head was carved from pau santo, a kind of tonewood. And the buttons were pau amarelo, or yellowheart. Ford's secretary thanked Johnston for the "nigger boy," saying that his boss was "very pleased" with the gift. "It is indeed a fine piece of work," Sorensen replied directly.[2]

Yet instead of unleashing the kind of mortal racism that gripped Kurtz, the jungle seemed to catalyze in Ford men another trait endemic to Americans: a blithe insistence that all the world is more or less like us, or at least an imagined version of "us." Here is the sawyer Matt Mulrooney commenting on workers, many of whom in the United States he would have undoubtedly considered black:

> Most of the people are white people. They are as white as we are. They are not colored up. Once in while you would run across a fellow and you could see he was smeared up with some other nationality. I wouldn't say it was Irish, or English, or Scotch or Dutch. I don't know what it was, but he'd have a different color on him. You couldn't tell. There was a color there. He wasn't a smokey or a white face. Them are the best workers. The rest of the 3,300 people were all the same, all white generally, they are all white, sunburned or tanned.

Nor were the Ford men seduced into thinking about the natural wonders of the Amazon in existential terms as markers of evil or human progress—as were so many travel writers. For Theodore Roosevelt, who valued the rough frontier or jungle life as character building, the Brazilian rain forest was simultaneously empty of the moral meaning created by civilization's advance and a cure for its corruption. But the men Ford sent down to build Fordlandia, and the women who went with them, largely avoided such musings. They did occasionally make mention of the tropical flora and fauna, yet often in the most prosaic way, commenting on the size of the bugs or the relentlessness of the heat and rain, and usually in mundane comparison with what they knew back in the States. Two decades after Constance Perini returned home, what still impressed her the most were the "black ants with claws just like lobsters" and the "largest flying cockroaches I've ever seen"—or, she said, "at least they looked like cockroaches."[3]

Charged with transforming the jungle into a plantation, company managers were of course concerned with the Amazon's natural dimensions. They had to consider many variables—quality of the soil and level of the land, irrigation, potential for hydropower, density of mosquitoes—when choosing where to plant rubber, where to build the workers' settlement and town center, and where to place the factory and dock. Dearborn sent a steady stream of questions to determine what equipment to ship: "What is the general tenacity of attachment of vines to trees and can they be readily pulled away from trees with heavy tractors or with a Fordson tractor?" "Is nature of soil such that trees will cling tightly to soil and carry a large portion of soil with roots if pulled up with tractors, or is soil loose and free enough to allow trees to be pulled out without leaving large holes which will require backfilling?" "What percentage of trees will be suitable for logging?" "What would be the cost of logging over 1000 board feet using native hand labor without machinery?" "Ascertain sources, quality and quantity of stone, gravel and sand for concrete. Crushing strength and chemical composition of clean sharp sand, gravel, and limestone should be determined." But the managers answered these questions with an unimpressed prose, unlike the kind of florid verse that the Amazon usually provoked.[4]

The jungle tended to produce not apocalyptic reflections on man's place in the universe but rather a wistful homesickness, a constant comparison of the Amazon with Michigan. Mulrooney got a "big kick" when, upon his return to Michigan, his friends would say to him, "Oh, gee, Mulrooney, it must have been a wonderful place to fish and hunt, all woods." "Yep, fine place," he told them, "you couldn't get out in the woods to hunt. If you caught a fish, it wasn't any good. They were just a bunch of grease. Give me the fish in Michigan!" Whether Ford managers, engineers, and sawyers may have thought the jungle a gothic hell or a window on to the consuming indifference of the primeval world to the hurriedness of man, they mostly kept it to themselves. When they looked up and saw vultures, as O. Z. Ide did upon arriving in Belém for the first time, they thought of Detroit pigeons.

IF JOHANSEN AND Tolksdorf were comical Kurtzes, they were pursued by their own Michiganian Marlow, John R. Rogge. An "old time lumber-jack" and a "natural born mill man" from the Upper Peninsula, Rogge had been at Fordlandia since the first tree was felled in early 1928, having been sent by Henry Ford to join Blakeley's advance team. Since he had survived with his reputation relatively intact both the opportunism of Blakeley and Villares and the ineptitude of Oxholm, Cowling, before he left the plantation, named Rogge assistant manager and told him to keep an eye on Oxholm.

Rogge was in a staff meeting when Francisco, the marooned cook, showed up at the office with a tale straight out of a "dime novel." It was night when Johansen and Tolksdorf put Francisco on shore, and he didn't realize until morning that he was on an uninhabited island. To stay meant to starve, so he lashed some driftwood together and floated a full day downriver until he came upon the hut of a rubber gatherer, who gave him some food and shelter. He then bargained for a canoe, taking twenty-four days to reach the Ford plantation, "through dangerous rapids, tropical rains, and all of the hazards of travel on the Upper Tapajós." After a short discussion among the staff, Rogge decided that the procurement of usable seeds was a top priority and that he would head an upriver expedition to search for the two wayward Ford agents.[5]

Rogge was happy to go. Born on a Wisconsin farm in Langlade County, he was one of nine boys, three of whom moved to northern Michigan to look for work in the timber industry. He felt at ease in the Tapajós valley, which, like Michigan's vast forests, was sparsely populated. If the Amazon was hot and humid, the eastern Great Lake plains of the Upper Peninsula were similarly swampy and moist and made miserable by horseflies and other insects during a good part of the summer. Rogge was also used to organizing life and work around the change of seasons: most of Upper Peninsular logging was done in the winter, when the cold hardened the roads and froze the swamps, allowing easier access into the forest. And

John Rogge with young rubber tree.

he was no stranger to water transport: Like the Amazon, the remote Upper Peninsula was cut through with rivers, which before the arrival of the railroad served as the main arteries for loggers, who built camps on their shores.[6]

Rogge thought his "sleuthing of a Scotchman" and "a German" would allow him to escape the familiar routine of the work camp and leave behind the relatively unimpressive lower Tapajós for the real Amazon. Northern Wisconsin, where he grew up, is steeped in Native American culture and history. Yet by time the "American lumberjack," as Rogge described himself, came of age in the early twentieth century, Great Lakes Indians like the Potawatomi, Menominee, and Ojibwa found themselves struggling to survive, victims of population decline, forced removal policies, and coerced assimilation. Rogge, therefore, hoped that his trip would provide an opportunity to encounter true Indians, of the kind that lived in the "real, untouched jungle." He gathered a team together, including a few Brazilians who knew something about seeds, and outfitted a small steamboat—open to the weather except for a small thatched sleeping cabin—with a two months' supply of food and equipment. As they set off from Fordlandia, Rogge and his men made the most of what anthropologist Hugh Raffles has called "hospitality trails," routes long used by European and American explorers, scientists, and businessmen as they traveled around the Amazon. On these routes, native labor did the hauling, cooking, cleaning, and poling (when rapids prohibited the boat's passage), and planters, merchants, town officials, and priests provided shelter and sustenance.[7]

Rogge was impressed with the skill of his barefoot and naked-to-the-waist boatmen, who occasionally had to jump overboard to push his boat through fast-moving water. He was less enthusiastic about his cook, also barefoot and dressed in a "pair of pants and a jacket that were so greasy and dirty that they interfered with his every movement on account of their stiffness." Rogge ordered him to put on clean clothes and to keep the cooking area neat and orderly, which he did, though he never learned to prepare eggs to the lumberjack's taste.

ROGGE LEFT FORDLANDIA in early December 1930, traveling during the last stretch of the rubber season, the six-month dry period when latex is tapped, smoked, and sent downriver. He passed riverboats and canoes taking balls of rubber to trading posts. He slept in the houses of local merchants and traders and negotiated with local tappers to allow his crew to string their hammocks around the trappers' huts. All of this gave him a firsthand view of the river's rubber economy.

As in other areas of the Amazon, rubber trees were not planted but rather grew wild along the 1,235-mile Tapajós, particularly in its upper headwaters and floodplains. Making his way to these thick, rubber-rich groves, Rogge found that the sloping banks framing the river's wide lower reaches gave way to forbidding jungle overhang. Within a few days up-river of Fordlandia, the jungle became dense and the Tapajós narrowed to a gap, flanked by limestone cliffs and dotted with tree-filled islands. The river then climbed over a series of white-water torrents and falls that only low-draft boats, light enough to be poled, pulled, or dragged overland, could travel. For the first couple of decades after the 1835 Cabanagem Revolt, when the rubber trade took off, these obstacles had discouraged commercial exploitation. A Frenchman who made this trip in the early 1850s described "roaring and terrible" rapids that "cross and recross and dash to atoms all they bear against black rocks" guarding the "deep solitudes" of the upper Tapajós. Yet by the 1870s, the diminishing yield of *Hevea* around the mouth of the Amazon, combined with increasing world demand, prompted merchants and traders to push farther and farther into the valley, avoiding the rapids and falls by building portage paths through the jungle. In the early twentieth century, most of the upper Tapajós latex trade was dominated by one man, Raymundo Pereira Brazil, whose family had migrated to the region from the state of Minas Gerais. At the height of the boom, Brazil owned two thousand rubber *estradas*, or trails. He controlled the river's workforce through debt bondage and monopolized trade and transportation routes.[8]

Brazil's bankruptcy in 1918, following the collapse of latex prices, left a power vacuum on the upper Tapajós. Although abuses of workers continued, river residents were now in a position to better their lot by playing the remaining traders, merchants, and trail owners off one another. At the same time, the decline of the rubber trade forced many tappers, including no doubt Rogge's boatmen, to broaden their survival strategies, supplementing their tapping by gathering nuts, planting, fishing, supplying riverboats with wood for their boilers, and hiring out as crews on steamboats.

Even with this diversification, the misery Rogge witnessed was intense. At every hut he passed, he saw poverty and disease, including chronic malaria and hookworm. Through a Portuguese interpreter he brought with him on the trip, Rogge heard the same kind of stories of abuse and exploitation LaRue told Henry Ford a few years earlier. Tappers complained about the low price of rubber and said that if they could save enough money for their passage they would leave their rubber trails and look for work in Brazil's industrializing south.

* * *

ROGGE SET OFF in search of the real Amazon, yet no matter how far he traveled his thoughts continually returned to America.

It took Rogge a few weeks to reach the trading post at Barra, the last reported location of Johansen and Tolksdorf, just below where the Tapajós breaks off into a number of lesser tributaries. The trip had been tedious, often taking hours to go just a quarter mile, with Rogge's crew straining muscles to pole the thatch-roofed boat through currents, navigating around rocks, trees, and shallows. At a number of places, small cataracts forced the party to disembark and walk, and bearers hoisted the vessel above the cascade with a makeshift pulley. The more the boat slowed and the narrower the river became, the thicker the swarms of bugs. "From the rising to the setting of the sun," another voyager along these waters had written, "clouds of stinging insects blind the traveler, and render him frantic by the torments they cause." Rogge, too, began to complain of what seemed like an inexhaustible variety of mosquitoes, flies, gnats, and midges, most so small that netting provided little protection. Exhausted and sick from two weeks of quinine and his skin inflamed by bug bites, the lumberjack welcomed the hospitality of Barra's principal citizen, José Sotero Barreto, a well-off rubber trader whom Theodore Roosevelt met on his journey over a decade earlier and described as a "gentleman of high standing." Barreto gave Rogge room and board and did everything he could to make the Ford agent comfortable.[9]

As he recuperated, Rogge enjoyed the pleasures of the manor, built high off the ground, with a broad veranda and glass windows. It was, he thought, the "best looking place" he had seen since leaving Fordlandia. Revived by a steady flow of tea, milk, and "plenty of chicken soup," he attended the nightly dances Barreto held in his parlor. During its golden years, the regional rubber aristocracy had been famous for its love of all things European, particularly Italian marble and Italian opera. But the bust dulled the old continent's appeal, and as the rubber lords looked north to America's booming car industry for salvation they also began to appreciate America's equally booming popular culture. The British explorer Charles Luxmoore, traveling up the Tapajós in early 1928 in search of the lost Colonel Percy Fawcett, reported arriving at the small village of Villa Nova to find people doing the Charleston.* And on offer every night on Barreto's Victrola were, among other American standards, "My Ohio Home" and "Ramona," both recorded just the year before. To the recovering Rogge, the 78s "sounded rather good hundreds of miles from home."[10]

At the end of Werner Herzog's *Fitzcarraldo*—that other tale of upriver obsession—the title character, played by Klaus Kinski, stands on the deck of his decrepit riverboat as the turntable plays tenor Enrico Caruso singing "O Paradiso." The scene is meant to invoke civilization's fragile beauty in the face of what the Brazilian writer José Maria Ferreira de Castro described as the Amazon's "overpowering sensation of the absolute." But it's also meant to convey a deep resonance, a harmony, between that enormity and the opera's emotional baroque. Despite the foreign provenance of the aria, the image is inescapably embedded in the Amazon.

Here, though, the music that Rogge listened to was purely nostalgic, not so much grounding him in the jungle as transporting him back home, or more precisely back to an America that was fast disappearing. In contrast to the sexualized, insinuating wooing of Rudy Vallee that reached Mulrooney and his wife in Fordlandia, the lyrics that helped restore Rogge's spirits conveyed a restless discomfort with the artificiality of modern times. "I want to wake up in the mornin' and hear the birdies say good morning, the way they always say good mornin' in my Ohio home. . . . I want to wander in the moonlight and meet my sweetie in the moonlight." Such wanderlust waltzes or ballads, often set in the American West (and just as often penned by European immigrants, as was the case of Gus

---

*Historian Bryan McCann, who has written widely on Brazilian music and popular culture, notes that at this time the upper Tapajós was only tenuously linked to southern Brazil and relatively recent migrant communities were receptive to new dance and music trends coming in from the Atlantic. The animated, African-based swing of the Charleston would have lent itself to the kind of informal communal celebration Luxmoore describes at Villa Nova. Residents of the village probably had seen one of the many short films or cartoons from the mid-1920s featuring the dance, either in Santarém or in one of the moving cinemas set up by itinerant movie men who roamed the backlands (figures memorialized in *Bye Bye Brasil* [1979] and *Cinema Aspirina e Urubus* [2006]). McCann also reports that the Charleston was a dance form that could easily be translated into many different cultures; in 1927, Jean Renoir's *Charleston Parade* featured an alien who lands in postapocalypse Paris and learns to do the Charleston (Devon Record Office, Exeter, UK, Charles Luxmoore, Journal 2, 1928, 521 M–1/SS/9).

Kahn's "My Ohio Home") provided an antidote to the urbane, topsy-turvy world of aggressive women and pleading men that populated Jazz Age crooning. They harkened back to an earlier era of proper courtship, before the coming of the electronic technologies that allowed soft-voiced effetes like Vallee—no "old time lumberjack" he—to become sex objects, reaching directly into homes, bedrooms, and, starting in 1933, Ford cars.[11]

"Ramona" wakened similar longings for authenticity. The song was based on the wildly popular 1884 Helen Hunt Jackson novel of the same name that transformed Native Americans into objects of nostalgia and Southern California into a major tourist destination, as generations of fans continue to this day to search out the places Jackson used as settings. Filmed three times by 1928, *Ramona*, which draws from Jackson's experience as a government agent investigating abuses against Native Americans, is an indictment of Anglo racism. Its title character represents Old California's vanishing Mission Indian culture, a victim of white depredation brought by the Gold Rush, by "Americans pouring in, at all points, to reap the advantages of their new possessions" and driving the Indians off their land "as if they were dogs." As in the novel, the song yearns for a pastoral idyll, always just out of reach beyond the next valley or, if Rogge stretched his imagination, river bend:

> I wander out yonder o'er the hills
> Where the mountains high, seem to kiss the sky
> Someone's up yonder o'er the hills
> Waiting patiently, waiting just for me.
> . . . .
> Ramona, when the day is done you'll hear my call
> Ramona, we'll meet beside the waterfall
> I dread the dawn
> When I awake to find you gone
> Ramona, I need you, my own.

Such melancholy provided a particularly apt sound track for Rogge's travels in search of "real Indians," the ones who had long ago retreated deeper into the jungle, in flight from the kind of violence *Ramona* dramatizes as having had decimated Native Americans in Southern California and, for that matter, in Wisconsin and Michigan. A "sad legacy," Jackson wrote, "indissolubly linked with memories which had in them nothing but bitterness, shame, and sorrow from first to last."[12]

As HE CONVALESCED in Barra, Rogge gathered evidence confirming Johansen and Tolksdorf's Ford-financed drinking and whoring. He learned that the two men had headed up the Cururu River to its *Hevea*-heavy floodplain. There, they had set up a work camp, hired about forty Mundurucú Indians, and started clearing the forest undergrowth in order to gather rubber seeds. Though not fully recovered, Rogge was resolved to finish his assignment. "I had yet," he told himself, "to see the first time that I was given a job that I couldn't handle." So he continued on their trail. The Cururu is tighter than the Tapajós, with a mesh of thick tangled creepers obscuring its banks. After a month of December rains, the forest was covered with water, and as the river narrowed, flies and mosquitoes grew denser and the sound of croaking frogs louder—Rio Cururu means River of Frogs, from the Tupi name for the poisonous and loquacious giant cane toads found throughout the region. It took Rogge about a full day to get to the Catholic mission, established by German Franciscans in 1912 in the wake of the boom. Still not feeling well, Rogge rested a few more days, dusting off his childhood German and enjoying heart-shaped Christmas pastry, or *Kuchen*, made by the nuns.

Here then was as close as Rogge would get to the "real, untouched jungle" and the "Indians that were reported to be living there." The lumberjack observed the Mundurucú with a keen ethnographic eye. They lived mostly naked, he noted, tattooing their bodies from "head to foot with the juice of some berry and a thorn." Each had three ear piercings, filled with "wooden plugs." Women also pierced their lower lips, and mothers nursed their babies until they were three years old. Children married as early as nine years of age, and it was the "squaw" who did all the "heavy carrying" while the male followed behind with "his hammock, bow and arrow." Ford once observed that people don't "stay put," and neither did the Mundurucú, who moved closer to the river during the dry season and inland during the wet. Those not settled in the mission lived in small, itinerant groups of ten to fifty, "scattered throughout the forest in large palm huts," under which they entombed their dead. When there was no more room for further burials, they abandoned the hut and established a new community elsewhere. Yet "untouched" the Mundurucú were not.

Portuguese troops had defeated the contentious Tupí-speaking Mundurucú a century and a half earlier, in 1784 in a battle that helped open up the Tapajós valley to Europeans, not just because it ended over a century of raids on colonial settlements along the river but because the defeated Mundurucú offered their services as mercenaries to pacify other uncooperative indigenous groups, including those who joined the 1835 Cabanagem Revolt. "And God requite the Mundurucu," wrote George Washington Sears, in his "Tupi Lament" commemorating the rebellion, "for on their heads shall rest the guilt of Indian blood by Indians spilt." This alliance with government forces, along with a reputation for "unalloyed, untempered savagery," as Robert Murphy, an anthropologist who worked in the region in the 1950s, put it, helped the Mundurucú survive the ravages of the rubber boom—unlike those starving refugees on the banks of the Xingu that Fordlandia managers considered, and then rejected, as a source of labor. Yet their numbers did decline rapidly over the course of the nineteenth century, by as much as 75 percent, leading to the abandonment of warfare as a way of life and an increasing dependence on the Franciscans for survival (though well into the 1950s, according to Murphy, "war was the favorite topic" of conversation among Mundurucú men, who traded stories of military strategy "as if it were yesterday"). By Rogge's visit, only a few thousand lived along the Cururu and in the inland savanna, along with a couple of hundred more around the Catholic settlement.[13]

The Franciscans' objective, like Fordlandia's, was a civilizational one. The mission supplied clothing to its charges and set up separate schools for boys and girls. It also encouraged the establishment of permanent villages—urging what had been nomadic families to live in settled homes with individual garden plots—inoculated children with the latest vac-

Mundurucú mission children, with German nuns.

cines, and promoted sanitation and hygiene. The homes directly under the Franciscans' care, Rogge noticed, "were very clean." Yet unlike Ford, the priests and nuns went about their evangelism with "some degree of tact and restraint," at least according to Murphy. It was not the kind of rash assault Ford hoped to launch on the preindustrial relations and sentiments of the people who lived in the Amazon but rather a slow subversion that transformed the ideas and social bonds that held them together as a people.[14]

The Mundurucú Rogge saw were nominally Catholic and accepted the authority of the mission as an institution. Yet Christian rituals and theology remained subsidiary to indigenous practices and beliefs. Priests baptized and confirmed Mundurucú children and established a proper Christian burial ground. Those Mundurucú, however, who lived outside the mission's jurisdiction ignored the admonitions of the missionaries and continued to inter their dead under the floor of the communal hut. The

Franciscans urged their wards to take public Catholic wedding vows, and Rogge said the priests refused to perform marriage ceremonies unless the girl was at least fourteen and the boy sixteen years old. This was fine with the Mundurucú, who thought the public ceremony "embarrassing and shame-provoking" and made "every effort to avoid it."

On Sundays, when outlying Mundurucú traveled to the mission to trade their rubber, the priests and nuns urged them to attend mass. Most did, motivated less by faith than by deference to the respected Franciscans. Children sat in the front with the nuns, men took the pews, remaining in a "rigid kneeling position" throughout the service, and women sat cross-legged on the floor of the center aisle, nursing their babies as the priest said mass.

Well into the 1950s, the Mundurucú continued to have their own creation myth, as well as enchanted explanations for the mundane suffering and joys of life, some of which harmonized with Catholic theology: During the time before the beginning of time, they believed, gardens bloomed without labor and axes cut of their own accord and the only requirement was a divine injunction not to look directly at the work taking place. But the Mundurucú looked. The "axes stopped chopping, the tree trunks grew hard, and men thereafter have had to swing the axes themselves."

Yet the idea of original sin did not take hold, nor did the concept of damnation. To the degree the Mundurucú believed in hell, they thought it a "particular destination of white people."[15]

ROGGE FINALLY CAUGHT up with Johansen and Tolksdorf a day upriver from the mission. He found the two men presiding over a large Mundurucú work crew and paying them in kind, with material purchased from a downriver trading post. After all the derelictions of the two renegades, it was their defiance of the company directive to pay wages that put an end to their adventures. Ford was adamant on this point. Indeed, when he discussed the benefits his rubber plantation would bring to Amazon dwellers, he usually did so in terms of wages. "What the people of the interior of Brazil need," Ford declared, just at the moment Captain

Oxholm was bungling the unloading of the *Ormoc* and *Farge* in Santarém, "is to have their economic life stabilized by fair returns for their labor paid in cash."[16]

Among the Mundurucú, however, money as a standard of value was unknown. Gift giving was the defining feature of their culture and economy; the exchange of food, knives, guns, and cooking utensils created a sense of identity and bound individuals, households, and settlements together in a diffuse network of reciprocity. By the time of Rogge's arrival, the Mundurucú system of generalized sharing was being increasingly replaced by barter relations whereby individuals negotiated their exchange item for item.* Still, throughout the 1920s and 1930s, each transaction remained highly personalized, unlike the kind of cold, faceless exchanges associated with cash economies.†

Rogge himself was well aware of Mundurucú custom in that regard. An observant Catholic, he had attended Christmas Eve mass at the mission and was particularly fascinated by the nuns' handing out presents after the service ended. Over the years, the Catholic outpost had accumulated a large collection of dolls of "all shapes and sizes," which had been donated by "every country on the globe." And each Christmas the nuns would gather up the dolls distributed the previous year, dress them in newly sewn clothes, and hand them out to the next generation of girls. Rogge understood that the nuns were trying to imbue gift giving with a specific religious

---

*It would not be until the 1980s, when gold was found on their land, that the Mundurucú would completely adopt money as a universal standard of value and exchange.

†There is a temptation to think of this kind of personalized network of gift giving as the antithesis of the rationalized industrial wage system the Ford Motor Company helped pioneer back in Michigan. Yet "wages" for Ford were always more than a simple unit of value. They were a state of mind, the key to his success both as a manufacturer and as a social engineer, as enchanted and filled with cultural meaning as was Mundurucú gift giving and bartering. "On the cost sheet," Ford said, "wages are mere figures; out in the world, wages are bread boxes and coal bins, babies' cradles and children's education — family comforts and contentment." Nor was he above using gifts to create personal bonds of loyalty. He paid Harry Bennett, for instance, only a small yearly salary yet showered him with presents, including several yachts, houses, and even an island mansion in the Huron River. "Never," he once tutored Bennett, "give anything without strings attached to it" (Collier and Horowitz, *The Fords*, p. 132; "Life with Henry," *Time*, October 8, 1951).

meaning to celebrate the birth of Christ (as well as to teach young children the virtue of wearing clothes). But when he was confronted with the wayward agents, Rogge's ethnographic sensibility failed him. He accused Johansen and Tolksdorf of theft, of paying their indigenous laborers with cheap goods and pocketing the money. The two tried to defend themselves, insisting that the Mundurucú didn't "want money." Rogge would not relent, and after reciting the litany of scandalous stories he had heard about the men during his travels, he stripped them of their account book and discharged them. Yet whatever the motives of Johansen and Tolksdorf, when Rogge requested that the Mundurucú continue collecting rubber seeds, they refused to be paid in cash and instead demanded merchandise for the labor. So he negotiated exactly what they wanted in order to continue their gathering.

It was late January when Rogge finally headed back to Fordlandia. Carried quickly on waters made swift by the seasonal rains, the lumberjack descended in twenty minutes rapids that took three or four hours to climb. He thought about the gifts he had received from the Franciscan missionaries, which included a photograph of "Indian life," a small wooden toy, and "some Indian relics," and pledged to always keep them as a "remembrance of my Christmas spent among the Mundurucú Indians in the interior of Brazil." As he approached Fordlandia, Rogge felt satisfied that he had accomplished the job that he had been "sent into the heart of Brazil to do." Dearborn, perhaps kept in the dark about his accommodation to local custom, was too. Henry Ford named him plantation manager shortly after his return, following Victor Perini's sudden departure owing to health reasons.

"WE LIVE AS we dream, alone," is just one of the many thoughts that move Marlow, the narrator of *Heart of Darkness*, as he journeys upriver in search of Kurtz. Rogge, too, found the jungle educative, although decidedly less existential. "One of the things I learned on this trip," he recounted a few years later as he reflected on his travels in the upper Tapajós, "is that no white man can live and be healthy on native diet and no matter how much good food you may have with you it is advisable to have a cook along that is known to be clean and can prepare food under trying conditions." The lesson could seem trivial, except for the fact that food was indeed a significant source of woe, and often conflict, in the jungle. In fact, exactly one year after his pursuit of Johansen and Tolksdorf, a fight over food, sparked by a hastily made decision by Rogge himself, nearly caused the destruction of Fordlandia.

CHAPTER 15

KILL ALL THE AMERICANS

IN DECEMBER 1930, WORKERS HAD FINISHED PAINTING THE FORD logo on the landmark that distinguishes Fordlandia to this day: its 150-foot tower and 150,000-gallon water tank. "When the view is had from the deck of a river steamer," wrote Ogden Pierrot, an assistant commercial attaché assigned to the US embassy in Rio, of his trip to Fordlandia, "the imposing structures of the industrial section of the town, with the tremendous water tank and the smokestack of the power house, catch the view and create a sensation of real wonderment."

He went on:

This is not unusual when it is considered that for several days the only signs of life that have relieved the monotony of the trip have been occasional settlements consisting of two or three thatched huts against a background of green jungle. A feeling akin to disbelief comes over the visitor on suddenly seeing projected before him a picture which may be considered a miniature of a modern industrial city. Smokestacks belching forth a heavy cloud formed by waste wood used as fuel, a locomotive industriously puffing

Industrial sublime: Fordlandia's powerhouse turbine.

along ahead of flat cars laden with machinery just received from the United States, steam cranes performing their endless half turns and reverses for the purposes of retrieving heavy cargo from the holds of lighters moored alongside the long dock, heavy tractors creeping around the sides of the hills dragging implements behind them for loosening and leveling the earth, others heaving at taut cables attached to stumps of tremendous proportions—all combine to increase the astonishment caused in the uninitiated visitors to this district, who had no conceptions of what had been accomplished in the brief space of slightly over two years.

Much of the piping that would provide indoor plumbing to the town was scheduled to be completed the following year. But as Christmas approached, workers bolted to the tower one feature that had nothing to do with water.[1]

IT TOOK DEARBORN'S purchasing agents some effort to find a factory whistle that wouldn't rust from the jungle humidity. Once they did, they shipped it to Fordlandia, where it was perched on top of the water tower, above the tall trees, giving it a seven-mile range. The whistle was piercing enough not only to reach dispersed road gangs and fieldhands but to be heard across the river, where even those not affiliated with Fordlandia began to pace their day to its regularly scheduled blows. The whistle was supplemented by another icon of industrial factory work: pendulum punch time clocks, placed at different locations around the plantation, that recorded exactly when each employee began and ended his workday.[2]

In Detroit, immigrant workers by the time they got to Ford's factories, even if they were peasants and shepherds, had had ample opportunity to adjust to the meter of industrial life. The long lines at Ellis Island, the clocks that hung on the walls of depots and waiting rooms, the fairly precise schedules of ships and trains, and standardized time that chopped the sun's daily arc into zones combined to guide their motions and change their inner sense of how the days passed.

But in the Amazon, the transition between agricultural time and industrial time was much more precipitous. Prior to showing up at Fordlandia, many of the plantation's workers who had lived in the region had set their pace by two distinct yet complementary timepieces. The first was the sun, its rise and fall marking the beginning and end of the day, its apex signaling the time to take to the shade and sleep. The second was the turn of the seasons: most of the labor needed to survive was performed during the relatively dry months of June to November. Rainless days made rubber tapping possible, while the recession of the floods exposed newly enriched soils, ready to plant, and concentrated fish, making them easier to catch. But nothing was set in stone. Excessive rain or prolonged periods of drought or heat led to adjustments of schedules. Before the coming of Ford, Tapajós workers lived time, they didn't measure it—most rarely ever heard church bells, much less a factory whistle. It was difficult, therefore, as David Riker, who performed many jobs for Ford, including labor recruiter, said, "to make 365-day machines out of these people."[3]

Fordlandia's managers and foremen, in contrast, were mostly engineers, precise in their measurement of time and motion. One of the first things the Americans did was set their watches and clocks to Detroit time, where Fordlandia remains to this day (nearby Santarém runs an hour earlier).* They scratched their heads when confronted with workers they routinely described as "lazy." Archie Weeks's daughter remembers her father throwing his straw hat on the ground more than once in frustration. With a decided sense of purpose that grated against the established rhythms of Tapajós life (David Riker liked to say that *hurry* was an "obscene" word in the valley), proudly affiliated with a company renowned for its vanguard interlocking efficiency, Ford's men tended to treat Brazilians as instruments. And called them such. Matt Mulrooney gave his workers nicknames. "This fellow I had named Telephone. When I wanted to send a message or an order down front, I'd just holler, 'Telephone!' and he'd show up."[4]

And they used themselves as standards to measure the value of Brazilian labor. "Two of our people easily carried some timbers which twelve Brazilians did not seem to be able to handle," observed a Dearborn official at the end of 1930. What a man could do in a Dearborn day "would take one of them guys three days to do it down there."[5]

These American managers and foremen did, after all, work for a man whose obsession with time long predated his drive to root out "lost motion" and "slack" in the workday by dividing the labor needed to build the Model T into ever smaller tasks: 7,882 to be exact, according to Ford's own calculations. As a boy, Ford regularly took apart and reassembled watches and clocks. "Every clock in the Ford home," a neighbor once recalled, "shuddered when it saw him coming." He even invented a two-faced watch, one to keep "sun time" and the other Chicago time—that is, central standard time. Thirteen when his mother died giving birth to her ninth child, Henry later described his home after her passing as "a watch without a mainspring."[6]

He also knew that attempts to change the measure of time could lead to resistance—again, well before he met labor opposition to his assembly

---

*Brazil resisted for over a decade an international agreement that would set the Greenwich meridian as the base for reckoning international zones, holding out for the use of its own coordinates to standardize time. It dropped its opposition in 1913 and accepted Greenwich time, though most interior regions, especially those without train lines such as the Amazon, continued to keep "God's time."

line speedup. He was twenty-two when, in 1885, most of Detroit refused
to obey a municipal ordinance to promote the "unification of time," as
the campaign to get the United States to accept the Greenwich meridian
as the universal standard was called. "Considerable confusion" prevailed,
according to the *Chicago Daily Tribune*, as Detroit "showed her usual
conservatism in refusing to adopt Standard Time." It took more than two
decades to get the city to fully "abandon solar time" and set its clocks back
twenty-eight minutes and fifty-one seconds to harmonize with Chicago
and the rest of the Midwest (the city would switch to eastern standard
time in 1915, both to have more sunlight hours and to synchronize the
city's factories with New York banks).[7]

In Fordlandia, industrial regimentation entailed a host of other initiatives besides whistles and punch card clocks. The paying of set bimonthly
wages, based on those punched cards, was the most obvious. So was a conception of the workday that made as little concession as possible to the
weather, keeping workers "on the clock" when rain poured down in sheets
and the temperature soared past 105 degrees. The effort to rationalize life
reached into the smallest details of a worker's day. As in Dearborn, plantation employees were required to wear a metal Ford badge, embossed with

Men line up to receive their pay.

A worker's badge depicting the Fordlandia ideal.

their ID number and an industrial panorama that included a factory complex, an airplane, two ships (the *Ormoc* and *Farge*?), and a water tower. The fieldhands who cleared the jungle and tended to the young rubber trees often took off their shirts in the heat, and so they pinned their badges to their belt buckles. The cost of a lost badge was deducted from wages.

Regimentation also extended into hygiene and health. The company required workers to submit to blood draws to test for disease and injections to vaccinate against smallpox, yellow fever, typhoid, and diphtheria. When workers went to punch out at the end of the day, they were met at the clocks by members of the medical team, who gave them their daily quinine pill. They were often reluctant to take it, though, as the high dosage prescribed by Ford's doctors caused nausea, vomiting, stomach pain, skin rashes, and nightmares. Hiding the pills under their tongues, the workers, once out of sight, would compete to see who could spit theirs the farthest. Plantation doctors also insisted that all workers take the antiparasitical chenopodium, without, as one employee complained, examining them to see if the medicine was required. "The Americans suppose that we are all full of worms," he said.[8]

AT DAWN, WHEN the whistle gave its first blast summoning workers to their stations, Fordlandia was often still shrouded in mist. Its managers would soon learn that the fog that wafted off the Tapajós early in the morning accelerated the spread of the rubber-destroying fungi. Yet in those early days, before the blight hit, they thought it beautiful, especially when the mist mingled with light's first rays through standing trees. The undulating hills and hollows of the planting area no longer looked like a wasteland, as over two thousand acres of six-feet-tall rubber trees, lined up in neat rows, had begun to sport young crowns of leaves. The estate was especially enchanting around the American compound. Though it was set back from the dock about a mile and a half, the row of houses nestled on a rise above a bend in the Tapajós, gave its residents a panoramic sunset view of the broad river. Behind the houses, as a buffer to the rest of the plantation, Archie Weeks had left a stand of forest, creating what residents described as a "nature park." With most of the jungle's dangers removed, it was easier to contemplate its pleasures. Paths raked clean of the rank, rotting leaves that normally cover the forest floor meandered through ferns, tropical palms, false cedars, and kapoks garlanded with climbers, bromeliads, bignonias, and other tropical flowers; large morpho butterflies flitted over the blossoms, their wings shining blue and black. And that December, Dearborn had sent down about a dozen live pines, to be used as Christmas trees in the American houses, so its homesick American staff could have a proper American holiday.

Slowly, before the second whistle signaled the official start of the day, the morning sounds of the forest would give way to the noise of waking families, women grinding manioc, and the chatter, first subdued and then playful, of assembling men. Most came from the bunkhouses or the plantation settlement. But a contingent commuted from the other side of the river, their canoe paddles splashing the water, oil lamps piercing the thick fog, helping them navigate, as did the occasional soft whistle if one drifted off course. Others walked from Pau d'Agua or one of the other small settlements on the plantation's edge that had so far withstood the company's attempts to buy them out or shut them down, continuing to offer a degree of nighttime autonomy to Fordlandia's workers. Time cards were punched, ignitions turned, instructions given, and the workday commenced.

By the end of 1930, then, it seemed as if Fordlandia had made it through its rough start and had settled into a workable routine. Most of the physical plant was built, and crews were pushing into the jungle, clearing more land, planting more rubber, and building more roads. John Rogge, named acting manager following his return from the upper Tapajós and Victor Perini's sudden departure, had arranged for a steady supply of seeds to be sent down from the Mundurucú reservation. Rogge had also sent David Riker earlier in the year to the upper Amazon, to Acre in far western Brazil, to secure more seeds, some of which had arrived and had been planted. Sanitation squads still policed the plantation's thatched settlement where workers with families lived, inspecting latrines and kitchens and making sure laundry was hung properly, waste was disposed of in a hygienic manner, and corrals were kept dry, well drained, and free of feces. But managers had their hands full getting the plantation and sawmill running, so they had mostly given up insisting that all single employees live on the estate proper, though they did try to force unmarried workers to eat lunch and dinner in the company's newly built dining hall. Nor did the administration in those early years provide much in the way of entertainment. For most employees, the workday ended at three. Apart from dinner there wasn't much else for single men to do but to drift to the cafes, bars, and brothels that surrounded the plantation, where they could eat and drink what they wanted and pay for sex if they liked. On Sundays, small-scale traders and merchants from nearby communities arrived on canoes, steamboats, and graceful sailboats, still widely used at the time, setting up a bustling market on the riverbank, selling fruit, vegetables, meat, notions, clothes, and books.

The strikes, knife fights, and riots that marked Fordlandia's first two years had subsided, and for all of 1930 there were no major incidents. Rogge decided that the detachment of armed soldiers that had been stationed at the camp since the 1928 riot was no longer needed. Fordlandia's end-of-the-year report, compiled in early December 1930, praised if not the work ethic then the "docility" of Brazilian workers, who do "not resent being either shown or supervised by men of other nationalities."

Still, Rogge kept a tug and a smaller launch at the ready—not at the main dock but up the river, accessible by a path from the American village.

THE TROUBLE STARTED in the new eating hall, a cavernous concrete warehouselike structure inaugurated just a few weeks earlier. To enforce the regulation that single workers had to take their meals on the plantation—both to discourage the patronage of bars and bordellos and to encourage a healthy diet—Rogge, back from a four-month vacation, decided after consulting with Dearborn that the cost of food would be automatically deducted from bimonthly paychecks.

The new system went into effect in the middle of December. Common laborers sat at one end of the hall, skilled craftsmen and foremen at the other; both groups were served by waiters. Workers grumbled about being fed a diet set by Henry Ford, consisting of oatmeal and canned peaches imported from Michigan for breakfast and unpolished rice and whole wheat bread for dinner. And they didn't like the automatic pay deductions, which meant they couldn't spend their money where they wanted. It also meant they had to form a line outside the dining hall door so that office clerks could take attendance, jotting badge numbers in their roll book. But the arrangement seemed to be working.

Then on December 20, Chester Coleman arrived in the camp to oversee the kitchens. Before having spent even a day at Fordlandia, he suggested that the plantation do away with waiter service. Fresh from his job as foreman at River Rouge, with its assembly lines and conveyor belts, Coleman proposed having all the men line up for their food "cafeteria-style." Rogge agreed, and the change went into effect on the twenty-second. Rogge also charged the unpopular Kaj Ostenfeld, who worked in the payroll office, with the job of deducting the cost of meals from workers' salaries and with making sure that the new plan went smoothly. Dearborn believed Ostenfeld a man of "unquestioned honesty," though they did think he could use some refinement and suggested that at some point he be brought to Detroit for "further development." Workers had long been unhappy with his condescending, provocative manner.[9]

During the first hour or so, eight hundred men made it in and out without a problem. Ostenfeld, though, heard some of the skilled mechanics and foremen complain. "When they came from work," he said, they expected to "to sit down at the table and be served by the waiters"—and not be forced to wait on line and eat with the common laborers. As the line began to bunch up, the complaints grew sharper. "We are not dogs," someone protested, "that are going to be ordered by the company to eat in this way." The sweltering heat didn't help matters. The old mess hall had been made of thatch, with half-open walls and a tall, airy A-frame roof that while rustic looking was well ventilated. The new hall was concrete, with a squat roof made of asbestos, tar, and galvanized metal that trapped heat, turning the building into an oven.[10]

Cooks had trouble keeping the food coming and the clerks took too much time recording the badge numbers. Outside, workers pushed against the entrance trying to get in. Inside, those waiting for food crowded around the harried servers, who couldn't ladle the rice and fish onto plates fast enough. It was then that Manuel Caetano de Jesus, a thirty-five-year-old brick mason from the coastal state of Rio Grande do Norte, forced his way into the hall and confronted Ostenfeld. There was already animosity between the two men from past encounters, and as their words grew heated, workers in dirty shirts and ratty straw hats and smelling of a day's hard work gathered round. Ostenfeld knew some Portuguese from his previous work at Rio's Ford dealership. But that didn't mean he fully understood de Jesus, who most likely spoke fast and with a thick working-class north Brazilian accent. Often Ford men had just enough Portuguese to get by, which could be a dangerous thing, creating situations where both parties might easily mistake obtuseness for hostility. In any case, Ostenfeld grasped what it meant when de Jesus took off his badge and handed it to him.

Ostenfeld laughed. As de Jesus later testified, "it was as if he was making fun," which "infuriated" those who were standing close by, following the argument. For his part, Ostenfeld claimed that de Jesus turned to the crowd and said: "I have done everything for you, now you can do the rest."[11]

The response was furious, one observer recounted, like "putting a match to gasoline." The "horrible noise" of the breaking pots, glass, plates, sinks, tables, and chairs served as a clarion, calling more workers to descend on the mess hall armed with knives, rocks, pipes, hammers, machetes, and clubs. Ostenfeld, along with Coleman, who had watched the whole scene unfold not knowing a word of Portuguese, jumped in a truck to escape. As they sped away to tell Rogge what was happening, they heard someone yell: "Let's break everything, let's get hold of Ostenfeld."

With Ostenfeld in flight, the crowd went on a rampage. Having demolished the dining hall, the rioters destroyed "everything breakable within reach of their course, which took them to the office building, power house, sawmill, garage, radio station, and receiving building." They cut the lights to the rest of the plantation, smashed windows, dumped a truckload of meat into the river, and broke pressure gauges. A group of men tried to pull out the pilings holding up the pier, while others set fire to the machine shop, burned company records, and looted the commissary. The rioters then set their sights on the things most closely associated with Ford, destroying every truck, tractor, and car on the plantation. Windshields and lights were shattered, gas tanks punctured, and tires slashed. A number of trucks were pushed into ditches, and at least one was rolled down the riverbank into the Tapajós. Then they turned to the time clocks, smashing them to bits.

One group broke away and headed to Pau d'Agua to get liquor, while another ran to rouse other protesters. Unaware of what was going on, Archie Weeks nearly drove a "touring car" straight into a group of men armed with clubs and knives. He spun the steering wheel hard and sped away, but not fast enough to avoid a rain of rocks that shattered his back window. Gaining some distance, Weeks ditched the car and made his way back on foot to where the Americans lived.

Learning of the uprising, Rogge, who himself was getting ready to eat dinner at his home in the American compound, dispatched a trusted Brazilian to cable Belém for reinforcements before the mob got to the radio. He then ordered Curtis Pringle, who by this point was in charge of Fordlandia's rubber planting, to evacuate most of the Americans from the estate, especially the women, who were "in a very nervous condition." Some left on the launch Rogge kept at the ready. Others availed themselves of "all means of transportation such as canoes, motor boats, horse back, etc."

Rogge, with his remaining staff, headed out to meet a group of about forty workers who were advancing on the American houses.

Smashed time clock.

"What are your grievances?" he asked them.

"We are mechanics, masons, and carpenters, not table waiters," they replied.

Rogge said he was sympathetic and promised to address their concerns, but only if they would go and calm their fellow workers. But the men sent to find liquor had returned, and the riot was "in full swing." When Rogge heard a group of drunken workers chanting "Brazil for Brazilians. Kill all the Americans," he decided that it was time to leave. He ordered his men to make for the tugboat, but David Riker, just back from Acre, and Archie Weeks found themselves cut off from the evacuation route. Fleeing into the jungle, they hid out for two days while the riot raged on.[12]

Rogge and the rest of his staff made it on the boat safely, passing the night anchored in the middle of the Tapajós. As the river's waves lapped against the hull, the "tremendous noise" that signaled the destruction of Fordlandia continued into the morning.

* * *

FORDLANDIA'S UPRISING WAS an aftershock of the revolution that had rocked Brazil a few months earlier, the one that brought Getúlio Vargas to power. Vargas's ascension was relatively bloodless, yet the frisson generated by his insurrection created a sense that the old rules no longer held and the old hierarchies no longer had to be respected. In the weeks before the December riot a number of Fordlandia's staff made mention of the charged atmosphere that enveloped the plantation—which is, perhaps, why Rogge kept a tug waiting. "A few radicals among the skilled workers," wrote Fordlandia's Belém agent, James Kennedy, to Dearborn, "misinterpreted the successful revolution all over Brazil which occurred in October and these radicals began agitating against anything pertaining to foreigners." Workers even hoisted red flags over their bunkhouses, which the Americans decided to let fly. But the ascension of Vargas also undoubtedly saved Fordlandia, for the man he named to replace Pará's governor, Eurico de Freitas Valle, who had led the campaign to revise Ford's concession, immediately agreed to provide whatever aid was needed to retake the plantation.

The riot began on Monday, and that night Kennedy wired Juan Trippe, the legendary founder of Pan American Airways, at his office in New York to tell him that Fordlandia had fallen to "mob rule." Trippe had recently established a trunk line between Belém and Manaus, with a mail and refueling stop in Santarém, and Kennedy asked if one of his planes could fly him and a few soldiers to the plantation. If they didn't get there soon, Kennedy warned, the "place will be a total wreck in 24 hours." Trippe immediately agreed.

The next morning, Tuesday, having secured a military detachment from the local army base, Kennedy, a Brazilian lieutenant named Ismaelino Castro, and three armed soldiers boarded a Pan Am twin-engine Sikorsky hydroplane, taking off from Belém's riverfront. It took about seven hours for the plane to reach the area, and when it landed in the early afternoon outside the town of Aveiros, just downriver from Fordlandia, Kennedy and Castro were greeted by Rogge and a few other Americans (the rest of the staff had fled to Santarém). Kennedy and the lieutenant decided to spend the night in Aveiros and travel to Fordlandia the following day. The next morning, they received word that the plantation had awaked quiet. But later that day, "irate" residents of Pau d'Agua and other villages that ringed Fordlandia's periphery marched on the estate's office with guns and machetes. Angry at the company's efforts to evict them, they were perhaps urged on by Francisco Franco, who after Oxholm's departure had developed an increasingly antagonistic relationship with Fordlandia, aggravated by Kennedy's heavy-handed efforts to force him to sell his property in Pau d'Agua.

Kennedy and Castro had the pilot of the Sikorsky swoop down and buzz the protesters, dispersing the threat. The plane then landed in the Tapajós and pulled up along Fordlandia's dock. Calm seemed to be restored, though Castro and his men went ashore on their own, telling Kennedy to wait behind.[13]

A delegation appointed by the workers received the lieutenant with a list of grievances they wanted to be presented to the company. High on the list was the demand that Ostenfeld be fired. The rest of the complaints had to do mostly with the right of free movement. Workers demanded to eat where, and what, they chose. They were tired of being fed whole wheat bread and unpolished rice "for health reasons," as per Henry Ford's instructions. They wanted to be able to frequent the cafes and restaurants that had sprung up around the work camp and be allowed to board steamboats, presumably to buy liquor, without first having to obtain permission. Single men complained about being jammed fifty to a bunkhouse.[14]

In the weeks after the riot, regional newspapers ran stories featuring other criticisms of the plantation's management. Manuel Caetano de Jesus, the mason fingered as the riot's instigator, told the *Estado do Pará* that the workers hated the time clocks, not just because they were unaccustomed to such regimentation but because the clocks were impractically placed too far from their work stations, making it difficult to punch in as required to do "under penalty of losing wages." Mario Pinheiro do Nascimento complained not just about being charged for food, which was not part of the deal when he contracted for work, but about the "very poor quality" of the food itself. The kitchen staff, he said, often served "rotten" fish "not fit for a dog kept hungry for three days."[15]

Others groused that come payday, the company, dependent on shipments of cash from Belém, was frequently short. So it handed out "cards" as markers. But if someone tried to leave, the plantation made it difficult to "exchange those cards for money." The hospital and medical staff had done much to improve the health conditions of the residents in the center of Fordlandia. Yet the death rate remained high from "beri-beri and other unknown fevers" for those who worked on the estate's outskirts building roads, gathering palm for thatch and timber, or clearing forest to plant more rubber. Pit vipers—large, thick-bodied snakes with a triangle-shaped head and rounded snout—continued to strike at the hands of workers as they chopped at the jungle's undergrowth.* Others made mention of cramped living conditions, of being made to work in the rain, or of mandatory trips to the hospital without reason or explanation.[16]

only the good of worker if in his best interest

FORD VISCERALLY OPPOSED the notion of workers representing themselves collectively; he once called unions the "worst thing that ever struck the earth." And as unions gained in popularity and strength, he seamlessly added labor leaders to his gallery of enemies. At the time of the 1930 riot, Ford could claim a series of victories against organizing campaigns led by the militant Industrial Workers of the World and the AFL-affiliated Carriage, Wagon, and Automobile Workers Union, and he would settle for nothing less in the Amazon. The men he sent down to Brazil, along with their supervisors back in Dearborn, were well versed in their boss's thinking when it came to labor unrest, and they took it as an article of faith that, as Sorensen would repeatedly remind Fordlandia's management, the company would not "let any strikers dictate how our business must be run."

So Kennedy told Lieutenant Castro flat out that he would not meet the protesters' demands "under any circumstances." Instead, he decided to use the opportunity presented by the riot to, as the sawyer Matt Mulrooney put it, "clean house." He wired José Antunes, owner of the namesake riverboat *Zeantunes*—Zé being short for José—who was in Belém waiting to bring a shipment of goods recently arrived from New York, along

---

*Also known as a bushmaster, this snake is among the most lethal in the world. Its Latin name, *Lachesis muta muta*, derives from Lachesis, one of the Fates in Greek mythology who decides individual destiny, and can be translated as "bringing silent death in the night," since, though it vibrates its tail prior to striking, it has no rattle.

with two hundred newly contracted employees, to Fordlandia. Kennedy told him to unload the cargo, dismiss the workers, and go to the Bank of London and withdraw an emergency shipment of cash.

As Kennedy waited for the money, a boat carrying thirty-five soldiers "fully armed and equipped with machine guns" docked at Fordlandia on Christmas Eve. The troops inspected the plantation, confiscating knives, guns, and any other implement that could be used as a weapon. Kennedy then ordered the soldiers to evict the residents of Pau d'Agua and the other shantytowns that surrounded Fordlandia and close down the bars, restaurants, and brothels that had long bedeviled the plantation. "Entirely clean them out," he told the soldiers. After the families were forced out and their houses torn down, Kennedy sent in the sanitation squad to "clean it up," to burn the latrines and pour quicklime into the pits. Shortly thereafter, with the backing of Vargas's government, he finally forced Francisco Franco to sell him the land where Pau d'Agua had stood for, as Eimar Franco puts it, "the price of a banana."[17]

The *Zeantunes* arrived on New Year's Day with the requested cash. Flanked by armed Brazilian soldiers, Kennedy gathered the plantation's workers together and paid them "for all time up to and including December 22." He then fired the entire labor force save a skeleton crew of a few hundred men.[18]

With Fordlandia in ruins and damages estimated to run over twenty-five thousand dollars, he waited to hear from Dearborn what to do next.

Part III

RUBBER ROUGE

Part III

RUBBER ROUGE

CHAPTER 16

AMERICAN PASTORAL

IT TOOK TIME FOR THE GREAT DEPRESSION TO REACH THE Tapajós, where Henry Ford's massive infusion of money and resources into the cash-poor economy offset the effects of plummeting commodity prices, capital flight, high interest rates, and declining exports that had shocked Brazil—and the rest of Latin America—immediately after the stock market collapse of October 1929. But back in Detroit, the impact was immediate. The crash hit the city hard, destroying more than two-thirds of its economy. In the years prior to the Depression, city and suburban factories had produced 5,294,000 cars worth $3.7 billion; four years later, the number had fallen to less than two million valued at $1.1 billion. Over 50 percent of the city's workforce was laid off. Hundreds of thousands of its residents either went on relief or simply packed up and left. Hundreds of thousands became homeless, many finding a bed in an abandoned factory the city had converted into a shelter. The suicide rate skyrocketed; four thousand boys and girls stood on breadlines for their daily meals; and 18 percent of schoolchildren suffered from severe undernourishment. The welfare department was reporting 7,500 monthly evictions. People were found dead on the street, poisoned by putrid food they had scavenged out of garbage cans. At night, men looted grocery stores while children prowled the streets, breaking shop windows and stealing goods. Some families dug holes in the ground for shelter, protected by nothing other than some laid-over brush.[1]

Ford at first restrained himself from using the crash to scold Wall Street and lash out at the money interests. He instead responded in a way many deemed responsible, preaching his gospel of consumer spending as a way out of the downturn. To back it up, he pledged that not only would he continue production at the Rouge full bore but he would raise his daily minimum wage from $6 to $7 a day. Ford seemed well positioned to lead the recovery: he himself had little invested in stocks, so his personal fortune was untouched, and his company, unlike General Motors, whose share price plummeted, wasn't publicly traded. Yet demand for the new Model A gradually slowed, and inventories backed up. Ford lowered its price, taking the difference out of dealers' commissions. But by the end of 1930, there was no margin left for any more reductions. The company quietly began to cut production and to buy more and more parts from outside low-wage suppliers—thus beginning the erosion of the fearsome self-sufficiency of the Ford Motor Company. By early 1931, the company had slashed the number of weekly hours of most workers, rendering meaningless Ford's vaunted Seven Dollar Day. Later that year, the company officially reduced that as well. And then in August the assembly line ground to a halt—Ford had more cars than customers to buy them. Just four years after its introduction in late 1927, the Model A, which Ford had hoped would have as long a run as the T, was history.[2]

As Ford approached his seventh decade, the destruction unleashed by the Depression and the fact that his company had been vulnerable to its effects accelerated his cultural conservatism. His worldview grew gnarled and knotted with fear and mistrust, and his mind, as the former head of his Sociological Department once put it, continued on its path to isolation. Forced to recant his anti-Semitism a few years earlier, he never again publicly criticized Jews. But the kind of optimism Ford had expressed early in the Depression took on a hectoring, recriminating tone. He began to link the nation's economic problems to his critique of the corrosive nature of America's modern consumer society. With Detroit children digging through garbage cans for food less than ten miles from his Fair Lane estate, Ford said he welcomed the recession's cleansing destruction, believing it would wash the excesses of the 1920s from the land. He pronounced the Depression a "wholesome thing in general," the "best times we have ever had." "It's a good thing the recovery is prolonged," Ford said, "otherwise the people wouldn't profit from the illness." His spokesman, William Cameron, who had previously penned many of the *Independent*'s anti-Semitic tracts, said on the Ford *Sunday Evening Hour*, a weekly radio show produced in a Ford studio, that the Depression was sent by "good Providence" to force atonement for "our former false prosperity." "The bad times were back in 1929 and before," Ford told a reporter. "That was the real panic—that so-called prosperous period. Business, at bottom, never was so bad as it was in what we called boom times."[3]

This last comment appeared in a long interview in the *New York Times* whose headline pronounced that Ford "Sees the Dawn of a Bright Future." Perhaps the interview, published in February 1933, was timed to preempt the momentum building around the cousin of his departed nemesis, Theodore Roosevelt. Franklin Delano Roosevelt took office a month after the interview, and Ford probably found much to like in his inspirational inaugural address. FDR condemned the stubborn incompetence of Wall Street's "unscrupulous money changers" and admitted that there was an "overbalance of population in our industrial centers." And he called for the "restoration" of "ancient truths" and "social values more noble than mere monetary profits." Yet early in his speech, the new president said that only a "foolish optimist can deny the dark realities of the moment," which the thin-skinned Ford must have taken as a reprimand.

It increasingly seemed to many that Ford's social criticism was a form of self-rebuke. His reformer image was wearing thin, as he and his company became implicated in many of the modern vices he condemned. Throughout the 1930s, Ford stepped up his jeremiads against crowded, dirty, crime-ridden cities. Yet even before the ruin of the Great Depression, Ford had contributed to the slow decline of Detroit's downtown by transferring much of his production and administration to Dearborn, paving the way for Chrysler and General Motors to likewise abandon the center of the city.

Ford lobbied for Prohibition, saying that Detroit's distilleries could be converted to make biofuels. Yet the criminalization of alcohol served only to deliver Detroit to gangsterism. Ford railed against finance capitalism even though his company was heavily invested in Detroit's Guardian Group, a banking house that, when it went bankrupt in 1933, helped spark a nationwide bank panic. Ford aggravated the crisis by first offering to bail out Detroit banks and then, perhaps acting on advice from Harry Bennett, withdrawing the offer. The collapse of the Guardian Group led to a wave of foreclosures of businesses and homes that would devastate the Motor City's downtown.[4]

Ford's social interventions were similarly corrosive. Ford complained about the ease with which technology could be used to manipulate mass society. But through the early 1930s, he lunched regularly with the fascist Catholic "radio priest" Charles Coughlin, who roused his listeners to fits of anti-Semitic rage and defended German Nazi violence against Jews during *Kristallnacht*. Evidence even suggests Ford funded the priest's campaign. Ford imagined himself a friend of African Americans, hiring them in large numbers—more than his competitors were—and paying them the same as he did whites. Yet most of his African American employees were confined to the Rouge's worst work, in its foundry, rolling mill, or paint shop, with little opportunity for advancement, while his gradual pullout from Detroit contributed to that city's deepening poverty and intensifying white vigilantism. And even as he expanded in Dearborn, he refused to challenge that county's system of segregation, which was considered the worst north of the Mason-Dixon line and lasted into the 1970s. He hired few African Americans outside the Rouge and practically none in his village industry program, designed to give workers a fuller, more balanced life. In his operations in Iron Mountain in the Upper Peninsula, a "concilium" of the KKK organized by Ford mill workers, who used Ford wood and kerosene to build and burn their inaugural cross, drove African American migrants looking for jobs out of town. The plant's manager issued a statement: "Mr. Ford wasn't employin' no colored people."[5]

Ford continued to preach pacifism. Yet not only had he already once turned his plants over to wartime production, his system of mass production helped make modern mechanized warfare possible.* Ford believed in community, but the highway system that developed in tandem with his car set small-town America on the path to destruction (to save his own childhood farm, he had to pry it from its foundations and move it wholesale). Ford celebrated self-reliance, though he did more than anyone to turn man into a cog in a machine. And of course he valued individualism even as he denied individuals the right to join a union if they wanted, responding to demands for industrial democracy by unleashing Harry Bennett, who throughout the 1930s would leverage his boss's paranoia and increasing divorce from reality to tighten his grip on the company. Bennett was well known in Detroit and its environs, where he maintained close connections with both law enforcement and the criminal underworld and where the local press treated him affectionately, like a colorful character out of a Damon Runyon story. But the stepped-up brutality committed by Bennett and his men during the Great Depression began to prompt other comparisons—namely to the fascist shock troops then on the march in Germany and Italy.

On Monday, March 7, 1932, Bennett's "service men" opened fire on a march of laid-off Ford workers and other protesters who arrived at the River Rouge to demand jobs and hunger relief. When the smoke cleared, five protesters were dead, another nineteen seriously injured, and the world outside the Rouge's gates got a close look, thanks to reporters and photographers on the scene, of what life was like for those who worked for the "despot of Dearborn," as the writer Edmund Wilson described Ford in *Scribner's Magazine*. Both Ford and Bennett escaped legal responsibility for the deaths, yet, as historian David Halberstam notes, the worldwide press coverage of the "Dearborn Massacre" was the beginning of the end for Ford's reputation as a benevolent reformer.[6]

Since his peace ship, Ford's philosophizing had been the subject of a good deal of ridicule and his industrial method the focus of serious

---

*This point was underscored after Ford's death when the president of Ford Motor Company, Robert McNamara, joined the John F. Kennedy administration as secretary of defense, a position in which he used industrial "systems theory" to rationalize warfare and wage "mechanized, dehumanizing slaughter" from the skies over Vietnam. See Gabriel Kolko, "On the Avoidance of Reality," *Crimes of War*, ed. Richard Falk, Gabriel Kolko, and Robert Jay Lifton, New York: Vintage, 1971, p. 15.

criticism, but starting in 1932 negative portrayals began to outweigh the positive. Aldous Huxley's *Brave New World*, with its forecast of a future made perverse by Fordism, was published just a month before the carnage; Jonathan Leonard's *The Tragedy of Henry Ford*, which came out a few weeks after, was greeted with a *New York Times* review headlined "Ford, the Small-Town Man Who Killed Small-Town Life." In 1937, Upton Sinclair's *The Flivver King: A Story of Ford-America*, asked: "What is Henry Ford? What have the years done to him? What has his billion dollars made of him?" Sinclair charged Ford with providing financial support to Hitler in Germany, and his accusation gained credibility a year later when the Nazi consul to Detroit bestowed the Grand Cross of the German Eagle on Ford on his seventy-fifth birthday. After the massacre, there also appeared a number of exposés of "the little man in Henry Ford's basement"—that is, of Harry Bennett, "general of the gangster army, and boon companion of the old man sitting in his estate on the hill, well within hearing of the shooting."[7]

Early 1932, then, with breadlines wrapping around corners, banks failing, factories closing, and protesters being shot in the street, would hardly seem like a promising moment for Diego Rivera to begin work on a celebration of the innovative "spirit of Detroit."

DIEGO RIVERA WAS relatively well known in the United States as the leading light of Mexico's muralist revival, an art movement that captured the energy of the 1910 Mexican Revolution. A leftist, Rivera was expelled from Mexico's Communist Party in 1929 after having been expelled from the Soviet Union the year before for his critical stance against Stalin. He came to the United States in 1930 to paint a series of frescoes for the San Francisco Stock Exchange and the California School of Fine Arts and to stage a retrospective of his work at New York's Museum of Modern Art. It was around this time that the Detroit Institute of Arts contacted him and asked him to "help beautify" the walls of its garden courtyard.

Rivera arrived in the city in April, a month after Bennett's massacre, with a free hand to take as the subject of his mural anything he wanted. The letter commissioning him merely suggested as a theme "something out of the history of Detroit, or some motif suggesting the development of the town." Edsel Ford, who sat on the DIA's board, offered to help the artist gain admittance to study any city business or factory that was still running. Rivera, though, knew exactly what he wanted to see and paint: the River Rouge.[8]

Despite the slowdown, the Rouge was still the grandest achievement of industrial capitalism to date. Rows of machines and belts at the Rouge were placed even closer together than they were in the old Highland Park factory, which meant that the Dearborn compound was larger than it seemed: had its machinery been spaced as it was at Dodge or Chrysler, or Highland Park, the physical plant would have had to be almost double in dimension. The genius of the Rouge, though, was not its size but its synchronized flow, with raw materials and finished parts moved from station to station by lorries, cranes, freight bins, assembly lines, and criss-crossed conveyor belts. The interchangeability of parts had become an obsession for the Ford Motor Company, and in the Rouge, as one employee put it, "every machine tool and fixture was fitted for the production of a single product whose every part had been standardized to the minutest detail." This is why it was so enormously expensive to switch over from the Model T to the A a few years earlier. Ford had to scrap or refurbish more than three-quarters of the plant's 45,000 specialized tools (valued at $45 million) and spend millions more buying 4,500 new ones. And the fact that Ford insisted on placing the Rouge's machines and workstations as close together as possible added to time and cost overruns because, as one worker put it, "the machines were in so tight that sometimes if we had to move a machine, we'd have to move four or five different machines to get that one out."[9]

Rivera, who never learned to drive, spent a month inside the River Rouge, visiting every one of its plants and sketching its operations. In his autobiography, Rivera tells of losing himself for whole days and nights in the Rouge's more than ninety buildings, observing the movement of its seventy thousand workers, "making literally thousands of sketches of towering blast furnaces, serpentine conveyor belts, impressive scientific laboratories, busy assembling rooms, also of precision instruments, some of them massive yet delicate, and of the men who worked them all." What others thought a deafening roar—like the British journalist Julian Street, who likened the sound of Rouge's predecessor Highland Park factory to Niagara Falls—Rivera heard as a "new music," a "wonderful symphony." His time in the labyrinth awakened his childhood "passion for mechanical toys," which had matured into an appreciation of the machine, "for its meaning to man—his self-fulfillment and liberation from drudgery and poverty." It was a sentiment Ford—who titled a chapter in one of his coauthored books "Machinery, the New Messiah"—surely would have recognized, for he similarly and repeatedly insisted that mechanization meant emancipation from material drudgery, more time to enjoy the finer things of life. "For most purposes a man with a machine is better than a man without a machine," he said. "Unless we better understand the mechanical portion of life, we cannot have the time to enjoy the trees, and the birds, and the flowers, and the green fields."[10]

After one month in the Rouge, Rivera spent another eight painting his masterwork. He saw his commission, financed mostly by Edsel Ford, as an opportunity to take the machine as an object of modern art, not in the gauzy, distant way that impressionists depicted trains running through a green valley or steam rising from a factory mill. Rather, he wanted, in his words, to bring the Rouge's "noise, smoke, and dust" directly into the institute's "charming sanctum," to unsettle the city swells. When he had finished, the museum's patrons did complain of the rudeness of his work. Asked why he hadn't chosen a more "traditional" subject, a still life, say, or a landscape, Rivera said that he "found any factory more significant and beautiful than any of the subjects they suggested." Collectively known as *Detroit Industry*, Rivera's murals are perhaps the most faithful tribute ever composed not just to the Rouge's power but to the holism of Henry Ford's thinking, even though Ford makes only a cameo appearance, in a small panel where he is teaching a trade school engine class.*

The murals comprise two major panels, along with a series of minor ones, mixing techniques drawn from cubism and futurism, social realism, classical and Renaissance art, and traditional Aztec, Mayan, and Olmec

---

*Four years earlier, in his Ministry of Education mural in Mexico City, Rivera painted a ghastly Ford sitting at a banquet table, along with J. P. Morgan and John D. Rockefeller, reading a stock market ticker tape.

motifs to depict over fifty major Rouge operations. The courtyard's north wall features towering spindles, casting boxes, sand blasters, rolling mills, and all of the ovens and machines needed to make the recently inaugurated V8 engine and transmission. In the background looms a volcano-like blast furnace, illuminated by flares of yellow, red, and orange. Rivera called the making of steel a thing of "plastic beauty," as "beautiful as the early Aztec or Mayan sculptures." The south wall mural, which depicts the finishing work of making a car, the stamping, pressing, welding, painting, and testing, is more restrained in terms of color and technique. Elsewhere in the courtyard, Rivera portrays other elements of the Rouge, its aviation and boat production, railroads, and powerhouses.

Unlike the haunting, unpeopled work of Charles Sheeler, who around the same time was capturing the Rouge in a series of widely publicized photographs and paintings, Rivera's frescoes are jammed with overall-clad workers—painters, welders, forgers, female spark plug testers, and even accountants—all the human energy that went into building a car. Productive motion is conveyed by contraposition. On the north wall, men, particularly those in the foreground, all seem to be bending backward, their muscular bodies pulling one thing or another. On the south, they lean forward, into their work. "I thought of the millions of different men by whose combined labor and thought automobiles were produced," Rivera said in his autobiography, "from the miners who dug the iron ore out of the earth to the railroad men and teamsters who brought the finished machines to the consumer," conquering "space and time" and winning "ever-expanding victories . . . against death."

Rivera, the Marxist, painted a few notes of dissent, including a small panel depicting workers leaving the factory over the pedestrian overpass where Bennett's men had gunned down the hunger marchers. While everywhere else in the murals humans run into one another, with no clear line fully separating one person from the next, suggesting connectivity and solidarity, here the solemn processional figures are distinct, implying that the alienation other critics of capitalism attributed to assembly production begins, for Rivera, at the factory's exit. The general mood of the frescoes celebrates determination, portraying workers energized by strenuous activity rather than enervated by machines. Rivera himself took great

From Charles Sheeler's 1927 series of River Rouge photographs. "The silence is awesome," wrote historian Leo Marx of another of Sheeler's works. "By superimposing order, peace, and harmony upon our modern chaos, Sheeler represents the anomalous blend of illusion and reality in the American consciousness."

pride when an engineer representing a group of Chrysler workers praised him for capturing the essence of the production process, fusing "together, in a few feet, sequences of operations which are actually performed in a distance of at least two miles, and every inch of his work is technically correct." The only thing missing, another group of workers told Rivera, was the factory whistle.

How Rivera managed this compression is the point where his frescoes move from merely representing the Rouge to embodying the idea behind it. Fordism is defined as an industrial process that breaks down the human movement that goes into making a product—in Ford's case a car—into its simplest component and then uses assembly lines to choreograph that movement to achieve maximum efficiency. It is a process that is impossible to observe sequentially over time, that is, by following the steps needed to transform raw material into finished product, since Fordism in its totality combines multiple subassembly processes that take place simultaneously— like a "river and its tributaries"—before converging in a main trunk line. Rivera achieved this effect by applying the medieval technique of polyscenic narrative, in which multiple scenes are placed together in a unified space. Such polyscenic narration usually tells a story over time, with the same characters appearing in different scenes that take place chronologically, that is, one after the other. The Detroit murals, however, illustrate specific tasks taking place in different places during a single moment, compressing into an integrated visual image the Rouge's intense interconnectivity and unrelenting flow. While medieval painters separated scenes with columns, archways, and windows, Rivera made use of Albert Kahn's snakelike conveyor belts and steel girders to move viewers from one discrete job to another, from foregrounded die and press workers to the foundry men deep in the painting's recesses, the whole thing backlighted orange by the forge fire.[11]

If Rivera's two principal panels sought to freeze in a single instance the multiple, simultaneous motions needed to produce a car (a defining feature of modernism is its reduction of experience to an explosive "now"), he also, in a series of surrounding paintings, revealed an appreciation of the millennia it took to produce both the raw materials and the human labor needed to make a Ford car. Above each of the two main

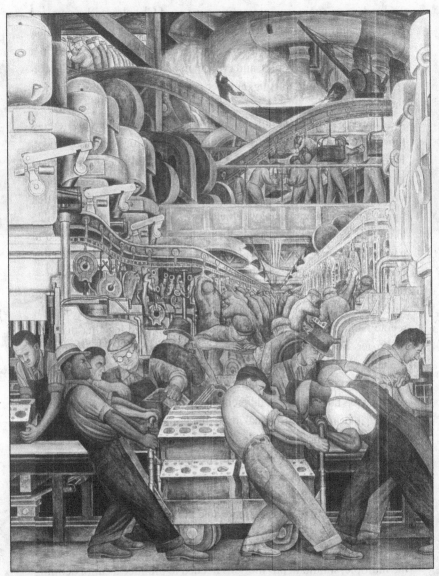

Auto workers thought the only thing missing from Diego Rivera's Detroit murals was the factory whistle.

frescoes are narrow oblong frames depicting geological sedimentation, layers of rock, fossil, crystals, limestone, crustaceans, and sand—in other words, the prehistory of much of the raw materials that fed the Rouge's forges, ovens, and furnaces (as well as the frescoes themselves, as tons of sand and limestone were needed to mix plaster and pigments). Elsewhere, Rivera included what could be a scene from an Upper Peninsula forest and a rubber tree being harvested by what appears to be Brazilian tappers (though no Fordlandiá latex had yet made it to the Rouge). And at the top of the walls, above the oblong geological panels, Rivera painted four nude females, allegorical representations of the world's great races, which produced the workers needed to extract the resources from the earth. In both style and sentiment, these allegories connect Rivera's Detroit frescoes to his Mexican murals, which often contained idealized, romantic portrayals of the glories of Aztecs or Olmecs, progenitors, in Rivera's epic visual history, of Mexico's revolutionary nationalism.

Neither Rivera nor Ford saw a contradiction in celebrating the power of machinery and science while at the same time idealizing a lost past. Ford shared Rivera's sense that his factory resulted from the collision of multiple time frames: industrial, geological, mytho-historical. Influenced by the eclectic spiritualism of his time, as well by his favorite author, Ralph Waldo Emerson, he repeatedly voiced beliefs that resonated with Rivera's upper panels—in reincarnation, in the existence of an "oversoul" composed of the accumulated experience of past lives, in the idea that "memory never dies." "We remember things from past lives in our present life," and not just individually but collectively, Ford said. He believed that the earth had nourished and lost many civilizations over millions of years—like Rivera's Aztecs and Olmecs—and that the knowledge produced by these civilizations had, in some mystical way, been handed down, culminating in the advancements of modern industry. "What survived is wisdom—the essence of experience."[12]

RIVERA LOST HIMSELF not just in the River Rouge in preparation for his Detroit murals but also in Greenfield Village, Ford's elaborate homage to rural America. By the time the Mexican painter arrived in the Motor City, Ford had added antique collecting to his many other late-in-life passions.

He had begun acquiring historical curios since at least 1906, when he started buying pieces of Edisoniana, anything to do with the life and work of his mentor and friend Thomas Edison, as well as copies of his beloved childhood school textbook, William Holmes McGuffey's *Eclectic Reader*. But collecting became a much more intense occupation following his humiliating 1919 trial, which was convened to settle a suit he filed against the *Chicago Tribune* for calling him an "anarchist." Ford's lengthy testimony became the talk of the country, as newspapers reported on his apparent illiteracy and his ignorance of historical events such as the American Revolution and the War of 1898. Asked to say who Benedict Arnold was, Ford replied: "He's a writer, I think," prompting hoots of laughter from the courthouse audience. It was around this time that he first proclaimed that "history is bunk," an opinion he would repeat throughout the 1930s and 1940s. "I say history is bunk—bunk—double bunk," he said in 1940. "Why, it isn't even true."

Ford was condemning not so much all references to the past as a particular interpretation of history, one that emphasized great men and their deeds. As historian Steven Watts has noted, Ford saw history in "surprisingly modern terms," not as an "empirical recovery of absolute truth but as *interpretations* of the past." If history was being "rewritten every year from a new point of view," how then, he asked, could "anybody claim to know the truth about history?" Ford's answer was to reject "great-man" history in favor of an account rooted in the slow evolutionary changes that occur in the "everyday life and work of ordinary people." He might not have been able to say what the War of 1898 was, but Ford was sure that stories of the kind that hailed the heroics of Theodore Roosevelt charging up San Juan Hill, even if they were true—which he doubted they were— had little to do with what drove progress. "The real history of a people was not expressed in wars," he said, "but in the way they lived and worked. . . . The history of America wasn't written in Washington, it was written in the grass roots." And any history book that celebrated "guns and speeches" but ignored the "harrows and all the rest of daily life is bunk," Ford insisted.[13]

Driving home from the trial, which he won, though the six-cent settlement he received was more a rebuke than a vindication, Ford turned to his secretary, Ernest Liebold, and said, "I'm going to start up a museum and give people a true picture of the development of the country." He also soon decided to build a town to go with the museum, asking without any prior conversation Edward Cutler, an architect in his employ, to draw him plans for a village. It was, said Cutler, "purely imaginative."

Over the next decade, Ford became the most famous antique collector in the world. Crates arrived daily in Dearborn, filling up the bays and warehouse of Building 13 of his now vacant tractor plant (production had been moved to the Rouge). Trucks and Michigan Central boxcars delivered anything one could imagine related to the mechanical or decorative arts—cast-iron stoves, sewing machines, threshers, plows, baby bottles, scrubbing boards, saucepans, vacuum cleaners, inkwells, steam engines, oil lamps, typewriters, mirrors, barber chairs, hobby horses, fire engines, kitchen utensils, Civil War drums, trundle beds, rocking chairs, benches, tables, spinning wheels, music boxes, violins, clocks, lanterns, kettles, cradles, candle molds, airplanes, trains, and cars. "We are trying," Ford told a *New York Times* reporter, "to assemble a complete series of every kind of article used or made in America from the days of the first settlers down to now. When we are through we shall have reproduced American life as lived."[14]

In October 1927—just a few days after Pará's legislature ratified Ford's Tapajós concession—Ford began work on both his town and his museum, modeled on Philadelphia's Independence Hall, to house and display his collection. Bulldozers cleared a two-hundred-acre lot and leveled off a knoll overlooking the Rouge River and workers started to lay the foundation for the Martha-Mary Chapel—built with bricks from the church where Clara and Henry were married and named after their respective mothers. Just upstream lay Ford's Fair Lane estate, a few miles downriver stood the Rouge factory, and the new town was built almost in the shadow of the smokestack crown of the complex's Powerhouse No. 1—eight chimneys as harmonious in their proportions as the eight columns holding up each of the Parthenon's two façades. "Life flows," Ford liked to repeat, but he would have a say in its course. Just as Blakeley and Villares were felling the first trees at Boa Vista, surveyors squared the site of a village green and workers began to lay railroad tracks and reassemble the scores of buildings that had been shipped from all over America—an 1803 Connecticut post office, the Wright brothers' bicycle shop, Abraham Lincoln's Illinois courtroom, Luther Burbank's botanical lab from California, Edgar Allan Poe's New York cottage, the homes of Patrick Henry, Daniel Webster, and Walt Whitman, Ford's childhood family farm, the Detroit shed where he built his first gas-powered "quadricycle," and, of course, Thomas Edison's Menlo Park, New Jersey, laboratories.[15] Ford named the settlement Greenfield Village, after his wife's childhood county, which by then had been absorbed by Detroit's sprawl.

Ford demanded historical faithfulness, ordering his engineers to rescue as much original detail from the structures and their surroundings as possible. For Edison's Menlo Park complex, he had seven boxcar loads of red clay shipped from New Jersey, along with the stump of an old hickory tree that was on the grounds. "H'm!" said Edison upon seeing the restoration, "the same damn old New Jersey clay!" Greenfield Village had everything that one could imagine as defining an American town before the arrival of Fordist mass production—a town hall, schools, a fire station, a doctor's office, a blacksmith, covered bridges, clapboard residences with neat flower gardens, and even liquor bottles (filled with colored water) in the inn's taverns, which Ford the teetotaler only grudgingly allowed after being urged by his wife. There was one detail, though, one mainstay of nineteenth-century small-town America, that Ford refused to replicate: a bank. The Ford Motor Company may have been forced to go into the lending business by setting up its Universal Credit Corporation, but Ford's vision of Americana would remain pure. His Main Street would stay forever untainted by Wall Street.[16]

Many in the press judged Ford's antiquarianism with contempt, pointing out the irony of the man singularly responsible for the disappearance of small-town America now claiming to be its restorer. "With his left hand he restores a self-sufficient little eighteenth-century village," wrote the Nation, "but with his right hand he had already caused the land to be dotted red and yellow with filling stations." "It was," said the New York Times, "as if Stalin went in for collecting old ledgers and stock-tickers." The New Republic chimed in: "Mr. Ford might be less interested in putting an extinct civilization into a museum if he had not done so much to

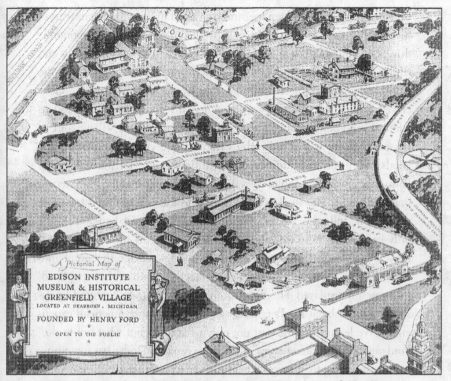

When an interviewer asked Edward Cutler, the architect of Greenfield Village, rendered above in a 1934 tourist map, if it was true that "just out of the clear sky one day, Ford asked you to draw a village," Cutler replied "yes."

make it extinct." And many intellectuals were particularly disapproving of his museum. Ford refused to consult curators to guide his collecting (even as in the Amazon he was forswearing botanists to help with his rubber plantation). One assistant remembers that Ford was "afraid of bringing in experts whose opinions might run counter to his." When his museum finally opened, it looked like, as one historian put it, "the world's biggest rummage sale," organized with no rhyme or reason.[17]

There was, however, logic at work. The vision of technological progress on display in Ford's museum and village — from the crafts era through mechanical steam engines to industrial manufacturing — was obviously self-serving, ending in the revolution in mass production that he presided over. Yet there is also a deep weariness revealed in this vision, a distrust of the flash of consumerism that had overtaken the American economy, driven by dotted-line loans and the induced demand of "trumpery and trinkets," as Ford put it, goods which performed "no real service to the world and are at last mere rubbish as they were at first mere waste." Conceived during the roiling twenties when his company was forced to adopt yearly model changes and easy loans, Greenfield Village and its museum, along with Ford's obsessive, massive collecting of material goods and historical buildings, was an antidote to the fetishism of cheap consumer products that had overtaken the economy, and the hucksterism that sold them. The stock market crash and the onset of an intractable depression, followed by the aftershocks of successive banking crises, only heightened Ford's desire for solidity. The items in his village and museum embodied the social relations and knowledge that went into making them, preserving the essence, in fact the breath—when it opened, his museum displayed Thomas Edison's last exhalation, captured by his son in a test tube at Ford's request—of a more durable American experience. "We learn from the past not only what to do but what not to do," Ford once told an interviewer. "Whatever is produced today has something in it of everything that has gone before. Even a present-day chair embodies all previous chairs, and if we can show the development of the chair in tangible form we shall teach better than we can in books." He said that one shouldn't "regard these thousands of inventions, thousands of things which man has made, as just so many material objects. You can read in every one of them what the man who made them was thinking—what he was aiming at. A piece of machinery or anything that is made is like a book, if you can read it. It is part of the record of man's spirit."[18]

DIEGO RIVERA DIDN'T share the scorn other intellectuals and artists heaped on Greenfield Village. During his stay in Detroit, Rivera visited the model town, wandering around its streets, houses, mills, and workshops from seven in the morning to one thirty the next. He recognized its sense of proportion and how it related to the nearby River Rouge plant. "As I walked on, marveling at each successive mechanical wonder," he recalled in his memoirs, "I realized that I was witnessing the history of machinery, as if on parade, from its primitive beginnings to the present day, in all its complex and astounding elaboration."[19]

The holism that Rivera identified in Ford represents a particular kind of pastoralism, an American pastoralism that didn't oppose nature and industrialization, or man and the machine, but saw each fulfilling the other. Much of Ford's faith that industry and agriculture could be balanced and that community would be fulfilled rather than overrun by capitalist expansion drew specifically from Ralph Waldo Emerson. Yet it's a conviction that had deep roots in American thought. As historian Leo Marx has pointed out, with the exception of the Southern slave states, American history reveals little opposition to mechanization and industrialization. America itself, Marx wrote, has often been held up by many of its celebrants as a machine in the New World garden, representing both a release of historical energy through the "seizure of the underlying principles of nature" and a domestication of that power through its Constitution—described as a "machine that would go of itself," a self-regulating, synchronized system of checks and balances.[20]

The main struts of Henry Ford's philosophy all had antecedents in eighteenth- and nineteenth-century American political and literary concepts: that mechanization marked not the conquest but the realization of nature's secrets and thus the attainment of the pastoral ideal; that history is best understood as the progress of this realization, of the gradual liberation of humans from soul-crushing toil; and that America has a providential role to play in world history in achieving this liberation. It was from such wellsprings of technological optimism that Ford was drawing when he predicted that his Muscle Shoals project would "make a new Eden of our Mississippi Valley, turning it into the great garden and powerhouse of the country." Against Marxists who warned that an impending "crisis of overproduction" would bring down capitalism, Ford countered by predicting that "the day of actual overproduction is the day of emancipation from enslaving materialistic anxiety." To those who thought industrialization deadened mind and spirit, Ford responded by saying that want was the true cause of alienation. "The unfortunate man whose mind is continually bent to the problem of his next meal or the next night's shelter is a materialist perforce," he said. "Now, emancipate this man by economic security and the appurtenances of social decency and comfort, and instead of making him more of a materialist you liberate him."[21]

These and similar pronouncements were not merely self-aggrandizing conceits on Ford's part. Many saw the cheap, durable car he made available to the multitudes as the "spontaneous fruit of an Edenic tree," to quote the Spanish philosopher José Ortega y Gasset's description of the quickness with which man embraced the automobile. What else could explain the effortlessness with which the Model T, after its demise, could be transformed into an object of pastoral nostalgia, as ornery as the animal it replaced? "If the emergency brake hadn't been pulled all the way back," E. B. White wrote in a 1936 *New Yorker* essay titled "Farewell, My Lovely," "the car advanced on you the instant the first explosion occurred and you would hold it back by leaning your weight against it. I can still feel my old Ford nuzzling me at the curb, as though looking for an apple in my pocket."[22]

As a response to the Great Depression, Ford's drive for balance and holistic self-sufficiency manifested itself in a number of ways: he increased his commitment to village industries and hydroelectricity; he said small household gardens would do more to offset poverty than government relief and urged his River Rouge workers to grow their own food; and he promoted his "Industrialized American Barn" at the 1934 Chicago World's Fair as a solution to the farm crisis. Ford also stepped up his funding of "chemurgical" (a neologism coined in 1934, combining the Greek words *chemi*, or the art of material transformation, and *ergon*, work) experiments, many of which took place in Greenfield Village's laboratory, to find new industrial uses for agricultural products. Many of his ideas were harebrained, an industrial version of medieval alchemy. Ford once had a truckload of carrots dumped in front of Greenfield Village's lab and told its chemists to find useful properties from their pulp. But he did have some significant successes. Iron Mountain chemists figured out how to use wood chips to make artificial leather, while the lab at Greenfield Village developed many new uses for soy meal and soy oil.

There is symmetry at work in what Ford thought he was doing at Dearborn and what he hoped to accomplish on the Tapajós, and the progress of both Greenfield Village and Fordlandia proceeded on remarkably parallel tracks, functioning almost as counterweights to each other in a pendulum clock, counting out the last long stretch of Henry Ford's long life. Ford's experience with model towns and village industries in the Upper Peninsula and lower Michigan set the stage for his frustrated Muscle Shoals proposal and then for both Greenfield Village and Fordlandia.

This evolution of thought partly explains why Ford never bothered to seek the guidance of other corporations such as Hershey or the United Fruit Company, even though they had long experience building and running company towns in Cuba, Central America, and elsewhere. Fordlandia was to benefit from the combined knowledge of Ford's many village projects in the United States. In the Amazon, Ford fully expected that chemists would turn the minerals, oils, and plants found on his estate into lubricating grease, fuels, paints, soaps, rope, fertilizers, and insecticides. Fordlandia's managers sent hundreds of samples back to Dearborn, as well as to Chicago's Field Museum, and today one can find dusty boxes in the Ford Archives filled with seeds, barks, and leaves of a variety of tropical flora, accompanied by notes indicating their acidity and nitrogen levels, as well as their ash, sodium, and lime content. Just as Ford hoped his village industries would achieve self-sufficiency through hydroelectricity, he thought that the Tapajós would provide enough power to limit the use of purchased gasoline; that the sawmill would cut hardwood not just for local use but for sale to support the plantation; that not just proper hygiene and decent health care but flower gardens and square dancing—which Ford would promote in Fordlandia as a response to the December 1930 riot—would cultivate virtuous workers; and that all of this applied craftwork, supplemented by Ford-founded and -funded schools, would produce a new generation of skilled workers. This is why so many of the men—Rogge, Mulrooney, Weeks, Perini, and others—along with their wives and children, who went down to start and run Fordlandia were from the Upper Peninsula, where the Ford Motor Company had first tried to combine the rational and efficient harnessing of nature with the orderly and aesthetic organization of humans.

OVER THE COURSE of the 1930s, Ford's vision began to turn in on itself. Before the Great Depression, the Ford Motor Company could seriously have claimed to have solved many of the most pressing problems that arose from the Industrial Revolution. It proved that capitalism could benefit not just the banker or the monopolist but the masses. And it showed how mechanization could not just drive down labor costs but increase buying power and free individuals from menial labor, allowing them more time for personal enjoyment and satisfaction outside the factory gates. But modern consumer capitalism created a whole new set of problems, aggravated by a depression seemingly without end.

Ford lived long enough to see himself and his system of production implicated in many of the vices he preached against. He also witnessed the ascendancy of Theodore Roosevelt's cousin Franklin as head of a political coalition—the New Deal—that was setting America's reform agenda. Ford's opposition to FDR and his program of government regulation flowed from the same kind of pastoralism that powered his technological optimism: a view of industry and nature as existing in fundamental harmony by extension tends to take even the mildest form of government interference as perverse.* Of course, his exhortations to self-reliance and patronage of village industries had as little chance of solving the problems revealed by the Great Depression as Fordlandia managers had of taming the Amazon. Yet Ford never relented in his condemnation of the New Deal's solution to the crisis: the promotion of unionism, government regulation of industry, and establishment of federal relief.

Specifically, Ford refused to warm to Roosevelt and his New Dealers. "People like that," he told Charles Lindbergh, "always get what's coming to them." But Ford not only saw the country elect FDR four times but witnessed the federal government complete its Tennessee Valley Authority project, in effect carrying out the Muscle Shoals proposal Ford made a decade earlier.† It would be Roosevelt and not Henry Ford who would bring cheap electric power to the farmers of the lower Appalachian Valley.[23]

---

*Ford's patronage of chemurgy, for instance, was an attempt to provide a corporate, private-sector alternative to government remedies for the rural crisis; if the industrial market for crops could be enlarged, there would be no need to regulate agricultural production, as the New Dealers proposed (Howard P. Segal, *Recasting the Machine Age: Henry Ford's Village Industries,* Amherst: University of Massachusetts Press, 2005, p. 34).

†Roosevelt signed the TVA Act on May 18, 1933, shortly after his inauguration. The legislation was sponsored in Congress by none other than George Norris, the Nebraskan senator who led the campaign that successfully denied Ford Muscle Shoals nine years earlier. The

In the last years of his life, Ford responded to these setbacks by losing himself in the past, in the details of Greenfield Village. Even as the Chrysler Corporation was pushing ahead despite the financial crash with its namesake modernist masterpiece in the busy heart of New York City, Ford was fussing over spinning wheels and rag dolls. And as GM and other businesses were rationalizing the modern corporate management structure, Ford's once revolutionary company was turning gothic, presided over by a gangster who ran the labor force as if he were a medieval lord.[24]

Ford fell into a depression when his longtime friend Thomas Edison died in late 1931. The carmaker would preside over one more breakthrough

act created the Tennessee Valley Authority, which soon became a working laboratory for many of the New Deal's rural initiatives and a testing ground for a new aesthetic style that sought to reconcile regionalism with modernism. Spectacularly successful, the TVA brought together hydraulic and electrical engineers, doctors, architects, economists, teachers, artists, and thousands of well-paid, unionized workers to carry out an enormous experiment in social planning. As Arthur Morgan, the engineer in charge of the project, put it, the "Tennessee Valley is the first place in America where we can sit down and design a civilization." Despite Ford's antipathy, many New Dealers drew inspiration from the carmaker's village industries and used the TVA to complete an ambitious agenda that included many of Ford's favorite ideas: dam building for flood control and hydroelectricity, dredging to improve navigation, reforestation, efforts to stem soil erosion, and prevention of disease, including malaria and hookworm. They even created a model town, Norris, Tennessee, named after Ford's adversary and described as a "rural-urban community where 1000 to 2000 people can have four-acre family gardens, modern city conveniences of pure water, electricity for cooking and heating, attractive homes, and the added interest of a town forest." Like Ford, FDR imagined the development of the Tennessee Valley having an exemplary effect on the whole country. He said that Muscle Shoals would become "part of an even greater development that will take in all that magnificent Tennessee River from the mountains of Virginia to the Ohio," benefiting "generations to come" and "millions yet unborn." In many of the discussions surrounding the TVA, an implicit analogy was drawn between the raging, uncontrolled, and flood-prone river with an unregulated boom-and-bust economy and the need for government intervention and planning to put both in service to human beings. FDR drew a similar comparison in his 1935 dedication of another large-scale public works project, the Hoover Dam in Nevada: "As an unregulated river, the Colorado added little of value to the region this dam serves. When in flood the river was a threatening torrent. In the dry months of the year it shrank to a trickling stream. For a generation, [residents] had lived in the shadow of disaster from this river which provided their livelihood, and which is the foundation of their hopes for themselves and their children. Every spring they awaited with dread the coming of a flood, and at the end of nearly every summer they feared a shortage of water would destroy their crops." See William E. Leuchtenburg, "Roosevelt, Norris, and the 'Seven Little TVAs,'" *Journal of Politics* 14 (1952): 418–41; Arthur Morgan, *Log of the TVA*, New York: Survey Associates, 1936, p. 19; Tim Culvahouse, ed., *The Tennessee Valley Authority: Design and Persuasion*, New York: Princeton Architectural Press, 2007.

engineering triumph: the V8 engine, introduced in 1932, would serve as the industry standard for decades to come. But Ford's body and mind began to yield. He continued to dress with precision, his back revealing only the slightest of stoops. And in interviews, he could still rouse himself to gracious animation of the kind he displayed to the Brazilian consul José Custódio Alves de Lima years earlier. He was charming when hosting Diego Rivera and his wife, Frida Kahlo, for dinner during their stay in Detroit, even after Kahlo asked him if he was Jewish. Yet those close to him noted that he was losing his sense of humor, and the malevolent side of his personality was becoming more manifest. Ford had renounced his public anti-Semitism, but in his private conversations with his old *Independent* staff, as well as with friends like Charles Lindbergh, the main point of conversations remained "the Jews." They, along with the Communists, GM, the Du Ponts, and FDR, Ford was sure, were trying to take over his factory. And though, as some have noted, his anti-Semitism remained detached from the close relations he had with many Jews, the nastiness he began to show his close associates, including the sadism with which he treated his son, Edsel, was visceral. As was his stoking of Harry Bennett's brutality. "Harry, let's you and him have a fight," Ford would gleefully whisper to his enforcer, siccing him on a troublesome worker.[25]

The balance Ford tried to achieve between industry and agriculture, society and community, gave way to a full-on retreat into antiquarianism. Between the River Rouge and Greenfield Village, Ford increasingly preferred the latter. Nearly every morning found him at its Martha-Mary Chapel, where the village schoolchildren started their days singing hymns. "He spent so much time around the village," remembered Edward Cutler, the architect who had planned Greenfield. "It was a relief for him to get down there." Ford would walk the village streets, sit under a tree and play his mouth harp, or warm himself by a fireside hearth. He refused, at least during the village's early years, to have a telephone installed. "He didn't want any way for them to get a hold of him," remembered Cutler.[26]

Frank Lloyd Wright, who earlier had praised Ford's vision for Muscle Shoals, was less understanding than Rivera of what he condemned as Ford's unrestrained traditionalism. Speaking of a trip he made to the River Rouge early in the Depression, Wright praised a building designed by

Albert Kahn as a perfect synthesis of form and function. "It was really a fine thing," he said, "eight hundred feet long, beautifully lighted. The sun was shining in it, and over about half of the shining surface of maple flooring was planted with wonderful machinery, with men working at the machines." But Ford—"the captain" as Wright called him—was nowhere to be found. He was "out playing" in his museum with his "old things, . . . reprehensible enough in themselves, and now worthless." Such antique "slumming," Wright thought, was part of a general escape from the innovative modernism of the 1920s into a sham traditionalism (an escape likewise represented by the wanderlust ballads that so entranced John Rogge on the Tapajós). Besides, Ford's "old cast-off things" weren't even American. Real Americanism was vital and organic, like Kahn's River Rouge. What Ford was collecting was "Georgian" carried over "to this new freedom by the Colonials because they had none other or better to bring."

Wright couldn't explain Ford's turn. "This is a man," he said, "from whom the future had a right to expect something more than sentimentality."[27]

In the Amazon, too, Ford's vision began to split apart. He took a personal hand in many of the decisions involved in rebuilding Fordlandia after the 1930 riot, particularly as they related to education and recreation. Yet as the attainment of the original motive for the project—to grow rubber—became increasingly elusive, Fordlandia became more and more a museum piece, Ford's vision of Americanism frozen in amber.

CHAPTER 17

GOOD LINES, STRAIGHT AND TRUE

BACK IN BRAZIL, A "PALL" SETTLED "OVER EVERYTHING" IN FORD-landia once the immediate threat of the December 1930 riot passed, a report back to Dearborn said. The Americans returned to their homes, but in the months after the clash they felt "intimidated" and "not sure that they cared to remain" on the plantation. They seemed paralyzed, "waiting for something to happen." The women were nervous, the men on edge. The skeleton crew of workers retained by James Kennedy had begun rebuilding the plantation's physical plant. Electricians got the generator working again, and laborers installed windows, hung doors, and fished trucks out of the Tapajós. Yet a sense of distress, of impending trouble, remained. It was as if the shock of the Great Depression, held at bay through 1930 by the magic of Ford wealth, had finally arrived on the Tapajós.

Even before the uprising, Ford had feared that his namesake plantation was spinning out of control into a cesspool of waste, vice, and ridicule. For a brief period after the departure of Oxholm, under first Victor Perini's and then John Rogge's supervision, the situation seemed to be improving. But the riot created a new sense of concern and urgency. So in February

1931, he once again sent Victor Perini, who a year earlier was forced to leave the plantation due to chronic edema, to make things right. This time Perini was accompanied by W. E. Carnegie, Ford's head accountant, and Archibald Johnston, a Sorensen man from the River Rouge.

Many on staff thought the team had come to shutter the plantation. In the United States, Ford was spending much of his company's savings on keeping his American business running and one newspaper after another announced that he was planning to abandon his Brazilian operations. "Report Ford Ending Para Rubber Work," ran a February 1931 headline in the *New York Times*. "Americans Assert Tropical Laborers Cannot Be Made to Punch a Time Clock as in North." Yet the Dearborn representatives did not announce, as many thought they would, the end of Fordlandia. They instead reaffirmed the company's commitment to build a "model city" in the jungle, one complete with restaurants, shops, churches, schools, decent, well-maintained houses, and "places of amusement." Once the town was established, Carnegie told a reporter from the *Times*, it would "elect its own Mayor, maintain its own fire department and police force and levy and collect its own taxes. In other words, it will manage its own affairs as a strictly independent community."[1]

"The plan is one of expansion," Carnegie continued, "by which the Brazilian people and the company will be brought together in a closer union of interests."

FOLLOWING A COSTLY riot, in the midst of a worldwide economic contraction seemingly without end, with his company for the first time ever running a deficit, even as rubber prices were tumbling, Ford decided to allot even more resources to his Brazilian venture. He did quietly send out feelers to see if any Brazilian interests would purchase the concession but was told that no one "would put money into the Rubber Company where there was no prospect of obtaining a profit for many years to come." And he continued to fund the efforts of the now eighty-four-year-old Thomas Edison, right up to Edison's death in 1931, to extract industrial-quality latex from goldenrod and other plants. Yet while Edison announced to the press that he was drinking an all-milk diet so that he would live long enough to find an alternative to tropical rubber, he told Ford that the production of synthetic latex was not feasible. When Soviet scientists issued a report around this time claiming that they had synthesized industrial-quality rubber from petroleum, the inventor, insisting that oil could not be turned into latex, denounced it as a fake. "It just can't be done," he said. Edison's opinion might have influenced the carmaker's decision to keep Fordlandia going.[2]

In truth, Ford couldn't just abandon a project literally linked to his name, one so grandiloquently proclaimed to the world. And here the Depression actually reinforced the decision to stay in the Amazon. Back home Ford was spending even more money on his village industry projects, which by this point had evolved from a remedy for the dislocations of the twenties to a strategy for surviving the 1930s. "There may be no immediate business reason for decentralization," admitted a Ford spokesman in 1935, "but there may be a human reason . . . and it would seem that our life is such that what is humanly desirable and morally right presently justifies itself as being economically practical." And though shop-floor reality was quite different—with stalled assembly lines and drastically reduced hours for workers—Henry and Edsel, through 1930 and 1931, repeatedly told the press that not only would they not cut wages, they would invest even more money in the River Rouge. The same boosterism took place in the Amazon.[3]

A miracle was needed in those bleak first years of the Depression. And Ford was only too happy to supply one. His company reversed its previous tight-lipped policy regarding Fordlandia, which it had adopted in the wake of the concession scandal, and began issuing press releases and supplying facts and statistics to any reporter interested in Ford's operations on the Tapajós. And sure enough, there began to appear after the riot a series of articles in US and Brazilian papers reprising the fanfare that had announced the original settlement a few years earlier.[4]

"No Business Depression Here," ran a headline in the *New York Times* two days after Christmas 1931, over a photograph of Ford's Tapajós town. "This is Fordlandia," the caption said, "where the automobile manufacturer is spending millions of dollars on the scientific growing of rubber. The settlement, once a waste, has been converted into a model city where high wages prevail." Around the same time, the *Washington Post* wrote that "electricity and running water in native homes were miracles undreamed before Henry Ford went to the tropics to develop his own sources of rubber supply." The *Chicago Tribune* likewise reported on the "modern city" rising in the jungle, one that would soon boast hundreds of "Swiss cottage type" homes, along with shops, parks, a church, a bank, a movie theater, and bus service: "Fordlandia, an up-to-date town with all modern comforts, has been created in a wilderness that never had seen anything more pretentious than a thatched hut. Water is supplied under pressure after it has been thoroughly filtered to remove dangers of fever infection, and electric light illuminated bungalows in a region where such inventions are proof of the white man's magic." And in the Upper Peninsula, the *Iron Mountain Daily News* told its readers, many of them Ford employees, that "Henry Ford has transplanted a large slice of twentieth century civilization" to the Amazon.[5]

This was increasingly the justification for Fordlandia, broadcast in the material supplied to the press as well as in international company correspondence. The longer it took the plantation to achieve its original purpose and produce latex, the more it was defended as a missionary project, a model for what Ford, and by extension America, could accomplish in the world. "Mr. Ford," said the *Washington Post* in 1932, "not only intends to cultivate rubber but the rubber gatherers as well." "A civilizing mission," agreed Major Lester Baker in a note published in the *Times*, a "dream."[6]

For Gerald Drew, who replaced John Minter as the American consul in Belém, Ford's utopianism was the "only theory" that could explain what he saw unfolding on the Tapajós. "Mr. Ford considers the project as a 'work of civilization,'" he told his superiors in Washington, including the secretary of state. Nothing else, he said, could explain the extravagant sums of money the company was spending on Fordlandia.[7]

Over the next decade, the company downplayed the need for rubber as providing Fordlandia's rationale and instead emphasized its civilizing mission. On Ford's Sunday *Evening Hour*, broadcast nationally, Linton Wells, the baritone-voiced foreign war correspondent, told listeners how the "skill and wits" of the Ford Motor Company had triumphed over the "tricky" and "perverse" Amazon jungle. Wells, who during World War II would be tapped by FDR to find a possible homeland in Africa for European Jews (he recommended Angola), described the creation of the town "on the edge of nowhere" almost "like magic" and praised it for containing all the "traditional essentials for health, happiness, and well-being." There were "churches, schools, and a splendid hospital, with a medical staff from Detroit's famed Henry Ford Hospital. Shops, movies, restaurants, and comfortable homes lined palm-fringed streets. There were electricity, telephone and sanitary services and an 18-hole golf course."[8]

Such cheerleading was not just for public consumption. Dearborn officials were telling one another the same things throughout the 1930s. After visiting the estate, Charles Sorensen wrote to Henry Ford that he should be proud of Fordlandia, for it was indeed a "school of civic education."[9]

"I think you would be well advised," wrote one Dearborn manager responding to an economics professor who asked for information on Fordlandia to include in a lecture, "to point out to your listeners that Mr. Ford's whole project is still in an experimental stage—that his experiment is as much sociological as industrial. Indeed, it is in the sociological field that he has thus far registered his finest achievements in Brazil."[10]

PERINI AND CARNEGIE, in consultation with Rogge, laid out an ambitious plan to have the reality catch up to the promise. The first thing they had to do was rebuild the workforce, which had shrunk to a few hundred workers. The plantation began to hire again, topping off at about fifteen hundred workers and their families—bringing Fordlandia's population up to around five thousand—within half a year. This time, though, the employment office took pains to vet applicants more systematically than in the past, when managers were only too eager to receive boatloads of job seekers, hiring anyone who was close to healthy, to offset the high turnover rate. Perini and Carnegie came to believe that during Fordlandia's first year or so, Einar Oxholm had unknowingly employed labor radicals, along with a "large number of criminals." The plantation therefore began to work more closely with the new Vargas government, itself involved in an attempt to consolidate its authority. Back in the States, the Ford Motor Company, which distrusted the government when it came to policy or regulation, had no problem with law enforcement. During the first Red Scare, from 1919 to 1921, it had regularly opened its files, including all the information on the personal lives of workers gathered in the wake of the Five Dollar Day announcement, to local police and the FBI, as a way of rooting out potential subversives. At Fordlandia, Perini and Carnegie put a similar system of vigilance into place, with a file opened on every job applicant, to be shared as needed with the police and military. Each worker was henceforth required to carry a "small book similar to a passport," which would include a photograph, fingerprint, signature, and previous police records.[11]

The next step was to complete as quickly as possible the "irradiating center of civilization," as Edsel described Fordlandia, long promised by Henry Ford himself. On the eve of the riot, beyond the American compound and the handful of well-built bungalows the skilled workers occupied, Fordlandia as a town existed only on the Dearborn blueprints rolled out for reporters two years earlier. The bawdy shantytowns on the edge of the plantation had been reduced to ashes and quicklime right after the December riot, though the bunkhouses and ramshackle village where married workers had lived still stood. As Fordlandia began to hire again, single workers and families moved back in. But Perini and Carnegie decided that this village was unacceptable, that a proper town needed to be raised, with a "civic center" complete with stores, movie theaters, and "all other utilities usually found in a city." They also recommended a significant expansion of Fordlandia's school system so that it could enroll all the children of the plantation's large labor force. And since it was no longer practical for the Ford Motor Company, dependent as it was on riverboat operators, local purveyors, and foreign banks, to be, as it had been to that point, the sole source of daily necessities, from shoes and clothing to coffee and food, Perini and Carnegie recommended that the plantation contract out to local "concessionaries" the right to establish businesses in the new town, with the company remaining responsible for health inspections and keeping prices fair and low. In keeping with their vision of small-town America, they recommended a series of small Main Street shops, each one specializing in providing a specific item or service, such as shoes and haircuts.[12]

But before they had a chance to put much of their plan into effect, Victor Perini was struck sick again. He tried but just couldn't take the wet Amazon heat. As occurred during his first visit, his legs and face swelled up, his eyelids grew puffy, and his skin broke out in a rash that refused to be soothed by lotions or steroids. He returned to Michigan, again just after a few months on the Tapajós, and soon after retired from the company, settling with Constance in Detroit. Carnegie also had to get back to his accounting

Archibald Johnston.

responsibilities. And Rogge, while considered by Dearborn to be trustworthy and efficient, was thought an ineffective supervisor of men, a fact underscored by the events of December. He stayed on as an assistant manager, but Archibald Johnston was put in charge of rebuilding Fordlandia.

Johnston was forty-seven years old when he took over in the middle of 1931. Born in Scotland, he had a thick brogue, intelligent eyes, and brushed-back tawny hair and was dubbed the "White Tiger" by the Brazilian press, as much for his swift adaptation to jungle living as for his poise in navigating through Belém's political scene. Not only did he rebuild the labor force and reestablish Ford's authority (with the help of the Brazilian police and military) but it was he who finally secured the company's long sought-after tax and tariff exemptions.[13]

With Rogge and Curtis Pringle as his assistants, Johnston also made some progress on turning Fordlandia into a real town. At first he had a hard time finding the kind of concessionaires Perini and Carnegie recommended to meet the settlement's needs. Local merchants were reluctant to specialize in one or two items. Francisco Franco, for instance, across the river, kept a small warehouse stocked with knives, rifles, ammunition, rope, candles, grains, sugar, shoes and sandals, cooking utensils, and perhaps a guitar or two to advance on credit, or to sell outright if cash was on hand, to rubber tappers and other river dwellers. But he was hardly likely to open a butcher shop or a shoe store typical of an American Main Street. As Victor Perini reported to Dearborn just prior to his departure, merchants "all want to conduct a general store" because in "small towns like Santarém it seems to be the custom for a merchant to sell everything that he can stock, including liquors of all kinds. They do not look so favorably upon the idea of one man running a shoe store, another a grocery, and a third man a meat market, as all felt that they should be permitted to sell whatever they can."[14]

Johnston eventually did contract with enough concessionaires to open a bakery, barber shop, shoe store, tailor, a store selling "notions and perfumery," two grocery stores, a vegetable and fish market, and a butcher. He also found someone to take over the repaired dining hall, now divided between the larger "Ford Restaurant" on one side and a slightly more upscale eating place for skilled workers on the other.[15]

Then he turned to Fordlandia's housing crisis. The plantation's original plans from 1928 called for the building of four hundred two-room houses "per Ford Motor Co. drawings," at a cost of $1,500 each—clearly

"There was nothing down there to absorb their earnings," said Ernest Liebold.
So Fordlandia opened a series of shops, including a shoe store.

Started w good intentions, became ab responsibility + benefiting him insufficient for the thousands of workers and their families who had come to the settlement. In truth, this failure to address workers' housing needs was not that different from what was happening in Michigan. Despite his famed paternalism and acquisition of towns like Pequaming, Ford, except for a small experimental community of 250 homes, largely tried to avoid providing houses for his Dearborn and Detroit workers, believing his high wages would be enough to create prosperous neighborhoods. He steadfastly ignored the city's mounting housing problems, which had dogged the automobile industry since the beginning of its expansion. Workers lived in overcrowded slums, flophouses, and tenements, most without decent plumbing, electricity, or heat, with African Americans consigned to the worst of the lot.[16]*

But on the Tapajós, the Ford Motor Company recognized that it couldn't escape the responsibility for supplying decent living quarters, and Johnston, in the wake of the riot, was determined to get it right. He demolished the "disreputable straw village" where workers with families had crowded, replacing it with over a hundred new palm-roofed adobe houses equipped with water and electricity and laid out in "good lines, straight and true." He cleaned up the riverfront and graded, paved, and named the streets that ran through what was finally beginning to look like a midwestern town, with sidewalks, streetlamps, and red fire hydrants. Dearborn, though, wasn't happy with the thatched houses and

---

*Urban poverty in America is often presented as a result of industrial decline. Yet historian Thomas Sugrue, in his *The Origins of the Urban Crisis: Race and Inequality in Postwar Detroit* (Princeton: Princeton University Press, 1996), argues that the roots of poverty and housing discrimination are inextricably linked to the consolidation—not the decline—of American industrial capitalism, not only to the refusal of corporate leaders like Ford to take responsibility for providing adequate housing for a growing urban working class but to specific choices made by companies to relocate in suburbs and other hard-to-unionize rural areas. Meanwhile, in Dearborn, Ford's River Rouge African American workers, 12 percent of his total workforce, were isolated in poor surrounding townships like Inkster, living in pitiful bungalows, with little access to basic services like decent schools for their children. The Great Depression finally forced Ford to spend tens of thousands of dollars to rehabilitate Inkster. But it was too little, too late and served only to reinforce segregation in Dearborn, which the Ford Motor Company never contested and which lasted well into the 1970s. Detroit continued its slide into urban poverty as Ford, General Motors, and Chrysler moved more and more of their work out of the city.

A snug bungalow on the Tapajós.

ordered Johnston to build proper midwestern-style clapboard bungalows. Johnston tried to reason with his superiors, saying that the huts
were "no disgrace to the Amazon region." He explained that "the natives
are quite happy and willing to live in them and as long as they are no
detriment to the health of Boa Vista, we feel that they should be allowed
to use them so why build more wood houses now?"[17]

But it was not thatched roofs and mud walls that impressed visiting reporters, who inevitably pointed to Fordlandia's handful of "Swiss cottage
type" homes and "snug bungalows" as exemplars of a "model colonial
town." So Johnston and Rogge got to work, and by the end of 1933 there
were over two hundred "modern houses" for laborers and foremen.

Designed in Michigan, the houses proved to be totally inappropriate
for the Amazon climate. Brazilians objected to the window screens that
Ford officials insisted be used, believing that they served not to keep bugs
out but to trap them in, "much as an old-fashioned fly-trap collects flies."
Amazon dwellers also preferred dirt floors, which were cooler than wood
or concrete ones. But Victor Perini, who during his first visit had inspected
housing conditions with Dr. Beaton, believed that beriberi was caused by

Straight and true: Fordlandia's Riverside Avenue, with Tapajós River to the right.

sleeping in low-slung hammocks with one's back close to the cold clay. So Dearborn ordered that all houses have poured concrete for flooring.[18]

Metal roofs lined with asbestos, chosen by Ford engineers to repel the sun's rays, in fact kept heat in. The "workers' houses were hotter than the gates of hell," recalled a priest who ministered in Fordlandia, "because some faraway engineer decided that a metal roof was better than something more traditional like thatch." They were "galvanized iron bake ovens," said Carl LaRue, commenting on Fordlandia's foibles years later. "It is incredible that anyone should build a house like that in the tropics." Another visitor described them as "midget hells, where one lies awake and sweats the first half of the night, and frequently between midnight and dawn

undergoes a fierce siege of heat-provoking nightmares." They seemed to be "designed by Detroit architects who probably couldn't envision a land without snow."[19]

Ford managers, said the priest, "never really figured out what country they were in."

They never really figured out who their workers were, either. In addition to inappropriate housing, Ford managers laid on a program of civic education and wholesome recreation that had little to do with the Amazon—and everything to do with America, or at least Henry Ford's understanding of America.

CHAPTER 18

MOUNTAINS OF THE MOON

THE FIRST TIME CONSTANCE PERINI MET HENRY FORD WAS IN 1926 as she was lying in bed in his namesake Detroit hospital, recovering from a long illness. "Stay right there," he said to family members who made to leave when he came in. "I'm not going to hurt anybody."

"Are you comfortable here?" Ford asked Mrs. Perini.

"Very much."

"How do you like Iron Mountain?" he inquired.

It was winter when the Perinis arrived in the Upper Pensinsula, having come from Manchester, England, where Victor worked in the Ford plant, and the Michigan town was covered in twelve feet of snow.

"I don't know what Iron Mountain looks like. All I've seen is roofs and snow. They don't even have sidewalks."

"Oh yes, they have sidewalks up there. You'll see them when the snow goes away."

"I don't know . . . we'll see when the snow goes away."

"You'll see," Ford replied, "there are plenty of sidewalks there and dandelions. You will be able to put flowers in and show them how to do it."

On his way out, she heard Ford tell her husband, "I knew she would come out all right. You can be proud. You've got a good wife. She is a good housekeeper and a good mother. Take care of her."

Constance recovered her health and returned to Iron Mountain, where she took Ford's advice. She planted flowers that spring, and sure enough, she said, "the idea must have taken hold on the rest of the town because the next year everyone got to work planting flowers and bushes. You would be surprised at what a difference it made." Ford, when he visited, "was quite pleased with the looks of the places on this visit," said Mrs. Perini. "He said so to several people."[1]

Here then, summed up, is Ford's civilizing injunction, issued in his home state years before he made his move into the Amazon: Go forth and plant flowers.

FOR HENRY FORD, gardening captured his vision of holistic Emersonian self-sufficiency, in which aesthetics and economics, nature and mechanics worked as one. At his Fair Lane estate in Dearborn, his wife, Clara, presided over twenty gardeners, three greenhouses, a sprawling general garden, a ten-thousand-plant rose garden, and the restoration, under the guidance of the naturalist John Burroughs, of a great portion of their land to its forested state. Ford also promoted gardening as an integral part of the curriculum of the many schools he supported in the United States, including those in Greenfield Village and his village industries. He gave his Upper Peninsula lumberjacks, jobbers, sawyers, and other mill workers plots of land to grow vegetables for their own use. In Dearborn, starting in 1918, the company began to make 35-by-60-foot plots available to employees on Ford property and encouraged homeowning workers to keep flower and vegetable gardens in their yards. Colored posters appeared around the Highland Park and Rouge plants letting workers know about Ford's Garden Education Service. A "company-gardener" was "on hand during all daylight hours to answer all questions" on how best to lay out plots, when to plant, and how to prepare and fertilize the soil. Workers paid a dollar for these services, which included the provision of seeds. The fee was "totally inadequate to cover the cost," noted an internal memo, but "sufficient to give each participant a 'stake' in the project." Through the Great Depression of the 1930s, Ford pushed gardening as an alternative to government relief. And by the end of the decade, some fifty-five thousand of his employees kept home gardens and another three thousand workers maintained garden plots on Ford-allotted land.[2]

And so in Fordlandia, as part of the post-riot rebuilding program, both Henry and Clara Ford became personally involved in promoting gardening, saying that it was their "expressed wish that the planting of flowers and vegetables be incorporated into the estate's school curriculum and encouraged among its workers." Roy McClure, chief of surgery at Detroit's Henry Ford Hospital, wrote to Archie Johnston that "Mr. Ford expressed considerable interest in the schools and in the hope that the medical program and perhaps gardening projects might be started as they have been at Dearborn, Georgia, Northern Michigan, as well as Wayside Inn."[3]

As with housing, Archie Johnston did what he could to comply. But here, too, he found the gap wide between Dearborn principles and Tapajós practice. "We are aware that Mr. Ford wants every home to have a small plot of ground in connection with same," Johnston wrote Carnegie in Dearborn, "but we wonder if the picture of Boa Vista has been properly presented to him." He pointed out that because the Brazilian settlement was nestled tight between the river and a hill, to give each house the 12,000 square feet of land Ford suggested would stretch out the population center. "One might say, what does that matter, but let us consider the costs, this means miles and miles of water mains, electric poles, wire, sewers, time lost in maintenance."

Johnston fudged when it came to spacing the houses. He bunched them up closer than Ford demanded. As to gardening, he told Dearborn that "we will do the best we can." But it was the dry season and there was much work to be done and ground to be cleared. Workers had made considerable headway during the 1930 rainy season, with the seed supply secured by Rogge on his trip up the Tapajós. And a good deal of forest had been cleared in the dry months leading to the December riot, with much of it planted by the skeleton crew kept on after the clash. Yet Johnston felt that too much time had been wasted in the months after the uprising, and he wanted to focus his energies on what he felt he had been put in charge to do, grow rubber. He was learning quickly that he had to spend a lot of resources dealing with the insects that attacked the maturing rubber trees, and he didn't want to expend any more of them trying to fend off the creatures that fed on fruit and vegetables. "Bugs," Johnston wrote, "both crawling and flying, are a great handicap." In addition, it wasn't easy to acquire the seeds for the kind of horticulture Henry and Clara suggested.[4]

He did try. Every new house was given a quarter acre of land to plant, and households were provided seeds and seedlings. Many of Fordlandia's workers had experience in maintaining *roças*, small jungle clearings where they grew vegetables, tubers, beans, fruits, and herbs. Others had farmed on the seasonally enriched floodplains.[5] And well before Ford started promoting gardening in the Amazon, many of Fordlandia's workers who lived in Pau d'Agua and other villages had raised pigs and chickens and kept vegetable and manioc plots. This ended up being a problem for the plantation, since too much access to land made Ford employees less dependent on Fordlandia's wages, restaurants, and commissaries. It also contributed to a high turnover rate among workers, as many would just quit and go back to their home communities to plant or to fish.[6] As in Michigan, Ford preached decentralization, and he hoped his garden program in Fordlandia would encourage a "sense of propriety and personal pride"—yet not so much pride that his workers would be able to forsake a cash salary altogether. So even as Johnston was encouraging residents to plant flowers and vegetables he was ordering families to dismantle their corrals—as his counterparts in the Upper Peninsula had done a decade earlier in Pequaming—thus prohibiting them from keeping livestock in their yards. Gardening, he said, should be geared to the "improvement of the street in general instead of small individual squares."[7]

Eventually, the plantation established a garden club and posted notices around town, translated into Portuguese:

Many persons here have expressed their wish that there be a concerted effort to beautify our streets and houses. It seems that this wish is shared, more or less, by every family and every person on the plantation, but up until now this wish has not been publicly shown and therefore has not been generally recognized. The cultivation of gardens contributes greatly to the general well-being of any community and is a source of pleasure to the owner as well as an improvement to the neighborhood. . . . With these thoughts in mind there has been inaugurated a Garden Club to which any family and any individual may join.

This announcement was followed by the "Best Home Garden" contest. The first-place prize would be twenty-five dollars, with the highest score given to the garden that was "attractive as well as practical, that is, it should have a combination of vegetables and flowers."[8]

JOHNSTON DIDN'T REALLY believe gardening would achieve self-sufficiency or even contribute to the moral improvement of character. He did think, though, that it could occupy children and stop them "from being destructive with trees already planted"—after school, they had a habit of trampling through just-planted fields and nurseries, and a gardening club, Johnston hoped, might otherwise absorb their energies through the afternoon.[9]

How to keep people busy—Americans so they didn't feel like "prisoners," Brazilians so they wouldn't decamp out of boredom or, worse, revolt—had become a major worry of Fordlandia's managers. It was a concern before the 1930 uprising. Right after the first food strike in 1928, Oxholm purchased six soccer balls, hoping that the sport would allow his men to blow off steam. And following every subsequent labor conflict, some Ford official would come up with a new remedial amusement. But after the 1930 riot, with the razing of the bordellos, bars, and casinos that had entertained workers during their off-hours, the provision of recreation became a more pressing issue for plantation officials. In their report back to Dearborn, Perini and Carnegie suggested setting up a "soft drinks and ice cream shop" and a "bandstand," so that the "natives would soon organize a band among themselves."[10]

As to the Americans, the company worried that they "have practically no diversion, and get extremely tired of seeing the same faces at all times and places." Dearborn urged its plantation staff to take vacations, to visit Belém or Manaus. Roy McClure, head of Detroit's Henry Ford Hospital, wrote a note to Edsel suggesting that Fordlandia residents take a railroad

New roads to roam: A Ford touring car stuck in Fordlandia mud.

trip through the jungle on the near defunct Madeira line "or wherever they wish to go in order to clear their minds of petty grievances which arise in some people who get to feeling they are prisoners."[11] Workers built playgrounds for children and a tennis court for adults, and Carnegie and Perini thought that if enough road was rolled—by 1934 there were close to thirty miles of paved and dirt thoroughfares—then "an automobile trip," in Ford "station wagons," of "several miles will also be possible."[12]

Back in the United States, golf had grown in popularity in the years after World War I, and like many other corporate managers Ford Motor Company officials, including Reeves Blakeley, who while in Belém negotiating the terms of the Tapajós concession could often be found shooting holes on a jungle range outside the city limits, had become avid players. And the *Dearborn Independent*, reflecting Ford's growing cultural conservatism, particularly his distrust of large, easily manipulated urban crowds, promoted

"The golfer never looks backward": Fordlandia's Winding Brook Golf Course.

golf as a substitute for baseball. Ford's paper criticized America's pastime for concentrating "ten thousand people" in one place while giving them little to do other than to sit in "cramped-up positions watching nine men handling a bat and a ball. . . . A large portion of our so-called sportsmen are mere shouters and noise makers, and have no more claim to be regarded as exponents of any particular game than the Roman mob which attended the gladiatorial contests in the arena." Golf, in contrast, got "people out of the crowded city to the pure air of the seaside or the country." It encouraged spectators to become participants themselves, not as part of a "team" but as individuals. The paper urged municipalities throughout the country to build golf courses as a way of promoting civic virtue, since a "community playing golf in its leisure moments should have no time for less edifying pursuits." Golf develops "foresight and perseverance," as the "golfer never looks backward; 'Fore' is his slogan, and his aim is to drive his ball clear of all traps and pitfalls." And so Ford workers on the Tapajós moved forward, laying out a nine-hole course adjacent to the American compound and the "nature park." Archie Weeks's daughter, Leonor, dubbed the links the "Winding Brook Golf Course," since it ran along an *igarapé*, or stream.[13]

Hunting was another sport that the Michigonians brought with them to the Amazon. In the forest they shot jaguars, panthers, and large snakes. The staff was allowed the "occasional use without charge of company boats," and men went out on the river on shooting expeditions. Opening fire into large congregations of caimans provided a way more to vent frustration than to test hunting prowess, though it took more skill to kill manatees and *botos*, the river dolphins that Brazilians affectionately and mischievously blamed for otherwise unexplainable pregnancies. The Americans were also encouraged to go on boating trips, yet the Tapajós was treacherous. Violent storms could be conjured out of a blue day, with afternoon wind heading up the valley crossing with the downstream current to create more than a meter-high chop. Santarém's Catholic cathedral is adorned with a gilded life-size iron Christ on a cross made of local itauba wood, a gift from the Bavarian naturalist Karl Friedrich Philipp

Ford workers and administrators, including, in the center, James Kennedy, John Rogge, and Dr. and Mrs. Smith, view a "sea cow," or manatee. A note on the back of the photograph says it weighed 600 pounds.

Ford tugboat trapped in a river-grass island.

von Martius for his having narrowly survived a fierce storm just off the shores of the town in 1819. The inscription thanks "divine pity" for saving him from the "fury of the Amazonian waves." Floating islands, as big as twenty acres and ten feet deep, posed another threat, able to encircle a craft and paralyze its propeller with their underwater vines. Swimming in the river was likewise dangerous, filled as it was with "alligators, piranhas, electric eels, sting rays, and large water snakes, sometimes as long as 30 feet." So once the houses Johnston had built, complete with indoor bathrooms and showers, were ready for occupancy, and two swimming pools, one for common laborers, the other for skilled workers and staff, were excavated, the company discouraged river bathing.[14]

There was radio reception, of the kind that brought Rudy Vallee to the

Mulrooneys. The company made sure that the Ford *Sunday Evening Hour*, which broadcast wholesome American music as well as safely exotic fare, such as the Ford Hawaiians, reached the plantation. But reception was often ruined by static. And with "victorola records and books" slow to arrive, managers continued to sponsor community-wide public activities, mostly on Saturday evenings and Sunday afternoons but also occasionally during the week. Brazilian workers participated in competitive sporting events, such as soccer, boxing, and foot races, which helped not only to keep them occupied but to entertain the Americans, particularly bored women. But all enjoyed the vaudeville show staged by the managers. One extravaganza was such a "big success," wrote Archie Johnston to Dearborn, that "everyone says it is the best ever here."[15]

At the end of 1931, Johnston built an open-air dance hall where the plantation held, at Henry Ford's urging, traditional American dances. Back in Michigan around this time, Ford, as part of his broader antiquarianism, began to sponsor fiddling contests and sent agents to scour the nation to record the steps of traditional dances before they disappeared or were corrupted by the "sex dancing" that was sweeping America. He also established his own private record label, Early American Dances, and hosted balls in Dearborn and in his growing collection of inns, farmhouses, and village industries throughout the country. Employees understood invitations as "thinly disguised commands" to attend, and they did their best to maneuver through waltzes, polkas, minuets, square dances, as well as the quadrille and the ripple. All guests—even Harry Bennett, who liked to wear bow ties so that in a fistfight his opponent couldn't get a hold on him—were expected to follow proper decorum: men, not women, were to initiate the dance and there was to be no cutting in and no crossing the middle of the dance floor. Benjamin Lovett, the instructor Ford contracted to organize these balls, wrote in his *Good Morning: After a Sleep of Twenty-Five Years, Old-Fashioned Dancing Is Being Revived by Mr. and Mrs. Henry Ford*, published in 1926, that protocol dictated that the man was to guide the woman without embracing. There would be no bodily contact except for the thumb and forefinger, which were to touch the woman's waist as if "holding a pencil." Boxes of the book were shipped up to Ford's towns in the Upper Peninsula, to Alberta, Pequaming, and other villages, where for a time the local schoolchildren took daily dance classes.[16]

In his encomium to Ford's music patronage, Lovett linked specific dances to "the racial characteristics of the people who dance them." Modern American dancing, with its flappers moving to the fox-trot, shimmy, rag, Charleston, and black bottom, not to mention the obscenely sensuous tango, had been sullied by influences "that originated in the African Congo, dances from the gypsies of the South American pampas, and dances from the hot-blooded races of Southern Europe." But Ford was rescuing a truer tradition of dance that "best fits with the American temperament, . . . a revival of the type of dancing which has survived longer among the Northern peoples." Ford himself traced the rot not to Africa, Argentina, or Italy but to Jews. The *Independent*, during its run of anti-Semitic articles, complained that the "mush, the slush, the sly suggestion, the abandoned sensuousness of sliding notes are of Jewish origins."[17]

Ford's dance revival clearly reflected his conservative turn. As the historian Steven Watts writes, the industrialist "deployed swirling, waltzing couples and stamping square dancers as skirmish lines in a larger cultural campaign to reclaim and defend American values and practices from an earlier day." Fordlandia allowed Ford to go on the offensive, to advance his campaign into the Amazon and reclaim its inhabitants, some of them already under the sway of dances like the Charleston, for a more virtuous sociability. In the rain forest, Ford made his counterthrust against Jazz Age culture not only with dance but also with verse. The man many the world over blamed for "trampling down individuality, beauty, and serenity, and erecting machine altars to Mammon and Moloch" sponsored in Fordlandia readings in Portuguese translation of Emerson, Henry Wadsworth Longfellow, and, ironically, William Wordsworth, the poet who declaimed against the mechanical "fever of the world" leading a "rash assault" on English greenery.[18]

IN ADDITION TO buying soccer balls to keep workers busy, Captain Oxholm also asked Charles Sorensen to send him a "moving picture outfit." Sorensen did, and Fordlandia began to screen films. But the projector the

Fordlandia dance hall, with movie screen on back wall.

Rouge sent down was outdated and the movies available from Belém's distributor were old, "terribly scratched, warped and dried out." And workers complained of boredom if the same picture was screened too many times. When Johnston took over management, he secured a better sound projector, which allowed him to feature more up-to-date films. He found a Fox agent in Recife who could supply the plantation with B action pictures, the "type that is best liked down there," said Johnston. Rio's movie industry was just getting started in the 1930s, and Johnston tried to show Brazilian films whenever he could, especially the popular *chanchadas*, slapstick musicals, including a few starring a young Carmen Miranda. "We intend putting on a good show for our workers," Johnston said. It's unknown if he ever had the opportunity to screen *Law of the Tropics*, a Warner Bros. picture partly based on a 1936 *Collier's Weekly* article on Fordlandia. The film, released in 1941, was a bust in the United States, panned by the *New*

"We intend putting on a good show": John Rogge, second from left, Curtis Pringle in the middle, and James Kennedy with camera, filming scenes of family life.

York Times for unrealistically depicting a "verdant" jungle where "mosquitoes never bother any one."[19]

Fordlandia also put on a good show for Dearborn. By the 1930s, Henry Ford had embraced celluloid as a way to link together his far-flung empire. Film crews would document his camping trips with Thomas Edison, Herbert Hoover, and John Burroughs; aerial shots of Mexico; scenes of street life in Bridgetown, Barbados; Diego Rivera painting the Detroit Institute of Arts; surgeries in the Henry Ford Hospital; Ford mines, mills, and dams; and each and every subassembly process that went into making a Ford car. Fordlandia, too, was filmed, as a decision was made early to "build up a complete history of our development in detail," for "a ready reference to any given operation." Henry Ford specifically asked to see "action, pictures, etc. etc." of Fordlandia's garden program.[20]

Johnston sent roll after roll of raw 16 mm footage to Dearborn, to be screened for officials, including Henry and Edsel, so they might get a sense of the plantation's progress and everyday life. These reels were largely made up of random, uncaptioned images: men sawing trees and clearing jungle, Americans shooting caimans and gutting manatees, chunks of meat dangled in the river to provoke a piranha frenzy, lingering head shots of workers, who seemed to have been chosen to illustrate the region's racial diversity, schoolchildren listening courteously to their teacher, and workers lining up to receive their paychecks, undergoing a medical examination, or playing soccer as women and children looked on. Many of these images were folded into in-house documentaries detailing different facets of Ford's vast holdings or into films focused on latex, such as *Redeeming a Rubber Empire*. In exchange, Dearborn sent news and documentary shorts down to Fordlandia, familiarizing Brazilian workers with other branches of the Ford family. *New Roads to Roam* and *Streamlines Make Headlines* introduced them to the Lincoln Zephyr, a luxury car made by a company Ford purchased in 1922, and let them know they were living in a new, aerodynamic age. *Making Wooden Wheels for Autos* gave the estate's residents a picture of the Rouge's state-of-the-art machinery that made the spokes and rims that would soon be framing tires made from Fordlandia latex.

Dearborn also provided films capturing the age of discovery, which was largely made possible by the rapid advances in transportation technology. Fordlandia workers and managers watched *Bottom of the World*, about Admiral Richard E. Byrd's expedition to Antarctica, a "rare, unbelievable record of the strangest and queerest things on earth" in which "not a scene" was staged (Byrd, partly funded by Edsel, named a mountain range after his patron). *Some Wild Appetites* let them enjoy "monkeys, alligators, tortoises, otters, opossums disporting themselves at feeding time." And *Hell Below Zero* took them to central Africa on an expedition commissioned by the Milwaukee Museum in search of the legendary Mountains of the Moon, a snow-capped 16,000-foot-high range separating what is today Uganda and the Democratic Republic of Congo. Deep in the sweaty sea-level Amazon, clackity film projectors beamed onto an outdoor screen the "fantastic sight of natives shivering before a campfire on the mythical line of the Equator."[21]

A whole set of films featured the heroism not of explorers but of Ford's cars, which could put the most remote places within the imaginative reach of the common man. Increasingly after World War I, newspapers reported on global expeditions that tested the endurance of the Model T. How far into the Amazon could it penetrate, how far up Machu Picchu could it climb? *Ford News*, an in-house paper for company employees, regularly ran stories about the adventures of the T along the Inca Highway or into the Mayan jungle. If Ford's car could make it, then anyone could, and so the age of exploration gave way to the age of tourism. In Fordlandia, in addition to documentaries about expeditions to the South Pole or up the Mountains of the Moon, the estate screened Ford-produced films such as *Yellowstone National Park* and *Glacier International Park*, promoting automobile leisure travel and introducing plantation workers to America's natural wonders, accessible as never before thanks to Ford.

Most of the company's historic film stock is stored in the United States National Archives in Washington, D.C., and judging from the sharp juxtapositions of otherwise unrelated shots—footage detailing, say, the synchronous industrial choreography of the Rouge followed by a bucolic panorama of farm life, or scenes illustrating the glacial pace of rubber tapping preceding images of dizzying assembly lines and conveyor belts—Ford officials and managers seemed to revel in contrasting the primitive with the modern, which highlighted their role in speeding up the world. In early 1928, for example, the *Ford News* ran a story reporting on a momentous event: the world's first in-flight movie. Outfitted with a projector and screen, a Ford TriMotor, the first mass-produced metal-clad airplane, took off from a Los Angeles airfield with curtains drawn as eight "theatrical people" settled into comfortable wicker chairs. The movie selected for the occasion, Harold Lloyd's *Speedy*, was a sly choice. Unlike Charlie Chaplin's later *Modern Times*, which offered a dark critique of Depression-era industrial speedup, Lloyd's movie is a Jazz Age celebration of the velocity of modern life. The plot of the film involves Lloyd's fighting not to save Manhattan's last horse-pulled tram but to make sure its owner gets a good price for selling his route to a motorized trolley monopoly. As the Ford TriMotor circled over Los Angeles, its passengers probably laughed at the opening scene of a tourist guide pointing out a "vehicle that has defied the rush of civilizashun—the last horse car in New York."[22]

* * *

ON THE TAPAJÓS, Johnston had finally succeeded in replicating a shiny American town, with neat houses, clean streets, shops, and a town square. It was, one traveler said, a "miniature but improved Dearborn Michigan in the tropical wilderness." He even managed to re-create some of the social conventions of Main Street America, at least as Ford imagined them, with weekly dances, movies, and other forms of recreation, including golf courses, tennis courts, swimming pools, and gardening clubs. Fordlandia paid good wages, provided decent benefits, including health care, and tried to cultivate virtuous workers. Yet Johnston was still finding it hard to usher in Ford's vision of modern times. In Dearborn, Ford's famed paternalism was diluted by the diverse resources available to workers in an urban, industrializing society. But in the Amazon, running a remote plantation with impoverished labor in a hostile environment, Fordlandia's managers found themselves presiding over an extreme version of cradle-to-grave capitalism — literally.[23]

Hundreds of babies were born each year in Fordlandia, creating a whole new set of problems for its managers. Amazon residents were used to giving birth at home under the care of a midwife. Ford doctors frowned on the practice, yet did not want to tie up hospital beds for obstetrics. So they didn't push the issue until a woman died in childbirth in late 1931. From then on, medical and sanitation squads added a new responsibility to their ever growing list, as they checked women for pregnancy and made sure no illicit midwifery was taking place.

Once born, children needed care. Dr. McClure had hopes that Dearborn chemists would soon find a "satisfactory substitute for cow's milk with soy bean milk" that could be used to feed infants and toddlers. But until then, Fordlandia's hospital distributed Borden's Klim, a powdered whole milk, to new mothers. The staff quickly learned that utensils had to be provided as well, since most workers didn't own dishes, or "even a spoon," to prepare the powdered milk, using instead their fingers to mix the powder in empty cans. Before long the plantation, on instructions from Edsel, had established a day-care center, named after Darcy Vargas, President Vargas's wife. Working mothers could leave their children in the care of company nurses, under the supervision of doctors who made daily visits. Johnston complained that the center "cost considerable money to operate." Children also needed to be educated, and before long the company was running seven schools in the Amazon, named after Ford's son and grandchildren, teaching home economics for girls and vocational training for boys, and gardening and ballroom dancing for all. "Shades of Tarzan!" ran the caption under a photograph of children in a company brochure celebrating the plantation. "You'd never guess these bright, happy healthy school children live in a jungle city that didn't even exist a few years ago!"[24]

Despite such cheery publicity, children on the Tapajós, including many who lived in Fordlandia, continued to suffer. Malnutrition remained one of the plantation's most obdurate problems. "The cemetery," McClure reported to Edsel, "contains children's graves far in excess of adults."

After the December riot, Dearborn attempted to hire more married than single men, with the idea that men with families would be less transient and more dutiful. But married men often trailed behind them not just a wife and a few children but an extended network of relatives, ever in danger of becoming wards of Ford's largesse. "These *caboclos*," wrote Johnston, "all seem to have a lot of hangers on." To discourage them from coming to Fordlandia, he suggested that they be provided with nothing "other than food."

Johnston was finding it difficult to abide by his own judgment. He tried to cut off commissary credit to the wife of an injured worker laid up in the hospital, since she was using the food she purchased on the credit to feed her extended family of three cousins and three nieces and to prepare meals for sale to unmarried workers. But when Johnston went to speak with her, she pleaded hardship. "God only knows my worries," she told the engineer. The "poor woman is probably correct," Johnston admitted, fearing that if he cut her off her immediate family would go hungry. He relented. "It is hard to know where to stop," he said. "We take care of all cases which actually need help."

Workers were still dying, leaving widows behind. "Widow Francisca Miranda" was an "old timer" who has "caused plenty of trouble" for the staff, insisting that she had the right to tap Fordlandia's wild rubber trees. Johnston concluded it was probably "easier" just to give her some money.

And there remained the issue of burials, which the company still paid for, though it did try to pass off responsibility for the cemetery to Santarém's Catholic bishop. But the bishop's priests were stretched thin throughout the Tapajós valley, and he was already annoyed that Fordlandia refused to place its schools under his authority or pay for the construction of a proper church. So he demurred, consenting only to have his clerics occasionally pass through the plantation to say mass and minister the sacraments. Without a resident priest, Fordlandia would have to continue to bury its own dead.[25]

All these social problems, though, would pale beside the one looming just ahead with nature.

CHAPTER 19

ONLY GOD CAN GROW A TREE

HENRY FORD ONCE CALCULATED, AS PART OF HIS QUEST TO REDUCE the complexities of the production process to their simplest components, that it took 7,882 distinct tasks to make a Ford car, and he divided the number by the physical and mental capabilities of his workforce. "Strong, able-bodied and practically physically perfect men" were required for 949 jobs; 670 could be done by "legless men," 2,637 by "one-legged men," 2 by "armless men," 715 by "one-armed men," and 10 by "blind men." The remainder required able-bodied workers, but of "ordinary physical and mental development."[1]

Yet the Amazon was a place where 7,882 organisms could be found on any given five square miles, the most diverse ecological system on the planet, one that did not move toward simplicity but stood at the height of complexity. One tree alone could serve as home to a dazzling variety of insects, along with an array of animals, orchids, epiphytes, and bromeliads. About 10 percent of the world's five to ten million species are found in the Amazon, and there are, as one observer puts it, more "species of lichens, liverworts, mosses, and algae growing on the upper surface of a single leaf of an Amazonian palm than there are on the entire continent of Antarctica." The region is home to 2,500 kinds of fish, about an equal number of birds, 50,000 plants, and an incalculable number of invertebrates. In 1913, it took one year to reduce the time needed to make a Model T from twelve hours and eight minutes to one hour and thirty-three minutes. Yet it is estimated that half of all the Amazon's species remain undiscovered, and after centuries of observation scientists are still not exactly sure why the Amazon—unlike other forests, where leaves turn brown during the dry season—grows green and lush when the rain stops or how this reversed pattern of photosynthesis contributes to the broader seasonal distribution of water throughout the region. The slightest intervention could produce changes beyond the ability of Ford's engineers to foresee, much less control: clearing the forest for rubber removed the leaf cover that sheltered the small creeks running to the river, with the added sunlight enriching the algae, which in turn increased the snail population. The snails were the vector for the small parasitic worm that causes schistosomiasis, a disease that affects human bladders and colons and didn't exist anywhere in the Brazilian Amazon until it appeared in Fordlandia.[2]

The clash between Ford's industrial system and the Amazon's ecological one, Chaplinesque in its absurdity when it took place over logistics, labor, and politics, grew even sharper when it came to the nominal reason for Fordlandia's founding: to grow rubber.

EVEN AS ARCHIE Johnston struggled through 1931 and 1932 to comply with Dearborn's social planning directives, he never lost sight of why he was sent to the Amazon, and at the end of his first year at Fordlandia he wrote to Charles Sorensen about how to move forward. "Everyone agrees that a great amount of work has been done at Boa Vista, and a great deal of money has been spent," Johnston said, yet "very little has been done along the lines of what we came here to do, namely plant rubber." He lamented that, having planted 3,251 acres after nearly four years of work, "we have merely scratched the surface. We have provided comforts for the sick, the staff, and the caboclo, but have done very little towards creating an early income for the Companhia Ford."[3]

Johnston shared the belief of his predecessors—Blakeley, Oxholm, Perini, and Rogge—that the sale of milled wood could potentially cover the plantation's expenses until rubber was ready to be tapped. Not all of the trees logged could be used or sold. "We are aware that Mr. Ford dislikes very much to burn down timber," he told Sorensen, "but it has to be done." Felled trees either too soft or too hard piled up, "rotting in the skidway." Milled wood, unable to be shipped until the rainy season swelled the Tapajós enough to allow an oceangoing cargo ship to get to the plantation, warped in the humid climate, infested with termites. Once again caught between the ideals of Ford and the reality of the Amazon, Johnston pleaded for practicality: "We do not consider it wrong to burn this timber, simply because we cannot saw it. When we consider the whole question logically and seriously, it is just a question of whether we burn good American dollars (gasoline to get the timber) or burn the lumber."

Johnston believed that if proper drying and storage facilities were built there were enough viable trees on the plantation to export three million board feet of milled, kilned hardwood a year. "We think the United States will be a splendid market," he said. "We have lumber that will delight the eye of the American architects." And to demonstrate, Johnston sent Ford and Sorensen that carved "little nigger boy" made out of Tapajós trees.

Johnston proposed a program of rapid expansion: he planned to run logging roads through 200,000 acres of the Ford concession, felling as many trees as the mill could cut and the market would bear. As the jungle gave way to machetes, broad axes, and cross saws, his men would burn the underbrush and prepare the ground to plant rubber. It would be only a few years, Johnston thought, before he had 100,000 acres planted with over 10,000,000 trees, producing 54,000 tons of rubber a year. That is, he hedged, "if all the trees were 100%."

Sorensen responded quickly to Johnston's letter, impressed with its determination and clarity. As to his planned "clearing of large areas and burning of same," the head of the Rouge wrote, "you have outlined this in a manner that we all understand, and everybody here is in accord with your program."[4]

Success seemed in reach. After the initial troubles adapting Michigan sawing techniques to Amazonian wood, Mulrooney, Rogge, and Fordlandia's other Upper Peninsula lumbermen had finally managed to get the sawmill and kiln to produce enough timber for the plantation's basic needs. And though the mill would have to be refitted to produce lumber for export, Johnston was confident that all obstacles could be surmounted. "The lumber is there," he told Sorensen, and "we know that the Ford organization can order any equipment and do anything within the power of man." Though he did concede that "only God can grow a tree."[5]

But it was the Great Depression, and Dearborn was having trouble selling cars, much less exotic veneers. The company tried to find mills and furniture manufacturers in Michigan, North Carolina, and New England interested in Amazonian hardwood. Ford put out a glossy brochure highlighting the wide variety of wood and veneer available from Fordlandia's

Fordlandia's sawmill, with lumber stacked and waiting to be shipped.

mill. Sucupira, with its "unusual blend of colors," resembled fumed oak. Massaranduba was an unusually strong wood, good for structural work on docks, railroads, and dance floors. Pau d'arco was attractively dark, while andiroba, a mahogany, would be perfect for radio cabinets and caskets. Spanish cedar lent itself to hand carving, as well as to cabinetry, and the mottled and striped muiracoatiara would nicely accent wall paneling where variation in color was desired.[6]

There were few takers, however. "The banking system is still very much of a muddled state" and the Rouge was running at reduced capacity, wrote the head of the Purchasing Department to explain why he hadn't been fully devoted to finding a market for his wood. By 1933, Dearborn worked the numbers and concluded that, assuming it found a market and assuming that the mill could produce four million board feet of lumber a year, it would still lose $12,000 a month.[7]

RUBBER WAS AN even bigger problem. From Fordlandia's inception, it was assumed that the company that had perfected mass industrial production would grow plantation rubber. Observers of Ford noticed that he treated machines as "living things," so in the Amazon it was to be expected that his men would treat living things—rubber trees—as machines. The model naturally was a Ford factory, either Highland Park or the Rouge, with its close-cropped rows of machinery, which cut down wasted movement, and its enormous windows and glass skylights, through which sun poured in, saving electricity by bathing the factory floor in cathedral-like radiance.

"You know," Ford once said, "when you have lots of light, you can put the machines closer together."[8]

Johnston strove to apply the same kind of regimentation to the plantation that Ford did to the factory, spacing the trees close together and insisting that with the right discipline two men could plant between 160 and 200 trees in eight hours, at 2½ to 3 minutes per stump. But he soon admitted that he had trouble making the math work, as the pace of planting rubber was subject to more uncontrollable conditions—bad weather in particular—than was the tempo of an assembly line.[9]

There is a reason rubber in the Amazon isn't planted close together but rather grows wild, scattered among other trees. *Hevea* is native to the Americas, which means that its natural predators, including its most deadly foe, South American leaf blight, are also native to the region. Thus rubber trees in the Amazon grow best when they are relatively far removed from each other, about two or three to the acre, slowing the propagation and spread of fungi and bugs that feed off their leaves. In contrast, in Southeast Asia, free from the presence of native predators, they can be planted in tight, well-ordered rows, hundreds to the acre. In his drive to plant as much acreage as possible to meet the terms of the contract, Captain Oxholm did space out the trees of Fordlandia's first planting somewhat farther than was the custom in Southeast Asian plantations. But those trees came up sickly as a result of Blakeley's scorched soil and Oxholm's reliance on hastily gathered seeds and seedlings of unproven quality, planted at the worst possible moment, when the air was dry and the heat high. "Stuck in the ground anyhow," most of Oxholm's frail, sunbaked plantings had to be plowed under.[10]

This meant that when Johnston took over management of the estate, most of its trees were young, a little over a year old, having been planted in early 1930, in the months after Rogge returned from up the Tapajós. Some of the trees in this second planting showed signs of blight. As their crowns had yet to form a canopy, though, there was still space enough separating each tree to slow the spread of the contagion. But there were already other concerns.

Despite the Amazon's relatively consistent dry and wet seasons, the specific ratio between sun and rain can change significantly from one region to the next. Fordlandia's average rainfall, about eighty-seven inches per year, was well within rubber's tolerance. Yet within this average, there is considerable variation. In 1929, 102.5 inches of rain fell in Fordlandia. The next year saw only 70 inches. Such fluctuation is another reason in Brazil *Hevea* thrives in the wild but suffers in plantations: the dense, diverse root systems of jungle foliage guard against erosion during particularly wet seasons and regulate the distribution of water during dry ones. Fordlandia's hilly terrain was made up of flat-topped plateaus surrounded by steep declines leading to deep undulating hollows and ravines. It was fine for jungle rubber when it stood alongside other trees buffered in a dense forest. But stripped bare, it magnified the power of the rain and sun. Hilltop seedlings proved vulnerable to the strong Tapajós wind, and the sun beat down on the fields like rays through the glass planes of Ford's factories, scorching exposed leaves and desiccating the plateaus (1930 was an exceptionally dry year). Clear-cut and free of roots, the inclines, with slopes thirty degrees or more, lost their topsoil to the eroding rains, exposing stony sterile soil, while the ravines flooded from poor drainage.[11]

Johnston tried to compensate by terracing the slopes and planting cover crops, mostly calopogonium, both to hold the topsoil and add nutrients. But this was costly and ultimately wasted labor. Terracing added nearly an extra twenty-five dollars of expense per acre, and ground cover often dried out from too much sun and risked catching fire.

In Fordlandia, then, managers were obsessed with the vagaries of Amazon weather, to a much greater degree than were the traders and merchants who profited from wild rubber, tucked away as it was under jungle cover. During his near decade tenure, Johnston would issue a steady stream of weather reports to Dearborn:

"The unusual dry weather continues . . ."

"The unusual drought continues . . ."

"Crop is very dry and dangerous from a fire point . . ."

"The plantation is exceedingly dry, cover crop in many places burned brown . . ."

"We have not had a drop of rain in 42 days . . ."

"During this period we have had an unusual amount of rain . . ."

"Everything is bone dry, there has been no rain for approximately 120 days . . ."

"We had three small fires . . . but managed to get them out . . ."

"The river draws rain clouds from the plantation . . ."

"Due to more rain than usual for this season of the year, we have not made as good progress as we would have liked . . ."[12]

In early 1932, after less than a year at Fordlandia, Johnston reassessed his options. His building program was progressing reasonably well. Yet the difficulties involved in both rubber growing and managing labor relations led him to revise his original proposal to Sorensen.

He now suggested that, in place of rapid expansion at Fordlandia, all major planting operations be moved about fifty miles upriver, to a flatter location that he, John Rogge, and Curtis Pringle had scouted out. Johnston recommended planting only on level land that didn't need terracing and leaving the hills, streams, and ravines wild to absorb the rainfall. The location Johnston and his men surveyed offered longer stretches of unbroken plateau than did Fordlandia, with its "terrible contours" that made the grading and paving of roads costly and prohibited the extension of the railroad, which had stalled at a few miles. It would be easy, said Johnston, to build bridges over the *igarapés*, or streams, the valleys of which would be left wooded as sources of firewood.[13]

Johnston was searching not only for flatter land but for a way to lessen the social burden on the company. Since the proposed site was close to an already established town, Itaituba, all the company had to do was build a small clinic, warehouse, office, and radio station. His idea was to outsource the clearing of the jungle to a local contractor, with Ford's medical department supervising the housing and sanitary conditions at the work site. Johnston could arrange for a "first class hardware store" from Belém to provide cutlasses, axes, saws, files, and grinding stones, so that Ford would not have to supply the "wants of any contractor."

"This means," Johnston said, that the company would be relieved of the responsibility of caring for its workers, for once the land was cleared the "contractor would burn down his palm huts, fill in the toilets, and leave us a cleared area." All that would be needed was a few hundred hired men to maintain the plantation, who while at work would be "subject to our policy in every way." Yet they would reside in Itaituba and "be allowed to live in the Brazilian style while not at work." Johnston concluded his case to Sorensen by saying that his job would be to "look after the health of our men, see that we get eight hours work each day and let someone else look after their minor needs."

Sorensen, perhaps after consulting with one of the Fords, would have none of it. He curtly dismissed Johnston's proposal, writing in its margin: "I don't want to see this done."[14]

Johnston had no choice but to try to make Fordlandia work. But he did finally ask for help. For nearly five years—from early 1928 through

1932—despite the occasional employ of Tapajós rubber men, Fordlandia had proceeded without expert counsel. Evidence suggests that its managers spurned the use of *mateiros*—native naturalists who possessed invaluable knowledge about the jungle.* Johnston himself was a structural engineer and knew nothing of the land. But as a Ford man, he represented a company that prided itself on having revolutionized industrial production through hands-on experience. He was a quick study, fast accumulating a store of rubber knowledge. And he was practical, constantly trying to deflate Henry Ford's "utopian ideas" by reminding him of the reality on the ground. Yet he also suffered from the occupational hazard common to Ford men, a kind of crackpot realism where decisions supposedly justified by observation were really shaped by a sense of infallibility born of success, a belief that the company could, as Johnston put it, "do anything within the power of man."

Charles Lindbergh, Ford's friend, described his experience working for the Ford Motor Company's aviation division thus: "Once they get an idea, they want to start in right now and get action tomorrow, if not today. Their policy is to *act* first and *plan* afterward, usually overlooking completely essential details. Result: a tremendous increase of cost and effort unnecessarily." And indeed Sorensen once told Lindbergh, "Don't forget, when you want to do something, the most important thing is to get it started." Don't let the experts, the head of production at the Rouge advised, "keep it on the drafting board; they'll keep on drawing lines as long as you'll let 'em."[15]

It was this "edict engineering," as one frustrated manager described Ford's development policy at the Rouge, that explains why it took four years for someone in Dearborn to raise a question that should have been asked in 1928. Was it "fair to assume," Ford's accountant W. E. Carnegie asked Archie Johnston in 1932, "that seeds which grew up in a forest will do as well when planted in a totally denuded area under a hot tropical sun?"[16]

Mateiros were often Portuguese-speaking, either married to Indians or raised in native communities; to this day, they serve as guides to outsiders, imparting otherwise inaccessible indigenous knowledge to those hoping to unlock the secrets of the forest either for science or for commerce (Susanna B. Hecht, "Last Unfinished Page of Genesis: Euclides da Cunha and the Amazon," *Historical Geography* 2:43–69, esp. p. 56; David Campbell, *Land of Ghosts: The Braided Lives of People and the Forest in Far Western Amazonia*, New York: Houghton Mifflin, 2005, p. 109).

It also explains Johnston's answer. Starting with "yes" and then working backward from there, here's how Sorensen's protégé justified his reasoning:

1) When the seeds of the rubber trees that now exist in the jungle were washed down in the flood era, there was probably no jungle and the rubber plants were probably subject to the same exposure as all other trees.

2) Rubber trees never spring up in the jungle from seeds dropping from the rubber trees, as it is too shaded.

3) We planted several hundred thousand seeds in the shade four years ago and last year when Mr. Rogge went there to collect them he found that they were in most cases a sickly bunch of stumps.

4) Rubber, we are informed, is planted successfully in the East under the same conditions as ours.

"All of the above deductions are by questioning people and observations," wrote Johnston. Therefore, in response to Carnegie's question, he had "every reason to believe yes."[17]

Reasoning by observation was in fact central to the way the Ford Motor Company, and Henry Ford himself, operated. "Learning by doing" was the core of the pedagogy Ford promoted in the numerous schools he patronized in the United States, and it accounted for the success of the scientific "experts" he trusted and admired, men like Thomas Edison, George Washington Carver, and Luther Burbank.

As his company evolved and grew, however, exhortations to use "common sense" to achieve success became less instructive than inspirational. As Albert Wibel, head of Ford's purchasing department, told Johnston, "you are going about this new work with a good common sense idea of the difficulties you have to overcome. About the finest asset one can have when in charge of a job such as you have at the rubber plantation is good horsesense and sound judgment. The ability to be careful and think things over quietly before going off half-cocked, to my mind, is a wonderful characteristic for an executive to have."[18]

Henry Ford himself was often invoked in letters between Dearborn and Fordlandia, his oracular pronouncements used not just for public consumption but to encourage intracompany striving. Concerned about cost overrides and the slow pace of progress, Wibel wrote to Johnston on another occasion to say that he was glad that finally "things seem to be shaping themselves very much for us instead of the other way." But, the head of purchasing went on, Dearborn was hard-pressed to understand why the "venture is costing us such a tremendous amount of money, with no return whatever for a great number of years." Still, Wibel assured Johnston, the general consensus was that he was doing very well: "Mr. Ford states that we only need to do what is right, and the rest of the situation will take care of itself."[19]

Or again: "Mr. Ford is optimistic as to the future, and feels that it is only a matter of time until business conditions will be normalized. He tells us that what we are going through is for the good of all parties concerned."

Johnston soon came to believe he needed something more than reassurance. This led him to do what Ford men were loath to do: request the help of an expert. "We are entering a gigantic proposition," he wrote Sorensen, and "we feel that it would be well to have the opinion of the highest expert on rubber planting."

He soon came to rue this moment of weakness.

CHAPTER 20

STANDARD PRACTICES

THE PLANT PATHOLOGIST JAMES R. WEIR WAS IN SUMATRA DIRECT-
ing research at a Goodyear Tire Company plantation when he was re-
cruited by Edsel Ford. Previously Weir had worked with the Department
of Agriculture's Bureau of Plant Industry, studying fungi on trees in the
western United States, as well as on sugar cane in Cuba, Haiti, and the Dominican Republic. Bearded, tall, and, in the opinion of one American
diplomat, conceited and cranky, Weir knew the Amazon well, having
been part of the same Department of Commerce rubber expedition that
included commercial attaché William Schurz and the botanist Carl
LaRue. From research he did on that trip, Weir had published a pamphlet
that became the authoritative reference on South American leaf blight,
known in Brazil as *mal-das-folhas* and in the technical journals as *Doth-
idella ulei* or *Microcyclus ulei*.

Weir arrived at Fordlandia in March 1933 and quickly impressed
Johnston with what appeared to be a sound assessment of the plantation's
problems and an aggressive proposal for expansion based on the modern
techniques used on Southeast Asian plantations. He told Johnston that he

had written a manual of standard practices for Goodyear and that one should be prepared for Fordlandia. "As rapidly as possible a series of Standard Practices on planting and general agriculture work is to be drawn up," Weir wrote in his preliminary report, advising that after they had been approved they should "become law." He counseled Johnston that "standard practices are as important in planting work as in the factory. They insure uniformity of result."

"At least," Weir said with just a hint of hesitation, "as far as this work of planting can be uniform."[1]

PRIOR TO WEIR'S arrival, the Ford Motor Company, which in Michigan prided itself on state-of-the-art everything, was using planting techniques, as one employee put, "as antiquated as the Model T."[2]

After Rogge's return from his upriver pursuit, Fordlandia managers used the seeds gathered by the Mundurucú in the second planting as well as to cultivate a "mother seed bed." *Hevea* was planted in a circumscribed area and the seeds thrown off from these "mother trees" were transferred to the plantation proper. This was a cumbersome, unpredictable system. The bed was nearly ninety miles away, isolated from the main plantation and accessible only by boat up the Cupary River and then by mule. The company had to maintain a camp of men at the site, both to keep the undergrowth of the trees clear and to hunt the wild boars and other jungle animals that fed on the seeds. More critically, Johnston and his men could not know if the seeds used to plant the mother bed would, in fact, produce trees that would yield high volumes of latex or would resist blight—the two characteristics that would make or break Fordlandia— until they matured considerably. There were too many variables at play: plantation workers believed that the seeds gathered by the Mundurucú at the headwaters of the Tapajós were generally better than those around Fordlandia. But the quality of any given seed was unknown. And even if a "mother tree" could be identified as a potential high yielder of latex or a strong resister of blight, that didn't mean that the seeds it threw off— products of pollination and thus composed of the genetic material of two trees—would likewise be so. Many trees grown from seeds gathered from Ford's mother bed, as Weir warned in his report, might prove to be "duds."

The alternative was asexual reproduction. As Johnston assured Dearborn, one could simply stick a rubber branch in the ground and it would "take root almost without fail."[3] That was one way of doing it. But Dutch botanists more than a decade earlier had pioneered the technique of bud grafting, which by the early 1930s had become the exclusive method in use on Southeast Asian rubber plantations. Bud grafting entailed taking a hearty rubber rootstock and grafting onto it a bud from a selected tree, or scion, with the desired properties—in this case high yield and strong resistance. The result is an amalgam, or clone, comprising two distinct genetic systems: sturdy roots and a resistant, high-yielding trunk. After the tissues of the two systems grafted and the bud produced a new shoot, the clone could be uprooted and planted as a whole tree or the grafted bud could be lopped off and the stump rooted. It was an efficient method of producing plantation stock because most rubber trees had a serviceable root system, and once a valued scion (high yielder, strong resister) was identified, it could provide multiple buds ready to be grafted.

This kind of genetic work was but a step removed from Fordism's mapping of the social genome, the manipulation of individual movement into precise motions to achieve maximum productivity. And Dearborn would eventually embrace bud grafting with enthusiasm. Yet a few years prior to Johnston's and Weir's coming, when a company official wrote to Fordlandia to ask if anyone there had ever heard of the technique, Rogge, the lumberjack from Upper Michigan then in charge of the estate, wrote back saying that, while he knew of the method, he didn't "consider bud-grafting necessary."[4]

In fact, Fordlandia's managers knew embarrassingly little about pollination, much less about asexual reproduction and bud grafting. In October 1932, the humorist Will Rogers, on a tour of Brazil and hearing that things were not going well for his friend Henry Ford, gave him a good-natured ribbing in the form of a letter to the *New York Times*:

To the Editor:
Pará, Brazil, October 24, 1932. Brazil ought to belong to the United States. We like to brag about everything big. We been flying up its coast line for five solid days and still got another day.

If any of you see the Rockefellers, kiss 'em for me. There is not a mosquito up this coast.* If they can just hear of one trying to get a start down here there is ten Rockefeller Foundation men got him singing the blues before sundown. No sir, you got to wait till you get to "God's country" to get eat up by insects.

Rio Janeiro is the prettiest city in the world from the air. We are just circling Para where we land for the night. It's right at the mouth of the great Amazon River.

Up from here is where Mr. Ford's rubber plantation is but somebody sold him all male trees and they are having a little trouble getting 'em to bear. I bet they couldn't fool him on carburetors but he didn't know sex life in the forest.

Yours,
Will Rogers

It was a joke: rubber trees did not reproduce by gender. The humor, though, was lost on Rogge, who sent a letter to the US Department of Agriculture asking if it was true that rubber trees were divided along male and female lines. "Rubber does not have male and female trees," someone from the department wrote back, before giving the lumberjack a fast lesson in insect cross-pollination.[5]

So Johnston decided that with Weir's impending arrival he better study up. In Fordlandia's office he came across a report on Southeast Asian rubber production detailing the technique of bud grafting (Dearborn had commissioned the study in 1928, though it seems that no one on the estate had bothered to consult it). As Johnston was reading, Curtis Pringle came into the office and mentioned that he knew how to do the procedure. Johnston was surprised to hear that an ex-sheriff from Kalamazoo had ever bud grafted, so he asked for a demonstration. Pringle proceeded to do exactly what the report "said must be avoided." Whittling the rootstock where the bud was to be attached, Pringle cut clear through the cambium, the thin layer of generative tissue found between the bark and

---

*The Rockefeller Foundation had launched a mosquito-eradication program in Brazil a few years earlier.

the wood, responsible for the production of secondary shoots. Johnston told Dearborn that this might just have been carelessness on Pringle's part but he was convinced more than ever that he needed an "expert's opinion and advice, on all our rubber operations and this as early as possible."[6]

"It might be in order," he said, "to have Mr. James Weir give our people a course of instruction."[7]

WEIR DID TEACH the staff how to bud graft properly. But the real problem, the pathologist said, was that Fordlandia had no sure scions from which to graft. So Edsel Ford agreed to Weir's request to travel to Southeast Asia, to Sumatra and Malaysia, to find trusted stock. Weir set out in June 1933 and quickly obtained 2,046 budded stumps grafted from an assured selection of high-yielding trees. Packed in sterilized sawdust, the cache left Singapore at the end of December, sailing across the Indian Ocean and through the Suez Canal in early 1934, then out into the Mediterranean, over the Atlantic, and up the Amazon.[8]

These stumps were, as all Southeast Asian rubber was, the direct descendants of the seeds spirited out of the Amazon more than fifty years earlier by Harry Wickham. Indeed, Weir, who didn't suffer from an excess of modesty, saw his mission as a bid to reverse history's course and restore Brazil to its former rubber glory.

In his letters back to Fordlandia and Dearborn, posted from different ports of call, Weir made much of his adventure. He told of the "breakbone fever" he contracted in Kuala Lumpur and of smuggling some seeds out of Malaysia with false customs certificates. He reported on the increasing restrictions placed by the Dutch and British on rubber production, which he predicted would lead to a market shortage that could be filled by "tropical America," with its constant, steady supply of latex. He repeatedly forecast success not just for Fordlandia but for all of Brazil. "The chances," Weir wrote, "of making Brazil a very large factor in the rubber world are good." Within a year, he told Johnston, the bud grafting of just eighteen of his more than two thousand stumps would produce thousands of seedlings. A second round of bud grafting could, conservatively calculated, "breed up to 120,000 trees" more, which in a decade would yield 3,600,000 pounds of latex.[9]

Johnston was encouraged not just by the information Weir sent him but because the pathologist, who seemed aloof at first, appeared to be loosening up a bit. From his Singapore hotel Weir wrote Johnston a letter teasing him about his Scottish brogue and reporting that his "blood brothers" from the "Land of the Mountains and the Flood" were kicking up a racket on the floor below. "The clans," he wrote, his own blood up from the success of his mission, "are marching under the banners of their chiefs, the pipes are sounding their wild and thrilling music, the old war cries make the hotel tremble and their tartan in fancy is still steeped in the blood of the brave. Vive le Scott!"

Then Weir did an inexplicable about-face. Prior to departing for Singapore, he had praised Johnston's management. "It is very gratifying to an agriculturalist," he said, "to see the amount of good work that has been done at Boa Vista." In time, he said, the plantation would no doubt be "a very great success," bringing "prestige for American business and for the name of the organization behind the project." He dismissed concerns that Fordlandia was too hilly, pointing out that numerous Southeast Asian plantations were just as rolling.[10]

But suddenly, upon his return toward the middle of 1934, he urged Edsel to "abandon" Fordlandia, insisting that it would never be profitable. He suggested that the company move operations seventy miles downriver, to Belterra, a flat 150-foot-high plateau slightly drier than Boa Vista but with richer soil and better drainage.

Weir's proposal caught Johnston off guard. Just two years earlier he himself had suggested moving operations upriver, yet by this point he had become invested in Fordlandia. His overhaul of the plantation was largely finished, and there now existed the orderly town that had long been imagined. He bristled at Weir's cavalier use of the word *abandon* to discuss Fordlandia's fate. "We do not think," Johnston wrote Dearborn, "that word should have been used and if you could see Fordlandia today you would see new shoots showing everywhere."

But Weir insisted to Dearborn that he could make a go of things only at a new site, especially with the clones he obtained in Sumatra. Having spent six years and $7 million on an enterprise that no one would take off their hands, the Fords now decided to heed the advice of an expert, even if it meant starting anew. In May 1934, their agents in Belém traded a little over 500,000 acres of Fordlandia—from a section that had yet to be fully explored—for an equal amount in Belterra. The rubber groves at Fordlandia were to be maintained as they were, with no further expansion, and the estate was to be used primarily as Weir's research station and "to produce budwood" for the new plantation, which the Fords apparently resisted calling Edselville, or Edselândia, as Jorge Villares had originally proposed when he met with the two Fords in Dearborn. The new settlement kept its original Brazilian name, Belterra, which means beautiful land.[11]

Johnston never forgave Weir his treachery, and for the remainder of Weir's four years with the Ford Motor Company, he issued a steady stream of criticism about him to Sorensen and to any other company official who would listen.

Weir refused to admit his mistakes, even when they led to serious setbacks. When "mites and other bugs had almost taken control" of Fordlandia's budwood nursery in 1935, Weir recommended that they be repelled with "sulphur, tobacco smoke, and finally soap." But because the pathologist had misidentified the pests this treatment didn't work and that year's cultivation of "clones and budwood was shot."[12]

Weir was expensive. "To date, with salary and expenses, trips, etc.," Johnston wrote Dearborn, "we have paid out to Mr. Weir $70,000 and for this amount he has never assumed, or had to assume, any responsibility." Weir came and went as he pleased, accountable to no one, Johnston reported. That was why the plantation had had such poor luck with the Southeast Asian clones, half of which had died. "Mr. Weir was here when they arrived, and although planting is the most important function in plantation work, Mr. Weir did not actually see or take part in the planting of one stump." Johnston and a helper did the planting. "We did our best," he said, but admitted that "it might not have been good enough."

Weir was haughty, and he couldn't get along with the rest of the staff. He clashed constantly with Johnston, but there was "one employee in particular" he really didn't like. That was Sheriff Curtis Pringle. Johnston had put Pringle in charge of the new plantation—the clearing of forest and construction of buildings having gotten under way in early 1935—where he and Weir wrangled over every aspect of its development, from the location and size of the nursery to how much pruning should be done of existing wild rubber trees, from what kind of ground cover to use to whether it was better to transplant budded stumps from the nursery to the field (Weir's position) or to graft desired buds directly to rootstocks already in the field (Pringle's).

Pringle, "like the rest of us, is by no means perfect," Johnston wrote to Dearborn, but if he "never took a cooperative attitude with Mr. Weir" it was because the pathologist "never took this attitude with Mr. Pringle; one cannot assume that all superior air and command either attention or respect." Johnson tried talking to Weir several times, telling him that his attitude was antagonizing the rest of the staff. But Weir shrugged it off. "At present," Johnston told Dearborn, Weir "can neither work in harmony with Pringle nor the writer."[13]

Weir was a prima donna. Though he presumed to tell Pringle how to build Belterra, he refused to spend a night there because the site was still under construction and there was no "privacy" and "no good bathroom." Johnston tried to order Weir to move to the new plantation. But Weir said he wouldn't until a proper house was built for him. Until then, he insisted on staying at Fordlandia, where Johnston ordered him to bunk with other single men and work in the "engineering office." Weir balked, adamant on remaining in one of the well-equipped houses built for married American managers. Johnston unsuccessfully tried to get Dearborn to back him up, writing that if Weir was allowed to work from home there would be no way to make sure he wasn't slacking. "We cannot control a man if he is at home," he said, since "he might be in bed."

Weir took credit for the accomplishments of others. "There is little or nothing in what he writes, nothing we do not already know, nothing we are not doing or intend on doing in the proper season," Johnston complained. "Everything he writes is meant to convey the idea to Dearborn that no one here knows anything about rubber. This condition does not exist, we know what we are doing." Weir even claimed to be the first to extract the poison rotenone, found in the roots of the timbo plant and used locally to kill piranhas, as an insecticide. "The timbo business is our idea," said Johnston, who claimed to have developed the pesticide himself.[14]

But Weir's worst vice, in Johnston's eyes, was that he valued theory over practice. Weir never stayed at Fordlandia for long periods of time, the manager said, always finding one reason or another to travel to Belém or Rio, or even back to the States. Therefore he hadn't actually observed the complete Tapajós annual planting cycle. That didn't stop him, Johnston said, from making sweeping generalizations about Fordlandia's planting methods. Weir, he told Dearborn, "is not acquainted with the conditions here through an entire season," making him "scarcely qualified to talk on certain subjects." Johnston heaped particular scorn on Weir's planting instructions, which the company had adopted as "law" shortly after Edsel had hired him. "He continually refers to his General Letters, and Standard Procedures, etc.," Johnston groused, accusing Weir of having imposed practices common on Southeast Asian plantations "before he had an opportunity to qualify as an expert about what should be Standard Practices in Brazil."

To support his cause, Johnston enlisted the services of another expert, Walter Bangham. A former colleague of Weir's who worked for Goodyear in Central America, Bangham supported Johnston's contention that they could make a go of rubber at Fordlandia. Johnston asked Bangham if Weir had indeed written Goodyear's "Standard Practices," as he claimed he had. "No, not one," replied Bangham. Johnston's new ally reported that Weir, having taken the Ford job, wrote him several times asking to be sent copies of Goodyear's plantation handbook, which he then passed off to Dearborn as his own work. Bangham also confirmed Johnston's suspicion that Weir was treating the whole operation more as an opportunity to conduct experiments than as a practical business venture. Weir's "Standard Practices as written are not standard practices, but experimental practices," Bangham said, "and the way you have done things here is more practical than what is written."[15]

"So it makes you wonder," complained Johnston to his Michigan superiors, "if Mr. Weir is sincere, does he know what he is talking about?"[16]

WEIR, FOR HIS part, sent Dearborn a series of progressively gloomier reports, blaming the plantation's lack of success on a combination of pestilence and incompetence. In early 1936, he "threw quite a bomb," in his words, at Dearborn officials, recommending that Fordlandia be scaled back dramatically and that planting in Belterra be extended only gradually. Contradicting his own initial enthusiasm, Weir declared that "no rubber man would have gone to Brazil in the first place to build estates." Having already convinced the company to move the whole operation downriver to Belterra—at this point still under construction—the pathologist now recommended to Dearborn that it start over in Central America.[17]

There may be some truth to Johnston's claim that Weir was taking advantage of his employment with Ford to test pet theories. Not only had the pathologist managed to convince Dearborn to turn Fordlandia into his own personal research laboratory, Weir himself admitted in his original survey that Ford's operations presented a wonderful opportunity to research a question that had long preoccupied rubber specialists: Did the seeds gathered by Henry Wickham represent Amazon's best *Hevea*, or could a sturdier and more profitable variety be identified? He wrote:

> It is a common opinion among those, familiar with rubbers of the Amazon and the East, that certain very characteristic forms, known to exist in Brazil, are not found in the population of trees on eastern plantations. With the possession of the eastern, tested, material to serve as standards and comparison, Boa Vista would have an unusual opportunity to accomplish what every planting Company in the East has planned to do, viz: investigate genetically the wild rubbers of the Amazon River drainage.

"Every effort," Weir said, "should be made to study the rubbers of the Amazon, for it is not unlikely, that some of the finest families of trees escaped the first collection of seeds that went to the East."

By getting Edsel Ford to finance his trip to Sumatra, Weir did exactly that, securing representative samples of Southeast Asian *Hevea* to test against Brazilian varieties so as to identify blight-resistant strains that might not have been included in Wickham's original seed consignment. In retrospect, it is perplexing why Weir, one of the world's foremost experts on rubber blight, should have downplayed its danger as he did in his first positive report, the one where he praised all of Johnston's "good work" and predicted a "great success" for Fordlandia. In that document, Weir recommended not only that rubber planting be expanded but that the trees be placed closer together than they so far had been. Where Oxholm and his successors spaced them about a hundred to an acre, Johnston, acting on Weir's advice, doubled up in 1934, planting two hundred to the acre. It could be the case that Weir was actually hoping for an epidemic of South American leaf blight as a way of isolating truly resistant stock, which he believed existed throughout the Amazon basin but had yet to be identified. Since blight is not a problem in Southeast Asia, none of the clones he brought back were specifically bred to withstand fungi; if they proved to be susceptible, while other, locally gathered seeds demonstrated resistance, it would confirm that there existed in the Amazon a wider variety of *Hevea* than that currently available to plantations in Asia.

Weir, despite his work with Goodyear and other corporations, was at heart a government agronomist, with a long and active affiliation with the Department of Agriculture. Just as State Department diplomats tended to cultivate a broader, stable investment climate rather than advance the immediate interests of specific companies (as did Commerce Department attachés), Weir seemed concerned less with making Fordlandia, or Belterra, work than with figuring out how to grow plantation rubber in the Amazon, even if it meant that a company other than Ford's would benefit.

So Johnston continued to fume. Weir, he said, has never been held accountable for his actions. Having left "others to carry on what he proposed," he "returns and criticizes what has been done." Johnston begged Dearborn to put Weir in charge of planting and insect control, letting him run "matters to suit himself." This would at least make him responsible for results. Give him a "definite job," he begged, "otherwise he will carry on as in the past."[18]

Caught up in his feud with Weir and pressed into not just running one plantation but building a second, Johnston probably missed the irony of what by late 1935 had become his main line of criticism about Weir, that the scientist had repeatedly advised the plantation to adopt methods not appropriate to the specific conditions of the Tapajós. "One does not have to be an expert," Johnston said, "to know that a standard practice in one country can be detrimental to good practice in another."[19]

CHAPTER 21

BONFIRE OF THE CATERPILLARS

As Weir and Johnston bickered, the foliage of Fordlandia's maturing trees began to close, forming a bridge over which South American leaf blight could march. Plantation managers had noticed the fungi, which feed off and spread among rubber leaves, from the moment the first trees began to bloom. But the Tapajós's long dry season allowed workers to slow its spread through constant pruning and leaf washing. Then in 1935, the crowns of most of Fordlandia's trees began to touch one another, and what was troublesome turned catastrophic.

The spores hit the older groves the hardest. "Practically all the branches of the trees throughout the estate," Weir wrote in a report to Dearborn, "terminate in naked stems. Each successive elongation of the shoot becomes smaller and smaller." The fungi don't kill trees straight out. But as they fight to refoliate, they grow successively weaker, either producing dwarf shoots or dying back altogether. Spores also attacked the estate's nurseries, including the new budwood bed. None of Weir's Dutch colonial clones, which held the hope of so many, proved resistant to the blight—expectedly so since South American leaf blight doesn't exist in

Fordlandia rubber planting.

Southeast Asia and therefore planters there had no reason to select for resistance.[1]

Upon arriving at Fordlandia two years earlier, Weir had minimized the threat of blight and the valley's erratic rain distribution and urged Johnston to plant even closer rows. Yet he now declared unequivocally that the disease had assumed "epidemic proportions with every change of humidity." Fordlandia's proximity to the Tapajós accelerated the disease, as the morning fog nurtured the fungi, which were now "spreading directly from tree to tree, without some intermittent controllable stage" and could not "be combated at Fordlandia successfully or economically." The Ford Motor Company, with the endorsement of a well-respected pathologist with experience on three continents, had in effect created an incubator.

SOUTH AMERICAN LEAF blight was well known to tropical botanists and planters at the time of Fordlandia's founding. By the early 1910s, pathologists had identified different manifestations of blight that had occurred throughout the Amazon basin as variations of a single disease. The blight is spread by airborne spores that move from leaf to leaf, entering their epidermis and reproducing between their cells. The fungi attack seedlings and mature trees alike, as well as a variety of latex-producing trees, not just *Hevea brasiliensis*. New leaves turn black and wither, while mature ones become pockmarked, with the infected tissue turning greenish black before rotting away completely.

Hevea is what botanists call a *climax* plant, meaning that it developed in an ecosystem—in this case the Amazon—that was at the apex of its complexity. Unlike relatively new *pioneer* crops like wheat, corn, or rice, which grow rapidly and throw off many fertile seeds and flourish in a variety of habitats, including large plantations, *Hevea* is not so adaptable. Its genetic composition is as old and evolved as the jungle that surrounds it. To use a metaphor associated with human behavior, *Hevea* is set in its ways. It grows slowly, its girth is thick, its seeds need coaxing, and it likes to hide from predators by mixing with other jungle trees. Yet despite these survival strategies, rubber, like many other tropical plants, can be a successful commercial crop when completely removed from its home environment, freed from the pests and plagues that evolved and adapted with it. While Southeast Asia was similar enough in climate to the Amazon, its native insects, parasites, and spores ignored South American rubber and so trees could be planted in close rows. In their original context, on the other hand, rubber trees grown near one another proved susceptible to pestilence, as Weir put it, with "every change of humidity."

South American leaf blight appeared in epidemic form in 1915 along the Caribbean coast, in Suriname, British Guyana, and the island of Trinidad, where planters first tried to grow estate rubber. In Suriname, it took just one year to decimate a two-year-old plantation of twenty thousand trees. *Hevea* can survive by shedding its leaves to shake off an infestation. But grouping trees in close-cropped rows made them vulnerable to not just one bout of blight but an endless barrage: even as an infected tree drops its leaves from the first assault, spores amassed on a neighboring tree attack again after a new bloom, then again and again.

This is why by the late 1910s estate rubber production had largely been abandoned in the Americas—until Henry Ford came along.

Johnston tried to fumigate with antifungal pesticides, but *Hevea* grows tall, up to thirty meters in height, and requires special water-powered sprayers that, since rubber was not a plantation crop in the Amazon, Belém merchants didn't have in stock. Dearborn shipped some down, but the plantation's hilly terrain made their use a time-consuming, costly, and ultimately ineffective response. By mid-1936, Fordlandia stood patchy and ragged, just at the moment it should have begun producing latex for export. Weir condemned large swaths of the plantation and Johnston couldn't argue.

The construction of Belterra was just about finished. Workers had built a city center and residential houses and cleared and planted thousands of acres with rubber. So a decision was finally made to switch the bulk of operations to the new site, with Fordlandia converted into a research center, budgrafting school, and nursery for hybrid clones to be planted at the new estate. The train stopped running along Fordlandia's three-mile stretch, as workers packed up the locomotive and cars and shipped them back to Detroit. A few staff families remained, rattling around the American neighborhood, as did a skeleton crew of Brazilian laborers. Some of them learned how to bud graft, while others kept up the nurseries, surviving rubber groves, and the Henry Ford Hospital, as well as their own lawns, gardens, and sidewalks.

"The growth of the rubber on Fordlandia is in striking contrast," Walter Bangham said after a visit in 1936, "to the excellent town site and industrial buildings that have been erected on the Fordlandia estate." But soon the town, too, began to take on a ghostly cast. A few years later, a visitor reported that the "jungle was beginning to creep back over it and blot out the signs and lines of a supercivilization which men had transported and transplanted at the cost of incredible effort, money, and human life."[2]

WHEN HENRY FORD approved Weir's proposal to acquire Belterra, it provided an opportunity for Weir and Johnston to find at least a narrow slip of common ground, as both men thought a successful rubber plantation did not need a concentrated company town along the lines of Fordlandia. Johnston was tired of caring for workers and their families from cradle to grave, while Weir believed "decentralization of the field force . . . . would save much time in going to and from distant parts of the estate." Rubber tapping had to begin at dawn, when sap flowed the freest. So Weir suggested that when the time came to tap latex at Belterra the company give plots of land to workers where they could build a house, close to a designated grove they would be responsible for maintaining and harvesting— in other words, he proposed a labor system pretty much like what existed in the Tapajós before the establishment of Fordlandia.

Ford disagreed, and once he authorized the swap of a piece of his original concession for land farther down the Tapajós, he sent instructions to build a new town, centered on a city square, complete with a church, a recreation room, an outdoor movie theater, a golf course, a swimming pool, a water tower, and even windmills to produce electricity. Ford had once told a village reporter, more than a decade earlier, when he was just getting started promoting decentralized "village industries," that he was strictly opposed to the idea of building "model towns" from scratch. "I'm against that sort of thing," he insisted, saying that he would instead locate his factories and mills in already established communities like Pequaming, which he purchased in 1923. But throughout the late 1920s and 1930s, as his village industry projects became less a realistic remedy for the dislocations of boom-and-bust capitalism and more a symptom of his intensifying obsessions, he did exactly "that sort of thing"—in the Upper Peninsula with his logging camps, in Dearborn with Greenfield Village, and in the Amazon with Fordlandia. At nearly the precise moment he was telling Johnston to proceed with the building of Belterra, Ford, upon driving through an Upper Peninsula forest he found especially pretty, sent a work crew to dig a mill lake and raise a prim twelve-bungalow town surrounding a village green. Named by Ford after the daughter of the manager of his UP operations, Alberta became the newest addition to his village industry program, its workers expected to divide their time lumbering, milling, and farming.[3]

Over the next couple of years, Alberta and Belterra proceeded on similar lines, with the company promoting wholesome living in both, through gardening, education, health care, and recreation. Even the clapboard bungalows of the two towns looked alike. White with green trim, they were Cape Cod style, with steep roofs and front gables. Alberta, which today stands intact and is run by Michigan Technical University as a forest research station and tourist attraction, would prove to be marginally more successful than Belterra—it provided a steady, if inconsequential, amount of milled timber to be kilned in Iron Mountain. But it was ultimately as unsustainable as Ford's Amazonian venture. Over the next decade, company executives were forever trying to quietly close the money-draining town, only to be countermanded by Henry Ford himself. "Get it running by Monday," he told his Upper Peninsula manager on Thursday, upon learning that the mill had been shut down.[4]

BACK IN BRAZIL at Belterra, hundreds of boys dressed in shorts, shirts, and caps and girls in white blouses and dark skirts began attending schools named after Henry's son and grandchildren: Edsel, Henry II, and Benson. Belterra was indeed flat, which was good not just for planting rubber but for laying out level, symmetrical streets. Even more than Fordlandia, which made some concessions to the ups and downs, backs and forths of river topography, Belterra looked like a squared midwestern town. Model Ts and As rolled down its straight streets, which were lined with fire hydrants, sidewalks, streetlamps, and white-and-green worker bungalows, with neat lawns and front gardens.

Belterra schoolchildren.

Cape Cod traditional I: Alberta.

Cape Cod traditional II: Belterra.

A new hospital, dubbed the "Mayo Clinic of the Amazon," was even more modern than Fordlandia's Henry Ford Hospital, complete with X-ray machines and blood transfusion equipment. The hospital serviced the workforce and the surrounding area, which was more populated than Fordlandia; its staff received the latest medical journals with the mail, which arrived daily from Santarém by horse—much quicker than the chuggingly slow riverboats needed to reach Fordlandia. Doctors performed more innovative operations than they did at Fordlandia, such as the removal of cataracts, an eye condition prevalent in the Amazon owing to the strong equatorial sun. Belterra medical personnel, chemists, and lab technicians made important advances in treating parasitical diseases and other infections that in later years would help other enterprises maintain a large force in the jungle. "In the interest of science," all of Fordlandia's Brazilian employees had to sign a waiver allowing the hospital to perform autopsies if they passed away on the estate.[5]

The sanitation squad continued to hunt wild dogs, drain swampy areas and cover them with oil so that mosquitoes couldn't breed, and inspect company houses to make sure kitchens and bathrooms were clean and laundry was hung to dry on lines. Still, Belterra represented a lessening of the feudal control that the company instituted, or at least tried to institute, at Fordlandia, more closely approximating modern labor relations based on wages and benefits—of the kind often extolled by Ford even as he was undercutting them with his social engineering and paternalistic manipulation. The town was set back from the river a few miles, providing it with a natural buffer from the riverboat liquor trade; the company didn't have to enforce Prohibition as strictly as it did upriver, which helped reduce conflict. The settlement was within relatively easy reach of Santarém,

Opposite page: The houses at Belterra were more self-consciously traditional than the ones at Fordlandia, as if mirroring Ford's increased cultural conservatism. The bungalows built by Archie Johnston at Fordlandia in the wake of the 1930 riot, though inappropriate for the climate, sported simple, clean, and functional lines. In contrast, Belterra's residences seem mannered, with gabled roofs, shutters, and painted trim. They were also, except for want of chimneys, indistinguishable from the houses Ford had built in Alberta, in Michigan's Upper Peninsula, around the same time.

so Belterra workers enjoyed some leverage in dealing with the company: at Fordlandia, accessible only by river, workers often felt trapped and utterly dependent on the plantation, especially after the razing of Pau d'Agua and other shantytowns did away with potential refuges for those who wanted to quit. At Belterra they could just walk away. At the same time, proximity to Santarém lightened the social burden of the plantation management. Though they still showed movies and provided other forms of recreation, finding something to alleviate worker boredom was no longer a pressing concern of the American staff.

For the Americans, too, life felt a little less isolated at Belterra than it did at Fordlandia. The mail, including American newspapers and magazines, got there quicker and it was easier to get to Santarém or even Belém for a visit. They lived in comfortable dwellings along a shady thoroughfare, not as picturesque as Fordlandia but more familiar, level, like a proper "American suburb." They were attended to by Barbadian servants and played golf on a "completely flat 9 hole, par 38 course." And they celebrated Christmas, New Year's, and July Fourth with parties and dances.[6]

With the switch from Fordlandia to Belterra, Archie Johnston began to supervise operations from Belém, leaving Curtis Pringle and John Rogge to oversee the construction of the new town and plantation. Setting aside his irritation with Weir, Sheriff Pringle, named general supervisor of Belterra, turned out to be reasonable and pragmatic. He faithfully built the new town center, along with houses for laborers and staff, but he tempered the puritanism that nearly wrecked Fordlandia, going easy on attempts to regulate the social life and eating habits of the plantation's workforce. As a reporter for *Harper's* put it after a visit, "Mr. Ford and Brazil are still somewhat in disagreement in matters of doors, screening, and heights of ceiling, but the ex-sheriff has proved himself an excellent arbiter. He does not insist upon square-dancing or wholesome Detroit-style cooking."[7]

The medical staff, too, learned to accommodate. After first trying to enforce a ban against midwifery, the hospital relented and allowed for home births. "There was so much resistance that half the people didn't obey it," recalled Emerick Szilagyi, a surgeon from Detroit's Henry Ford Hospital who did a tour of duty on the new plantation, "so I lifted the rule and made it voluntary."[8]

As a result of this newfound willingness to adapt rather than impose, labor problems were much less acute at Belterra than at Fordlandia. There were no more kitchen riots and nighttime evacuations of the Americans, no more urgent telegrams to Juan Trippe asking for Pan Am hydroplanes to shuttle in detachments of soldiers and disperse armed crowds by flying in low over their heads.

Nature, though, refused to be subdued.

IN LATE 1936, Belterra's plantation seemed to be in relatively fine shape. Pringle had cultivated a nursery with over 5,000,000 seedlings to serve as rootstock, cleared and blocked out a good part of the estate, and planted 700,000 trees. These trees came from a mix of the surviving Southeast Asian stock, clones from Fordlandia trees that had weathered the epidemic relatively unscathed (thus indicating that they had some immunity to blight), stumps obtained in Panama, and seeds gathered from trees around the mouth of the Amazon, mostly from Marajó Island, that showed strong resistance. Blight began to make an appearance on the leaves of Belterra's young trees, yet it seemed like workers would have a better chance at controlling it than they did on Ford's first plantation. The new estate had good soil and was much flatter than Fordlandia's rolling hills, which made it easier to fumigate and prune. Set back from the river, it experienced less morning fog than Fordlandia, and the winds were drier, which also slowed the growth of fungi.

The main threat to Belterra's rubber, at least at first, was not blight but bugs. The company had great success in eradicating mosquitoes and flies by draining and oiling wet areas where they could breed and maintaining a rapid-response team of swatters. But as with blight, the concentration of *Hevea* accelerated the reproduction of insects that fed off rubber, leading to wave after wave of infestations. "The bugs have never been seen before in such quantities," wrote Johnston of an early mite epidemic, "the reason being there has never been a Rubber Estate before with such large nurseries."[9]

The lace bug was rubber's worst predator. In normal jungle conditions, the natural food chain kept the population low and the threat contained. But as the entomologist Charles Townsend, brought in on more than one occasion to respond to an outbreak, observed, the "extensive

Dusting nursery at Belterra against leaf fungi and insects.

planting of rubber . . . has created a greatly increased food supply and the bugs took advantage of it to multiply in proportion."

Dearborn officials received a crash course in tropical entomology, having asked Townsend to compile an "insect census" for Fordlandia. Townsend started with lace bugs, noting that they deposited their "eggs on the underside of the rubber trees and these hatch into small spiny larvae, which pierce the leaf epidermis with a sharp proboscis and suck the juices of the leaves, thus greatly weakening the seedlings."[10]

He went on to register scores of other problem pests. Red mites sucked the sap from leaves, as did the white flies, which fed on a variety of plants but preferred rubber. They "fly freely" about, Townsend observed, and "it is only a matter of time" before they "extend over the whole plantation." The flies were "attended" to by "small black ants," which likewise drained sap from the rubber leaf. Then there were the white weevils, ten millimeters long with light blue legs, bluish to pinkish leafhoppers, treehoppers with broad bodies and two short, sharp horns, spanworms, mandarova moths, green roaches and green grasshoppers, large locusts, and generic broad and flat "plant bugs." A similar multicolor palette of scale insects — green, white, and black — attached their long stylets to leaves, draining them of their vigor and leaving a brown or black crust when they were done.

Caterpillars are especially harmful to rubber, and they thrived on Ford's estates. There were pale caterpillars and small yellowish to greenish caterpillars with erect pointed dorsal tubercles sporting stinging hairs. And there were plenty of tussock caterpillars, slug caterpillars, sphinx caterpillars, and hairy caterpillars with "slender tufts of black hair near the head." For a brief period, fire and suava ants, which swarm from September to November, ate caterpillars, but like the white flies they came to prefer rubber. This cavalcade of insects attacked not just rubber but machinery as well. "Nocturnal spiders," for instance, would "spin webs from wire to ground during wet weather," causing the telegraph equipment to short-circuit.[11]

The protocol to fight such an array of threats was exhaustive and included placing a standing bounty on the "head" of a "mole-type animal that eats stumps." Reports back to Dearborn extensively detailed the activity of "ant men making their regular rounds," teams of women who pulled weeds and picked insects, new experimental techniques to deal with lace bugs, and weekly inspections of trees for Fomes lignosus, a root fungus, and Diplodia dieback, another fungus distinct from leaf blight.

The company mobilized Belterra's whole population to respond to outbreaks. During one early caterpillar assault on a block of the first trees to be planted on the estate, "every available person, man and women, was lined up to do an effective handpicking." In five hours, they collected an estimated 250,000 caterpillars, filling fifty one-gallon containers. When no more caterpillars could be found, they emptied the containers into a pile, threw gasoline on it, and torched the pyre.

Beyond bounty hunting and bonfires, Belterra chemists did come up with innovative insecticides. They extracted poison from timbo and cassava, concocted a fish oil wash laced with kerosene, mixed a compound of nicotine sulfate and arsenate, and boiled a "poisoned syrup" that was effective against fire ants, "designed to kill the whole nest including the

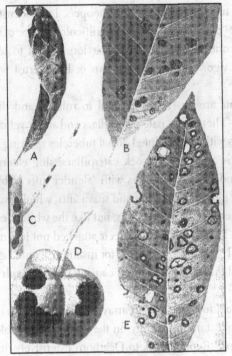

Effects of South American leaf blight on rubber tree.

queen." The fight against insects added even more expense to what it would cost the company to produce a pound of latex.

BUT WORKERS WERE holding the insects at bay, and Belterra was progressing. The key to success, as always, was to find stock that both yielded profitable amounts of latex and had strong immunity to fungi and pests. Pringle and others involved in planting the new estate had identified high yielders (mostly from strains found at the headwaters of the Tapajós, as well as on the upper Amazon River, around Acre) and strong resisters (many from Marajó Island, at the mouth of the Amazon). But the staff soon came to realize that these two traits tended to be mutually exclusive in wild *Hevea*: high yielders had low immunity, while strong resisters produced too little latex.

It was ostensibly to search for an ever elusive strain of high-yielding and hardy *Hevea* that James Weir, in late 1937, organized yet another seed-gathering expedition to the state of Acre. But the pathologist had no intention of returning. "This is my last day on the Tapajós," he wrote a confidant. "I did not tell anyone at Fordlandia that I did not plan to return after I finish with the Upper Amazon. I will drop you a line from God knows where." Perhaps Weir had decided to quit the plantation because the appearance of blight had convinced him of the futility of trying to grow estate rubber in the Amazon. Or maybe he left because he was peeved that Dearborn denied him permission to make a second trip to Southeast Asia. Whatever the case, in keeping with his aversion to team-work, he said not a word to anyone at Fordlandia or Belterra.[12]

Johnston was glad to be rid of him. Once it was clear that Weir was not returning to Fordlandia, Johnston told Dearborn he would welcome a replacement, so long as he didn't have previous experience in Asia and thus wasn't steeped in assumptions that "might not apply" in Brazil. "Some young Harvard graduate in Botany and Genetics, one that came from the West with a farm background," was his idea of a suitable candidate. "Bring him here," he said, and "let him learn plantation practices, and through time he will develop into the man you want." Actually, Johnston didn't have to look far, for two individuals with the qualities he described, short of a Harvard pedigree, were already on the plantation.

Edward and Charles Townsend—sons of the entomologist—had been Weir's assistants, and now they took over research. They focused on selection and controlled cross-fertilization to try to produce hybrids that had both desirable traits. They made some progress, particularly using bees as pollinators. Yet they had trouble finding just the right combination. One hybrid proved resistant to blight *and* a high yielder, but its leaves were thin and unusually vulnerable to lace bug. Another, with thicker leaves, ran unimpressive amounts of sap.[13]

Even as they worked to cultivate hybrids, the Townsend brothers be-gan experimenting with crown, or top, grafting, a technique that had been developed in Southeast Asia to control leaf mildew but never put to large-scale commercial use. Once a tree created by grafting a high-yielding strain of *Hevea* to a healthy rootstock attained a height of seven feet, planters would perform a second graft higher on the trunk, this one from *Hevea* that had demonstrated strong resistance. After this splice took, the old crown would be lopped off and the result would be a tree formed of three distinct genetic compositions: durable roots, a high-yield trunk, and a full, verdant crown of blight- and bug-resistant leaves.[14]

To Johnston's delight, the experiment was working. The grafts were holding, even against the Tapajós's strong winds, and the circumference of twice-grafted trees grew at the same rate as did an unspliced tree's. The procedure was time-consuming and costly and entailed building bulky scaffolding in the field to perform the operation and to support the graft until the tissue fused. And since only about every other graft took, the process had to be performed twice or sometimes three times until the graft bonded. But until a suitable hybrid could be created and multiplied in sufficient quantities, crown-grafted rubber was the only potentially competitive alternative to mass-produced Southeast Asian latex. And it held enough promise that US agricultural scientists—who, with Japan on the march through China and Germany gearing up its military and munitions industry, had once again been mobilized by Washington to find a secure source of "war rubber"—began to copy the method in experimental stations in Costa Rica and the Panama Canal Zone.

After Weir's departure, Johnston stepped up planting at Belterra. Over the next couple of years, work crews cleared over twenty thousand acres and planted close to two million trees, about a third of them top grafted. The plantation continued to suffer from chronic insect invasions, yet Belterra finally began to look like a true commercial estate, with its level groves blocked out in twenty-acre sections in an orderly fashion and its technicians keeping precise records of where they planted which seeds, seedlings, and bud grafts, so as to control for and develop better strains of *Hevea*.

But then Johnston lost his two best men. In late 1937, as John Rogge was traveling to Fordlandia to deliver a payroll, his boat was tipped by a late afternoon Tapajós storm, the kind that can come out of nowhere and call up oceanlike waves. Rogge fell overboard and drowned. A year later, Pringle, who had survived his fight with Weir relatively unscathed, had a nervous breakdown. He had been in the Amazon for a decade, having taken very little of his assigned vacation time. He became entangled in a series of petty fights with fellow staff members and started to suffer from insomnia, aggravated by drinking cup after cup of coffee "day and night, and through the night," and chain-smoking strong Brazilian cigarettes. Belterra's doctor diagnosed him as having all the symptoms of a "very nervous condition." His hands grew cold despite the heat, "denoting," the doctor said, a "general let down." The sheriff's wife also began to let herself go, ignoring a tooth abscess until the infection spread to her jaw.

"So much for the Pringles," wrote the doctor to officials in Dearborn, who ordered the couple to return to Michigan at the end of 1938.[15]

MEANWHILE, OPINION MAKERS in Rio and São Paulo continued to clamor for a visit from Henry Ford. As they heard reports that his Amazon enterprise had solved many of its social problems only to be beset by natural ones, it seemed all the more important that he come to see his namesake plantation. Brazil's Chamber of Commerce and Industry published an open letter in a Rio newspaper advising him to gain firsthand knowledge of the town that bore his name:

> Everything in life has its right and left side, its good and bad turn. With the wonderful enterprising spirit characteristic of Henry Ford, which makes him one of the greatest men of our times, he is ready to do everything in order to develop his large rubber plantation. . . . Unluckily, however, there was one principal element lacking for the success of his enterprise: personal knowledge of the region. . . . It would be very advantageous if Ford, who is already invited officially to visit Brazil, would visit the Tapajós, and give instructions to his representatives personally, instructions which would be capable of guaranteeing the success of the operations being undertaken in Pará.

The invitations kept arriving. The president of a small college in São Paulo invited him to do a radio interview:

> Your books have been widely read in Brazil, and aside from your commercial interests in the country, through the automobile that bears your

name, or your properties at Fordlandia, what you say and write is always read with very great interest. It has long been hoped that you would visit the country some day. The least that could be done to bring you in direct contact with the people would be a short fifteen minute interview over the radio, where your voice would be heard, expressing your own ideas on subjects of mutual interest to you and the Brazilians.

"I think," the president concluded his invitation, "this offers you a real opportunity to in some way establish a little more personal contact with the Brazilian people."

But as Ford advanced in years, the man who claimed to have invented the modern world began to develop a mild case of technophobia. Despite his promotion of air flight—PR for his company's aviation division—he didn't really like airplanes, so his long-promised arrival on Charles Lindbergh's *Spirit of St. Louis* was out of the question. As was, apparently, a radio interview.

Ford's secretary cabled the college president, simply saying, "Sorry Mr. Ford unable to comply with your request. Does not broadcast."[16]

CHAPTER 22

FALLEN EMPIRE OF RUBBER

THE FINAL YEARS OF FORDLANDIA AND BELTERRA MIRRORED THE final struggles of Ford's life; one can read in the letters and reports Archie Johnston sent back to Dearborn the history of the Ford Motor Company during the Great Depression—particularly the battles fought against unions and the growing reach of the federal government into its economic affairs. Though a protégé of Charles Sorensen, who competed with Harry Bennett for Ford's favor, Johnston was sympathetic to Bennett, writing him letters complaining of his graying hair and the jungle heat and sending him jaguar skins, hammocks, and other Amazonian curios. Bennett, who kept a number of tigers and lions as pets at his "castle"—as his house on Geddes Road in Ann Arbor was called—was grateful, and he kept Johnston updated on his efforts to beat back unionism at the Rouge.

Ford was not alone in his opposition to collective bargaining. When Congress passed the Wagner Act in 1935, leveling the playing field somewhat in the fight between capital and labor by protecting workers engaged in organizing from arbitrary dismissal, Detroit's Big Three all stated their resolve to remain union free. The United Automobile Workers, founded in 1935 and led by Walter and Victor Reuther, was small and practically penniless. But its members found a powerful weapon in the sit-down strike, halting production not by picketing on the outside but by refusing to leave their workstations, a move that stopped owners from hiring scabs. GM fell in 1936, signing a contract with the UAW, followed shortly by Chrysler. That left only Ford.[1]

The Rouge went into lockdown. Harry Bennett added more men to the ranks of his already bloated Service Department. His gunsels stepped up their surveillance, searching lockers and lunch pails for UAW literature, following workers into bathrooms to make sure no union talk occurred, and breaking up gatherings of two or more employees. Ford wouldn't let instruments of war be exhibited in his museum. Yet he let Bennett place machine guns atop the Rouge plant. The campaign against the UAW created a siege mentality among Ford's managers, and Bennett used his free rein to go after not just labor organizers or potential union supporters but anyone showing any sign of disloyalty. Bennett's men went undercover in the bars, markets, and churches that Ford workers frequented, reporting back on union sympathy and general grousing. In 1937, Bennett made front-page national headlines—just as he had five years earlier with the "Dearborn Massacre"— when photographers captured him and about forty of his men attacking Walter Reuther and other UAW members as they handed out union literature outside the factory's Gate 4. The thugs beat Reuther bloody and then threw him down a set of stone steps. They stomped on other organizers and broke the back of a minister. One woman vomited blood after being kicked in the stomach. The assault took place outside the same gate where Bennett and his men murdered the hunger marchers.

Edsel, who not only believed unionization to be inevitable but was broadly sympathetic to the New Deal as a step toward corporate rationalization, tried to intervene to limit Bennett's power. But Henry Ford, now seventy-four and in failing health—he would suffer a stroke in 1938— repeatedly reaffirmed Bennett's authority over labor issues. "He has my full confidence," he told his son. "The Ford Motor Company would be carried away," Henry said, "there wouldn't be anything left, if it wasn't for Harry."[2]

Archie Johnston watched these developments from afar, and he read his own ongoing battles with labor and the Brazilian government into them. He certainly was more partial to Bennett than was Edsel, whom he equated with James Weir. "FDR's actions," he wrote to Charles Sorensen following GM's and Chrysler's surrender, are "pitifully weak." He reported his successful defeat of Fordlandia's "first sit down strike" in June 1937, when about seventy-one men who cut wood for the boilers occupied the powerhouse. Johnston settled it in Bennett-like fashion, depriving the strikers of food and water until they vacated the building. "Now all is in order," he wrote.[3]

But Johnston in the jungle—stymied by a chronic labor shortage despite the global depression—found himself much more vulnerable than Bennett at the Rouge. Like FDR, Brazil's president, Getúlio Vargas, presided over a process of economic and political modernization, challenging the extreme power of landed elites and provincial politicians—power roughly analogous to the autonomy of states in the United States prior to the New Deal.* Johnston had welcomed Rio's intervention when it was used to rein in the local Amazonian elite, who had made life difficult for the company. Now, though, Rio had become part of the problem.

Vargas's government promoted new labor laws that made it easier for workers to unionize and required companies to provide paid vacations, severance pay, and pensions. Taking advantage of the new situation, workers at both Belterra and Fordlandia organized a union in early 1937 and began to file a growing number of complaints—mostly related to disputes over what union leaders described as arbitrary firings or efforts to claim newly mandated benefits—in federal labor court. As a result, government inspectors were regularly showing up at the plantations to demand access to company records and take testimony from employees. After a judge ruled that the company was subject to the jurisdiction of the Ministry of Labor—and not the Ministry of Agriculture, as Ford lawyers tried to argue as a way to

---

*The New Deal's most radical proposals came early, in a burst of laws Roosevelt shepherded through Congress soon after his 1933 inauguration, only to be diluted as time wore on; Vargas, in contrast, moved slowly, proposing only moderate changes upon taking power in 1930. But as opposition emerged, Vargas and his supporters, after suppressing a rebellion staged by São Paulo elites opposed to his efforts to concentrate federal power in Rio, became more aggressive. They adopted a new centralizing constitution in 1934 and then three years later declared the Estado Novo, or New State, best thought of as a fusion of Mussolini-style corporatism and New Deal social welfare.

exempt Ford from a new labor code—activists had become increasingly "bold," as Johnston wrote Dearborn, in their demands. Belterra was easily accessible to the Brazilian press, so he had to act with circumspection in dealings with organizers. At the more remote Fordlandia, though, Johnston fired a number of the most vocal, including the president and vice president of the union. But they continued their activities, simply moving offshore to set up their "headquarters on an island in the river."[4]

This was not the Island of the Innocents that held the brothels and bars but rather Francisco Franco's Urucurituba, which became a refuge for Fordlandia's labor leaders. In general terms, Vargas's prolabor legislation, as part of his broader political and social agenda, was designed to undercut the local power of rural potentates like Franco. It was a Vargas appointee who in the weeks after the December 1930 riot not only forced Franco to sell Pau d'Agua to Ford for a pittance but also removed him from his position as mayor of the nearby municipality of Aveiros. But these actions had one consequence that Fordlandia managers could not have foreseen: in retaliation, Franco began to support Fordlandia's labor organizers, creating an unlikely alliance between the modernizing thrust of unions and the feudal reaction of a provincial don.[5]

As did his counterparts at the Rouge, Johnston tried to keep the union at bay. "The Company," he warned his workers, "will not tolerate labor organizations." But after Rogge's death and Pringle's collapse, Johnston found himself shorthanded. The replacements Dearborn sent down lacked hands-on experience in running a plantation labor force, leaving Johnston in Belém to rely on a team of untested managers. And the law was against him. Johnston had no choice but to yield when a local judge ruled in 1939 that Ford's rubber plantations were indeed subject to Vargas's new federal labor law guaranteeing workers the right to organize; that same year a federal judge in the United States found the Ford Motor Company guilty of violating the Wagner Act.

Years before the River Rouge was forced to negotiate a contract with the United Automobile Workers, Fordlandia and Belterra had a union.

VARGAS REMAINED APPRECIATIVE of Ford, despite the support his administration gave to the plantation's workers. Like Ford, the Brazilian president considered himself a modernizer. During his administration, Brazil's road network doubled in size and the number of airports increased from 31 to 512. In any case, once it was established that Ford's plantations were subject to new labor and social welfare legislation, government arbiters usually dismissed most of the specific complaints brought against the company by employees. Dependent on the goodwill of a president who by the end of the 1930s had assumed dictatorial powers, Edsel Ford, upon learning that Vargas intended to tour northern Brazil in late 1940 to promote the development of the region, sent him a telegram inviting him to review Belterra. Since Archie Johnston was out of the country on vacation, he asked Harry Braunstein, executive manager of Ford's Rio assembly plant, to receive Vargas in his and his father's name.[6]

Vargas arrived at Belterra on October 8 in a hydroplane, circling overhead a few times to survey the town and planting fields before landing. As the plane pulled up to the dock and the president stepped out, Braunstein gave the signal to the band to strike up Brazil's national anthem, sung by several hundred children from the Henry Ford and Edsel Ford schools, "properly dressed in uniforms." When Vargas and his staff climbed into a waiting Lincoln to drive the ten miles to the plateau where Belterra was located, a number of men in the crowd asked that the motor be turned off and they be allowed to pull the president to the plantation, "signifying in that way their happiness and joy." Braunstein prevailed on them to abandon the idea as impractical, suggesting instead that sixty or so bicyclists form an escort. Along the way, cheered by crowds of onlookers, Vargas commented on the neatness of the children's dress and the "excellence of the road," noting that Brazil "certainly needed more such roads." His aide-de-camp remarked that he himself was from northern Brazil and he had never seen "as healthy a group of men as greeted the President" anywhere in the region. Once in Belterra, Vargas found much else to praise—the hospital, the dentist's office, schools that supplied books, pencils, and uniforms free of charge to the students, a spacious dance hall and other recreation facilities, and clean, tidy houses with colorful front gardens. The presidential entourage went on a "mosquito hunt" in a number of the plantation's screened buildings and found not a one.[7]

That afternoon, Vargas gave a speech in Belterra's new park, telling Ford's workers that the main objective of his government was to "create social laws which would serve to establish social harmony among all, to establish frank and sincere collaboration and co-operation between employer and employee, with all working toward the same end." Of course, he said, if there were "more men like Mr. Ford in this world no social legislation would be necessary." He then led a round of cheers for Henry and Edsel Ford. That night at dinner, Braunstein apologized that the two Fords couldn't be there in person to welcome him but presented Vargas with their signed photographs. He raised his glass to the president's commitment to progress and to advancing the well-being of workers. "Mr. Ford," Braunstein said, was the "first industrialist in the world who revolutionized the relations between worker and employer by giving them that which contributed to a life of comfort and equality, and we are doing everything within our power to follow in his footsteps in the treatment of those who work, produce, and co-operate in this project." One day, he said, admitting that the long-promised recovery of the latex trade had so far remained elusive, it "may possibly mean the re-birth of the Amazon Valley," the revival of the "fallen Empire of Rubber."

Vargas rose to share his impressions of the plantation, expressing "great satisfaction" that Ford was doing so much to "plant" not just rubber but "health, comfort and happiness." Echoing Braunstein's admission that so far the project had proved viable more in humanitarian terms than in economic ones, he emphasized the carmaker's generosity: Ford had not "as yet received any material compensation" despite his considerable expenditure. The rest of the evening and the next day involved more mutual expressions of admiration. There was, though, one piece of business Braunstein wanted to bring up with the president. Just before Vargas left, Braunstein, speaking in the name of Henry Ford, requested that he transfer Belterra and Fordlandia out of the jurisdiction of the Ministry of Labor and place them under the supervision of the Ministry of Agriculture—which would in effect make the company immune to labor law. Vargas said he would consider the request but promised nothing as he boarded his plane to fly to Manaus.

There, Vargas gave a speech that is considered by historians to mark the beginning of a long campaign by Brazil's federal government to populate and industrialize the Amazon. The address echoed Ford's technological optimism and advocacy of large-scale development projects. Yet perhaps influenced by his visit to Belterra, where he witnessed the failure of Ford's millions to revive the rubber economy, Vargas seemed to repudiate the kind of rural/industrial holism, driven by a respect for nature, the carmaker believed he could achieve in the Upper Peninsula, Muscle Shoals, the Tapajós, and elsewhere. Known as the "March to the West," Vargas's speech gave nature no quarter. "The highest task of civilizing man," the Brazilian president said, was to conquer and dominate the valleys of the great equatorial torrents," transforming their blind force and the extraordinary fertility into disciplined energy. The Amazon . . . shall become a chapter in the history of civilization."[8]

Following Vargas, one administration after another established government agencies and announced new schemes to rapidly modernize the region, to achieve "fifty years in five," as one of Vargas's successors put it, or to send "people without land" to a "land without people," as the military government of the 1960s described its colonization plan. Most of these efforts would fail on their own terms—that is, they did not bring sustainable, humane development to the region. They did, however, accelerate rapid deforestation, beginning what William Woodsworth might have called a "rash assault" on the largest intact tropical rain forest left on the planet.

IN DEARBORN, SOCIAL relations were decidedly less harmonious than either Braunstein or Vargas had painted them that night in Belterra. The UAW had grown rapidly at the River Rouge and other Ford plants since its founding in 1935. Having forced GM and Chrysler to the table, organizers could harness the union's resources in their fight against the lone holdout of the Big Three. In early 1941, activists shut down the Rouge in protest over the widespread firing of labor activists. It was the first strike ever called against Henry Ford and union leaders were not sure how his employees would respond. Only a third of the Rouge's workforce had by then signed with the UAW—Bennett's "terrorism," as the National Labor Relations Board described his reign, had its effects.[9]

As the strike spread throughout the Rouge's many divisions, Bennett first tried to label it communistic, an act of treason since the Ford Motor Company had just signed an agreement with the Roosevelt administration to begin war production. Workers answered by carrying pickets emblazoned with swastikas, equating Ford with Hitler. Why, one sign asked, did "Ford get a Nazi medal?"—a reference to the Grand Cross of the German Eagle bestowed by the German consul on Ford three years earlier on his seventy-fifth birthday. Unable to red-bait, Bennett next tried to race-bait. He hoped to capitalize on the loyalty some African American workers had for Ford based on his equal opportunity hiring (as well as their distrust of an all-white union leadership) to convince them to go back to work. This, too, failed. Most workers, including many African American workers, refused to return to their jobs.[10]

Ford threatened to shut the plant down rather than bargain collectively with his workers. Yet within a few weeks, in one of the greatest about-faces in US labor history, he not only agreed to recognize the results of a union election but, after the UAW won that election with an overwhelming majority, signed a contract that gave the union everything it wanted, including job security, the highest wages in the industry, and back pay to more than four thousand wrongfully fired workers. Historians debate what led Ford, who once moved a whole factory from New England to Michigan to thwart a union drive, to relent. Some point to Edsel's pleading, backed up with Clara Ford's threat to leave Henry if he didn't settle. Whatever the specific combination of motives that drove him to the bargaining table, when Ford finally met with Walter Reuther to congratulate him on his victory, he spun his surrender in the same conspiratorial web he used to explain most things in life. "You've been fighting General Motors and the Wall Street crowd," he said, now "we fight General Motors and Wall Street together, eh?"[11]

The deal also included a strong and binding grievance procedure that, considering what historians Peter Collier and David Horowitz call the "bizarre combination of feudal laws and naked power" that arbitrarily governed Ford's factory floor, was the industrial equivalent of enforcing due process on the divine right of kings. Ford often said his company was revolutionary, yet it took militant labor organizers to make it so.[12]

BACK IN THE Amazon, Johnston was having no better luck with rubber than he had holding off the union. By the time of Vargas's visit, plantation workers at Belterra had cleared nearly thirty thousand acres and planted close to three million trees. About a third of them were top grafted, still too young to give latex but showing promising vigor and fortitude. Then in late 1940, leaf blight, always present yet contained at Belterra, turned epidemic. Johnston, back from vacation, responded by ordering his crew to quickly top graft all tainted trees. But by the following year, blight had infected 70 percent of the blocks with closed canopies, killing most of the estate's trees.[13]

After the entry of the United States into World War II in 1941, Johnston was recalled to Dearborn, where he joined Ford's aviation division as it converted to the production of bombers and other wartime planes. But he remained the principal administrator of Ford's Amazon plantations and enjoyed talking with reporters and other Ford workers about his ten years in the jungle. "No white man," he liked to say, "can live in that country." He also remained committed to the expansion of rubber production and continued to hold out hope that top grafting, given time, could overcome blight, pest, and scales. Partial vindication came earlier the next year when, despite two years of epidemic blight, Belterra yielded 750 tons of latex. It wasn't high-quality rubber, and it was a far cry from Ford's annual consumption of fifty million pounds. But Johnston thought it a start.[14]

Then, on a return trip to Brazil in October 1942, Johnston witnessed what he called "the greatest swarm of caterpillars that has ever been seen in this area." For years, Fordlandia's caterpillar battalions had performed extensive and relentless handpicking to contain the pests. Now a new generation of moths had evolved and adapted to the threat by laying their eggs "only on the new shoots at the top of the trees." At that height, pickers couldn't see the hatched caterpillars until it was too late, until they had swarmed "down the tree eating all before them."[15] The trees recovered somewhat, putting out another shoot of leaves. But in what seemed to

Johnston to be a coordinated follow-up, the leaves were then assaulted by leaf blight—the "most severe attack in the history of the plantation." This time there was no rallying. "In many cases [the trees] had not strength to put out a third flush of foliate. With the excessive dry weather the trees started to die back. Some have died half way down the trunk and may die completely."[16]

"Some areas," Johnston reported to Dearborn, "are now as bare as bean poles."

CHAPTER 23

TOMORROW LAND

"My dear Harvey," Edsel Ford wrote to the namesake son of his father's old friend Harvey Firestone shortly after the United States had entered World War II, "I think I mentioned to you once something about selling our rubber plantation property on the Tapajós River in Brazil. If you would consider buying it, or have anything like that in mind, would you care to discuss the matter with me?" Firestone, who had taken over his deceased father's company, had nothing like that in mind. He was already getting about ten thousand tons of latex a year from his plantation in Liberia. The tire maker politely declined the offer.

By this point, Fordlandia and Belterra had practically become a subsidiary of the US government. Throughout his life, Ford had steadfastly opposed the fusion of business and government even as other American industrialists, particularly during the Great Depression, embraced it. But now in his late seventies he could do little but watch the marriage go forward.

The Japanese occupation of Southeast Asia and its rubber fields led to a renewed interest among Washington officials, not just in the Departments of Commerce and Agriculture but in the Pentagon as well, to find new sources of "war rubber." There had been advances over the last decade in the production of synthetic rubber, yet its production used up too much petroleum, an equally scarce resource. After war broke out, the Roosevelt administration signed treaties with sixteen Latin American countries to promote rubber production, promising government and private invest-ment and guaranteeing high prices for their latex. Vargas, who flirted with fascism but quickly lined up with the Allies, signed on.[1]

The Brazilian Amazon, despite the millions of dollars invested by Ford, was supplying less than 1 percent of the world's latex. In exchange for a $100 million loan, which included $5 million to invest in Amazon rubber, Vargas promised to sell all of his country's exportable rubber to the United States at a fixed price until December 1946. Rio began to work closely with US government agencies such as the Rubber Develop-ment Corporation, the Board of Economic Warfare, and the Office of Inter-American Affairs—headed by the peripatetic Nelson Rockefeller, who because of his deep business ties in the region became FDR's most influential envoy to Latin America. The idea was to encourage the migra-tion of tens of thousands of laborers to the Amazon in the hope of jump-starting rubber production. These "rubber soldiers" were promised credit and tools, decent housing, clothing, medical attention, beefed-up labor protection against local rubber bosses, and a fixed, honest, and livable price for their latex—in short, a New Deal–style guarantee to protect them against all those miseries cataloged so vividly in Carl LaRue's 1927 report, miseries that the coming of Henry Ford to the Amazon was supposed to have ended.

Archie Johnston by temperament and training was ill-disposed to welcome the attentions of the federal government—be they Rio's or Washington's—into Fordlandia's affairs, and he still resented having been forced to recognize the plantation worker's union. Yet having just witnessed the last, consuming blight infestation and caterpillar invasion at Belterra, he had run out of ideas about how to move forward in Brazil. He told Edsel that partnership with the government could per-haps finally make Ford's rubber estates profitable and that Washington's promise to pay an above-market price for latex could offset the estate's cost overruns. He also thought the hyped "war for rubber" might provide much needed labor.

So at the same time that Ford Motors in the United States was suspending production of civilian vehicles to meet the exclusive needs of its now single customer—building jeeps, planes, and tanks and allowing federal representatives to monitor production—Fordlandia, too, was opened up to Washington. Botanists from the Department of Agriculture set up shop in Fordlandia and Belterra to study Ford's top-grafting and cross-fertilization techniques. Federal scientists watched workers furiously bud graft trees in an attempt to outrun leaf disease and caterpillar infestations, and they took samples of the plantation's rubber stock back with them to US government tropical research stations in the Panama Canal Zone. In May 1942, Edsel wrote a letter to Johnston, certainly not vetted by his father, saying he had "no objection" to the Department of Agriculture's distributing Fordlandia clones to other Latin American countries.[2]

As the American press geared itself toward promoting the war effort, Ford's Amazon plantations assumed their final incarnation: useful embassies of FDR's wartime Good Neighbor Policy, staging grounds for New Deal diplomacy in the Amazon. As part of the war effort, Johnston ordered plantation managers to push forward on a frantic program of expansion. By the end of March 1943, field workers had top grafted more than 820,000 trees and performed about 60,000 hand pollinations to breed high-yielding, disease-resistant stock. The nursery had produced enough clones to graft hundreds of thousands of crowns onto trees already planted in the field, and for a stretch of 1944, workers were performing tens of thousands of top grafts a month. "Mr. Johnston and assistants are soberly confident," wrote one journalist, "but without overflowing enthusiasm. They have battled Amazonia too long for that. The successful trees I saw, their leaves glistening and green as they should be, confront the Amazonian jungle as forerunners of millions of scions being prepared for other advance bases. Someone close to the development of plantation rubber in the Amazon Basin told me that anyone except Henry Ford would have surrendered long ago." Admittedly, Ford's rubber output might be but a "drop in the bucket," but it was enough to "help plug the serious leak in our stock pile." And it would "increase geometrically year after year." As late as 1945, one writer was forecasting that Fordlandia would be producing five hundred tons of latex by 1950.[3]

But the blight and the bugs continued to undermine all efforts. Though Belterra and Fordlandia were finally producing some latex, their operating cost was much higher than what rubber was trading for on the international market, despite the war. With large blocks of rubber trees ravaged by leaf blight, Belterra workers were collecting only about 165 pounds of latex per acre, a woefully low yield considering the amount of capital that had been invested. Peasants in Sumatra in the 1930s, in contrast, tapped about twice that amount in the same acreage.[4]

Yet while the two plantations were economic failures, their well-ordered towns stood as shining examples of the American dream. Travel writers poured into Latin America to report on the state of the wartime Good Neighbor Alliance, and for those traveling through the Amazon, Fordlandia and Belterra became obligatory layovers, places where they gladly traded the promise of a good story for a good bed. After a rough time up the Tapajós, Henry Albert Phillips was happy to find at Belterra a "guest house that might have been in Dearborn, Michigan, or even in Paradise, after what I had come through to get there. Hot shower, frozen fresh food dinner, electric fans, Beauty Rest Mattress, and the first sleep in weeks that was not like a steam bath." Ford's first Amazon plantation might have been a "multiple-million-dollar failure," Phillips wrote in a book called *Brazil: Bulwark of Inter-American Relations*, but in Belterra he found the "*living* image of the ghostly Fordlandia," a place where "Fordlandia's brightest dreams were being substantiated."

Walt Disney visited Fordlandia in 1941 on a tour organized by Nelson Rockefeller's Office of Inter-American Affairs, as part of the agency's mission to promote the commercial, cultural, and scientific integration of the Americas. Three years later, using film footage supplied by the Ford Motor Company, Disney released a documentary under the auspices of Rockefeller's agency called *The Amazon Awakens*, which celebrated the Ford town as one of the Amazon's four great cities, along with Iquitos, Manaus, and Belém. The film, typical of others made during the war to highlight pan-American goodwill, included images of Americans playing golf on a course that looked like it could have been located in California, right where Disney after the war would build his own namesake model town. Like Fordlandia, which promised to wrench the Amazon into modernity while simultaneously organizing square dances and pastoral poetry readings for its workers, Disneyland's themed parks would mix and match different experiences of time: the stage coaches, riverboats, and railroads of Frontierland, along with Main Street USA, modeled on Disney's hometown of Marceline, Missouri, captured a bygone America, while Tomorrowland pointed to the future. Adventureland featured a jungle river cruise on a boat called the *Amazon Belle*.[5]

Fordlandia's and Belterra's laboratories and hospitals were put to use as federal experimental stations, in an effort to improve the health and nutritional conditions of the Amazon and support large-scale migration. Plantation doctors cooperated closely with the Office of Inter-American Affairs, which in support of the war for rubber was carrying out a large-scale campaign to eliminate the diseases that stood in the way of maintaining a large, concentrated labor force in the jungle. They shared their research with government public health reformers on how to fight malaria, hookworm, and other infectious diseases. Johnston even ordered a new building constructed to house a corps of Brazilian nurses who would work under the auspices of Rockefeller's health program.[6]

In 1942, air force officials requested that the Ford Motor Company build a runway in Belterra to conceal a stash of planes. German U-boats had been targeting Allied ships off Brazil's coasts, and the air force was nervous that Belém's airport—considered one of the most critical along the US–Latin American–African route—was vulnerable. After consulting with Edsel, Johnston agreed. But he hoped at least to get some labor in exchange for this cooperation. "You of course are aware," he wrote to Lieutenant Colonel Charles Wooley, "that there is a great shortage of labor, and the entire project is only possible if more men are obtainable." But no help was forthcoming, and he had to build the airstrip with the plantation workers he had on hand.[7]

Fordlandia and Belterra were in effect nationalized, both practically—their clones distributed to other plantations to support the war effort, their doctors and technicians placed under the command of Rockefeller's government health campaign, and their land and labor put to the serv-ice of the US military—and symbolically. Henry Ford of course in-tended Fordlandia to be an example of his particular American dream, of how Ford-style capitalism—high wages, humane benefits, and moral improvement—could bring prosperity to a benighted land, free of gov-ernment meddling. Yet by the early 1940s, Fordlandia's economic failure actually strengthened the hand of those who advocated for increased gov-ernment investment in, and regulation of, the rubber industry, while its clean streets, functioning utilities, and impressive record in hygiene and health care made it an effective symbol of what the New Deal–style politi-cal and economic cooperation could accomplish abroad, even in a place as remote and underdeveloped as the Amazon.

Though nothing came of it, James G. McDonald, head of FDR's Ad-visory Committee on Political Refugees, even secured Henry Ford's tenta-tive permission to resettle European Jewish refugees at Fordlandia. McDonald met with Ford at Dearborn on April 1, 1941, along with Harry Bennett, Archie Johnston, and Albert Kahn, to discuss the matter. The Nazis had overrun Eastern Europe and invaded North Africa, but Pearl Harbor was still a few months in the future, so the River Rouge had yet to be turned over to wartime production. As McDonald laid out his proposal, Bennett kept interrupting the conference to take phone calls. As it turned out, the meeting was taking place on the very day the UAW launched its strike of River Rouge, and Bennett was issuing a series of urgent orders in an effort to contain the situation. Ford himself didn't look well, McDonald thought. He had "aged markedly" since the last time the two had met. He was "vague" in his responses and seemed distracted, drifting off on tan-gents. "We are on this earth to work and for nothing else," he said; laziness was the cause of most of the world's ills, including the war. Archie John-ston related the history of Fordlandia to FDR's emissary and said that he wasn't optimistic about settling large numbers of European Jews on the plantation, since "for them to work the land would be to lose caste because almost all of the laborers today are colored natives." Johnston thought it would be better to send them to southern Brazil, around São Paulo. Three times in the conversation, Ford let McDonald know that he thought syn-thetic rubber would replace natural latex and that his Brazilian plantations would be better used for the large-scale relocation of small farmers. He agreed in principle to settle Jewish exiles on them, though he refused to commit to a specific plan for action. And at a number of points, both Bennett and Ford interrupted the discussion to declare "they were not interested in this scheme in any sense as a means of easing criticism at Mr. Ford's alleged anti-Semitism."[8]

EDSEL DIED IN 1943, and for a dangerously long moment Harry Bennett tottered on the edge of taking complete control of the Ford Motor Company. After the first UAW contract was signed in 1941, Bennett had managed to retain and even tighten his hold over the increasingly senile Ford. He even dubiously claimed that Henry added a codicil to his will putting him in charge of the company upon his death—which, after Ford's passing, Bennett claimed to have burned. Yet the recognition of the UAW and the establishment of a grievance procedure began to erode Bennett's power, whose chief source of authority—the ability to terrorize workers— was taken away from him. After another, this time major stroke, Henry, again urged on by his wife, Clara, turned over the company to his grandson. In this, she had a little help from the Roosevelt administration. Alarmed that the company it depended on for war matériel was being crippled by infighting and mismanagement, the White House had arranged the early release of the young Henry from the navy, hoping that he might be able to bring some sanity to his grandfather's company.

Henry Ford II took over a business worth over a billion dollars and employing more than 130,000 workers—75,000 of them in the Rouge alone. Yet it had no system of oversight (a few years earlier, Henry Ford had abolished the Accounting Department when he learned that Edsel had, without consulting him, ordered the construction of a new office building) save the remnants of Bennett's vast spy network, and it was wracked by years of corruption and pilfering. Millions of dollars of material were stolen yearly from Ford plants. Bennett himself siphoned a substantial cut from numerous contracts. With "no cost control, no mechanism for establishing or checking plans," the Ford Motor Company was not just a metaphorical labyrinth. It actually had secret lairs where midlevel thugs enjoyed illicit pleasures. Henry II busted one up personally, using an iron club to break down the door. The internal disaster of the Ford Motor Company actually made Fordlandia look like a model of efficiency and transparency. And the company hadn't made a civilian vehicle in over three years.[9]

So considering the pressure on Henry II to rebuild the company and get it ready for postwar production, his decision to sell off his grandfather's many money-losing village industries, including holdings in the Upper Peninsula, didn't take much thought. The economic boom that took place in the decades after World War II would "decentralize" American life, but in its own way—through the growth of the interstate highway system, suburban development, and the migration of industry from the Northeast and Midwest to the South, the Southwest, and then abroad. And it wouldn't be propelled, as Ford once predicted, by "little factories along the little streams" or powered by waterwheels, steam, or beet juice.

The Ford Motor Company's board of directors named Henry Ford II president on September 21, 1945. One of his first acts, in early October, was to fire Harry Bennett. Then, on November 5, he turned Fordlandia and Belterra, valued at nearly $8 million, with $20 million invested in them, over to the Brazilian government for $244,200—which covered the amount the company owed its plantation workers under Vargas's laws guaranteeing severance pay.

HENRY FORD TOOK Edsel's death hard. The carmaker had taunted his son during his last years, as he wasted away from what is now called Zollinger-Ellison syndrome, stomach tumors that overproduce corroding acid. Ford told Edsel that his symptoms were caused by his Grosse Pointe "high living," by what he ate, or didn't eat, how he chewed, what he drank, and when he exercised. Shortly after Edsel died, Ford told the wife of an employee, as they wandered around Greenfield Village, that he knew that "in life, he and Edsel had not always understood each other and at times could not see eye to eye." But Ford, the perfecter of mechanical reproduction, believed in spiritual reproduction, that is, reincarnation, and he hoped that "before too long, he and Edsel would be together again" and that "there would be better understanding and they could continue working together."[10]

Ford's health declined rapidly. He spent more and more time in Greenfield Village, as well as in some of the other towns and mills he

Ruins of the sawmill at Iron Mountain in the Upper Peninsula.

owned throughout Michigan. But even before Henry II began to unload Ford's village industries, company officials, trying to consolidate operations to make wartime production more efficient, had quietly closed two of his favorites. Both were located near his summer home, on the shore of Lake Superior in Michigan's Upper Peninsula: Pequaming, which Henry purchased in 1923, and Alberta, which he had constructed from scratch in 1936, around the time that he and Edsel approved the creation of Belterra.

Though the company increasingly distanced itself from its controversial founder—for more than half a century, Ford Motors would rarely mention Henry in its advertising—many in the Upper Peninsula continued to invoke Ford's name. "Everybody is calling our village a ghost town," said one Pequaming resident in 1942, after the company began to remove equipment from its mill. Yet its residents still held out hope. "As long as there's a Henry Ford, Pequaming will still be here."[11]

Ford did visit Pequaming once more, in the summer after Edsel's passing. No one in the company told him that the mill had been shut down,

Ruins of Pequaming sawmill.

so he was saddened to learn that the town's clapboard houses had been boarded up and its saw stilled. Ford walked around the village and talked with a few of its remaining families. Just a few years earlier more than four hundred people called Pequaming home. Now only a handful of its seventy-four houses were occupied. Its school had been a special source of pride for Ford, reminiscent of his own boyhood single-room school-house. But that day all he saw was a "shell of walls and floors," its desks sold off and its doors padlocked. The town's caretaker asked if he wanted to go in. Ford said no. He "preferred to remember it as it was with the sound of children's voices."

The Pequaming mill whistle blew one last time in 1947, an old-timer thinks she remembers, to mark Ford's death.

STILL WAITING FOR HENRY FORD

WHEN THE FORD MOTOR COMPANY ABANDONED ITS AMAZON holdings in November 1945, many of its workers didn't know the Americans were leaving until the day they boarded ship and embarked down the Tapajós. "Goodbye, we're going back to Michigan," said the wife of Fordlandia's last manager to her nanny, América Lobato. "They didn't take anything with them, they just left, like that," Lobato recalled.

In Belterra, the departure was just as quick. Workers from the rubber nurseries, some of whom had learned bud-grafting techniques from James Weir, were assembled and told that both plantations were being turned over to the Brazilian government's Instituto Agronômico do Norte, headed by Felisberto Camargo. A progressive agronomist, Camargo believed that the rational application of science, technology, and hygiene could bring about a peaceful, satisfied world—a view obviously related to Henry Ford's earlier technological optimism. Yet henceforth the agent of that application would be not an individual or a private corporation but a government organization of the kind Camargo worked for.

In Fordlandia, Camargo pulled up most of the rubber trees closest to the town, instead planting jute, cacao, and other experimental crops and grazing humpbacked, floppy-eared cattle imported from India. Fordlandia, he said in a report to the United Nations, was an "utter failure" due to "blank ignorance" and the refusal to "test its theories by experiment." But Camargo did credit Fordlandia with being the "true cradle of the technique of double grafting," which, while unable to save the plantation, had benefited others. "Above all," the Brazilian agronomist said, the place was an "object lesson in applied science and a proof of human capacity in the face of a demanding and ill-understood task on the largest scale." In Belterra, by the time the company left, Ford workers had planted thirty thousand acres of land with about two million rubber trees that were crown grafted and thus, finally, resistant to leaf blight. Camargo forecast that this one plantation would soon yield annually about a third as much rubber as all the Amazon did at the height of the boom. He also hoped that its large stocks of clones and hybrids could be sold to Goodyear and Firestone plantations, with the profits invested back into projects to develop the region.[1]

But though Belterra's twice-grafted trees were running sap, they couldn't compete with the low-cost latex that was flooding the world market following Japan's defeat in the war. America's revived auto industry was either buying its rubber from recaptured Malaysian, Indonesian, and Vietnamese plantations or synthesizing it from petroleum, now affordable as a result of Franklin Delano Roosevelt's 1945 deal with King Abdul Aziz of Saudi Arabia, who traded military protection for the cheap oil that fueled America's postwar economic expansion. Yet it wasn't just low-cost or synthetic latex that foiled Camargo's plans to continue the work started by Ford.

Camargo, an appointee of Getúlio Vargas, understood it as his task to increase the Amazon's agricultural output as well as to overturn its "semifeudal" social structure. He proposed that the government support the creation of tapper cooperatives and help them sell their latex on the international market, thus bypassing parasitical middlemen and ending once and for all the "most irrational exploitation of man and natural resources"—the very system that Ford so many years ago had promised to do away with. But once the war was over, Vargas's conservative opponents staged a coup and removed him from power. In the Amazon, old-guard merchants and traders, having waited out Ford, Vargas, and World War II, regrouped and went on the offensive. They lobbied Rio to stop subsidizing plantation rubber and reduce its assistance for health care, education, and other social services that threatened to undermine their power. Claiming there were millions of untapped wild rubber trees throughout the jungle, they said that the best way to revive the latex economy was to go back to the way things used to be, to forget about cultivating *Hevea* and paying wages and return to a reliance on "independent"—that is, indebted—tappers. Not content with having outlasted Henry Ford, the rubber barons wanted Belterra to be broken up into small lots and sold off.[2]

Belterra remained intact for the time being, yet the rubber merchants and traders got much of what they wanted. Camargo was eventually transferred out of the Amazon to a post in Rio and the federal government shifted its subsidies directly to rubber merchants, in effect reviving the old debt system that had ruled the region during the boom. But having won the skirmish against Camargo, the region's old rubber oligarchy lost a larger war. In May 1951, the first latex shipment from Singapore arrived in the Brazilian port of Santos, produced from trees that were the direct descendants of the seeds Henry Wickham sent to Kew Gardens exactly seventy-five years earlier. Brazil has ever since relied on imported latex to meet its rubber needs.[3]

In the 1950s, Fordlandia and Belterra were abandoned a second time, passed from one government agency to another, each in turn less committed to their management and upkeep. Some families moved out, others moved in. Camargo's "object lesson" in large-scale, industrial agricultural science reverted to an archipelago of small, dispersed hamlets where peasants, many of them former Ford workers, cultivated plots of land among the derelict rubber stands, then selling the fruits, vegetables, and other forest products in local markets.

IT WOULD BE tempting to read the story of Fordlandia and Belterra as a parable of arrogance, just one in a long line of failed bids to press man's will on the storied Amazon. But the parable is not quite right. Other would-be jungle conquerors tended to be motivated by the sublime vastness of the

Ruins of Fordlandia's powerhouse.

Amazon itself, entranced with the idea of taming its wildness. The "sociologist manufacturer," though, had his sights on a more formidable challenge. Ford, the man who in the early 1910s helped unleash the power of industrialism to revolutionize human relations, spent most of the rest of his life trying to put the genie back into the bottle, to contain the disruption he himself let loose, only to be continually, inevitably thwarted. Born more from political frustration at home than from the need to acquire control over yet another raw material abroad, Fordlandia represents in crystalline form the utopianism that powered Fordism—and by extension Americanism. It reveals the faith that a drive toward greater efficiency could be controlled and managed in such a way as to bring balance to the world and that technology itself, without the need for government planning, could solve whatever social problems arose from progress's advance. Fordlandia is indeed a parable of arrogance. The arrogance, though, is not that Henry Ford thought he could tame the Amazon but that he believed that the forces of capitalism, once released, could still be contained.

Those unfettered forces are most visible in Manaus, about three hundred miles west of Santarém. Once the gilded epitome of a rubber-boom excess, Manaus after the bust became a "city of the past," as the *Washington Post* observed, with the drop in latex prices "acting more slowly but as surely as the ashes of Vesuvius in Pompeii."[4] The city revived only in the late 1960s, when Brazil's military regime decreed it a free-trade zone. Exempt from import tariffs, Manaus became Brazil's national emporium. Cargo ships arrived at its deepwater port from the United States, Europe, and Asia to unload consumer goods. In 1969, the *New York Times* was reporting that a "feverish prosperity" had returned, as Brazilians from Rio, São Paulo, and other points south took advantage of improved, subsidized air flight, flying into the city to purchase duty-free toys, fans, radios, air conditioners, and television sets. At the same time, the military government provided subsidies and reduced export taxes to stimulate industry, turning the city into one of the world's first brand-name assembly zones—similar to the Mexican *maquilas* that were then beginning to press against the the southern border of the United States. Today, Manaus's industrial parks are home to about a hundred corporate plants, including Honda, Yamaha, Sony, Nokia, Philips, Kodak, Samsung, and Sanyo. In 1999, Harley-Davidson opened its first offshore factory in the city. Gillette has its largest South American facility here. When a consumer in Latin America purchases a DVD player, cell phone, TV, bicycle, or motorcycle, there is a good chance it was assembled in the middle of the world's largest tropical forest.[5]*

With the highest population growth rate in Brazil, Manaus has gone from less than 200,000 people in the mid-1960s to nearly 3,000,000 residents today. The city bursts out of the Amazon like a perverse Oz, steadily eating away the surrounding emerald foliage. Like many other Third World cities, Manaus is plagued by rising poverty and crime, child prostitution, gridlocked traffic, pollution, and poor health care. There is no

---

*Manaus is called a free-trade zone, but there is little "free trade" about it, at least in the way that term implies minimal government intervention in the market. With its remote jungle location deep in the continent's heartland, the city as a manufacturing center could not survive without significant government subsidies, needed to offset the high cost of transportation.

sewage plant in the city, and its waste flows untreated into the Rio Negro. Manaus accounts for 6 percent of Brazil's total manufacturing, and provides about a hundred thousand jobs. Yet no matter how dynamic its export sector, the city can't possibly give employment to all the migrants who travel from the rural Amazon and beyond, desperate for work. On flights in, visitors can see the luxury condominiums that rise high along the river's sandy banks and, pressed up against them, low-lying slums built on wobbly stilts to protect against river flooding, a dramatic landscape of inequality in one of the most unequal countries in the world. It makes the distance that separated the homes of American managers from those of Brazilians in Fordlandia negligible in comparison.[6]

Cities like Manaus, based on the assembly of corporate brand-name products, are the true heirs of Ford's legacy. Their economies are made possible by a process if not started than at least perfected by Ford's factory lines, that is, by the breaking up of industrial production into a series of reducible, routinized, and reproducible parts. Ford, of course, imagined his industrial method as leading to greater social cohesion. In his more utopian moments, he envisioned a world in which industry and agriculture could exist in harmony, with factories providing seasonal labor for farmers and industrial markets for agricultural products like soybeans. It's an easy vision to mock, especially considering the brutality and dehumanizing discipline that reigned at the River Rouge. Yet actual Fordism at its most vigorous albeit short-lived stage did result in a kind of holism, where the extraction and processing of raw materials, integrated assembly lines, working-class populations, and consumer markets created vibrant economies and robust middle classes. Anchoring it all was a belief that decent pay would lead to increased sales. Yet even as Ford was preaching his gospel of "high wages to create large markets," Fordism as an industrial method was making the balanced, whole world Ford longed for impossible to achieve.

Today, the link between production and consumption, and between good pay and big markets, has been broken, invalidated by the global extension of the logic of the assembly line. Harley-Davidson, for instance, does not make motorcycles from start to finish in Manaus but rather assembles bikes from parts manufactured elsewhere, which it then sells in the Brazilian market. Sony likewise uses free-trade zones (not just Manaus but Colón in Panama, Ushuaia in southern Argentina, and Iquique in northern Chile) as low-tax entrepôts into national markets. The final confection of the product in these cities is a formality, done to exempt the product from import taxes. In Manaus, Sony puts together TVs (over a million a year) and audio equipment from component parts made in countries with even lower labor costs and certainly less labor protection than in Brazil.

In other words, there is no relationship between the wages Harley-Davidson pays to make its products and the profits it receives from selling them. Instead of Ford's virtuous circuit of high wages and decent benefits generating expanding markets, a vicious one now rules: profits are derived not from well-paid workers affluent enough to buy what they have made but from driving prices as low as they can go; this in turn renders good pay and humane benefits not only unnecessary for keeping the economy going but impossible to maintain, since the best, and at times the only, place to cut production costs is labor. The result is a race to the bottom, a system of perpetual deindustrialization whereby corporations—including, most dramatically, the Ford Motor Company itself—bow before a global economy that they once mastered, moving manufacturing abroad in order to reduce labor costs just to survive.

Ford's River Rouge employees were once some of the highest-paid industrial workers in the world. But they now make a fraction of what they did three decades ago and, with Ford's continued existence as a company hanging by a slender thread, are continually asked for bigger and bigger givebacks. In 2007, the UAW, in an effort to convince Ford to make its new "world market" model Fiesta in the United States, offered to cut starting wages by half, to less than fifteen dollars an hour. It didn't work. In June 2008, the company announced that it would set up production in Mexico, where the union there agreed to cut wages for new hires to half of the prevailing salary of $4.50 an hour. In order to stay competitive with China, some factories have cut hourly wages to as low as $1.50 an hour. Poverty is not just a consequence but a necessary component of this new system of permanent austerity. In Ford's day, high wages, aside from their role in creating consumer markets, were needed to build a reliable labor force. Today, misery plays that role. "I guarantee you that if we advertise for 2,000 workers," admits Juan José Sosa Arreola, the Mexican union leader who helped negotiate wage cuts in order to convince Ford to make the Fiesta in Mexico, "10,000 people are going to show up." Every year, the same kind of desperation pushes tens of thousands of migrants into Manaus—and millions into cities like it across the globe. In the 1920s, Ford thought that the "flow" of history was moving away from cities. But in 2008, more than half of the earth's inhabitants were reported to be living in cities, a billion of them—a sixth of the world's population—in slums.[7]

In the lower Amazon, then, along about a three-hundred-mile axis, runs the history of modern capitalism. On one end is Fordlandia, a monument to the promise that was early-twentieth-century industrialization. "Ford built us a hospital; he paid his workers well and gave them good houses," a Fordlandia resident told a *Los Angeles Times* reporter in 1993. "It would be nice if the company would come back." On the other is Manaus, a city plagued by the kind of urban problems Ford thought he could transcend but whose very existence owes much to the system he pioneered. Trying to reproduce America in the Amazon has yielded to outsourcing America to the Amazon.[8]

As MANAUS CONTINUES its outward sprawl, Fordlandia, too, has experienced an influx of new migrants. They largely come not from the northeast, as Ford's men did eighty years ago, but from the south, from the Amazon state of Mato Grosso, arriving along an eleven-hundred-mile dirt highway that is an impassible mud trench for much of the rainy season. Many of Fordlandia's recent settlers raised cattle in Mato Grosso, a trade they brought with them to their new home. Ford's opinion that cows were the crudest, most inefficient machines in the world is not unjustified considering the amount of land and energy it takes to keep one alive. Between 2000 and 2005, cattle ranching accounted for 60 percent of deforestation, and today Brazil is the world's largest exporter of cows, with its 180,000,000-head herd equaling the size of its population. At least a thousand of them can be found at Fordlandia, grazing along the riverbank and on what was Fordlandia's golf course.

The town's tennis court has yielded to cattle stalls. But mostly the cows roam and ruminate on the hillsides previously planted with rubber, now converted to pastureland.[9]

Rather than marking a revival of Fordlandia, the new settlers signal a fresh wave of despoliation, part of a larger shift in the balance of power between man and nature. Many have observed the ironies involved in Ford's varied efforts to harmonize industry and agriculture, be it in the woods of the Upper Peninsula, along the waterways of southern Michigan, or in Appalachia's Tennessee Valley. But the most profound irony is currently on display at the very site of Ford's most ambitious attempt to realize his pastoralist vision. In the Tapajós valley, three prominent elements of Ford's vision—lumber, which he hoped to profit from while at the same time finding ways to conserve nature; roads, which he believed would knit small towns together and create sustainable markets; and soybeans, in which he invested millions, hoping that the industrial crop would revive rural life—have become the primary agents of the Amazon's ruin, not just of its flora and fauna but of many of its communities.

There's a new commercial sawmill in operation at Fordlandia, and though its technology is not much improved from what John Rogge and Matt Mulrooney had available eighty years ago, it's had much more success at exporting wood than Ford did. The mill's owner, Raymundo Donato, is amused when asked if he faces the kinds of problems that so vexed Ford, from termites and wood that is too hard or too soft to the valley's warp-inducing humidity. There are uses now for soft wood that didn't exist back then, he says. The kapok ceiba is one of the Tapajós's tallest trees, rising high above the forest canopy, but Fordlandia's sawyers considered its wood to be worthless pulp. Today, though, the majestic tree can be shredded and then pressed ignobly into particleboard. Many of Ford's other problems had to do with the fact that his wood sat at the plantation for weeks, often months, vulnerable to the weather until a big enough lot could be assembled to make a shipment back to the United States worth the cost of transportation. Donato only has to send batches of lumber a few hours to the town of Itaituba, where the boards are dry kilned, strapped with metal bands to prevent warping, and then floated downriver to be sold to one of the big timber multinationals.

Donato employs about 125 local residents and produces graded timber for export to the United States, Canada, Europe, and Asia. His permits are all in order, he insists, and he strictly follows environmental law, using techniques of selective timbering that allow the forest to reproduce. Most of the thousands of small mills that exist throughout the forest, however, operate illegally, and logging is responsible for about 6 percent of deforestation. In early 2008, satellite imagery showed a shocking increase in the rate of rain forest clear-cutting. "Never before have we detected such a high deforestation rate," said Gilberto Câmara, head of the National Institute for Space Research. The world was reminded that it had already lost 20 percent of the Amazon's 1.6 million square miles, and if the pace continued, 40 percent of what was left would be gone by 2050. In response, the federal government launched an operation to crack down on illegal logging. Woefully understaffed in relation to the size of the territory to be covered, government agents decided to focus on key towns or cities where contraband wood comes in from the jungle to be "laundered" and transformed, by bribery or faked paperwork, into legitimate export cargo, sold to multinationals like Japan's Eidai Corporation, China's Tianjin Fortune Timber, and the New Orleans–based Robinson Lumber Company, which enjoy the patina of legitimacy even though they operate at just a degree of separation from the lawlessness that plagues much of the Amazon's lumber industry.[10]

Tailândia, a fast-growing city of sixty-five thousand people located two hours south of Belém, is one such potential choke point, home to dozens of small mills and the offices of a number of large timber multinationals. Logging, legal or not, provides needed income to many in the state of Pará, and in Tailândia an estimated 70 percent of the city's population make their living off wood. So when inspectors arrived in town in February 2008, they were met by thousands of protesters, who burned tires, erected barricades, and took a number of government officials hostage. Rio sent in reinforcements, hundreds of heavily armed police, to retake the town. They restored order, confiscating five hundred truckloads of wood valued at $1.5 million and closing down dozens of unlicensed mills. Federal agents also destroyed hundreds of illegal ovens used to make bootleg charcoal, which is shipped to southern Brazil, where it is used to fire blast furnaces that smelt pig iron. This aspect of the illegal lumber industry is particularly devastating to the Amazon's future since these charcoal ovens burn young trees too small to be milled—the forest's most reproductively healthy and active generation. Tailândia's ovens alone consume tens of thousands of saplings a month.[11]

The charcoal industry also has horrific human consequences. In December 2006, a *Bloomberg News* investigation found that much Amazonian charcoal was made by starving, disease-ridden slaves. Lured to the region with promises of good-paying work, whole families were held captive in camps deep in the jungle, given polluted, parasite-ridden water to drink and miserable food to eat and forced to sleep in windowless corrugated tin shacks, unbearably hot on their own but even more so owing to their closeness to the kilns. Children were left to play in the mud, living with malaria, dying from tuberculosis and other illnesses. The Amazon is today home to an estimated twenty thousand modern slaves, "people who have absolutely no economic value except as cheap labor under the most inhumane conditions imaginable," says Marcelo Campos, an official with the Brazilian Ministry of Labor. The charcoal is used to make pig iron, which is exported to the United States to be turned into steel for consumer products manufactured by some of the world's biggest corporations, including the Ford Motor Company. This modern form of jungle slavery is, as Campos points out, a "key part of the globalized, export-oriented economy Brazil thrives on."[12]*

By some estimates, logging is a two-billion-dollar-a-year industry in Pará, with wood going for $275 a cubic meter, or about $1,300 a tree. It's a high-stakes business, and violence has become an elemental part of the trade. In 2005 in eastern Pará, gunmen hired by loggers killed Sister Dorothy Stang, a Maryknoll nun from the United States who had been working with local rural communities to oppose illicit logging. In early 2008, just southeast of where Stang was murdered, Emival Barbosa

---

*When it opened, the River Rouge not only made its own pig iron in furnaces heated with coal coke but recycled coke gas to make chemical byproducts, ore dust to make machine borings, and slag to make cement; today, the Ford Motor Company no longer molts its own pig iron, having long ago sold off its famed River Rouge foundry to a Russian company.

Machado was shot to death as he was leaving his house, probably for providing information to officials about criminal logging. A few years ago, gangs of armed loggers marauded through lands claimed by the Rio Pardo Indians, chasing them away, sacking valuable trees, and leaving desolation in their wake. Between 1971 and 2004, 772 activists working to either defend human rights or slow deforestation have been executed in Pará. Only three cases have been brought to trial.

ROADS, TOO, WHICH Ford promoted, have accelerated the devastation of the Amazon. With the announcement that the Ford Motor Company planned to establish a rubber plantation in the largely roadless jungle came much speculation in the local press that it would build major highways linking interior areas like Mato Grosso to ports and markets. Such projects never materialized, though plantation workers in both Fordlandia and Belterra laid out dozens of miles of roadbed, both to open up the estates' hinterlands for planting and logging and to allow staff members to go on short car trips to escape boredom. But in the years since Getúlio Vargas traveled from Belterra to Manaus to give his "March to the West" speech, road construction has increased rapidly. In the 1960s, the government built a 1,200-mile highway connecting Belém to the new capital of Brasilia, and the 3,000-mile Trans-Amazonian Highway was inaugurated in 1972, with the hope of promoting migration out of the drought-plagued northeast into the less populated rain forest.

Road building in the Amazon has created what social ecologists have described as a destructive "feedback cycle." Migrants move in and land values rise. Often, the construction of the road and the arrival of farmers, ranchers, loggers, speculators, and settlers bring disease to, and spark confrontation with, indigenous peoples. Always, the advance of roads puts sudden and rapid pressure on the local ecology. Forest is cleared, cattle are grazed, and crops are planted. Such activity fragments ecosystems—whose biological diversity depends on maintaining an extensive, uninterrupted mass of forest—into smaller and smaller sections, propelling the extinction of flora and fauna and increasing the risk of forest fires. The profits generated from the increased economic activity lead to additional road building, most of it illegal. Dirt spurs shoot off the main spine of the highway, creating a "fishbone effect" startlingly visible from the air. Meanwhile, poor settler farmers, enticed by the prospect of cheap, abundant land, quickly find that, once stripped of trees, the Amazon's soil becomes exhausted. So they push farther into the forest. And the process begins all over again. There are currently more than a hundred thousand miles of legal and illegal roads cutting through the Amazon, each at one time promising to bring prosperity and development but most often delivering bloodshed, displacement, impoverishment, and clear-cutting.

The road that brings Mato Grosso migrants to Fordlandia, BR-163, continues northeast, eventually reaching its terminus in Santarém. For much of the way, to the left on the northwest side of the highway, stands the Tapajós National Forest, which includes a good portion of the original Fordlandia concession. It's one of the Amazon's first protected areas, over a million acres of relatively intact forest and home to a number of indigenous communities. It was here that, starting in 2000, Daniel Nepstad, a scientist affiliated with the Woods Hole Research Center in Massachusetts, covered 2.2 acres of land with a clear plastic tarp for five years to simulate a prolonged dry period. The results of the experiment suggested that the kind of multiyear droughts that the Amazon has witnessed of late, along with a general decrease in precipitation during the rainy season—which many identify as an effect of the deforestation—will greatly hinder the jungle's ability to reproduce. Some trees showed a stubborn resilience, drawing water from more than forty feet in the soil. But the soil eventually dried out, and after four years the death rate of large canopy trees, those that reach up to 150 feet into the open sun, jumped from 1 percent to 9 percent. All trees demonstrated a significant slowing of growth, which means that if the drying trend continues, not only will the forest be shorter and stunted but its ability to absorb carbon, which plays an important role in cooling the earth's temperature, will be curtailed. "This experiment provides researchers with a peek into the future of this majestic forest," Nepstad says.[13]

THE FUTURE CAN be seen quite clearly on the other side of BR-163. Pushing against the road is what environmentalists call the Amazon's "soy frontier," open land clear-cut for pastures or plantations, dotted with tufts of trees and the occasional ramshackle hamlet. Ford spent millions of dollars trying to find new uses for soy, and his dream has been more than realized: today's corporate agribusiness is Ford's "chemurgy" on steroids. Soy can now be found in an array of mass-produced products, from animal feed, pet food, and baby formula to fast food and biofuels. Over the last two decades, industry scientists have gone beyond anything that Greenfield Village chemists could have imagined, as genetically modified soy can be found in about 60 percent of all processed foods, most often as oil or filler. As a result, growing European, Asian, and US demand has turned Brazil into the second-largest producer of soy.[14]

Soy is one of the Amazon's leading causes of deforestation. In one year alone, between August 2003 and August 2004, planters cleared over 10,000 square miles of the Amazon, roughly the size of Belgium. Most of this planting is in the southern scrublands of the Amazon basin, in the state of Mato Grosso. But in recent years, soy has crept north to the Tapajós, and as it does, it disrupts many more lives at a much quicker pace than does logging, notwithstanding all the cruelty and coercion that accompanies that trade. Where logging displaces settlements in scattershot fashion, soy devours communities more inexorably, displacing farming and ranching families with as much disregard as it fells trees. Because the crop is cultivated on large-scale, mechanized plantations, it doesn't provide much employment for those uprooted by its march. At the same time, the extension of monoculture squeezes out the planting of vegetables and fruits produced for local use, as land is more profitably used to grow soy than, say, papaya and so dramatically raises the price of what crops— more and more imported from outside the region—do get to market.

In 2002, the multinational agroindustry giant Cargill, hoping to induce the federal government to pave BR-163—and thereby make it easier for the company to export its Mato Grosso harvest—spent $20 million to build a granary warehouse and port in Santarém, with a protruding conveyor running to three deepwater chutes designed to fill the holds of the largest cargo ships with soybeans.* Santarém had until recently largely

---

*BR-163 remains unpaved for little more than half its run from Cuiabá, the capital of Mato Grosso—where most of Brazil's soy is grown—to Santarém. And in its current dirt and mud state, even during the dry season, it's too rough for major corporations like

remained a sleepy provincial town not that different from when the poet Elizabeth Bishop wrote about her "golden evening" on the Tapajós. That changed after Cargill built its terminal. Speculators and developers moved in, and the price of a hectare (2.47 acres) of land skyrocketed, from $25 in 2000 to more than $500 eight years later. Many poor farmers or ranchers were unable to resist such a payoff. Selling their land, they moved into Santarém proper, whose infrastructure was unprepared to handle the influx. This migration led not just to shanty sprawl but to a dramatic increase in the cost of basic grains, fruits, vegetables, and meat. With over three hundred square miles of surrounding farmland now used for soy, there's much less room, and considerably less financial incentive, to grow oranges, pineapples, manioc, and greens or to graze cows and pigs.[15]

Henry Ford placed great hope in soybeans, projecting that the crop would provide a much needed financial lifeline to farming communities struggling to survive as industrialization pushed agricultural prices lower and lower. His promotion of soy was part of his efforts to balance farm and factory so that mechanization would not destroy community but fulfill it. But in Belterra—Ford's last sustained effort to strike such a balance—soy has wiped off the map the dozens of small villages that had spread out from the center of the town over the last couple of decades and, along with them, the schools, churches, and family networks that are the heart of any community.

Belterra stands just off BR-163, about an hour south of Santarém, on a flat plateau perfect for mechanized soybean cultivation. In 2001, hardly any soy was grown in its boundaries. Today, tens of thousands of Belterra's flatland hectares are planted with soy. It is expensive to cut down virgin jungle. The former president of Cargill's Brazilian operations told me that it costs about $1,500 to clear one hectare, which means that a plantation of, say, five hundred hectares would take years to reap a profit, even

---

Cargill, Archer Daniels Midland, Bunge, and the Brazilian-owned Maggi Group to use. They instead ship their soy overland about 1,200 miles south to one of Brazil's two major Atlantic ports or truck it about 500 miles northwest on a paved two-lane highway to Porto Velho, load it on barges, and float it down the Madeira and Amazon rivers. Once blacktopped, the highway will be a quick and cheap way for landlocked Mato Grosso planters to get their product to Santarém's deepwater harbor, where it can be loaded on cargo ships and sent on its way. But environmentalists fear that an asphalt road will hasten the spread of soy, as well as logging and cattle ranching, deeper into the Amazon and quicken its destruction.

The soy frontier: Belterra.

considering the high price of soy. This expense is why growers like to move into land already cleared for cattle pastures and small farms (often pushing farmers and ranchers to initiate another cycle of deforestation). It is also what makes Belterra, in addition to its level soil, so attractive. Ford's men already did most of the work.*

Until recently, stories told about the Amazon tended to emphasize the jungle's unconquerable enormity, its immense indifference to man's puny ambitions, a plotline that captures well the history of Fordlandia. That has changed, of course. It's the forest that now appears frail, as Belterra vividly demonstrates. Nearly eight decades ago, Ford's men slipped and slid in the mud in their four-cylinder, 20-horsepower Model F tractors or 27-horsepower Model Ns—"iron mules" they were called—to prepare

---

*Belterra never sent much rubber back to Detroit, but soon its soy will be making its way into Ford cars. In July 2008, Cargill started construction in Chicago on a state-of-the-art factory designed to produce mass quantities of industrial-quality plastic made from soybeans, including soy shipped from the company's Santarém port. One of Cargill's customers is the Ford Motor Company, which plans to use the plastic in its 2009 Ford Escape ("Cargill Builds First Full-Scale BiOH Polyols Manufacturing Plant," Cargill press release, July 8, 2008, www.cargill.com/news/news_releases/080708_biohplant.htm).

the land to plant rubber trees. Today, developers use Caterpillar D-9s or D-11s, or Komatsu D275s, treaded behemoths weighing as much as a hundred tons and running on up to 900 horsepower to plow down those same trees. They are outfitted with special cutting blades angled to push the felled wood to the right as the machine advances. The protruding part of the blade is spiked, letting operators stab and twist the trunks of obstinate trees. At the rear of the dozers are mounted "rippers," multishank hydraulic plows to pull up trunks and break rocks. Once the downed trees are gathered in a pile with a backhoe, the same ground is passed over once again, this time by two tractors tethered together by a heavy chain weighed down by a rolling steel ball that yanks out root systems as it is dragged forward. Soy itself does its part in forcing the jungle to yield. Domesticated in temperate Asia, the bean is not native to Brazil, much less is it suited to the hot and humid Amazon. But advances in insecticides, pesticides, fungicides, and phosphate-heavy fertilizer, along with the creation of crossbred "tropical soy," have allowed Amazon growers not just one crop but two a year. And Brazil has just permitted farmers to use genetically engineered seeds—a logical extension of Fordism into the cellular structure—making possible the spread of soy ever deeper into the rain forest.

Some Belterra residents tried to hold out. But they found themselves, as described in a report in *National Geographic*, "encircled by an encroaching wasteland, as whining chain saws and raging fires consumed the trees right up to the edge of their land. Their yards were overrun with vipers, bees, and rodents escaping the apocalypse, and when tractors began spraying the cleared fields, toxic clouds of pesticides drifted into their homes." Their animals died. Family members became ill. João de Sousa has raised cattle for over four decades on his small ranch. His land is now an island in a sea of soy, as all of his former neighbors have sold their farms and moved out. "They never put a dyke up," Sousa complained of the new soy planters. "Chemicals went into the brook where the cows drank." He's lost 88 of his 120-head cow herd as a result. "Once when I was by the field and they were spraying, I started to feel odd and I collapsed on the track." Elsewhere, in what its former residents now describe as the "ghost village" of Gleba Pacoval, some families at first refused to sell their land. But hired gunmen set fire to their homes, driving them out. Union activists tried to organize against intimidation, only to be barraged by death threats.[16]

SPARED THE DESTRUCTION suffered by surrounding villages, Belterra's town center still looks much the way it did when Archie Johnston and Curtis Pringle built it, with white-and-green Cape Cod bungalows set back from straight streets, their front yards planted with neat flower gardens. And just as Ford, buffeted by the changes that swirled around him, looked to the past for solace, Belterra's municipal authorities, practically swallowed up by soy, have turned to history for relief. In recent years, they have tried to promote their town as a tourist attraction, putting out a brochure recounting its unique role as one of Henry Ford's most remote outposts, whose architecture "reminds one of a small American town in the Midwest in the 1920s." "The local people," it reads, "still preserve the custom of having gardens around their houses," because the "Ford Company gave prizes for the best garden." The brochure also calls attention to the well-maintained "House Number One," a spacious home with large rooms and a privileged view from the balcony. This "house of dreams" was "designed especially for the creator of the Project: Henry Ford." The industrialist was all set to travel to Belterra, the guidebook says, but forty days before the planned visit Edsel died. The trip was canceled, and "locals wonder if Henry Ford had come, then perhaps he would never have abandoned Belterra."

Back up the Tapajós at Fordlandia, removed for now from soy's onslaught, palpable neglect blankets the town, despite its recent bustle. Contrasted with the broad, well-kept streets on display in old photographs of the place found in the Ford Archives, many of its roads are today crowded by scrub and spindly trees, their branches overhanging potholed macadam. In one photo, concrete crosses line the settlement's cemetery in neat rows, with shorn hills and open skies in the background. Now the burial ground is overrun by forest and weeds, its crucifixes off-kilter. A clutch of fallen crosses, most dating from the 1930s, their inscriptions long worn off, have been gathered up and propped against a tree in the center of the graveyard. At Albert Kahn's decrepit hospital, the floor is

*América Lobato in front of her paintings of rubber trees and the
water tower.*

strewn with patient records from 1945, the year Ford turned the town over
to the Brazilian government, though the building has been used as a clinic
periodically over the last couple of decades.

Some residents have tried to keep up appearances. As in Belterra, in
front of many of the still inhabited bungalows, neat patches of rose bushes,
tangerine and peach trees, along with Spanish plums and palm fruits, accent the town's elegiac quality. And inevitably at some point in any conversation, residents will point out that Ford never visited Fordlandia, even
though he kept promising that he would. "Fordlandia was born and died

expecting a visit from its patron," writes yet another Brazilian travel guide. Its inhabitants, the guide says, keep "one of the rooms of the best house in the American neighborhood in a permanent state of preparation."

Given the waste, slavery, and ruination visited on much of the Amazon today their longing is understandable. Henry Ford's vision of an Emersonian arcadia rising from the jungle canopy, though preposterous, now seems relatively benign. The dream lingers in the sights and sounds of Ford's *cidades fantasmas*, ghost cities, haunting reminders of the early twentieth century's promise of humane development. In Belterra, in the building where Henry Ford never slept, the town has recently installed a "Henry Ford" library and organized a "Henry Ford" children's choir. And the factory whistle still blows four times a day, summoning workers who no longer live there to a plantation that has long been shuttered.[17]

The residents of Fordlandia and Belterra are still waiting for Henry Ford.

NOTES

Introduction: Nothing Is Wrong with Anything

1. "Police Protect Ford and Edison at N.Y. Auto Show," *Atlanta Constitution*, January 11, 1928.

2. Allan Nevins and Frank Ernest Hill, *Ford: Expansion and Challenge, 1915–1933*, New York: Charles Scribner's Sons, 1957, pp. 437–59; "Remarks," *Time*, January 16, 1928.

3. "No 'Price War' for His Concern, Mr. Ford Insists," *Christian Science Monitor*, January 9, 1928; "Henry Ford Coming Today," *New York Times*, January 9, 1928; "Remarks," *Time*, January 16, 1928.

4. "Ford Plans Plane Trip to Brazil Rubber Tract," *Washington Post*, January 10, 1928; "Ford Plans Brazil Flight," *Los Angeles Times*, January 10, 1928; "Henry Ford's Voyage," *Washington Post*, January 11, 1928; "Ford Met Marshall Here," *New York Times*, January 16, 1928; "Dr. Wise Proposes Inquiry on Jews," *New York Times*, January 9, 1928.

5. "Ford to Continue Effort to Produce Aero at Car Price," *Washington Post*, March 4, 1928.

6. "Ford Sees Hoover the Next President," *New York Times*, January 10, 1928; "Ford Gets Big Area to Grow Rubber," *New York Times*, October 12, 1927.

7. William N. McNairn and Marjorie McNairn, *Quotations from the Unusual Henry Ford*, Redondo Beach, Calif.: Quotamus Press, 1978, p. 101.

8. Arnold Höllriegel, "Ford in Brazil," *Living Age*, May 1932, p. 221, reprinted from the *Berliner Tageblatt*; Elaine Lourenço, "Americanos e caboclos: Encontros e desencontros em Fordlândia e Belterra-PA," master's thesis, Universidad de São Paulo, 1999, p. 38; David Grann, "The Lost City of Z," *New Yorker*, September 19, 2005.

9. "Ford Rubber," *Time*, October 24, 1927; "Fordlandia, Brazil," *Washington Post*, August 12, 1931.

10. See P. H. Fawcett, *Lost Trails, Lost Cities*, New York: Funk and Wagnalls, 1953, p. 267; Brian Fawcett, *Ruins in the Sky*, London: Hutchinson, 1958; and Peter Fleming, *Brazilian Adventure*, New York: Scribner's Sons, 1933.

11. Aubrey Stuart, trans., *How Henry Ford Is Regarded in Brazil; Articles by Monteiro Lobato*, Rio de Janeiro, 1926 (available in Yale's Sterling Library); Thomas Skidmore, "Brazil's American Illusions: From Dom Pedro II to the Coup of 1964," *Luso-Brazilian Review* 23 (Winter 1986): 77.

12. Theodore Roosevelt, *Through the Brazilian Wilderness*, New York: Cooper Square Press, 2000, p. 217. See also Candice Millard, *"The River of Doubt:" Theodore Roosevelt's Darkest Journey*, New York: Doubleday, 2005; Francis Gow Smith, "The King of the Xingu," *Atlanta Constitution*, December 16, 1928.

13. John Hemming, *Tree of Rivers: The Story of the Amazon*, London: Thames and Hudson, 2008, p. 203; Candace Slater, *Entangled Edens: Visions of the Amazon*, Berkeley: University of California Press, 2002, p. 46; Susanna B. Hecht, "The Last Unfinished Page of Genesis: Euclides da Cunha and the Amazon," *Historical Geography* 32 (2004): 43–69.

14. *Burden of Dreams*, documentary, dir. Liess Blank, Flower Films, 1982.

15. Jonathan Norton Leonard, *The Tragedy of Henry Ford*, New York: G. P. Putnam's Sons, 1932, p. 108; "Sober Thoughts on Things and Kings," *New York Times*, April 27, 1930; "Life in Fordlandia!" *Iron Mountain Daily News*, May 18, 1932.

16. *Washington Post*, September 5, 1928.

17. Kenneth Grubb, *Amazon and the Andes*, New York: Dial Press, 1930, p. 14; A. Ogden Pierrot, "A Visit to Fordlandia," *Rubber Age*, April 10, 1932.

18. http://www.cremesp.org.br/?siteAcao=Revista=247 (accessed May 8, 2008).

19. Frederick Upham Adams, *Conquest of the Tropics: The Story of the Creative Enterprises Conducted by the United Fruit Company*, New York: Doubleday, Page, and Co., 1914, pp. 9, 114.

20. Perry Miller, *Errand into the Wilderness*, Cambridge: Harvard University Press, 1975, pp. 1–15; Harry Bernstein, "Some Inter-American Aspects of the Enlightenment," *Latin America and the Enlightenment*, ed. Arthur Whitaker, Ithaca, N.Y.: Cornell University Press, 1961, pp. 53–55.

21. "Ford Tire Plants Planned in Brazil," *New York Times*, November 16, 1928; "The Ford Shutdown," *Washington Post*, September 18, 1922.

22. National Archives, microfilm 1472, roll 40, RG 59, 832.6176/58, Drew to State, February 14, 1930.

23. Douglas Brinkley, *Wheels for the World: Henry Ford, His Company, and a Century of Progress, 1903–2003*, New York: Viking, 2003, p. 232.

Chapter 1: Under an American Flag

1. "Churchill Defends Rubber Restrictions," *New York Times*, March 13, 1923; "Churchill Sarcastic over Debt Policy," *New York Times*, July 20, 1924; Charles R. Whittlesey, *Government Control of Crude Rubber: The Stevenson Plan*, Princeton, N.J.: Princeton University Press, 1931; Austin Coates, *The Commerce in Rubber: The First 250 Years*, New York: Oxford University Press, 1987, pp. 205–64; Barry Machado, "Farquhar and Ford in Brazil: Studies in Business Expansion and Foreign Policy," PhD dissertation, Northwestern University, 1975, p. 274.

2. "Hoover Contrasts Wheat and Rubber," *New York Times*, December 30, 1925; Machado, "Farquhar and Ford," p. 205.

3. "Rubber Manufacturers Discuss Supply Question," *Wall Street Journal*, February 28, 1923; "Rubber Men Record Protest to Britain," *New York Times*, February 28, 1923; Coates, *The Commerce in Rubber*, pp. 233, 232; Alfred Lief, *Harvey Firestone: Free Man of Enterprise*, New York: McGraw-Hill, 1951, pp. 228, 231.

4. Machado, "Farquhar and Ford," p. 245.

5. Machado, "Farquhar and Ford," p. 201; Nevins and Hill, *Ford*, pp. 396–97; Royal Davis, "Cycles in the Automobile Pneumatic Tire Renewal Market in the United States," *Journal of the American Statistical Association*, vol. 26, no. 173, Supplement: Proceedings of the American Statistical Association (March 1931), pp. 10–19.

6. Ford Bryan, *Friends, Families, and Forays: Scenes from the Life and Times of Henry Ford*, Detroit: Wayne State University Press, 2002, p. 247.

7. Benson Ford Research Center (BFRC), accession 65, Reminiscences, E. G. Liebold, ch. 10.

8. Lief, *Harvey Firestone*, p. 51.

9. BFRC, accession 285, box 545, June 8, 1926, Raskob to Ford; BFRC, accession 65, Reminiscences, E. G. Liebold, ch. 10.

10. BFRC, accession 65, Reminiscences, E. G. Liebold, ch. 10.

11. Warren Dean, *Brazil and the Struggle for Rubber: A Study in Environmental History*, New York: Cambridge University Press, 1987, p. 4.

12. E. Bradford Burns, "1910: Portrait of a Boom Town," *Journal of Inter-American Studies* 7 (July 1965): 410; "A Thousand Miles Up the Amazon," *Frank Leslie's Popular Monthly*, March 1897; "Valley of the Amazon," *New York Times*, July 23, 1899; Brian Lewis, "The Queer Life and Afterlife of Roger Casement," *Journal of the History of Sexuality* 14 (October 2005): 371; "Para and Manos," *Los Angeles Times*, June 18, 1899.

13. Hemming, *Tree of Rivers*, p. 202.

14. José Maria Ferreira de Castro, *A Selva*, Lisbon: Guimaraes Editores, 1991 (first published in 1930); Hemming, *Tree of Rivers*, pp. 203–5; Hecht, "The Last Unfinished Page of Genesis."

15. Robert F. Murphy, "The Rubber Trade and the Mundurucú Indians," PhD dissertation, Columbia University, 1954, 71.

16. Murphy, "The Rubber Trade," p. 8.

17. Joe Jackson, *The Thief at the End of the World: Rubber, Power, and the Seeds of Empire*, New York: Viking, 2008.

18. J. T. Baldwin, "David B. Riker and *Hevea brasiliensis*: The Taking of Rubber Seeds Out of the Amazon," *Economic Botany* 22 (October–December 1968): 383; Dean, *Struggle for Rubber*, pp. 7, 13–28, 90, 177–80.

19. Hemming, *Tree of Rivers*, pp. 96–97.

Chapter 2: The Cow Must Go

1. Roosevelt, *Through the Brazilian Wilderness*, p. 195.

2. Leonard, *The Tragedy of Henry Ford*, p. 120.

3. Brinkley, *Wheels for the World*, p. 141; David A. Hounshell, *From the American System to Mass Production, 1800–1932: The Development of Manufacturing Technology in the United States*, Baltimore: Johns Hopkins University Press, 1984, pp. 10, 217–62.

4. Robert Lacey, *Ford: The Men and the Machine*, Boston: Little, Brown, 1986, p. 109.

5. Brinkley, *Wheels for the World*, p. 155; Julian Street, *Abroad at Home*, New York: Century, 1914, pp. 93–94.

6. Keith Sward, *The Legend of Henry Ford*, New York: Rinehart, 1948, p. 37.

7. Brinkley, *Wheels for the World*, pp. 159, 373; McNairn and McNairn, *Quotations*, p. 47.

8. Lacey, *Ford*, p. 120; Brinkley, *Wheels for the World*, p. 174.

9. Lacey, *Ford*, pp. 123–24.

10. Neil Baldwin, *Henry Ford and the Jews: The Mass Production of Hate*, New York: Public Affairs, 2001, p. 39.

11. Brinkley, *Wheels for the World*, pp. 157–58, 275–78; Baldwin, *Henry Ford and the Jews*, pp. 41–42.

12. Stephen Meyer III, *The Five Dollar Day: Labor Management and Social Control in the Ford Motor Company, 1908–1921*, Albany: State University of New York Press, 1981, pp. 154–55; Lacey, *Ford*, pp. 129–31.

13. Leonard, *The Tragedy of Henry Ford*, p. 108.

14. Nevins and Hill, *Ford*, p. 604.

15. David L. Lewis, *The Public Image of Henry Ford: An American Folk Hero and His Company*, Detroit: Wayne State University, 1976, p. 213.

16. Peter Collier and David Horowitz, *The Fords: An American Epic*, San Francisco: Encounter Books, 2002, p. 49; Lewis, *The Public Image of Henry Ford*, p. 475.

17. Collier and Horowitz, *The Fords*, p. 49.

18. BFRC, Reminiscences, A. M. Wibel, pp. 1–7; Brinkley, *Wheels for the World*, p. 283.

19. Charles A. Lindbergh, *The Wartime Journals of Charles A. Lindbergh*, New York: Harcourt Brace Jovanovich, 1970, p. 712; Samuel Marquis, *Henry Ford: An Interpretation*, Boston: Little, Brown, 1923, p. 153.

20. T. E. Lawrence, *Seven Pillars of Wisdom*, London: Jonathan Cape, 1935, p. 6; Lacey, *Ford*, p. 127; David E. Nye, *Henry Ford, "Ignorant Idealist,"* Port Washington; N.Y.: Kennikat Press, 1979, p. 71.

Chapter 3: Absolute Americanisms

1. Lacey, *Ford*, p. 323; Brinkley, *Wheels for the World*, pp. 275–92; Nevins and Hill, *Ford*, pp. 279–99.
2. "Commercialism Made This War," *New York Times*, April 11, 1915; Ann Jardim, *The First Henry Ford: A Study in Personality and Business Leadership*, Cambridge: MIT Press, 1970, p. 131, "Henry Ford Still Thinks Soldiers Are Murderers," *New York Times*, July 16, 1919; BFRC, Reminiscences, Irving Bacon, p. 26.
3. *New York World*, July 18, 1919; "Commercialism Made This War," *New York Times*, April 11, 1915.
4. Nevins and Hill, *Ford*, p. 610.
5. Barbara S. Kraft, *The Peace Ship*, New York: Macmillan, 1978, pp. 49–52.
6. Philip Sheldon Foner, *History of the Labor Movement in the United States*, New York: International Publishers, 1994, p. 8; " 'Mr. Zero' Befriends 'Shorn Labor Lambs,' " *New York Times*, September 5, 1921; "Police Clubs Break Mobs of Idle," *New York Times*, September 20, 1921. Ledoux would later go on to help organize the 1932 "Bonus Army" march on Washington, during the Great Depression. See "Bonus Army Digs In," *New York Times*, July 18, 1932.
7. Millard, *The River of Doubt*, p. 337; Theodore Roosevelt to Henry Ford, November 30, 1914, in *The Days of Armageddon: 1914–1919*, vol. 8 of *The Letters of Theodore Roosevelt*, Cambridge: Harvard University Press, 1954, p. 851.
8. Brinkley, *Wheels for the World*, p. 190; "Roosevelt Urges Unity in America," *New York Times*, May 20, 1916.
9. Theodore Roosevelt, *The Winning of the West*, vol. 3, New York: G. P. Putnam's Sons, 1894, p. 45; Theodore Roosevelt, "The Strenuous Life," in Lewis Copeland et al., eds., *The World's Great Speeches*, New York: Courier Dover Publications, 1999, p. 345; T. J. Jackson Lears, *No Place of Grace: Antimoderism and the Transformation of American Culture, 1880–1920*, Chicago: University of Chicago Press, 1981, p. 134; Howard K. Beale, *Theodore Roosevelt and the Rise of America to World Power*, Baltimore: Johns Hopkins Press, 1956, pp. 37–38; John Judis, *The Folly of Empire: What George W. Bush Could Learn from Theodore Roosevelt and Woodrow Wilson*, New York: Oxford University Press, 2006; David Nasaw, *Andrew Carnegie*, New York: Penguin, 2006, p. 650.
10. BFRC, accession 1, box 135, "Pacifism"; "Ford Leads St. Louis Poll: Roosevelt Second in Straw Vote and President Wilson Fifth," *Washington Post*, May 28, 1916.
11. Reynold M. Wik, *Henry Ford and Grass-Roots America*, Ann Arbor: University of Michigan Press, 1972, p. 167.
12. Theodore Roosevelt to Henry Ford, February 9, 1916, in *The Days of Armageddon: 1914–1919*, p. 1022.

13. "Roosevelt Urges Unity in Defense," *New York Times*, December 6, 1915; "Roosevelt to Visit Detroit," *New York Times*, May 14, 1916; "Roosevelt Urges Unity in America," *New York Times*, May 20, 1916; Brinkley, *Wheels for the World*, pp. 230–31; Collier and Horowitz, *The Fords*, p. 87.

14. Kathleen Dalton, *Theodore Roosevelt: A Strenuous Life*, New York: Knopf, 2002, p. 448; Theodore Roosevelt, *Righteous Peace through National Preparedness: Speech of Theodore Roosevelt at Detroit, May 19, 1916*, Whitefish, Mont.: Kessinger Publishing, 2006, p. 19.

15. "Colonel Aloof, Ford Too," *Chicago Tribune*, May 20, 1916; "Ford Answers Roosevelt," *New York Times*, May 21, 1916.

16. Brinkley, *Wheels for the World*, p. 233.

17. "Roosevelt Bitter in Beginning War on the President," *New York Times*, October 29, 1918.

18. "Osborn Attacks Ford," *New York Times*, June 15, 1918; "To Michigan: Not Ford," *Chicago Tribune*, June 27, 1918; Theodore Roosevelt, "The Man Who Pays and the Man Who Profits," *Washington Post*, August 11, 1918. See also Theodore Roosevelt, "Test Wilson by His Own Tests," *Chicago Tribune*, June 26, 1918, and "Roosevelt Bitter in Beginning War on the President," *New York Times*, October 29, 1918.

19. BFRC, accession 65, Oral History, Irving Bacon, p. 45.

20. Leonard, *The Tragedy of Henry Ford*, pp. 48–49.

Chapter 4: That's Where We Sure Can Get Gold

1. Leonard, *The Tragedy of Henry Ford*, p. 170; "Henry Ford Still Thinks Soldiers Are Murderers," *New York Times*, July 16, 1919.

2. Baldwin, *Henry Ford and the Jews*, p. 17; Ford was quoting "Locksley Hall" as late as November 1941. See Charles A. Lindbergh, *The Wartime Journals of Charles A. Lindbergh*, p. 555. For the Victor Hugo quote, see Albert Schinz, "Victor Hugo, le Grand Poète Humanitaire; Champion de la Cause de la Paix Universelle; Promoteur de l'Idée des États-Unis d'Europe," *French Review* 9 (November, 1935): 11–25.

3. BFRC, Reminiscences, A. M. Wibel.

4. BFRC, accession 1, box 12, folder 8; Marquis, *Henry Ford*, p. 58.

5. Nevins and Hill, *Ford*, p. 605; Mary Dempsey, "Henry Ford's Amazonian Suburbia," *Américas*, March 1996, p. 44; Leo Marx, *The Machine in the Garden: Technology and the Pastoral Ideal in America*, New York: Oxford University Press, 1964, pp. 18, 241.

6. Howard P. Segal's *Recasting the Machine Age: Henry Ford's Village Industries*, Amherst: University of Massachusetts Press, 2005, is the most comprehensive study of Ford's village industries. See also Wik, *Henry Ford and Grass-Roots America*, p. 159; Ney, *Henry Ford*, p. 80.

7. "Soy Beans," *Edison Institute of Technology Bulletin*, April 1935; Farm Chemurgic Council, "Proceedings of the Second Dearborn Conference of Agriculture, Industry, and Science, Dearborn, Michigan, May 12–14, 1936."

8. Collier and Horowitz, *The Fords*, p. 106; William Adams Simonds, *Henry Ford and Greenfield Village*, New York: Frederick A. Stokes, 1938, p. 235; Ney, *Henry Ford*, p. 79.

9. Brian Cleven, "Henry Ford: Life and Logging," *Michigan History*, January–February 1999; Ford R. Bryan, *Beyond the Model T: The Other Ventures of Henry Ford*, Detroit: Wayne State University Press, 1990, pp. 118–29; William Stidger, *Henry Ford: The Man and His Motives*, New York: George H. Doran, 1923, p. 161.

10. Bryan, *Beyond the Model T*, pp. 45–58.

11. BFRC, accession 65, Reminiscences, Joseph Francois.

12. Tom McCarthy, "Henry Ford, Industrial Conservationist? Take-Back, Waste Reduction, and Recycling at the Rouge," *Progress in Industrial Ecology: An International Journal* 3, no. 4 (2006): 305; *Ford Comes to Iron Mountain: The Birth of Kingsford*, np, nd (located in Iron Mountain Public Library).

13. David L. Lewis, "The Rise and Fall of Old Henry's Northern Empire," *Cars and Parts*, December 1973, p. 92.

14. BFRC, accession 65, Reminiscences, Oscar G. Olsen.

15. Cleven, "Life and Logging," p. 20; BFRC, accession 65, Reminiscences, Alfred Johnson; Bryan, *Beyond the Model T*, p. 119.

16. Nevins and Hill, *Ford*, p. 219; BFRC, vertical file, Village Industries, General, 1920s, "Henry Ford Says Farmer-Workmen Will Build Automobile of the Future," published in *Automotive Age*, August 28, 1924; BFRC, vertical file, Village Industries, General, "One Foot in Industry and One Foot in the Soil."

17. "Ford Plans a New York for Alabama," *Chicago Defender*, May 20, 1922; "City All Mainstreet," *Literary Digest*, April 8, 1922; Littlee McClung, "The Seventy-Five-Mile City," *Scientific American*, September 1922.

18. "Rush for Muscle Shoals," *New York Times*, Febuary 12, 1922; "The Truth about Muscle Shoals," *Atlanta Constitution*, March 26, 1922.

19. Samuel Crowther, "Muscle Shoals," *McClure's Magazine*, January 1923; "Ford Determined to Secure Shoals," *Atlanta Constitution*, March 18, 1922; Nye, *Henry Ford*, pp. 32, 84.

20. "Ford Determined to Secure Shoals"; Nye, *Henry Ford*, p. 93.

21. Lacey, *Ford*, pp. 128–29; Leonard, *The Tragedy of Henry Ford*, p. 26; Louis-Ferdinand Céline, *Journey to the End of the Night*, trans. Ralph Manheim, New York: New Directions, 2006, p. 194.

22. Segal, *Recasting the Machine Age*, p. 76; Brinkley, *Wheels for the World*, p. 394; Lacey, *Ford*, pp. 368–70.

23. Sward, *The Legend of Henry Ford*, p. 314; Segal, *Recasting the Machine Age*, p. 76.

24. Phillip Bonosky, *Brother Bill McKie: Building the Union at Ford*, New York: International Publishers, 2000, p. 56.

25. Brinkley, *Ford*, p. 260.

26. The book was published in English as *The Crowd: A Study of the Popular Mind* by E. Benn in 1896, but Ford cited the exact translation of its original French title, published in 1895. See p. xvii for the quote.

27. BFRC, vertical file, Village Industries, General, 1920s, "Henry Ford Says Farmer-Workmen Will Build Automobile of the Future."
28. Collier and Horowitz, *The Fords*, p. 123; Brinkley, *Wheels for the World*, p. 426; Nevins and Hill, *Ford*, p. 536.
29. Henry Ford, *Ford Ideals: Being a Selection from "Mr. Ford's Page" in the Dearborn Independent*, Dearborn: Dearborn Publishing, 1922, pp. 357–60.
30. For the *Sunday Evening Hour*, see Lewis, *The Public Image of Henry Ford*, p. 453; "Farewell, Ford," *Time*, February 1942; Nevins and Hill, *Ford*, p. 598.
31. Nye, *Henry Ford*, p. 82.
32. Wik, *Henry Ford and Grass-Roots America*, p. 120; Sward, *The Legend of Henry Ford*, p. 129; Alvin Rosenbaum, *Usonia: Frank Lloyd Wright's Design for America*, Washington, D.C.: Preservation Press, 1993, pp. 60–62.

Chapter 5: Fordville

1. José Custódio Alves de Lima, *Recordações de homens e cousas do meu tempo*, Rio de Janeiro, 1926, pp. 373–77; BFRC, accession 38, box 61, "History of the Companhia Ford Industrial do Brasil since Its Inception"; BFRC, accession 285, box 420, de Lima to Ford, September 29, 1925.
2. Meyer, *The Five Dollar Day*, p. 40; Nevins and Hill, *Ford*, p. 600; Clayton Sinyai, *Schools of Democracy: A Political History of the American Labor Movement*, Ithaca, N.Y.: Cornell University Press, 2006, p. 66.
3. Nevins and Hill, *Ford*, pp. 485, 600; Brinkley, *Wheels for the World*, p. 250.
4. Brinkley, *Wheels for the World*, p. 202; see also Mira Wilkins and Frank Ernest Hill, *American Business Abroad: Ford on Six Continents*, Detroit: Wayne State University Press, 1964; Richard Downs, "Autos over Rails: How US Business Supplanted the British in Brazil, 1910–28," *Journal of Latin American Studies* 24 (October 1992): 551–83.
5. Barbara Weinstein, *For Social Peace in Brazil: Industrialists and the Remaking of the Working Class in São Paulo, 1920–1964*, Chapel Hill: University of North Carolina Press, 1997; Downs, "Autos over Rails"; Joel Wolfe, *Autos and Progress: The Brazilian Search for Modernity*, New York: Oxford University Press, 2009, ch. 3.
6. Paul Hoffman, *Wings of Madness: Alberto Santos-Dumont and the Invention of Flight*, New York: Hyperion, 2006.
7. National Archives, RG 59, decimal file 121.5632/6, Morgan to Secretary of State, May 25, 1926; William Lytle Schurz, *Brazil: The Infinite Country*, New York: E. P. Dutton, 1961, p. 64; Machado, "Farquhar and Ford," p. 262; Joan Hoff, *American Business and Foreign Policy, 1920–1933*, Lexington: University Press of Kentucky, 1971, p. 278, n. 33; Joseph Tulchin, *Aftermath of War and US Policy toward Latin America*, New York: New York University Press, 1971, p. 112; Herbert Hoover, *Memoirs*, New York: Macmillan, 1952, vol. 2, p. 79.
8. "U.S. Appoints Commission to Study South American Rubber," *Atlanta Constitution*, August 5, 1923; BFRC, accession 74, box 17, "Alleged Scandal about Our

Concession"; National Archives, RG 59, microfilm 519, roll 32, 832.52/22, "State of Pará Offers Gratuitous 370,000-Acre Concessions of Rubber-Producing Lands in Development Project," November 13, 1925; National Archives, RG 59, microfilm 0519, roll 43, 832.6176F75/1, Minter to State, July 5, 1927; RG 59, Microfilm 0519, roll 43, 832.6176F75/2, Minter to State, July 11, 1927; BFRC, Reminiscences, O. Z. Ide; Machado, "Ford and Farquhar," pp. 284–96.

9. BFRC, accession 285, box 20, letter from Schurz to Liebold, July 21, 1925; BFRC, accession 74, box 13, letter from Schurz to Henry Ford, September 12, 1925; Machado, "Farquhar and Ford," pp. 260–61. See also Hoff, *American Business and Foreign Policy*, pp. 206–7, for similar practices by attachés in Asia.

10. National Archives, RG 59, microfilm 0519, roll 43, 832.6176F75/1, Minter to State, July 5, 1927, enclosure 2.

11. National Archives, RG 59, microfilm 0519, roll 43, 832.6176F75/1, Minter to State, July 5, 1927, enclosure 4, National Archives, microfilm 0519, roll 43, 832.6176F75/3, Minter to State, July 22, 1927; Machado, "Ford and Farquhar," p. 306; National Archives, RG 59, microfilm 0519, roll 43, 832.6176F75/1, Minter to State, July 5, 1927, enclosure 1.

12. BFRC, accession 74, box 17, Villares to Greite, August 14, 1926.

13. National Archives, RG 59, microfilm 0519, roll 43, 832.6176F75/1, Minter to State, July 5, 1927, enclosure 4.

Chapter 6: They Will All Die

1. Machado, "Farquhar and Ford," p. 225; BFRC, accession 285, box 696, Henry Ford Office; Dean, *Struggle for Rubber*, pp. 72, 75.

2. BFRC, vertical file, "A Report of the Exploration of the Tapajós Valley by Carl D. LaRue," April 19, 1927.

3. Brinkley, *Wheels for the World*, p. 368.

4. Leon Jacobs, "Hookworm Disease," *American Journal of Nursing*, November 1940, pp. 1191–96.

5. Barbara Weinstein, *The Amazon Rubber Boom, 1850–1920*, Palo Alto: Stanford University Press, 1983, pp. 75, 250–60.

6. John R. Lee, "The So-Called Profit Sharing System in the Ford Plant," *Annals of the American Academy of Political and Social Sciences* 65 (May 1916): 305; Meyer, *The Five Dollar Day*.

7. Nevins and Hill, *Ford*, p. 614.

8. Michael Edward Stanfield, *Red Rubber, Bleeding Trees: Violence, Slavery, and Empire in Northwest Amazonia, 1850–1933*, Albuquerque: University of New Mexico Press, 1998.

9. Hounshell, *From the American System*, p. 276; David Halberstam, *The Reckoning*, New York: William Morrow, 1986, p. 90; Baldwin, *Henry Ford and the Jews*, p. 231.

10. Brinkley, *Wheels for the World*, p. 362; Segal, *Recasting the Machine Age*, p. 30.

11. Collier and Horowitz, *The Fords*, p. 99; Halberstam, *The Reckoning*, p. 94.

12. Marquis, *Henry Ford: An Interpretation,* p. 76.
13. "Mr. Ford's Opportunity," *New York Times,* March 20, 1927.
14. Lacy, *Ford,* p. 217; Baldwin, *Henry Ford and the Jews,* pp. 222, 237.
15. Baldwin, *Henry Ford and the Jews,* p. 237.

Chapter 7: Everything Jake

1. Royal Davis, "Cycles in the Automobile Pneumatic Tire Renewal Market in the United States," *Journal of the American Statistical Association* 26, Supplement: Proceedings of the American Statistical Association (March 1931): 10–19.
2. Roy Nash, *The Conquest of Brazil* (1926), New York: Biblo and Tannen, 1998, p. 200.
3. Sean Dennis Cashman, *America in the Twenties and Thirties: The Olympian Age of Franklin Delano Roosevelt,* New York: NYU Press, 1989, p. 19.
4. Collier and Horowitz, *The Fords,* pp. 122–23, 133; Thomas Bonsall, "Edsel: The Forgotten Ford," *Automobile Quarterly,* Fall 1991, p. 21, cited in Brinkley, *Wheels for the World,* p. 401.
5. "Life with Henry," *Time Magazine,* October 8, 1951.
6. BFRC, "Diary Kept by Judge O. Z. Ide during South American Trip to Investigate Possible Sites for Rubber Plantation, June–November 1927"; BFRC, Reminiscences, O. Z. Ide.
7. Ferreira de Castro, *A Selva,* p. 10; Thomas Orum, "The Women of the Open Door: Jews in the Belle Epoque Amazonian Demimonde, 1890–1920," *Shofar: An Interdisciplinary Journal of Jewish Studies* 19 (2001): 86–99.
8. National Archives, RG 59, microfilm 0519, roll 43, 832.6176F75/4, Minter to State, July 22, 1927.
9. National Archives, RG 59, microfilm 0519, roll 43, 832.6176F75/5, State to Minter, nd; National Archives, RG 59, microfilm 0519, roll 43, 832.6176F75/3, Minter to State, July 23, 1927; Machado, "Farquhar and Ford," p. 310.
10. BFRC, Reminiscences, O. Z. Ide; National Archives, RG 59, microfilm 0519, roll 43, 832.6176F75/5, State to Minter, nd; National Archives, RG 59, microfilm 0519, roll 43, 832.6176F75/3, Minter to State, July 23, 1927; Machado, "Farquhar and Ford," p. 310.
11. BFRC, Reminiscences, O. Z. Ide.
12. Wilkins and Hill, *American Business Abroad,* p. 169; BFRC, Reminiscences, O. Z. Ide.
13. National Archives, RG 59, microfilm 0519, roll 43, 832.6176F75/3, Minter to State, July 23, 1927; BFRC, "Diary Kept by Judge O. Z. Ide during South American Trip."
14. Machado, "Farquhar and Ford," p. 311.
15. First mention of "Fordlandia" in company records is in the *Ford News,* November 1, 1928; BFRC, accession 74, box 13, "Rubber Production."
16. BFRC, accession 196, "O. Z. Ide Fordlandia"; BFRC, accession 301, box 2.

Chapter 8: When Ford Comes

1. National Archives, RG 59, microfilm 0519, roll 43, 832.6176F75/3, Minter to State, July 23, 1927.
2. *Iron Mountain News*, February 11, 1930.
3. BFRC, Reminiscences, E. G. Liebold, p. 630.
4. David Cleary, "'Lost Altogether to the Civilised World': Race and the Cabanagem in Northern Brazil, 1750–1850," *Comparative Studies in Society and History* 40 (January 1998): 109–35; Hemming, *Tree of Rivers*, p. 122.
5. Hemming, *Tree of Rivers*, p. 122; Cleary, "'Lost Altogether to the Civilised World,'" p. 131.
6. Weinstein, *The Amazon Rubber Boom*, p. 42.
7. George Washington Sears, *Forest Runes*, Forest and Stream Publishing Company, 1887, pp. 157–58; Hecht, "The Last Unfinished Page of Genesis," p. 61.
8. Author's interview with Diogo Franco, March 14, 2008.
9. Henry Albert Phillips, *Brazil: Bulwark of Inter-American Relations*, New York: Hastings House, 1945, p. 63; James Orton, *The Andes and the Amazon*, New York: Harper and Brothers, 1870, p. 200; David Riker, "The Last Southern Seed," unpublished manuscript.
10. BFRC, vertical file, Rubber Plantations, Correspondence; Ford R. Bryan, "Henry's So-Called Rubber Plantation in Florida"; "Ford Plans Rubber Grove," *New York Times*, February 17, 1925, p. 10; Williams Johns Cummings, ed., *From Kingsford: The Town Ford Built in Dickinson Country, Michigan* (scrapbook of newspaper clippings in Iron Mountain's public library).
11. Eimar Franco, *O Tapajós que eu vi (memórias)*, Santarém: Instituto Cultural Boanerges Sena, 1998, p. 39; author's interview with Eimar Franco, March 16, 2008.
12. Aubrey Stuart, trans., *How Henry Ford Is Regarded in Brazil: Articles by Monteiro Lobato*, Rio de Janeiro, 1926 (available in Yale's Sterling Library); Thomas Skidmore, "Brazil's American Illusions: From Dom Pedro II to the Coup of 1964," *Luso-Brazilian Review* 23 (Winter 1986): 77; Machado, "Farquhar and Ford," p. 311; Lourenço, "Americanos e caboclos," p. 38; Edward Tomlinson, "Jungle Gold," *Collier's Weekly*, December 12, 1936.
13. Tomlinson, "Jungle Gold."
14. John P. Harrison, "Science and Politics: Origins and Objectives of Mid-Nineteenth Century Government Expeditions to Latin America," *Hispanic American Historical Review* 35 (May 1955): 189; John Homer Galey, "The Politics of Development in the Brazilian Amazon, 1940–1950," PhD dissertation, Stanford University, 1977, p. 2.
15. *Folha do Norte*, March 2, 1929.
16. BFRC, accession 74, box 14, "Black Book: Strictly Confidential." *Gazeta de Noticias* published Souza Castro's attacks throughout May 1928.
17. *O Jornal*, February 19, 1928; Assis Chateaubriand, *As nuvens que vêm: Discourses parlamentares*, Rio de Janeiro: Edições Cruzeiro, 1963, pp. 360–62.

18. *O Jornal*, February 19, 1928; Assis Chateaubriand, *As nuvens que vêm*, pp. 360–62; Lourenço, "Americanos e caboclos," pp. 35, 38.
19. BFRC, accession 285, box 420, Liebold to de Lima, October 28, 1925; de Lima, *Recordações de homens e cousas do meu tempo*, pp. 373–77.

Chapter 9: Two Rivers

1. BFRC, accession 74, box 13, "Rubber Production in Amazon Valley."
2. McCarthy, "Henry Ford, Industrial Conservationist?"; "Ford May Use Waste Fire," *Los Angeles Times*, April 11, 1928.
3. Bryan, *Beyond the Model T*, pp. 140–50, 155; Nevins and Hill, *Ford*, p. 610.
4. *Ford News*, March 15, 1928; August 1, 1928.
5. "Ford Rubber Plantation Ship Leaves Detroit," *New York Times*, July 27, 1928; "Ford Expedition Starts to Exploit Rubber Tract," *Washington Post*, July 27, 1928; "Ford Voyagers," *Detroit News*, July 28, 1928; *Ford News*, August 19, 1928.
6. BFRC, Reminiscences, Ernest Liebold.
7. "City That Lost Chance Offered It by Ford," *New York Times*, March 2, 1930; Howard Wolf and Ralph Wolf, *Rubber: A Story of Glory and Greed*, New York: Covici Friede, 1936, p. 239.
8. "Ford Sends Party to Start Rubber Culture in Brazil," *Christian Science Monitor*, July 27, 1928; "Ford Voyagers," *Detroit News*, July 28, 1928.
9. *Detroit News*, July 25, 1928; July 26, 1928; July 29, 1928.
10. "Henry Ford, 65, Pledges Speed," *Detroit Times*, July 30, 1928; BFRC, accession 1, box 11.
11. BFRC, accession 38, box 61, "History of the Companhia Ford Industrial Do Brasil since Its Inception."
12. BFRC, accession 74, box 17, Oxholm to Sorensen, September 28, 1928; "Ford Plan Arouses Acclaim in Brazil," *New York Times*, November 25, 1928.
13. Brett C. Millier, *Elizabeth Bishop: Life and the Memory of It*, Berkeley: University of California Press, 1995, p. 309.
14. Nash, *The Conquest of Brazil*, p. 201.
15. Hugh Raffles, *In Amazonia: A Natural History*, Princeton: Princeton University Press, 2002, p. 25; BFRC, accession 6, box 74, "The Ford Rubber Plantations."
16. BFRC, accession 74, box 2, "Report on visit of W. E. Carnegie, 1929."
17. "With Ford on the Amazon: The story of the Ford Plantation, an Eye-Witness," *Planter*, January 1931, in BFRC, vertical file, "Rubber Plantations"; BFRC, accession 285, box 748; BFRC, accession 74, box 13, "Black Binder."
18. Lourenço, "Americanos e caboclos," p. 40; "With Ford on the Amazon"; BFRC, accession 38, box 61, Oxholm to Sorensen, January 19, 1929.

Chapter 10: Smoke and Ash

1. BFRC, accession 74, box 13; National Archives, RG 59, microfilm 0519, roll 43, 832.6176F75/3, Minter to State, July 23, 1927.
2. BFRC, accession 74, box 13.

3. Machado, "Farquhar and Ford," p. 319; BFRC, accession 74, box 13; BFRC, accession 301, box 2; BFRC, accession 74, box 2, "Report on Visit of W. E. Carnegie."

4. Brinkley, *Wheels for the World*, p. 189.

5. Phillips, *Brazil*, p. 56.

6. Franco, *O Tapajós*, p. 81; author's interview, Eimar Franco, March 16, 2008.

7. Machado, "Farquhar and Ford," p. 318; BFRC, accession 74, box 17, "Alleged Scandal about Our Concession"; National Archives, RG 59, microfilm 0519, roll 43, 832.6176F75/14, Minter to State, November 25, 1927.

8. Machado, "Farquhar and Ford," p. 318; BFRC, "Alleged Scandal about Our Concession"; Minter to State, November 25, 1927; BFRC, accession 38, box 113; BFRC, accession 74, box 1, Roberge, November 23, 1934; BFRC, accession 301, box 2, "Notes of Rubber Company Matters"; BFRC, accession 38, box 113, Longley to Sorensen, July 2, 1928.

9. BFRC, accession 74, box 17, "Interplant Correspondence."

10. National Archives, RG 59, microfilm 0519, roll 43, 832.6176F75/2, Minter to State, July 11, 1927; 832.6176F75/29, Drew to State, April 22, 1929; BFRC, accession 390, box 86, Johnston to Wibel, October 9, 1933; "Ford Handicapped by Labor Scarcity," *New York Times*, October 20, 1929; Machado, "Farquhar and Ford," pp. 317, 358–63; BFRC, "Alleged Scandal about our Concession."

11. National Archives, RG 59, microfilm 0519, roll 43, 832.6176F75/22, Drew to State, December 15, 1928; Machado, "Farquhar and Ford," p. 343.

12. Hoffman, *Wings of Madness*, p. 279.

13. "Henry Ford Still Thinks Soldiers Are Murderers," *New York Times*, July 16, 1919; Wik, *Henry Ford and Grass-Roots America*, p. 253.

14. Hoffman, *Wings of Madness*, p. 302.

15. Hoffman, *Wings of Madness*, p. 300; David Omissi, *Air Power and Colonial Control: The Royal Air Force, 1919–1939*, Manchester: Manchester University Press, 1990.

16. "Air Crash Kills 14 in Rio," *New York Times*, December 4, 1928.

17. Hoffman, *Wings of Madness*, p. 310; Samuel Guy Inman, *Latin America: Its Place in World Life*, Freeport, N.Y.: Ayer, 1972, pp. 223–25; Matthew Hughes, "Logistics of the Chaco War, 1932–1935," *Journal of Military History* 69 (2005): 411–37.

18. Machado, "Farquhar and Ford," p. 344.

19. Dean, *Struggle for Rubber*, pp. 73–74.

20. BFRC, accession 74, Box 14, "Black Book: Strictly Confidential."

21. National Archives, RG 59, microfilm 0519, roll 43, 832.6176F75/22, Drew to State, December 15, 1928; 832.6176F75/29, Drew to State, April 22, 1929; 832.6176F75/32, Memo, Division of Latin American Affairs, May 3, 1929; BFRC, accession 301, box 21, Carnegie to Craig, March 27, 1931; BFRC, accession 74, box 13, "Report on Visit to Companhia Ford Industrial do Brasil," December 2, 1930; Machado, "Farquhar and Ford," p. 348.

22. *Folha do Norte*, March 2, 1929, and March 3, 1929.

23. BFRC, accession 74, box 2, "Personnel File 1930;" *Folha do Norte*, May 8, 1930.

24. BFRC, "Black Book: Strictly Confidential."

Chapter 11: Prophesied Subjection

1. McNairn and McNairn, *Quotations*, p. 51.
2. Brinkley, *Wheels for the World*, p. 102; BFRC, Reminiscences, A. M. Wibel, pp. 168–69.
3. BFRC, accession 38, box 61, Sorensen to Oxholm, July 5, 1929.
4. BFRC, accession 74, box 13, "Interplant Correspondence."
5. Wilkins and Hill, *American Business Abroad*, p. 172.
6. "Brazil Sending Arms to Ford's Plantation," *Washington Post*, January 3, 1929.
7. BFRC, accession 74, box 17, Oxholm to Sorensen, September 28, 1928.
8. Hemming, *Tree of Rivers*, p. 17; Roger D. Stone, *Dreams of Amazonia*, New York: Penguin, 1989, p. 47; BFRC, accession 65, Reminiscences, Victor J. Perini (as told by Constance Perini); Reminiscences, Matt Mulrooney.
9. Phillips, *Brazil*, pp. 68–69; J. T. Baldwin Jr., "David B. Riker and *Hevea brasiliensis*," *Economic Botany* 22 (1968): 383–84.
10. BFRC, accession 74, box 14, "Black Book: Strictly Confidential."
11. BFRC, accession 74, box 6, Miscellaneous Letters.
12. BFRC, accession 390, box 86, Johnston to Wibel, June 5, 1934.
13. BFRC, accession 74, box 9, Johnston to Stallard, April 15, 1940.
14. Edviges Marta Ioris, "A Forest of Disputes: Struggles over Spaces, Resources, and Social Identities in Amazonia," PhD dissertation, University of Florida, 2005.
15. BFRC, accession 74, box 6, "Indian Labor."
16. BFRC, Reminiscences, Carl LaRue; BFRC, accession 74, box 2, "Riot 1930"; BFRC, accession 74, box 2, "Report on Visit of W. E. Carnegie."
17. Franco, *O Tapajós*, pp. 82–83; BFRC, accession 74, box 13, "Report on Visit," December 2, 1930. See also the binder in accession 74, box 9, that contains a report on the land titles held within the boundaries of Fordlandia; "Armed Brazilians Raid Ford Rubber Plantation," *New York Times*, December 25, 1930; "Enjoin Ford Interests," *New York Times*, December 27, 1930; Segal, *Recasting the Machine Age*, p. 24.
18. *Iron Mountain News*, January 26, 1925; August 3, 1925.
19. BFRC, Reminiscences, Ernest Liebold.
20. BFRC, accession 38, box 64, Sorensen to Victor Perini, February 28, 1930.
21. Author's interview with Eimar Franco, March 16, 2008.
22. *Folha do Norte*, December 23, 1930.
23. BFRC, accession 74, box 7, Oxholm's monthly progress reports to Sorensen.
24. BFRC, "Report on Visit of W. E. Carnegie."
25. Grubb, *Amazon and the Andes*, p. 19.
26. BFRC, accession 38, box 61, "Rubber Plant Visit 1929."

Chapter 12: The Ford Way of Thinking

1. BFRC, accession 38, box 61, "History of the Companhia Ford Industrial do Brasil since Its Inception"; BFRC, accession 74, box 13, "Companhia Ford Industrial

do Brasil"; BFRC, accession 88, box 2, Mira Wilkins Research Papers, Interview with William Cowling.

2. Machado, "Farquhar and Ford," pp. 349–53.

3. BFRC, accession 38, box 61, Sorensen to Oxholm, July 5, 1929; BFRC, accession 74, box 17, "Cowling to Ford, et al.," August 20, August 23, and September 9, 1929.

4. For Bennett's role in Ford's subsequent firing of Cowling, see Bennett, *We Never Called Him Henry*, New York: Gold Medal Books, 1951, p. 61.

5. "Cowling to Ford, et al.," August 20, August 23, and September 9, 1929.

6. National Archives, RG 59, microfilm 0519, roll 43, 832.6176F75/55, Drew to State, October 1, 1929; Machado, "Farquhar and Ford," p. 361.

7. "Golden Jubilee," *Time*, May 27, 1929; Warren Sloat, *1929: America before the Crash*, New York: Cooper Square Press, 2004 (1979).

8. Kaj Ostenfeld, "The Family with the Red Roses," unpublished manuscript on deposit in New York Public Library, APV (Ostenfeld) 93-2371.

9. "With Ford on the Amazon: The Story of the Ford Plantation, an Eye-Witness," *Planter*, January 1931, in BFRC, Vertical File, "Rubber Plantations."

10. Ibid.

11. Wilkins and Mill, *American Business Abroad*, p. 171.

12. BFRC, accession 285, box 755.

13. BFRC, accession 6, box 74; BFRC, accession 74, box 10.

14. "Armed Brazilians Raid Ford Rubber Plantation," *New York Times*, December 25, 1930; "Opposition to Ford Dropped in Brazil," *New York Times*, May 3, 1931; Isabel Vincent, "Fordlandia: The Amazon Town That Henry Ford Built," *Globe and Mail*, March 20, 1993.

15. "Brazil Sending Arms to Ford's Plantation," *New York Times*, January 3, 1929.

16. BFRC, accession 390, box 86, Johnston to Wibel, December 31, 1932.

17. BFRC, accession 38, box 61, Oxholm, October 17, 1929.

18. John Galey, "Industrialist in the Wilderness: Henry Ford's Amazon Venture," *Journal of Interamerican Studies and World Affairs* 21 (1979): 271; author's interview with Einar Oxholm's son Einar, February 12, 2008.

19. "Ford Envoy Leaves Brazil," *New York Times*, October 4, 1929; BFRC, accession 301, box 21, W. E. Carnegie to B. J. Craig; BFRC, accession 74, box 13, "Report on Visit to Companhia Ford Industrial do Brasil," December 2, 1930.

20. BFRC, interview with William Cowling.

21. Dean, *Struggle for Rubber*, p. 73.

Chapter 13: What Would You Give for a Good Job?

1. Nevins and Hill, *Ford*, pp. 17, 536.

2. Ibid., pp. 14–15.

3. BFRC, accession 65, Reminiscences, Victor J. Perini (as told by Constance Perini).

4. BFRC, accession 65, Reminiscences, Matt Mulrooney.

5. BFRC, accession 74, box 7, Monthly Reports, December 1930.

6. José Maria Ferreira de Castro, *The Jungle*, trans. Charles Duff, Viking, 1935, p. 65; Nash, *Conquest of Brazil*, p. 201.

7. BFRC, accession 74, box 7, Progress Report.

8. BFRC, accession 74, box 1, "Tentative Scheme of South American Plantation Organization"; BFRC, accession 74, box 2, "Report on Visit of W. E Carnegie, 1929"; "Report on Visit of Messrs W. E. Carnegie and V. J. Perini, February 1931"; BFRC, accession 75, box 13, "General Plan of Operation for 1930 and 1931"; BFRC, accession 301, box 2, "Companhia Ford Industrial do Brasil"; BFRC, accession 38, box 61, "Report on the Second Visit of W. E. Carnegie, 1930"; BFRC, accession 74, box 7, monthly progress reports.

9. BFRC, accession 75, box 13, "General Plan of Operation for 1930 and 1931."

10. Isabel Vincent, "Fordlandia: The Amazon Town That Henry Ford Built," *Globe and Mail*, March 20, 1993.

11. Henrique Veltman, "Os Hebraicos da Amazônia," unpublished manuscript, 2005, p. 55; Baldwin, "David B. Riker"; BFRC, accession 47, box 13, "Report on Visit"; David Riker, "The Last Southern Seed," unpublished manuscript; author's interview with David Riker's grandson, David Riker, July 28, 2007.

12. Earl Parker Hanson, *Journey to Manaos*, New York: Reynal and Hitchcock, 1938, p. 73; Kaj Ostenfeld, "The Family with the Red Roses," unpublished manuscript on deposit in New York Public Library, APV (Ostenfeld) 93–2371.

13. Ostenfeld, "The Family with the Red Roses."

14. Hanson, *Journey to Manaos*, pp. 74–76.

15. Author's interview with Eimar Franco; Franco, *O Tapajós*, p. 79; Vera Kelsey, *Seven Keys to Brazil*, New York: Funk and Wagnalls, 1940, pp 222–23.

16. Vincent, "Fordlandia."

17. Author's interview with Leanor Weeks, August 2, 2007; author's interview with Charles Townsend, June 20, 2008.

18. BFRC, accession 74, box 5, Johnston to US Marines, September 19, 1942.

19. BFRC, accession 65, Reminiscences, Matt Mulrooney; Allison McCracken, "'God's Gift to Us Girls': Crooning, Gender, and the Re-Creation of American Popular Song, 1928–1933," *American Music* 17 (1999): 365–95.

20. BFRC, accession 74, box 18, miscellaneous reports and telegrams; BFRC, accession 74, box 16, "Gardens," McClure to Edsel Ford, August 3, 1939; BFRC, accession 74, box 14, Roberge, May 5, 1939.

21. William Cronon, *Nature's Metropolis: Chicago and the Great West*, New York: Norton, 1992, p. 202.

Chapter 14: Let's Wander Out Yonder

1. BFRC, accession 65, Reminiscences, John R. Rogge.

2. Elizabeth Esch, "Fordtown: Managing Race and Nation in the American Empire, 1925–1945," PhD dissertation, New York University, 2003, p. 97; BFRC, accession 285, box 1275.

3. BFRC, accession 65, Reminiscences, Matt Mulrooney.

4. BFRC, accession 301, box 2, "Companhia Ford Industrial do Brasil."

5. BFRC, accession 65, Reminiscences, Matt Mulrooney; BFRC, Reminiscences, John R. Rogge. Also see "Ford Plant Chief to Leave Here Tomorrow for Project in Brazil," *Iron Mountain News*, February 11, 1930, which summarizes a letter Rogge wrote home about his upriver trip.

6. Information on John Rogge's life and activities at Fordlandia comes from an interview with his nephew, Roger Rogge, July 17, 2007.

7. Raffles, *In Amazonia*, p. 138.

8. Weinstein, *The Amazon Rubber Boom*, pp. 53, 73, 126, 169, 185–87, 189, 237, 291; William Lewis Herndon and Lardner Gibben, *Exploration of the Valley of the Amazon Made under Direction of the Navy Department*, Washington, D.C.: Robert Armstrong, 1854, pp. 308, 311.

9. Roosevelt, *Through the Brazilian Wilderness*, p. 360; Herndon and Gibben, *Exploration of the Valley of the Amazon*, p. 309.

10. For a photograph of Baretto's house, see Devon Record Office, Exeter, UK, Charles Luxmoore, 521 M–1/SS/9.

11. McCracken, " 'God's Gift to Us Girls,' " p. 379.

12. Dydia Delyser, *Ramona Memories: Tourism and the Shaping of Southern California*, Minneapolis: University of Minnesota Press, 2005; "The Right Woman in the Right Place," *Washington Post*, March 26, 1883; Helen Hunt Jackson, *Ramona: A Story*, New York: Little, Brown, 1914, pp. 39, 46, 83.

13. Henri Coudreau, *Voyage au Tapajoz*, Paris, 1897, pp. 38–40; Cleary, " 'Lost Altogether to the Civilised World': Race and the Cabanagem in Northern Brazil, 1750–1850": John Hemming, *Amazon Frontier: The Defeat of the Brazilian Indians*, Cambridge: Harvard University Press, 1987, p. 236; Sears, *Forest Runes*, p. 157; Robert F. Murphy, *Headhunter's Heritage: Social and Economic Change among the Mundurucú Indians*, Berkeley: University of California Press, 1960, p. 1; Yolanda Murphy and Robert F. Murphy, *Women of the Forest*, New York: Columbia University Press, 2004, p. 105; for a short interview with a Mundurucú leader who helped put down the Cabanagem Revolt, see Herndon and Gibben, *Exploration of the Valley of the Amazon*, p. 311.

14. Robert F. Murphy, *Mundurucú Religion*, Berkeley: University of California Press, 1958, p. 8.

15. S. Brian Burkhalter and Robert F. Murphy, "Tappers and Sappers: Rubber, Gold, and Money among the Mundurucú," *American Ethnologist* 16 (1989): 105, 114; Murphy, *Mundurucú Religion*, p. 10.

16. "Ford Tire Plants Planned in Brazil," *New York Times*, November 16, 1928.

Chapter 15: Kill All the Americans

1. A. Ogden Pierrot, "A Visit to Fordlandia," *Rubber Age*, April 10, 1932.

2. Esch, "Fordtown," p. 115; BFRC, accession 74, box 2; author's interview with Eimar Franco, March 16, 2008.

3. For Riker's opinion, as interpreted by the traveler Henry Albert Phillips, see *Brazil: Bulwark of Inter-American Relations*, pp. 68–69; see also Baldwin, "David B. Riker and *Hevea brasiliensis*," pp. 383–84.

4. Author's interview with Leanor Weeks; Phillips, *Brazil*, p. 63; BFRC, accession 65, Reminiscences, Matt Mulrooney.

5. BFRC, accession 74, box 2, "Report on Visit of W. E. Carnegie."

6. Henry Ford, *Today and Tomorrow*, New York: Doubleday, p. 101; Mark Seltzer, *Bodies and Machines*, New York: Routledge, 1992, p. 157; Esch, "Fordtown," p. 48; Collier and Horowitz, *The Fords*, p. 11.

7. "The Clocks Put Back," *Chicago Daily Tribune*, September 19, 1885; "The Proposed Universal Day," *Scientific American*, May 20, 1899; "A Belated Reform," *Washington Post*, February 13, 1898; "News of the Week," *Michigan Farmer*, November 17, 1900.

8. *Estado do Pará*, December 27, 1930.

9. BFRC, accession 74, box 13, "Report on Visit to Companhia Ford Industrial do Brasil," December 2, 1930.

10. BFRC, accession 74, Box 2, "Riot 1930."

11. *Estado do Pará*, December 31, 1930.

12. Author's interviews with Leonor Weeks and David Bowman Riker (David Riker's grandson).

13. "Armed Brazilians Raid Ford Rubber Plantation," *New York Times*, December 25, 1930; "Enjoin Ford Interests," *New York Times*, December 27, 1930.

14. For the wheat bread and rice complaint, see BFRC, accession 75, box 17, "Interplant Correspondence," Kennedy to Dearborn, December 24, 1930. For the Dearborn company store, see Nevins and Hill, *Ford*, p. 347.

15. *Estado do Pará*, December 26, 1930.

16. *Estado do Pará*, December 27, 1930.

17. Franco, *O Tapajós*, p. 82.

18. *Folha do Norte*, December 28, 1930; "Report Ford Ending Para Rubber Work," *New York Times*, February 2, 1931.

Chapter 16: American Pastoral

1. Collier and Horowitz, *The Fords*, p. 102; Sward, *The Legend of Henry Ford*, p. 223; Richard T. Ortquist, "Unemployment and Relief: Michigan's Response to the Depression during the Hoover Years," *Michigan History* 57 (1975): 209–36; T. H. Watkins, *The Hungry Years*, New York: Macmillan, 2000; Joyce Shaw Peterson, *American Automobile Workers*, 1900–1933, Albany: State University of New York Press, 1987, p. 135.

2. Brinkley, *Wheels for the World*, pp. 380–88.

3. Collier and Horowitz, *The Fords*, pp. 102–3; Sward, *The Legend of Henry Ford*, pp. 224–25; "Times Good, Not Bad, Ford Says: Sees the Dawn of a Bright Future," *New York Times*, February 1, 1933.

4. Barrie A. Wigmore, *The Crash and Its Aftermath: A History of Securities Markets in the United States, 1929–1933*, Westport, Conn.: Greenwood, 1985, p. 444; Lacey, *Ford*, pp. 327–40; Thomas J. Ticknor, "Motor City: The Impact of the Automobile Industry upon Detroit, 1900–1975," PhD dissertation, University of Michigan, 1978.

5. Baldwin, *Henry Ford and the Jews*, p. 303; David Allan Levine, *Internal Combustion: The Races in Detroit, 1915–1926*, Westport: Greenwood, 1976, pp. 161–64. See also *From Kingsford: The Town Ford Built in Dickinson Country, Michigan*.

6. "The Despot of Dearborn," *Scribner's Magazine*, July 1931; Halberstam, *The Reckoning*, p. 65.

7. "The Little Man in Henry Ford's Basement," *American Mercury*, May 1940; Bonosky, *Brother Bill McKie*, p. 79.

8. Desmond Rochfort, *Mexican Muralists: Orozco, Rivera, Siqueiros*, San Francisco: Chronicle Books, 1998, p. 126.

9. Ford R. Bryan, *Henry's Lieutenants*, Detroit: Wayne State University Press, 1993, p. 284; Hounshell, *From the American System*, pp. 187, 288.

10. Diego Rivera, *My Art, My Life*, Mineola, N.Y.: Courier Dover Publications, 1991, pp. 111–22; McNairn and McNairn, *Quotations*, p. 76.

11. Lew Andrews, *Story and Space in Renaissance Art: The Rebirth of Continuous Narrative*, Cambridge, U.K.: Cambridge University Press, 1998, p. 5.

12. Steven Watts, *People's Tycoon: Henry Ford and the American Century*, New York: Knopf, 2005, pp. 320–21; Ralph Waldo Trine, *The Power That Wins*, Indianapolis: Bobbs-Merrill, 1928, p. 77.

13. Watts, *People's Tycoon*, p. 422; Geoffrey C. Upward, *A Home for Our Heritage: The Building and Growth of Greenfield Village and Henry Ford Museum, 1929–1979*, Dearborn: Henry Ford Museum Press, p. 2; Steven Conn, *Museums and American Intellectual Life, 1876–1926*, Chicago: University of Chicago Press, 1998, p. 156.

14. Conn, *Museums and American Intellectual Life*, p. 159; "Ford Builds a Unique Museum," *New York Times*, April 5, 1931.

15. Upward, *A Home for Our Heritage*, p. 26.

16. Simonds, *Henry Ford and Greenfield Village*, p. 134.

17. Lacey, *Ford*, p. 244; Watts, *People's Tycoon*, pp. 407–9, 422.

18. *New York Times*, January 12, 1936.

19. Rivera, *My Art, My Life*, p. 112.

20. Nevins and Hill, *Ford*, p. 605; Dempsey, "Henry Ford's Amazonian Suburbia," p. 44; Marx, *The Machine in the Garden*, pp. 18, 165.

21. Nevins and Hill, *Ford*, pp. 598, 610.

22. José Ortega y Gasset, *The Revolt of the Masses*, New York: New American Library, 1950, p. 59.

23. Lindbergh, *The Wartime Journals*, p. 712.

24. Brinkley, *Wheels for the World*, p. 422.

25. Collier and Horowitz, *The Fords*, pp. 121, 164.
26. Upward, *A Home for Our Heritage*, p. 22; Richard Bak, *Henry and Edsel: The Creation of the Ford Empire*, New York: Wiley, 2003.
27. Wright, *On Architecture*, pp. 145–46.

Chapter 17: Good Lines, Straight and True

1. BFRC, accession 74, box 2, "Report on Visit of Messrs. W. E. Carnegie and V. J. Perini," February 1931; "Opposition to Ford Dropped in Brazil," *New York Times*, May 3, 1931; "Ford Plans a Town on Brazilian Tract," *New York Times*, February 7, 1931.
2. "Report Ford Ending Para Rubber Work," *New York Times*, February 2, 1931; "Ford Men Deny Plan to Drop Rubber Work," *New York Times*, February 3, 1931; "Edison to Stay on Job Till He Makes Rubber," *New York Times*, March 18, 1930; *India Rubber Journal*, May 23, 1931, p. 671.
3. Segal, *Recasting the Machine Age*, p. 13; Brinkley, *Wheels for the World*, p. 380.
4. "Opposition to Ford Dropped in Brazil"; "Ford Plans a Town on Brazilian Tract"; "Fordlandia, Brazil," *Washington Post*, August 12, 1931; "Modern City Rises in Jungle," *Chicago Tribune*, March 30, 1932.
5. "Fordlandia, Brazil"; "No Business Depression Here," *New York Times*, December 27, 1931; "Life in Fordlandia!" *Iron Mountain Daily News*, May 18, 1932.
6. *Washington Post*, February 15, 1942; "Sober Second Thoughts on Things and Kings," *New York Times*, April 27, 1930.
7. National Archives, RG 59, microfilm 1472, roll 40, 832.6176/58, Drew to State, February 14, 1930.
8. BFRC, accession 23, box 17, "Rubber Plantation," "Ford Summer Hour," Sunday, August 24, 1941.
9. BFRC, accession 38, box 68, February 1931.
10. BFRC, vertical file, "Rubber Plantation; Brazil Correspondence," Letter to H. G. Moore, September 26, 1934.
11. Meyer, *The Five Dollar Day*, p. 176; Nevins and Hill, *Ford*, p. 537; "Report on Visit of Messrs. W. E. Carnegie and V. J. Perini."
12. Esch, "Fordtown," p. 120; "Ford Voyagers," *Detroit News*, July 28, 1928.
13. *Folha do Norte*, September 16, 1934.
14. "Report on Visit of Messrs. W. E. Carnegie and V. J. Perini."
15. "Report on Visit of Messrs. W. E. Carnegie and V. J. Perini"; BFRC, accession 390, box 86, Johnston to Wibel, October 9, 1933.
16. BFRC, accession 74, box 13, "Black Binder," "Brazil Rubber Plantation"; Levine, *Internal Combustion*, pp. 16–18; Nevins and Hill, *Ford*, p. 348; Joyce Shaw Peterson, "Black Automobile Workers in Detroit, 1910–1930," *Journal of Negro History* 64 (Summer 1979).
17. BFRC, accession 74, box 14, Johnston to Carnegie, May 25, 1932; Johnston to Carnegie, August 25, 1932; box 16, Johnston to Roberge, May 5, 1939.

18. BFRC, Reminiscences, E. G. Liebold, p. 626; Charles Morrow Wilson, "Mr. Ford in the Jungle," *Harper's*, July 1941.

19. "Ford's Dream Lies in Decay," *Los Angeles Times*, March 9, 1992; Wilson, "Mr. Ford in the Jungle"; Brian Kelly and Mark London, *Amazon*, New York: Harcourt Brace Jovanovich, 1983, p. 287.

Chapter 18: Mountains of the Moon

1. BFRC, accession 65, Reminiscences, Victor J. Perini (as told by Constance Perini).

2. Brinkley, *Wheels for the World*, p. 218; BFRC, vertical file, Village Industries, General, "One Foot in Industry and One Foot in Soil" (Ford Motor Co. Program).

3. BFRC, accession 74, box 16, Stallard to Johnston, January 13, 1940.

4. BFRC, accession 74, box 16, Johnston to Roberge, October 23, 1930.

5. Morgan Schmidt, "Farming and Patterns of Agrobiodiversity on the Amazon Floodplan," MS thesis, University of Florida, 2003.

6. Ioris, "A Forest of Disputes."

7. Ioris, "A Forest of Disputes"; Schmidt, "Farming and Patterns of Agrobiodiversity"; BFRC, accession 74, box 16, Groth to Johnston, April 27, 1940.

8. BFRC, accession 74, box 16, "To the Members of the Belterra Garden Club."

9. BFRC, accession 74, box 17, "Interplant Correspondence."

10. Ibid.

11. BFRC, accession 74, box 16, McClure to Edsel, August 3, 1939.

12. Ibid.

13. "Golf as Molder of Men," *Dearborn Independent*, August 2, 1924.

14. BFRC, accession 390, box 83.

15. BFRC, accession 74, box 14, Johnston to Roberge, March 14, 1939.

16. Wik, *Henry Ford and Grass-Roots America*, p. 224; Collier and Horowitz, *The Fords*, p. 86; BFRC, accession 65, Reminiscences, Oscar G. Olsen.

17. *Dearborn Independent*, August 6, 1921.

18. Watts, *People's Tycoon*, p. 421; Nevins and Hill, *Ford*, p. 605; Dempsey, "Henry Ford's Amazonian Suburbia," p. 44; Marx, *The Machine in the Garden*, p. 18.

19. BFRC, accession 74, box 14, Roberge to Johnston, May 5, 1939; BFRC, accession 74, box 17, "Film and Projectors," Johnston to Roberge, March 29, 1937; Edward Tomlinson, "Jungle Gold," *Collier's Weekly*, December 12, 1936.

20. BFRC, accession 74, box 16, Pringle to Johnston, November 16, 1937. Fordlandia footage can be found in the National Archives, Special Media Archives Services Division, College Park, Md.; BFRC, accession 74, box 16, Johnston to Roberge, October 23, 1930.

21. *New York Times*, June 27, 1931.

22. *Ford News*, June 1, 1928.

23. Phillips, *Brazil*, p. 54.

24. BFRC, accession 74, box 16, McClure to Edsel Ford, August 3, 1939; Johnston to Roberge, August 10, 1939; box 15, Johnston to Black, September 18, 1941; Esch, "Fordtown," p. 119.

25. BFRC, accession 74, box 13, "Black Binder," Meadowcroft to Rogge, March 17, 1931.

Chapter 19: Only God Can Grow a Tree

1. Henry Ford, with Samuel Crowther, *My Life and Work*, New York: Doubleday, Page, 1922, p. 108.

2. David Campbell, *Land of Ghosts: The Braided Lives of People and the Forest in Far Western Amazonia*, New York: Houghton Mifflin, 2005, p. 12; Stone, *Dreams of Amazonia*, p. 28; Harald Sioli, "My Life in the Amazon," *Biotropica* 11 (1979): 244–45.

3. BFRC, accession 390, box 86, Johnston to Sorensen, November 17, 1931.

4. BFRC, accession 390, box 86, Sorensen to Johnston, December 17, 1931.

5. BFRC, accession 390, box 86, Johnston to Heller, October 22, 1932.

6. BFRC, accession 38, box 61, "Distinctive Brazilian Hardwoods."

7. BFRC, accession 390, box 86, Wibel to Johnston, March 13, 1933; Wilkins and Hill, *American Business Abroad*, p. 176.

8. Nevins and Hill, *Ford*, p. 614; Brinkley, *Wheels for the World*, p. 138.

9. BFRC, accession 74, box 14, Johnston to Sorensen, October 18, 1937.

10. "With Ford on the Amazon: The Story of the Ford Plantation, an Eye-Witness," *Planter*, January 1931, in BFRC, vertical file, "Rubber Plantations."

11. Joseph A. Russell, "Fordlandia and Belterra, Rubber Plantations on the Tapajós River, Brazil," *Economic Geography* 18 (1942): 127; Joseph A. Russell, "Alternative Sources of Rubber," *Economic Geography* 17 (1941): 399–408.

12. BFRC, accession 74, box 6.

13. BFRC, accession 390, box 86, Johnston to Sorensen, February 2, 1932.

14. BFRC, accession 390, box 86, Carnegie to Johnston, February 16, 1932.

15. Lindbergh, *The Wartime Journals*, p. 710.

16. Nevins, *Ford*, p. 447, for "edict engineering."

17. BFRC, accession 390, box 86, Johnston to Sorensen, February 2, 1932.

18. BFRC, accession 390, box 83, Wibel to Johnston, July 17, 1934.

19. BFRC, accession 390, box 83, Wibel to Johnston, May 21, 1931.

Chapter 20: Standard Practices

1. BFRC, accession 390, box 86, Weir to Johnston, March 31, 1933.

2. BFRC, accession 1514, box 1, Roberge to Weir, July 29, 1937.

3. BFRC, accession 390, box 86, Johnston to Carnegie, September 16, 1932, in Dean, *Struggle for Rubber*, p. 75.

4. Dean, *Struggle for Rubber*, p. 64; BFRC, accession 390, box 86, Johnston to Wibel, December 31, 1932.

5. BFRC, accession 38, box 71, Department of Agriculture to Rogge, November 8, 1932.

6. BFRC, accession 390, box 86, Johnston to Wibel, March 13, 1933.

7. BFRC, accession 390, box 86, Johnston to Wibel, December 31, 1932.

8. BFRC, accession 1514, box 1, Johnston to Weir, May 9, 1933.

9. BFRC, accession 1514, box 1, letters in "1928–1933."

10. BFRC, accession 390, box 86, Weir to Johnston, March 31, 1933.

11. Dean, *Struggle for Rubber*, pp. 76–77; BFRC, accession 390, box 86, Johnston to Roberge, September 6, 1937.

12. BFRC, accession 390, box 86, Johnston to Roberge, September 6, 1937.

13. BFRC, accession 390, box 83, Johnston to Wibel, September 6, 1937.

14. BFRC, accession 74, box 14, Johnston to Roberge, October 16, 1936.

15. BFRC, accession 390, box 83, Johnston to Wibel, September 6, 1937; BFRC, accession 74, box 1, Johnston to Roberge, July 1, 1936.

16. BFRC, accession 74, box 1, Johnston to Roberge, July 1, 1936.

17. Dean, *Struggle for Rubber*, p. 78.

18. BFRC, accession 74, box 14, Johnston to Wibel, September 6, 1937; Johnston to Roberge, September 28, 1936, and October 16, 1936.

19. BFRC, accession 390, box 83, Johnston to Wibel, September 6, 1937.

Chapter 21: Bonfire of the Caterpillars

1. Dean, *Struggle for Rubber*, pp. 53–62, 78.

2. Phillips, *Brazil*, p. 54.

3. BFRC, vertical file, Village Industries, General, 1920s, "Henry Ford Says, Farmer-Workmen Will Build Automobile of the Future," published in *Automotive Industry*, August 28, 1924.

4. Brian E. Cleven, "Pequaming and Alberta: Henry Ford's Model Towns," master's thesis, Department of Social Sciences, Michigan Technological University, 1997, p. 131.

5. Gastão Cruls, "Impressões de Uma Visita a Companhia Ford Industrial do Brasil," *Revista Brasileira de Geografia*, October 1939, pp. 3–25.

6. "Fourteen-Year Effort to Produce Plantation Rubber in Brazil Is Showing Progress," *Washington Post*, January 31, 1943.

7. Kelly and London, *Amazon*, p. 290; Wilson, "Mr. Ford in the Jungle."

8. Dempsey, "Henry Ford's Amazonian Suburbia."

9. BFRC, accession 390, box 86, Johnston to Wibel, March 4, 1935.

10. BFRC, accession 390, box 83, "Insect Census of Fordlandia," March 29, 1935.

11. Galey, "Industrialist in the Wilderness," p. 275; BFRC, accession 74, box 13, "Rubber Production in Amazon Valley."

12. BFRC, accession 74, box 1, cited in Johnston to Roberge, April 23, 1937.

13. Author's interview with Charles Townsend, grandson of the entomologist and son of Charles Townsend, James Weir's assistant, June 20, 2008.

14. BFRC, accession 390, box 83, Johnston to Wibel, February 10, 1937.

15. BFRC, accession 74, box 14, Johnston to Roberge, November 30, 1938; BFRC, accession 38, box 91.

16. BFRC, accession 74, box 5, clipping; BFRC, Henry Ford Office, accession 285, box 2155, "Hun-Hunt."

Chapter 22: Fallen Empire of Rubber

1. Brinkley, *Wheels for the World*, p. 426.

2. Collier and Horowitz, *The Fords*, p. 129; Nye, *Henry Ford*, p. 93.

3. BFRC, accession 390, box 83, Johnston to Wibel, June 8, 1937.

4. BFRC, accession 74, box 12, correspondence.

5. BFRC, accession 390, box 83, August Report, Johnston to Sorensen; Franco, *O Tapajós*, p. 84; author's interview with Eimar Franco, March 16, 2008.

6. Andrew Revkin, *The Burning Season: The Murder of Chico Mendes and the Fight for the Amazon Rain Forest*, Washington, D.C.: Island Press, 2004, p. 88.

7. BFRC, accession 74, box 12; Galey, "Industrialist in the Wilderness," p. 282.

8. Alexander Cockburn and Suzanna Hecht, *The Fate of the Forest: Developers, Destroyers, and Defenders of the Amazon*, London: Verso, 1989, p. 105.

9. Brinkley, *Wheels for the World*, p. 430.

10. Baldwin, *Henry Ford and the Jews*, p. 284.

11. Brinkley, *Wheels for the World*, p. 433.

12. Collier and Horowitz, *The Fords*, p. 201.

13. H. G. Sorensen, "Crown Budding for Healthy Hevea," *Agriculture in the Americas*, October 1942.

14. "Ford Plantations a Chapter in Romance of Rubber," *Christian Science Monitor*, February 5, 1942; Wilkins and Hill, *American Business Abroad*, pp. 181–82.

15. BFRC, accession 74, box 6, "Plantation Report."

16. Ibid.; Wilkins and Hill, *American Business Abroad*, p. 182.

Chapter 23: Tomorrow Land

1. Seth Garfield, "Tapping Masculinity: Labor Recruitment to the Brazilian Amazon during World War II," *Hispanic American Historical Review* 86 (2006): 275–308; Pedro Martinello, A *"Batalha da Borracha" na Segunda Guerra Mundial e suas consequências para o vale amazônico*, Rio Branco: Universidade Federal do Acre, 1988; Frank D. McCann, *The Brazilian-American Alliance, 1937–1945*, Princeton, N.J.: Princeton University Press, 1974.

2. Dean, *Struggle for Rubber*, p. 97; BFRC, accession 6, box 74, May 13, 1942; Charles H. T. Townsend, "Progress in Developing Superior Hevea Clones in Brazil," *Economic Botany* 14 (1958): 189–96.

3. Roland Hall Sharp, *South America Uncensored: Jungles of Fascism, Genuine Good-Neighborliness, Portrait of a Continent, in Search of Frontiers*, New York: Longmans, Green, 1945, p. 270; Phillips, *Brazil*, p. 57; Karl Brandt, *Reconstruction of World Agriculture*, New York: Longmans, Green, 1945.

4. Dean, *Struggle for Rubber*, p. 97; BFRC, accession 134, box 4, Camargo to Stallard, December 1, 1944; BFRC, accession 74, box 12, Plantation Reports, January 1942–December 1943; BFRC, accession 7, box 5, Belterra Monthly Progress Reports, 1941 to 1945. See also the reports in accession 74, box 13, related to Belterra.

5. Steve Mannheim, *Walt Disney and the Quest for Community*, New York: Ashgate Publishing, 1983, p. 26; Barbara Weinstein, "Modernidade tropical: Visões norte-americanas da Amazônia nas vésperas da Guerra Fria," *Revista do IEB* 45, September 2007, pp. 153–76; "Film to Cite Riches of South America," *New York Times*, December 30, 1941.

6. BFRC, accession 285, box 2629.

7. André Luiz Vieira de Campos, "International Health Policies in Brazil: The Serviço Especial de Saúde Pública, 1942–1960," PhD dissertation, University of Texas, Austin, 1997, p. 75; BFRC, accession 6, box 74, Johnston to Wooley, October 26, 1942.

8. Columbia University, Rare Books and Manuscripts Collection, "James G. McDonald," "Confidential memorandum of McDonald-Ford Negotiations in Dearborn," April 1, 1941.

9. Brinkley, *Wheels for the World*, p. 501; Collier and Horowitz, *The Fords*, p. 161.

10. Bennett, *We Never Called Him Henry*, p. 285; Brinkley, *Wheels for the World*, p. 478.

11. Howard Segal, "What Bill Ford Is Learning from Great-Grandpa," History News Network, http://hnn.us/roundup/entries/20940.html, January 23, 2006; Earl L. Doyle and Ruth MacFarlane, *The History of Pequaming*, Ontonagon, Mich.: Ontonagon County Historical Society, 2002, p. 167; Cleven, "Pequaming and Alberta," p. 109.

Epilogue: Still Waiting for Henry Ford

1. "Amazonia—A Granary Out of the Jungle," *New York Times*, July 31, 1949; Felisberto Camargo, "Report on the Amazon Region," *Problems of Humid Tropical Regions*, Paris: United Nations Educational, Scientific, and Cultural Organization, 1958, pp. 11–22; "Wait for the Weeping Wood," *Time*, July 26, 1948.

2. Dean, *Struggle for Rubber*, pp. 102, 115.

3. Ibid., p. 115.

4. "Brazil's Famous City of Folly," *Washington Post*, February 15, 1914.

5. "Brazil's Famous City of Folly"; Joseph Novitsky, "Boom, Bust, and Now Boom Again in Amazon Town," *New York Times*, July 1, 1969.

6. "Jungle Trade Zone Tries to Survive, Far from Markets in a Changing World," Associated Press, July 5, 2005; "Brazil's Resurgent Amazon Powerhouse," *BBC News*, August 29, 2006.

7. "Race to the Bottom: Mexico Lowers Wages to Snag International Auto Production," *International Herald Tribune*, June 8, 2008; "Half of World's Population Will Live in Cities Next Year, UN Report Says," *International Herald Tribune*, June 27, 2007.

8. Jeb Blount, "Ford's Dream Lies in Decay," *Los Angeles Times,* March 9, 1993.

9. Rhett A. Butler, "Deforestation in the Amazon," http://www.mongabay.com/brazil.html#cattle (accessed May 8, 2008).

10. "Amazon's Rescue Reversed," *Guardian,* January 25, 2008; Alexei Barrionuevo, "With Guns and Fines, Brazil Takes on Loggers," *New York Times,* April 19, 2008.

11. Monte Reel, "Brazil Pursues Crackdown on Loggers," *Washington Post,* March 21, 2008; Tim Hirsch, "Brazilian Town at Centre of Crackdown," *Telegraph,* March 3, 2008.

12. Michael Smith and David Voreacos, "The Secret World of Modern Slavery," Bloomberg.com, December 2006, http://www.bloomberg.com/news/marketsmag/modern_slavery1.html (accessed May 12, 2008).

13. Woods Hole Research Center Press Release, "World's Largest Rainforest Drying Experiment Completes First Phase," http://www.eurekalert.org/pub_releases/2005-03/whrc-wlr032105.php.

14. Heidi Sopinka, "Spilling the Beans on Soy," http://www.commondreams.org/archive/2007/10/26/4832/.

15. Alex Bellos, "Blood Crop," *Telegraph,* October 13, 2007, http://www.telegraph.co.uk/earth/main.jhtml?xml=/earth/2007/10/13/sm_soya.xml&page=1 (accessed May 12, 2008).

16. Scott Wallace, "Last of the Amazon," *National Geographic,* January 2007, p. 70; Bellos, "Blood Crop"; Indira Lakshmanan, "Amazon Highway Is Route to Strife in Brazil," *Boston Globe,* December 27, 2005.

17. http://cps.aena.br/cps_arquivos/fg/provasanteriores_arquivos/provadiscursivaturismo.pdf (accessed May 8, 2008).

ILLUSTRATION CREDITS

Grateful acknowledgement is made to the following individuals and institutions for permission to publish images from their collections: Stephanie Lucas, Carol Whittaker, and Jim Orr of the Benson Ford Research Center at The Henry Ford (Dearborn, Michigan); Melanie Bazil of the Henry Ford Hospital; Silvia Inwood of the Detroit Institute of Arts; Matthew Westerby of The Metropolitan Museum of Art; Karen Hass of The Lane Collection of the Museum of Fine Arts, Boston; Jill Slaight of The New-York Historical Society; Jim Detlefsen at the Herbert Hoover Presidential Library and Museum; James Dompier at Baraga County Historical Society (Michigan); John Brunton of the Devon County Council Devon Record Office (UK); and Leonardo F. Freitas.

The material appears on the following pages:
From the collection of The Henry Ford: 36, 59, 129, 137, 139, 141, 154, 172, 174, 184, 187, 190, 195, 197, 200, 207, 221, 224, 231, 255, 270, 271, 273, 274–75, 281, 282, 283, 284, 287, 288, 297, 317, 321, 322, 326
Conrad R. Lam Archives & Historical Collections of the Henry Ford Hospital: 297
Daniel Schoepf, *George Huebner 1862–1935: Un Photographe à Manaus*: 27, 29
Collection of the The New-York Historical Society: 67
Devon Record Office (reproduced by permission of the owners of the Luxmoore papers [D.5121M]): 91, 131, 215
The Metropolitan Museum of Art, with permission from the Lane Collection: 248
Diego Rivera, *Detroit Industry, North Wall (detail, 1932–1933)*; Gift of Edsel B. Ford, photograph © 2001, The Detroit Institute of Arts: 250
James R. Weir, *Pathological Survey of the Para Rubber Tree*: 328
Baraga County Historical Society: 352
Leonardo F. Freitas: 368
Herbert Hoover Presidential Library and Museum: 24

ACKNOWLEDGMENTS

First thanks go to Sara Bershtel, as ruthless a rationalizer of words as Henry Ford himself of movement. It's a privilege, and enormous fun, to work with her. I'm also grateful to Riva Hocherman for helping to make all the right decisions and to Roslyn Schloss for her impressive copyediting skills. Megan Quirk was wonderful shepherding the book through editing and production. I want to thank Barbara Weinstein, Tom Rogers, Joel Wolfe, Seth Garfield, Bryan McCann, Karl Jacoby, Tom McCarthy, Karen Robert, Betsy Esch, and Joe Jackson for helpful discussions, leads, corrections, and suggestions. Michelle Chase, Rosalind Leveridge, Daniel Rodríguez, and Lindsey Gish assisted with key research. Susan Rabiner helped give shape to the project at its early stages and has been supportive throughout. Thanks also to the children of Fordlandia, as well as others who have memories of the project, for taking time to share them with me, including Charles Townsend, Leanor Weeks, Einar Oxholm, Raymundo Miranda, Diogo Franco, Eimar Franco, Roger Rogge, Douglas Riker, and David Riker. Gil Serique provided indispensible help navigating around the Tapajós, and for sharing the history of his family. I'm thankful for the support librarians and archivists gave me along the way, including Carol Whittaker of the Benson Ford Research Center, Melanie Bazil of the Henry Ford Hospital, and Jamie Myler of the Ford Motor Company Archives. Much appreciation also to friends and colleagues, including Marilyn Young, Sinclair Thompson, Jack Wilson, Ada Ferrer, Bob Wheeler, Steve Fraser, Molly Nolan, Corey Robin, Maureen Linker, Scott Saul, Robert Perkinson, Jolie Olcott, Laura Brahm, Deborah Levenson, Liz Oglesby, Gil Joseph, Harry Harootunian, Kristin Ross, Kieko Matteson, Carlota McAllister, Linda Gordon, Mark Weisbrot, Diane Nelson, Di Paton, Frank Goldman, Peter Brown, Gordon Lafer, Matt Hausmann, Rachel Kirtner, Debbie Poole, Gerardo Rénique, Toshi Goswami, and Tannia Goswami, for support in different ways. And Manu, who deserves thanks for this and everything. I'd like to dedicate the book to Emilia Viotti da Costa, who continues to be a wonderful teacher.

INDEX